Roland Barthes
Structuralism and After

Roland Barthes

Structuralism and After

ANNETTE LAVERS

Harvard University Press
Cambridge, Massachusetts
1982

Library of Congress Cataloging in Publication Data

Lavers, Annette.
Roland Barthes, structuralism and after.

Bibliography: p.
1. Barthes, Roland.   2. Structuralism.   3. Semiotics.
4. Languages — Philosophy.   5. Literature — Philosophy.
I. Title.
P85.B33L3   410'.92'4   81-13447
ISBN 0-674-77721-2   AACR2

To K., with love and gratitude,

Acknowledgements

I should like to thank Frank Kermode, for supplying part of the original impetus for this study and for many stimulating comments in conversation and seminar; Giulio Lepschy, who did not consider interdisciplinary interest 'an unwarrantable breach of privacy', for his many criticisms and suggestions — any remaining errors are of course purely my own; Jonathan Culler, for his acute and constructive observations; Jacqueline Lesschaeve and François Wahl at Le Seuil for bibliographical help; Janice Price, John Whitehead, Beverley Brown and Mary Cusack for their help and enthusiasm; my mother and my father, for their tireless co-operation in tracing material which helped me build a more balanced picture of a particularly confusing period; my husband, whose constant support went far beyond what a mere dedication can acknowledge; all the friends and students with whom I discussed the topics examined in this book when they still had a pioneering flavour, in the Sixties (which, we all know, include the Seventies); and *The Times Literary Supplement* for allowing me to use some paragraphs which originally appeared as reviews of most contemporary French thinkers.

My greatest debt must lie with Roland Barthes, and not only from an intellectual point of view which will be obvious enough. His open-mindedness and generosity with commentators and translators were proverbial. The theses put forth here, which often conflicted with what I have called the 'authorized version', were communicated to him during the years when this account of his career took shape against a changing ideological backcloth. Little did I know then that I would have to rewrite it in the past tense.

The author and publisher would like to thank the following for permission to reproduce copyright material:

C.K. Ogden and I.A. Richards, Routledge & Kegan Paul Ltd and Harcourt Brace Jovanovich, Inc. for one diagram from *The Meaning of Meaning*, first published in 1923; the Estate of Roland Barthes, Jonathan Cape Ltd and Hill & Wang, Inc. for one diagram adapted from *Mythologies* (translated by Annette Lavers) and two diagrams adapted from *Elements of Semiology* (translated by Annette Lavers and Colin Smith), both of which were first published in French by Editions du Seuil in 1957 and 1964 respectively.

Contents

All chapter titles are quotations from Barthes.

Part I Criticism begins with compilation   1

1   Where to begin?   3
2   The structuralist debate   13
3   A narrative with a hero   25
4   He is a writer, who wants to be one   32

Part II Something beyond language   45

5   The network (synchrony)   47
6   The voyage (diachrony)   66
7   The responsibility of forms   84

Part III A euphoric dream of scientificity   101

8   Everything, then, can be a myth?   103
9   Homo significans   128
10   Both diffident and rash   133
11   It is the path that makes the work, or, Between things
      and words   151

Part IV The science of literature is literature   165

12   In those days, intellectual history was going very fast   167
13   A whole landscape in a bean   178
14   The starred text   196
15   The body under the body   204

Appendix   217

I   Structuralism   217
II   Semiology, the sign, relations and functions   219
III   Synchrony, diachrony, the subject and society   228
IV   The units of language and the organization of meaning   231

Notes   240

Biography   266

Bibliography   268

Index   295

Abbreviations

These abbreviations refer to books by Barthes; articles by him are designated by their date (see Section I of Bibliography) except in the case of those included in *Image-Music-Text, The Eiffel Tower and Other Mythologies, New Critical Essays* and *Le grain de la voix*, which are designated by name, so as not to lengthen the Bibliography. Page numbers refer to the English translations when they exist, except in the case of *Leçon*.

C4, 8,	etc. *Communications* special issues
CV	*Critique et vérité*
E	*Essais critiques*
ES	*L'Empire des signes*
ET	*The Eiffel Tower and Other Mythologies*
G	Reprint of *Degré zéro* and *Eléments de sémiologie*, Gonthier, 1965
GV	*Le Grain de la voix*
IMT	*Image-Music-Text*
L	*Leçon inaugurale au Collège de France*
M	*Mythologies*
MI	*Michelet*
NEC	*Nouveaux essais critiques*
PT	*Le Plaisir du texte*
R	*Sur Racine*
RB	*Roland Barthes par Roland Barthes*
S	*Eléments de sémiologie*
SE	*Sollers écrivain*
SFL	*Sade, Fourier, Loyola*
SM	*Système de la Mode*
SZ	*S/Z*
T	Interview by Jean Thibaudeau, in *Tel Quel*, 47, winter 1971
Z	*Le Degré zéro de l'écriture*

C'est un garçon sans importance collective, c'est tout juste un
individu....
Céline. (Epigraph of Sartre's *Nausea*.)

C'est qu'un homme n'est jamais un individu.... Ainsi l'histoire nous
fait universels dans la mesure exacte où nous la faisons
particulière....'
Sartre.

Part I

Criticism begins with compilation

1

Where to begin?

'Life and times'

Roland Barthes is generally acknowledged, even by those not conversant with his books, as one of the leading figures of the French intellectual scene. Yet although his work would make far less sense cut off from its context, none of his contemporaries, perhaps, has managed to remain so essentially *singular*. Indeed, it may well be in the tension between the collective and the individual that the key to Barthes can best be found.

This book accordingly has a dual focus: it concerns itself with the various doctrines propounded by Barthes in the course of his career, chiefly in the fields of sociology and literary criticism; but it also attempts to place these doctrines as part of an existential search and the shaping of a self-image. To use a distinction which Barthes is fond of making, the first is the subject of the book, and the second is its object.[1]

There exists a familiar framework for the study of such masters of art or thought — their 'life and times'. Like many such traditional frameworks, it has much to recommend it: the modern reformulation of the long-term aim of the social sciences as a 'science of the subject and of history' shows that such a perspective is to some extent unavoidable.

Unfortunately, in the case of Barthes this approach runs into a number of theoretical and practical difficulties. To start with, it so happens that a major tenet of his theory of literature is that there is no automatic link between the work and either the 'life' or the 'times'. Such a link is intuitively assumed by everybody, but establishing it is a different matter. It is well known that Proust objected to certain types of biographical criticism which he saw as giving no clue as to the nature of the deeper creative self. And Barthes's comment on George Painter's biography of Proust himself was that such books teach us not that an author's work is illuminated through knowing all its 'sources' in real life but, on the contrary, that a writer (and here Barthes also speaks for himself) experiences his life through the prism of his future work, seeking obstinately in fragmented episodes the concrete embodiment of essences he already divines (1966a; see also Proust 1954 and Painter 1959). Still, a psycho-biographical reading need not always be so reductive: we are all 'thought-experiments' for one another.

Theoretical considerations aside, a second reason for not launching forthwith into a biographical sketch is that such an approach has one indispensable condition, that the life should be known; and that of Barthes is not. Or rather, what is known is mostly known through Barthes himself, which automatically trades its explanatory status for something that itself needs to be explained. The first biographical material, in a short book on his work by Mallac and Eberbach (1971), was supplied by him and concerned only his public life. A second source was the interview he granted the novelist Jean Thibaudeau in the same year (by far the most interesting and the most revealing he ever gave) and which appeared in the periodical *Tel Quel*, in the first of a series of special issues various French reviews devoted to Barthes.

Critics also use a book diversely referred to as *Barthes par Barthes* or *Barthes par lui-même* ('Barthes by himself') — the only one actually written by the author concerned in a series published by Le Seuil and paradoxically known as 'So and So by Himself'. Written on Barthes's own suggestion to his publisher, *Roland Barthes by Roland Barthes* takes us to a third reason for being cautious. The first page tells us that all that follows must be read as if it concerned a character in a novel; the pronouns alternate (as previously in *The Pleasure of the Text*) between 'I', 'he', and 'R.B.', rendering the possibilities of self-revelation. This makes these texts, above all, *literary* texts, aspects of a certain genre — partly autobiography and partly autoportrait — which is currently the object of intense theoretical interest. What is more, they are part of Barthes's *later* work and, as we shall see, chronology is especially significant in his case. But it also supplies a fourth reason for postponing a discussion of biographical elements: readers of *Barthes by Barthes* were surprised to find the author denigrating the major part of his own work. Obviously, these so-called 'admissions' should have been situated in their psychological and intellectual context; one cannot make use of the facts they contain in isolation, for they concern a new system. Regrettably, literary criticism did not rise to the occasion, and Barthes's autobiographical works have mostly been taken at face value. The reader of the present volume is therefore referred directly to the biography and bibliography appended at the end of this study; biographical elements will be mentioned in the main text only when they are relevant to a particular matter.

And now, what of Barthes's 'times'? My initial, loose, description, for those who have not read him, was as a literary critic and a sociologist.[2] To the initiated, the inadequacy of such typecasting will immediately be apparent, for two reasons. One is the paramount importance, in Barthes's own eyes, of his literary enterprise as such; indeed, his stylistic prowess lent further authority to his pronouncements. The second reason is that Barthes was one of those people who cannot think without exploring the foundations of their activity until this produces an extensive re-drawing of boundaries. This led to a more abstract reconsideration of his early reflections on literature and society until they came to be viewed as two parallel activities of deciphering signs, and subsumed under the common heading of *semiology*.

Semiology and structuralism

Semiology is the name of a projected general science of signs conceived by the Swiss linguist Ferdinand de Saussure, who taught in Paris at the turn of the century. Semiology was never developed by Saussure and made little progress after him; Barthes sought the cause of this relative sterility not only theoretically but through a tentative empirical application. Although the hope for a general science of signs may eventually prove illusory, semiology has proved extremely useful as a working hypothesis. An International Association for Semiotic Studies was constituted in 1969; it had its first, massively-attended, Congress in Milan in 1974 and its second in Vienna in 1979. The subjects discussed included logic and scientific languages, architecture and the visual arts, music, literature and behaviour; the preoccupations represented there would formerly have been classified as, for instance, linguistics, sociology, criticism or psychiatry.

In Saussure's idea, the difficulties of linguistics would one day be solved by a general semiology of which linguistics would be only a part. Yet, as he realized, language 'better than anything else, offers a basis for understanding the semiological problem' (*Course*,16). This is because linguistics has an unrivalled fund of theoretical and procedural experience, itself due to the unique properties of language among other sign systems, human, artificial or animal. Thus linguistics and semiotics mutually define each other, so to speak. Barthes's solution to this circle was to stand Saussure's order of priority on its head, making semiology a part of linguistics. While many theorists have found this untenable, Barthes could make such a suggestion because of his belief, almost a personal myth but credible enough in an era of mass culture, that in our society 'human language is not only the model of meaning but also its foundation' (*SM*,9).

Modern linguistics came to be called *structural* due to Saussure's view that language was made up of structures (the linguist Hjelmslev, a disciple of Saussure, defined a structure as 'an autonomous entity of internal dependencies (1959, 1) and Barthes took up this definition).

The attempt, pioneered by the anthropologist Lévi-Strauss, to use linguistics as a model for the study of other human symbolic systems, as well as the philosophy which some thought they could deduce from it (Barthes being one of the most prominent), was accordingly called *structuralism*. This term is now reputed to have gone out of fashion, and the explanation (if fashion ever needs one) may well lie in the evolution of linguistics itself. Early structuralist attempts took their inspiration from phonology, the study of the sounds of a given language. The emphasis has since then shifted to the other parts of linguistics: syntax (the study of the units formed by combining the words, namely sentences and now even discourses), semantics (the study of the meaning of words and their combinations) and finally pragmatics (the study of the uses and effects of signs). Structuralism certainly played a part in this process, albeit negatively: its intensive exploitation of the insights afforded by its chosen models inevitably highlighted their limits as well as its own.[3] *Semiology*, or its Anglo-American and Soviet rival *semiotics*, may show greater staying power, dissociated as they are from any reminder of either a philosophical movement or a possibly superannuated linguistic school.

Readers are referred to the Appendix of this book for an outline of the various connections between basic linguistic tenets and concepts derived from other fields; for the purposes of all that follows this Appendix will be taken as read. It is important, especially in the case of Barthes, to remember that many structuralists reached their central insights by non-linguistic routes, for structuralism is essentially transdisciplinary. Right from the start Barthes was anxious to show the confluence of all disciplines which could rank as sciences of symbolic activity: linguistics, psychoanalysis, modern historical methods, anthropology, Sartrean ontology and Marxist studies of social formations. He was eventually so successful in this that the assumed synthesis of all these 'human sciences' (this gallicism has special relevance in view of the debates during the structuralist period, see Chapter 2) could in turn be used to give a scientific status to some of the more questionable tenets in his later philosophy.

This book could not aspire — for reasons of space, let alone competence — to provide even an introduction to an immense and varied field which amounts to nearly forty years of contemporary thought. The next section will therefore simply be an enumeration of the thinkers and disciplines relevant to Barthes's work; this enumeration will be completed in Chapter 2 by a discussion of the philosophical debates affecting all these disciplines (this part of Chapter 1 as well as Chapter 2, which describe the background to Barthes's work, are thus rather more demanding than the others). These debates left a mark on Barthes's career, which is described in Chapter 3, while Chapter 4 examines the thematic and stylistic constants which, thanks to their counterpoint with more obviously intellectual topics, often give a clue to the deeper meaning of his work. After this introductory survey in Part I, the order of study is roughly chronological, although some of Barthes's works are dealt with across several chapters (this applies especially to Barthes's statements on reading, *Critique et vérité* and *S/Z*, his special and general theories of relativity, as it were).

Part II is chiefly concerned with Barthes's first works, *Writing Degree Zero* and *Mythologies*, and begins by examining the basic components (conscious and unconscious) of his system, the relation between his view of history (the 'something beyond language') and the status of language, literature and their users, as found in his various models of the good society. *Writing Degree Zero* is taken as a framework in Part II, showing Barthes's concern with the dialectics of freedom and constraint; emphasizing, on the one hand, that what might have seemed merely topical at the time of existentialism was in fact fundamental in Barthes's work and, on the other hand, that freedom and constraint were from the start treated as linguistic as well as social and literary questions. *Critical Essays* and various texts on literature are discussed in both Parts II and III. *Critical Essays* is shown to be a crucial turning-point both for the birth of a doctrine of literature and a correlated self-image. Part III is centred on Barthes's structuralist period, stretching from 'Myth Today' (as distinct from the essays which precede it in *Mythologies*), through some of the *Critical Essays*, to *Elements of Semiology* and *Système de la Mode*. Part IV describes how Barthes was led back to literature through a contestation of structuralism; the titles of Chapters 13 and 14 convey, in Barthes's terms, the respective principles of the structuralist and post-structuralist approaches: centripetal and centrifugal. The final chapter attempts to deal with Barthes's later career in the context of recent ideological upheavals.

'A vast translation of the world': models and difficulties

At the time when Barthes began to write in the mid-1940s, there is no doubt that the success of Marxism among French intellectuals was to a great extent due to its 'totalization', not unlike the syntheses later sought in structuralism; as we shall see, this debate around the notion of totalization may well epitomize the whole period. With its sources in German philosophy, English economics and French political theory, held together by its historical perspective, Marxism could claim to be just the kind of 'synthetic anthropology' Sartre had demanded since the early 1940s. Existentialism at that time was itself far too specialized to provide such a synthesis since Sartre (despite the vistas promised by the notion of 'situation') had not yet begun to bring social structures into the system of constraints on freedom, as part of the specification of an individual destiny. As for an analysis of the physical world, which was also found in Marxism, it was completely neglected in Sartre's system since what initially mattered to him was stressing matter's absolute ontological separateness from consciousness, the difference between *en-soi* (in itself) and *pour-soi* (for-itself). By contrast, Marxism explained at one stroke the laws of the world and those of the mind, in a historical perspective.

To this heady mixture Marxism also brought a political impact, constantly felt in this period of Cold War and decolonization. Thus, even for many thinkers outside its orbit, Marxism often had the status of 'privileged interlocutor'. Barthes and many others had hopes of being able to cling to this framework while improving, or at least 'modernizing', it with injections of psychoanalysis, Anglo-American sociology, genetic psychology, modern historiography and, finally, textual studies. Unfortunately, whoever wished to use Marxism had first to run the gauntlet of the Stalinist establishment, particularly rigid in France and never more so than when Barthes began to write. As a result it was on the fringes of orthodox Marxism that the most productive developments took place. Largely a Hegelian renaissance, kicked off by Alexandre Kojève's lectures in the 1930s, the debates of the period were well represented in the journal *Arguments*, to which Barthes was a contributor and in which his first structuralist article was published.[4]

The immediate source of structuralism was Lévi-Strauss's application of the methods of linguistics to anthropology; linguistics thus became the chief model, acquiring its image as a 'pilot science'. Linguistics of course had itself been greatly influenced by the 'aggregate of ideas' appearing under the rubric of cybernetics. The meaning of this term has been extended beyond the science of 'control and communication in the animal and the machine' to cover what is known as information theory (see Appendix, pp. 224-6), systems theory and theory of games, to which should also be added computer science and the study of artificial intelligence. Gregory Bateson called cybernetics 'the biggest bite out of the fruit of the Tree of Knowledge that mankind has taken in the last two thousand years' and these words reflect the high hopes of solving basic linguistic problems and succeeding in applications such as machine translation. Such hopes are rather deflated today, but this buoyant atmosphere was Barthes's first context.

When Lévi-Strauss began to apply the principles of structural linguistics to anthropology and culture, he was often literally following the suggestions made by the pioneers of linguistics. But something like the structuralist idea was already at work in anthropology, as is well shown by Jean Cuisenier in his article on 'Structuralism as word, idea and tools' (1967). Cuisenier demonstrated that the principle of structuralism (namely the systematic comparison of cultures seen as organized wholes by means of a search for constants and variables, followed by that of the syntax of transformations which allows one to pass from one to the other) had itself only been made possible by the methods of classification evolved in the mid-1940s. These methods, he argued, were already widely used by psychologists, sociologists, linguists and ethnologists in order to introduce a meaningful hierarchy into qualitative data.[5]

The decisive influence on Lévi-Strauss, however, was the linguist Roman Jakobson, whom he had met in the United States where both had emigrated during the Second World War. Jakobson had a major role in the development of phonology and had in addition made important theoretical suggestions about poetic language and the classification of genres, based on a classification of the functions of language which has come to dominate structuralist studies of literature and supplied an essential element of Barthes's own theories (see Appendix, p. 226). Several articles by Barthes are commentaries on Lévi-Strauss's various essays from the mid-1940s to the mid-1960s on the logic of myths, folk-tales and various symbolic aspects of modern culture. Barthes clearly derived considerable encouragement from these essays in both his literary and sociological pursuits but, as is obvious from his earliest works, the essential idea that cultures are overdetermined and that they utter several messages at once is also at the heart of his own experience.

Lévi-Strauss's example was soon followed in France by the psycho-analyst Jacques Lacan. Lacan's 'Fonction et champ de la parole et du langage en psychanalyse' sometimes called the 'Discours de Rome', after the 1953 Congress where its delivery announced his secession from the main French psychoanalytical society) advised all those interested in the unconscious to go and 'read Saussure'. Whatever the merits of his theory, his intellectualized approach turned out to be a breakthrough for psychoanalysis in France, a country whose particularly acute native school of psychological writers had until then been made singularly im-mune to the Freudian gospel.[6] Further cross-fertilization occurred in a series of articles by the Marxist philosopher Louis Althusser and his disciples, written between 1960 and 1965 and published in two collections, *Pour Marx* (*For Marx*) and *Lire le Capital* (*Reading Capital*). Psychoanalytic notions like overdetermination and the 'symptomatic reading' of a patient's discourse were used to give a more precise meaning to the Marxist 'reading' of society and Marx's own reading of classical political economy. Althusser played a major part in the generation of contemporary self-consciousness about epistemology, as well as in turn boosting the 'scientific' status of (particularly Lacanian) psychoanalysis as a result of its association with an avowedly scientific socialism.[7]

Marxism is, among other things, a philosophy of history, even if the Althusserian reassessment and the discussions among various thinkers around the notion of the Asiatic mode of production meant that this expression could no longer denote a unilinear evolution and progress.

'History' for them required an appreciation of plurality, whether a recognition of the stratified structure of social formations or the different rhythms at which each of these levels develops. History itself was, during this period, one of the most quickly developing branches of knowledge and the scene of much theoretical and methodological activity. A thinker like Michel Foucault, trained as a philosopher, nevertheless likes to think of himself as an historian. Barthes himself published some important articles in the main French historical journal *Les Annales* — which gave its name to a school of thought — and modelled his criticism of existing literary studies, 'History or Literature' (*R*,153), on the reflections of Lucien Febvre and Marc Bloch, the two founders of the school. Barthes also worked under one of the school's main representatives, Fernand Braudel, and gives as a source of his own thinking on semiology the range extended to certain linguistic concepts in historical studies.[8]

At the very centre of the turmoil, in a way, was the history and philosophy of science. For instance, the identification of the linguistic and the genetic 'messages' (even down to their 'punctuation') in the work of Nobel prizewinners François Jacob and Jacques Monod seemed for a while to make the supremacy of linguistics secure. Lacan found some corroboration of his views in Monod's declaration in his Inaugural Lecture to the effect that our view of evolution is quite consistent with a claim that man did not create language but, on the contrary, that language created man.[9] Philosophy itself had repeatedly in the previous twenty or thirty years been the subject of attacks from sceptical scientists or disappointed philosophers.[10] Yet, except for a brief moment in the heyday of structuralism and its stress on positive science, there was no perceptible decrease in the philosopher's conviction that he could go quite a long way by means of software alone, a reaction further encouraged by the increasingly insistent denunciations of the hegemony of technocracy, the insidious prestige of vulgarized popular science, and the power structure built into the very practice of modern science.[11]

Early philosophical works, such as Cassirer's studies of symbolic thought, Husserl's theory of the sign and its critique by Jacques Derrida, are of decisive importance in the latest developments of semiology. The blurring of boundaries between the discourses of literature, criticism and philosophy, so conspicuous in Derrida's work, is typical of a reassessment which acknowledges Heidegger and Nietzsche as its ancestors.

Meanwhile, the 1950s and 1960s saw the mutual acquaintance of the British and French brands of philosophy, thus testifying, if anything can, to the synthesizing zeal which followed a long period of autistic development on either side. The early and the later work of Sartre became better known on the other side of the Channel, thanks partly to Laing and Cooper's anti-psychiatry, while linguistic philosophers were at last crossing in reverse, helped in this case by the new prestige of all aspects of and approaches to language. It is no longer appropriate to use Wittgenstein or Popper as intercontinental missiles; together with Austin, Strawson, Searle, Grice and others they are an integral part of current French intellectual discourse. Reading their works, as against simply making use of their names, may well turn out to be as arduous as reading the French structuralists they are used to disparage.

This brief enumeration of recent developments in a number of disciplines is sufficient to point to a major problem facing Barthes's reader. Since his work, and structuralism generally, were born of a synthesizing ambition, an appreciation of Barthes's innovations ideally requires a familiarity with all that he attempts to synthesize. Thus one reader will approach his work from one particular discipline, encounter words belonging to another, and accuse Barthes (or his commentator) of using 'jargon'. Yet it is the concepts which are lacking, not the words. As Barthes once put it, answering his critics: Is the Freudian *superego* the same as the *conscience* of classical psychology?: 'Yes, if one removes all the rest' (*CV*,33). These objections are even sometimes levelled at words resurrected from the classical heritage; yet if *mimesis* and *praxis* are part of common educated speech, why not their Platonic and Aristotelian correlates, *diegesis* and *proairesis*?

But this situation can only be exacerbated by the notorious cleft between the two cultures. Even within faculties, transdisciplinary co-operation sometimes encounters other obstacles. As one of the fathers of cybernetics, Norbert Wiener, said, a specialist tends to regard another area as 'something belonging to his colleague three doors down the corridor' who will 'consider any interest in it on his part as an unwarrantable breach of privacy' (1948, 8). Thus it is not surprising that the first inkling granted to the public at large that a major intellectual shift was on the horizon took the form of a quarrel which broke out among literary critics and not in the closed circles of specialists. But it was paradoxical, in the case of such a complex movement, to find the 'Ancients' trundling out the familiar charges of ignorance in order to intimidate the 'Moderns'. Barthes responded in kind, giving in *Critique et vérité* an overview of all the research which should be applied to literary studies, and concluding, with the probabilities on his side: 'One doubts whether the "old criticism" is up to it' (*CV*,37).

The 'Quarrel of the critics' began in 1964, when Barthes had already published enough critical works on literature and society for their discussion to occupy more than half of the present book, with the first attacks against him by Raymond Picard, a professor at the Sorbonne who had specialized in Racine and particularly resented Barthes's work (and Lucien Goldmann's) on the same subject. There followed in 1965, Picard's violent diatribe, *Nouvelle critique ou nouvelle imposture*, whose main target was again Barthes. Using the technique of quibbling about a few factual details so well described by René Wellek (1963, 6) in its employment against the Anglo-American New Criticism, Picard at the same time passed judgment with the utmost assurance on questions of psychology and epistemology, apparently in blithe ignorance of the turmoil both had recently undergone. This self-appointed champion of French taste and intellect against the international disgrace caused by the *nouvelle critique* left no doubt as to the part played by literature and literary studies in the pattern of social power.

One of the best works which emerged out of this debate was Serge Doubrovsky's *Pourquoi la nouvelle critique?* (1966) which, appearing just after Barthes's *Critique et vérité*, can thus also serve as a commentary on it. Doubrovsky, practically alone and probably because he taught in the United States (most of the *nouveaux critiques* were forced by the academic ideology to teach abroad or in marginal institutions), saw that since Picard himself promoted an approach based on Valéry and the New Criticism (in theory at least, since as Doubrovsky observes, he devoted in fact most of his labours to tasks of historical scholarship), he might well have been called a potential formalist. Of the three weapons Picard used to fight against what he saw as pretentious narcissism, 'the certainties of language, the implications of psychological coherence, the imperatives of genre structure', the first two had an ironical ring in view of the researches which were then gathering momentum in linguistics and psychoanalysis, but the third denoted a well-known object of enquiry on the part of the Russian formalists, an anthology of whose texts had been published by Tzvetan Todorov in the year preceding that of Doubrovsky's pamphlet.

As for Doubrovsky's own position, which the rest of his book abundantly characterized as phenomenologist/existentialist (his avowed aim being to contribute to some future *What is Criticism?* on the lines of Sartre's *What is Literature?*), it was not even perceived by the most bigoted of the contestants. For it was beginning to appear that the term *nouvelle critique* covered in fact two very different types of practice. The first type aimed at recapturing the creative core of a literary work, and thus claimed parity with the philosophy of the period in taking lived experience as its foundation. The second type has been widely described as the 'irruption of the human sciences into the field of criticism', and its latent positivism was held in suspicion by the practitioners of the first. The whole episode in retrospect therefore looks like a comedy of errors, not least because this noisy Quarrel turned out to be a mere curtain-raiser for a far more important confrontation, the subject of the next chapter.[12]

2

The structuralist debate

More quarrels

The Quarrel of the critics and the furore it caused in Departments of Literature was in fact indicative of a wider malaise of definition and delineation concerning the nature of different possible discourses and their status in society. This was also central to the complex of questions, motivations, methods and doctrines which formed Barthes's problematic and thus there was a kind of poetic justice — whatever its attendant discomforts — in his being chosen as whipping-boy. Yet his opponents were totally unaware of the magnitude of the issues involved, and treated the whole affair as a local and transient disturbance; by contrast in *Critique et vérité* Barthes characterized the Quarrel as the index of a massive shift in intellectual discourse, a 'crisis of the Commentary' arising from the realization of what he later called the 'compromised' aspect of the human sciences, since they are conveyed by a discourse which can have an infinite semantic drift (1973a).

The recognition of the observer's involvement in what he observes is probably the main lesson of twentieth century thought, and when extended from perception to language, leads to the conclusion that all objects are created, and subjects constituted, by this same language (*CV*,46-9). The magnitude of this shift can be gauged by the puzzled and aggressive comments which greeted the idea that the discourse of science could be examined like any other discourse. Science was no longer to be a 'metalanguage' safe from the consequences of current enquiries about language. Thus the real confrontation[1] was carried out on a more fundamental epistemological level than the Quarrel: it involved practically every discipline, was conducted by better-matched protagonists and eventually centred on the question of humanism. What was involved was no less than an investigation of the nature, status and powers (conscious and unconscious) of the epistemic subject, the speaking and writing subject, and of possible subjects of science and of history — the now fragmented aspects of what used to be blithely known as 'Man', the object of both modern philosophy and of the 'human sciences', a term which from then on could only be written in inverted commas. The debate around literature and criticism appears as a precursor of the new controversy in another way, since perceptive analysts of structuralism could trace the sources of its anti-humanism back to the New Novel, especially Robbe-Grillet, and to the New Theatre of Beckett and Ionesco in the previous decade. This link is very important for the study of Barthes, who was a potent ideological source of the new developments.[2]

The two contending sides were eventually realigned as, on the one hand, the structuralists and, on the other, several sections of the intellectual world which until then had more often than not been at daggers drawn — phenomenologists, existentialists, personalists and non-Althusserian Marxists. The initiative for realignment, however, came entirely from the structuralists who could then with great verve denounce this unholy *union sacrée* while deriving immense publicity from this state of affairs. But the apogee of structuralism around 1966[3] was quickly followed up by an internal contestation, by thinkers like Jacques Derrida and Julia Kristeva; neither bigoted enemies of structuralism nor ignorant of its achievements, they had, on the contrary, been thoroughly conversant with it from the start. The new debate was centred around the ideological implications of the concept of sign. This reversal, which in practice coincided with the wider recognition of the structuralist myth (and the concomitant tidal wave of publications) understandably resulted in quite a few intellectual casualties; as Barthes put it, 'in those days, intellectual history was going very fast' (*T*,99). The main themes of the structuralist and post-structuralist debates must be briefly outlined since they are an essential background to Barthes's work.

During the rise of structuralism, that is, from the mid-1950s to the mid-1960s, a distinction was often made between structuralism as a method and structuralism as a philosophy. Its proponents tended to emphasize the former aspect. So, in a different way of course, did some of its most contemptuous detractors, but on the whole they preferred to show that philosophical attitudes, even a full-blown ideology, were discernible in structuralist works, and were even necessarily presupposed by its methods and procedures. The work of linguists, anthropologists, and even analysts of literature when their material allowed them to behave like mythographers, could be fairly easily presented as a positive contribution to the sciences of 'man'. Philosophical concerns were more explicit in Althusser, and his presuppositions thus served to highlight those of Lacan, whose work he had drawn on. As for Foucault, although he had brought to light historical primary source material, he was the most obvious philosopher of them all, and could hardly be defended consistently when, with provocative militancy, he described Man both as a recent invention and an obsolescent philosophical problem (see below, p. 19). Attitudes to structuralism were often determined by the extra philosophical burden put on acceptable scientific achievements, and especially of course where social and political consequences were inferred. But objections were also levelled at structuralism from a scientific point of view, as is shown by Jean Piaget's book *Structuralism*. In spite of its shortcomings,[4] I shall take it for the time being as a guideline. The fact that there is no single treatment of this debate which is at once comprehensive and balanced puts the onus on the reader and may well be symbolic of the whole situation.

Man and structures

Emile Durkheim's idea of *le fait social*, was that it exercised an external constraint over the individual. It could therefore be studied in the manner of Auguste Comte who wanted, as Piaget points out, to explain man by means of mankind and no longer mankind by means of man. Comte put sociology — a word he coined — at the summit of a hierarchy of all the sciences, and gave an account of their development (see Appendix, p. 230 for an account of Saussure's relation to Durkheim). Piaget, in like fashion, successively reviews all the structures found in mathematics and logic, physics and biology, psychology, linguistics and social studies, with an appendix on the philosophical conclusions which can be drawn from the study of these structures. This appendix points up Piaget's one-sidedness, since it is only here, at the end of the book, that major participants in the debate, like Sartre, Althusser and Foucault, make an appearance.

Despite the numerous and diverse polemical intentions in the different disciplines, all structuralists agree that the structures they claim to have discovered in nature share three properties: totality, transformations and self-regulation. These are abstracted by Piaget from what seems to be a common definition of a structure, namely a system of transformations, endowed with its own laws, without need of external elements. A structure is thus different from a mere aggregate of elements.

Although Piaget accepts this essential distinction between a structure and an aggregate, he thinks that the idea that structures are self-sufficient, and can therefore be studied as immanent, is no more than a postulate. It was obvious even from the outset, and despite its literary sources, that structuralism was a part of a general scientific trend which could be traced back to the end — for Piaget the beginning — of the nineteenth century. In particular, the notion of field in physics had served as a model in psychology for Gestalt theory which maintained that perception is a direct and instantaneous apprehension of wholes, whose properties cannot be reduced to that of their elements. According to the Gestaltists, the experimental discovery of such structures made unnecessary any study of their genesis (an exploration of the subject's mental activity and his interaction with the world). This attitude made the Gestaltist model particularly welcome to structuralists. Yet, as Piaget points out, it was a view which had already been seriously qualified by his own discovery of the importance of developmental factors. The argument for the autonomy of structures on grounds of their coherence, however, involves consquences, some of which he accepts, while rejecting the depreciation of the notion of causality (now replaced by laws of transformation), especially historical causality which until then had been the all-purpose explanation.

Piaget does go along with the corresponding depreciation of what phenomenologists called *le vécu*, 'lived experience'. Defined exclusively in terms of the conscious (although subject to varying degrees of awareness in practice) this notion of experience cannot recognize unconscious factors (although the word *unconscious* for Piaget refers to the laws of language or behaviour and not to Freudian dynamics). For phenomenologists it is possible to have direct access, through empirical facts, to essences and ideal significations; for structuralists the relationship with the world is mediate. Lévi-Strauss tells in his autobiography, *Tristes Tropiques*, of the three disciplines, his 'three mistresses', geology, Marxism and psychoanalysis, which gave him the original insight that the truth, the intelligible, was never found in what is immediately accessible to the senses. Oppositions like those of the manifest and the latent in psychoanalysis, of deep and surface structure in Chomskyan linguistics, of immanence and manifestation in semantics or of the double articulation in structural linguistics (where meaning results from a combination of elements themselves without meaning; see Appendix, p. 231) — all partake of the same idea for the structuralist.[5]

Special techniques are therefore necessary to get at the truth, which can only be read by a decoder or even a cryptanalyst or code-breaker, although the hope of evolving automatic discovery procedures (on the model of an algorithm) has been abandoned even in linguistics: each field must develop its own method of approach, designed to cope with its specific structuration. Thus even in human affairs structuralists reject the method of *comprehension* which for phenomenologists and existentialists was the only one suited to the nature of man who as subject and agent freely confers meaning and value (comprehension is the direct apprehension of the meaning of human behaviour, while *explanation* denotes the analytic method suited to the sciences of nature). Hence structuralism's inevitable and sometimes sadistically gleeful devaluation of the human project, a denial of the possibility of choice. Man does not act, think or speak, he is 'acted', 'thought' and 'spoken'. For Lévi-Strauss myths think themselves out in men and unbeknownst to them. For

Lacan, Descartes's *Cogito ergo sum*, 'I think therefore I am', taken by Western philosophy as the canonic form of the relationship of the subject to his thought, must be rewritten as 'I think where I am not, I am where I do not think'; the subject is subverted and man is defined by his 'radical eccentricity to himself'. Lacan stressed not the rationalist, therapeutic and optimistic aspects of psychoanalysis but the irreducible character of the unconscious, castration as the entrance into society and the primacy of language in the constitution of the subject, and of the signifier in language. Individual and collective subject are nothing more than the locus where the effects of organizations which escape them are manifested, the site of the combinatorial play of elements. Such an image, however, was welcomed by those who, like Lévi-Strauss, were growing tired of the posturings of the subject, a spoiled child which had hogged the centre of the stage for too long, playing, to use Bachelard's term, the part of 'epistemological obstacle'.[6]

A new positivism?

Where Sartre's dualism had emphasized man's radical rupture with the world, with structuralism the pendulum was to swing back to a long overdue emphasis on the link between man and the cosmos. Piaget correctly detects in structuralism an attempt to reach the ultimate reality of nature despite the stress it puts on mediating codes (Lévi-Strauss has even declared himself content with 'vulgar materialism'). Yet the movement was soon hailed as a 'new positivism', paradoxically since Comte invented the word *positivism* to denote a rejection of metaphysical attitudes in favour of a scientific methodology which could also be applied to the prospective human sciences. The answer to this paradox is double: first of all, the new intelligibility stressed synchrony and the simultaneous relations between elements, rather than diachrony and all questions of development from origins (just as linguists had stopped concerning themselves with the origin of language). This fresh perspective was productive in discovering structures, and initial success which was experienced as a positive and fertile acquisition contrasting happily with what had become a repetitive and pious restatement of 'man's condition' by phenomenologists. Secondly, the rejection of the genetic perspective as irrelevant offered a welcome liberation from the Marxist yoke and its increasingly dogmatic and sterile stress on history.[7] The structuralist validation of abstraction offered an emancipation from constant exhortations to think in concrete terms on the part of Marxism at its most dogmatic and sterile. Yet it is significant that at the time Lévi-Strauss still felt the need to present his autonomous structures as contributions to the neglected field of Marxist superstructure. For quite a long time, this latent schism was not felt; Lévi-Strauss as well as disciples of

Lacan and Althusser still went on publishing in Sartre's *Temps modernes* (although one must also remember the connection of this periodical with Maurice Merleau-Ponty, whose catholic views were clearly important for Barthes's thinking at the time).

The positivist outlook, which purports to defend science against metaphysics, invariably ends up impeding the progress of science itself, and this is very well shown by Piaget. One reason he starts his critique of structuralism with mathematics is that, according to him, the first example of a structure in the modern sense is found in the mathematical concept of groups, as conceived by the early nineteenth-century mathematician Evariste Galois. Piaget argues that the fruitfulness of the notion of group derives from an indissociable combination of transformation and conservation, whose utilization of the idea of equilibrium and tension makes it an incomparable instrument of constructivity. This allows Piaget to beat the structuralists at their own game. The idea of groups is the basis of set theory, a favourite structuralist model; but the concepts involved in the notion of groups can equally be used to show that sets could be considered not as relations but as 'beings' which have classifiable operations performed on them, thereby reaching the notion of *category* (see Badiou, 1969, 45, 56, 91). This indeed is the modern mathematical practice. In other words, the distinction between relations and elements, and its structuralist twist of stressing relations in order to depreciate the positive content of the elements, is itself ideological and out of date from at least one point of view: there is no such thing as a form in itself or a content in itself. Any content may be 'deconstructed' into an interplay of forms; but vice versa any form can in its turn be treated as a content.

Piaget concludes that the general conditions necessary to explain rational schemata are both a system of regulated transformations *and* an openness to the possible. Such a position transcends that of the structuralists for whom 'the possible' refers to a kind of Mendeleev periodic table of elements. For Piaget this 'possible' lies in the future and results in part from an interaction of the subject with the world. We shall see how Barthes oscillated between these two models. In the special 'Structuralism' number of *Esprit* (a personalist monthly), Jean Ladrière argues that formalization cannot be separated from interpretation, that neither exists before the other. In interpretation, the system, like an oracle, offers several possible worlds into which we can make reality fit; though it seems to impose its law on us, it is itself the product of a sovereign action.

Whatever final conclusions one wishes to draw from this consideration of scientific activity as reality, not myth, it is clear that there was nothing in it to terrify a personalist, as the least timorous of them soon pointed out. The same applied to those among the materialists who did not need the constant reassurance of an unmistakable material view of matter. The philosopher of science Georges Canguilhem put the debate into perspective when with tongue in cheek he titled his excellent review of Foucault's *The Order of Things* — 'Death of Man or Exhaustion of the Cogito?'[8]

Theory as strategy

Two books published around that time, *Qu'est-ce que le structuralisme?* (1968), edited by François Wahl, and *Panorama des sciences humaines* (1973), edited by Denis Hollier, exemplify the ambivalence with which the human sciences are now viewed. These books are valuable counterparts to Piaget's survey and should be read in conjunction with it.

Trying to answer his own question, Wahl declares that structuralism concerns those sciences that deal not with objects but with their signs, with *représentance*. Accordingly, he selects linguistics, poetics, anthropology and psychoanalysis. His introduction and essay on Foucault, Althusser and Derrida show beyond all doubt, however, that each field has benefited from a convergence and cross-fertilization whose effects are strictly speaking not scientific but ideological. This last word cuts particularly deep since the 'sciences of sign systems' were said to derive their privileged status from an 'epistemological break' marking the passage from an ideological discourse to a science (the epistemological break, a much-quoted phrase of Bachelard, occurs when the definition of a new 'object' opens the passage from the empirical to the theoretical, in which, according to a witticism by another epistemologist, Alexandre Koyré, experiment has to be verified by theory).

Hollier's *Panorama* is even more revealing, both in its preface and its table of contents. Structuralism purports to be a 'discourse where theory becomes *strategy*' (1973, 7). Hollier's book is more broadly based than Wahl's since its field is defined as 'the articulation of the facts of *production* and the facts of *signification*, that of the facts of *labour* and those of *language* in whose interplay sexuality finds itself enmeshed'. It redistributes the human sciences under the three headings of labour, unconscious, languages (corresponding to the three areas marked out for special study by Foucault in *The Order of Things*). Structuralism is presented polemically as the only truly modern and scientific answer to the question of 'man', a question positivism (which apes natural science) and hermeneutics (which interprets signs) had been vainly trying to answer with their opposing methods. Foucault had argued that since the much-publicized death of a God conceived as the locus of the truth, man has been attempting to define himself both as the *object* of new sciences modelled on the natural sciences (the famous 'human sciences') and also as the *subject* of science itself. In other words he had been considering himself some times as nature and sometimes as God without ever being able to bridge this constitutive gap — the term 'human sciences' in fact covers a series of disciplines (like linguistics, geography, psychology, etc.) conceived as completely heterogeneous and for which a common object is thus purely illusory. Hence Foucault's description of 'man' as 'un étrange doublet empirico-transcendental'.[9]

The debate around structuralism is thus centred on two notions: that of science and that of the subject. In practice the subject is more important, since the debate around science, which seemingly devalues the notion of truth and replaces it by that of a consciousness of history (thus the human sciences are said to be 'neither empirical nor dogmatic but historical') in fact ends up in an undeniable dogmatism. Wahl takes the new paradigm so much for granted that he describes himself and his collaborators as facing the problems typical of 'second generation' scientists, in Kuhn's notion of the puzzle-solving activity of what has become 'normal science'. Whoever does not agree is exposed to much punitive talk of 'regression'. But the major enigma (explicitly put to one side by Kuhn) namely the correspondence between these human and historical constructions and the real, is hardly touched on (just as it is avoided in J.-M. Benoist's interesting account, 1975). Any accumulation of knowledge would be unwelcome in a philosophy which seeks to separate the idea of history from that of linear progress, a conception which goes back to the Enlightenment.

A new Eleatism?

For this reconsideration of history is what was really at stake in the polarization around the question of humanism. In 1947 Sartre had defensively claimed that existentialism was a humanism. Althusser now aggressively claimed (against Sartre and others) that Marxism was not. In thus trying to give back to Marxism its epistemological edge he was successful in widening its horizon and starting a process of emancipation allied to the novel aspects offered by the Chinese offshoot, itself soon to generate a momentous schism. The idea of a Cultural Revolution could only strengthen the tenet that superstructures are relatively autonomous and act as a spur to structuralist research, as well as somewhat relieving the 'unhappy consciousness' of the intellectual.

For while some made scientific objections to structuralism, others found more to fear in the fatalistic despair which a belief in such an 'order of things' might produce. Lacan, in earlier and less polemical times, had stated in a remarkably ecumenical doctoral thesis (1975b) that 'the fact that the subject says "I", thinks he is acting to some purpose, makes promises and assertions' was something that could not be ignored (and he was not above making some recommendations which would today smack of social engineering). Such practical guidance on everyday matters and wider political issues was now of course out of the question. The notion of 'typical cure' is taken in *Ecrits* as a symbol of the 'abjection' to which French analysis had sunk. Pressed to ascribe an aim to analysis, Lacanians would never go beyond a general description, that it might enable the subject to 'advene', or gain access, to his desire. All this showed an admirable distrust of normative and prescriptive attitudes; yet somehow one never quite felt that it stemmed from a desire to give full play to unfathomed human possibilities, which had been unmistakable in the theories under attack, Marxism, surrealism and existentialism.[10]

The structuralist outlook, which asserts the primacy of structure over history, seemed in comparison essentially static and in effect conservative. Inevitably, there were some to suggest that structuralists were not in fact displeased with the current state of affairs and that their philosophy, whatever their professedly left-wing opinions, was in fact the ideology of technocracy. More charitable interpretations saw it as the consequence of a political impotence reinforced by the advent of Gaullism, which reduced intellectuals to the status of mandarins. Certainly, the period between the mid-1950s and the mid-1960s saw profound social changes in France, and for a while the 'speaking subject' gave every sign of actively choosing to be a passive subject of the consumer society. There are some who reject such socio-historical explanations and insist that the structuralist system must be discussed in its own terms; but this simply means that they have already endorsed this system, since structuralism is precisely defined by an immanent stance.

Structuralism was described by the independent Marxist philosopher Henri Lefebvre as 'the new Eleatism'. This reference to the Ancient philosophical school was meant to allude to the structuralists' constant stress on the constitutive role of established institutions and to their inability to account for change except as something accidental and irrational. To see change as brought about by men in charge of their fate would at least introduce some intelligibility. The 'illusion' that it was possible to act as a responsible subject was understandably reinforced in 1968 when, as someone put it, 'the structures took to the streets'.

With so many factors involved, the intellectual picture became very confused; even knowing someone's character, political affiliations, philosophical and religious opinions, personal style, daily newspaper and present place of work could not count as legitimate clues to his stand on any subject. On navigating any one individual's stance in relation to the many forms of *soixante-huitard* leftism, it is necessary to take into account the positions of the French Communist Party which, like a mighty planet, was deflecting quite a few trajectories. The scars left on Barthes by left-wing puritanism are obvious as early as *Writing Degree*

Zero but the defence of superstructure in Althusserian Marxism had been a welcome relief from *ouvriérisme*. Stalinist dogmatism, however, found a natural successor in the Maoist wave which followed 1968, convincing Barthes that the name of power is Legion. The need for a more sophisticated way to tackle it was 'brutally evident', as he put it in his Inaugural Lecture (1977) and the second preface (1970) to *Mythologies*; a statement which, like others, was widely misunderstood in spite of his having elucidated it several times. While Maoist dogmatism seems to have counteracted, for Barthes, the libertarian atmosphere which followed the *prise de la parole* (a definition of 1968, by analogy with the taking of the Bastille), the optimism of 1968 is no doubt at the source of the hedonistic release which produced *The Pleasure of the Text*.[11]

But the 1960s (and early 1970s) came to an end. The translation of Solzhenitsyn's *Gulag Archipelago*, together with the woeful story of Marxist regimes all over the world, and perhaps their own experience of dogmatism within their respective movements, made many former Maoists or even plain left-wingers change their tune, sometimes abruptly. This general feeling of revulsion against Marxism of all sorts gave rise to the wave known as the *nouveaux philosophes*. It also gave a new topicality to the traditional debate about the interpretation of 'the man and his work'. Just as Freud's life and character had been scrutinized as a possible source of bias in psychoanalysis, Marx has come in lately for this sort of biographical treatment. Attempts were made to show that concentration camps, xenophobia, anti-semitism and the tendency to embalm father figures were already present in embryo in Marx's selfish, narrow-minded, self-important, humourless, phallocratic and snobbish propensities. This theme was soon taken up by the entire French press; Gide's and Camus's objections to Marxism were unearthed. *Le pouvoir* (power), especially that of the state, Hegel's 'cold monster', became the omnipresent enemy. *Savoir* (a combination of science and *pouvoir*) did not have a good press either. There were those who complained that the idea of tracing the genealogy of tyranny from Stalin back to Lenin, Marx, Hegel and Plato is nothing but Karl Popper writ large; but they missed the main point, which is that the face of the world has changed since Popper wrote *The Open Society and Its Enemies* (1945).

Sartre had defined existentialism as an attempt to live out fully all the consequences of atheism; the structuralists had retorted that this claim was invalidated by existentialism's Promethean humanism. Now there was a new twist. The indictment of the Enlightenment, with its belief in reason and progress, led to a general denunciation of all *maîtrise*. This currently overworked word has complex connotations which make it an ideal vehicle for Barthes: it can mean mastery or control, but the immediate source of its recent usage is the Hegelian dialectic of Master and Slave in the *Phenomenology of Mind*. The belief that it is not possible or desirable ever to 'totalize' or 'master' anything, be it the unconscious, a literary text, or human history, has given a new meaning to dialectics which (in addition to its unwelcome Marxist connotations) is now seen as a synthesizing fantasy rather than an instrument of relativization. As against this, plurality, heterogeneity, and a recognition of the Other as other are praised. Another curious consequence is of interest in view of Barthes's later texts. One offshoot of Maoism had been feminism, since women on the left were finding little change in the way they were treated, and could see no harm in trying to speed up the revolution as far as their rights were concerned. Thanks to the Lacanian synthesis, the protest against unity and totality could be extended to a protest against all phallic values, not only in male-dominated society but, through the demotion of ego and reason, in the discursive approach itself and in all systematic thought as well.

Self-help, ethnic revivalism, a return to private life and a stress on ethics at the expense of politics had become the new values; but some still deplored the loss of a common belief. They saw the subversion of the subject in structuralism as a clearing of the ground for a religious rebirth. Hence Roger Dadoun, praising Solzhenitsyn's attitude as 'regredience' not regression, while Foucault envied Muslim spirituality — until Barthes pointed out that Khomeini was surely an archetypal example of *pouvoir*, while François George noted that Marx's paranoid tendencies were no less evident in the God of the Old Testament.

These rapid shifts produced a generalized scepticism and nihilism which undoubtedly went along with Barthes's own evolution to explain the feeling of artistic and intellectual isolation evoked in his autobiography. This succession of losses of values has also been reflected in the new inflationary atmosphere in publishing: in the last ten years intellectual objects have increasingly been treated as obsolescent commodities, a trend which has in turn been recognized by sociologists like Jean Baudrillard as a new object for their activity. The publishing waves come ever faster: structuralism, 1968, the *nouveaux philosophes*, the *nouveau romantisme*, the *nouvelle droite*, resembling the yearly upheaval of fashion studied by Barthes in *Système de la Mode*. One survival tactic, not available to Barthes himself, has been the development of the new torrential kind of writing style. At first a reaction to the Medusa-like fascination of the all-conquering Structure, it has proved itself adaptable, on the one hand as expression of a would-be specifically feminine approach to writing and, on the other, the new prophetic mysticism. This writing seeks to be both sensuous and to exhibit the 'logic of the signifier', the very law of the unconscious which, as was shown by Freud and exemplified by Lacan, is an indefatigable and tasteless punster. These Joycean practices have undoubtedly increased the general awareness of the reality and resources of the material side of language and what it reveals about the workings of the mind; but they often seem very mechanical in contrast with Barthes's inspired and subtle effects.[12]

As is well known, Sartre's own conception of literature was quite different, although it is all too easy to reduce it to a few formulae on 'committed' literature and to forget the lessons of his essays on imagination and above all his own practice as a writer. The dispute between structuralists and existentialists was not inevitable; the second of these two great post-war movements could have been conceived as a long overdue complement to the first to yield a total picture of man in society.[13] Both movements, after all, fought the same enemy, the positivism which, as Barthes notes in 'Myth Today' (*M*,151-2) denies both determinism and freedom. In *Search for a Method*, Sartre had deplored the prevalent impoverished version of Marxism for its neglect of the structures in individuals and society. For Sartre these were mediations of a project: Lacan's findings could be integrated into his own notion of the practico-inert. In Sartre's famous saying, what is important is to find out what man makes of what has been made of him. Structuralism's failure to recognize the central place of praxis was the object of Sartre's comment that 'geology' would be a more appropriate description of Foucault's work than Foucault's own term 'archaeology'. And yet, Sartre had seemed in the late 1960s to be poised to add his structuralist *aggiornamento* to his earlier phenomenological, Marxist and even psychoanalytical ones. And never more so than on the subject of structural approaches to the text, which he said he himself intended to use in his study on Flaubert. Controversy made him harden his positions, however. Goaded by a journalist about the spectrum of possible meanings allowed by the 'plural writing' advocated by Barthes, Sartre retorted that even a spectrum has a unity. The fact that it is very difficult to find metaphors for plurality which do not lend themselves to the same criticism suggests that we can perceive plurality only in a polar opposition with unity.

In the introduction to his book on Flaubert, Sartre, like Barthes, asks the question: Where to begin? He declares that owing to man's incessant labour of totalization, the main thing is to start exploring this symbolic whole from a given problem. Accordingly Sartre begins with Flaubert's 'native wound', which was eventually to turn him into a 'subject of writing'. A similar approach will be adopted here.

3

A narrative with a hero

Armature, code, message

The background to Barthes's career has now been sufficiently sketched. Equally, I must assume a reader who has a basic familiarity with Barthes's work: this is meant to be a book, not a textbook. The aim is to give a 'symptomatic reading', one for which the gaps and presuppositions in the discourse are as significant as what is explicitly stated.

What then is the symptom, this 'native wound' with which Sartre suggested one should begin? To anticipate — an awareness that society sends us messages within messages, that indoctrination and coercion are the price to pay for recognition, and in particular for recognition as a writer. And that, conversely, the image of the writer, and perhaps even the desire for recognition are fostered in us by society in the first place. Barthes tried for a time to solve this difficulty by adopting separate strategies as semiologist (that is, as scientist) and as writer, echoing the dual approach of the existentialists, their essays dealing with essences and their fiction with existence. Barthes was not satisfied for long by this arrangement, however, and his suspicion is proved right today when a more profound approach to the semantics of discourse seeks to account for fiction and system as elements of the same spectrum (see Lacoue-Labarthe, 1975).

The thesis of this book therefore concerns both the unitary thrust of Barthes's work and the chronology in which it was deployed. A distinction borrowed from Lévi-Strauss is useful at this point. In *The Raw and the Cooked* he distinguishes in the study of myths between the *armature*, a set of properties which remain invariant in two or several myths; the *code*, the system of functions ascribed by each myth to these properties; and the *message*, the content of any one particular myth (1964, 205). What Barthes himself identifies as problematic, and the basic concepts with which he tackles it — in short, the armature — will be examined first. Here we find three focuses in Barthes's activity: he seeks to provide a typology of discursive strategies, a theory of poetic language or the poetic Word, and a philosophy of literary studies in which the respective roles of imitation and innovation, style and method, can be reassessed within the framework of teaching and research. All these concerns can be traced back to Barthes's first published book, *Writing Degree Zero*, (1953) and will be found to foreshadow many ideas later associated with other theorists.

Barthes's *codes*, in other words the system of functions his 'myths' use to account for his universe (and the word *myth* does not here have the derogatory meaning it has for him) are two in number, co-existing throughout his work but alternating their relative dominance. An awareness of chronology is therefore essential in reading Barthes, since some words switch their content in the course of this alternation (the most obvious being *speech* and *writing*) while others, like *meaning*, exchange their initial positive connotation for a negative one. Foucault's notion of archaeology, as the discovery of staggered discontinuities, is thus more useful here than the idea of a linear development, which cannot account for all the facts observed. Finally, Barthes's individual works are the *messages* themselves, and the word applies here to the form at least as much as to the content.

Chronology

It comes as no surprise to find that all Barthes's exegetes are forced to adopt some sort of counterpoint, playing the logic of their argument against that of the various works studied and against the development of their author — hence a number of flashbacks in the following pages. As for 'flash forwards', which are indispensable for pointing up thematic constants, they have had a bad press since the existentialists argued that they robbed the characters of their freedom. They are good for drama, though, as has been known from time immemorial; and since Barthes invites us to read *Critical Essays*, for instance, as a narrative with a hero, we shall not deny ourselves this thrill.[1]

All commentators agree that Barthes's career falls roughly into four phases, but they disagree about their interpretation. The first phase is a statement of general attitudes, an elaboration of what I have called the armature of his thought. The second phase was characterized by him as a 'euphoric dream of scientificity', his structuralist period. The third he summarized as a passage 'from semiology to semanalysis', the word coined by Julia Kristeva to denote a new theory of signification. Thus the distinction between the second and third phases is partly at Barthes's own insistence: to the layman, a work like *S/Z*, typical of the third phase, still looks forbiddingly 'structuralist' and sufficiently remote from traditional ways of tackling a text to make the break imperceptible.

Indeed I shall argue that it is a mistake to view the themes of this period as entirely new, not, however, on the grounds of a structuralist hegemony but, on the contrary, because the third period often involves a return to some of Barthes's basic attitudes, visible in his first phase before the great scientific dream took complete hold. These attitudes were already fully expressed as a doctrine of literature around 1960, a date at which the texts show a marked change occurring in Barthes, for reasons which cannot be fully explained. This change, which caused the switch in Barthes's codes, was the result of an effort to resolve some conflicts which looked insoluble and is the source of the despondent tone of the preface to *Critical Essays* (1964). The significance, indeed the visibility, of these changes was, however, masked for a while by the rise of structuralism, which evoked in Barthes a tremendous surge of optimism and self-confidence, as existentialism and Marxism had done in his early career. When structuralism was in turn contested, the move from second to third phases, Barthes fell back onto these earlier positions, fortified now by the theories of Foucault, Derrida, Kristeva and the established ideology of the 'second generation' — all of which he had foreshadowed almost twenty years before. However, what is at stake here is not establishing intellectual ownership but a defence of these ideals and frame of reference Barthes espoused at the beginning of his career, a claim that the obvious tension of these early years corresponded to some genuine antinomies.

The fourth phase has been welcomed by those who were overawed by the technical complexity of his earlier work. Suddenly 'something seemed to have happened to Barthes', a mellowing which they could trace in subjects and attitudes. Undeniable as this may be, one is rather sorry for people who had to wait until then to realize that Barthes was human. This public response probably has another cause: a new importance granted to the reader. Barthes, from his third phase on, seemed to speak no longer as a 'message-sender' but as a 'message-receiver'; and the reader he had in mind was himself.

This in turn is part of the change which I have indicated above. But many have preferred to give an account centred on the notions of science and truth crucial to the structuralist debate. And indeed the dialectics of constraint and freedom, community and individual, prose and poetry, which govern Barthes's thinking can also be expressed as an opposition between writing and science. In the significantly entitled *Critique et vérité* (1966) Barthes analysed three stances which can be adopted towards a literary work (once the necessary socio-historical and philological research has been done). Ranging from the most objective to the most subjective, they are that of the 'science of literature' (or as it is generally known by now, *poetics*), that of *criticism*, and that of *reading*. Poetics studies the general conditions of literary meaning. Criticism 'fills' with various significations the abstract forms discovered by poetics and is therefore necessarily a kind of 'anamorphosis', involving different but limited points of view in a regulated transformation.[2] The critic's interpretations must be validated by their coherence and completeness and not by reference to the critic's own 'authenticity'. The existence of criteria of validation is Barthes's refutation of the labour-saving objection, on the part of critics who did not care to go into all these new and difficult systems of interpretation, that the new critics said anything that came into their minds: 'One does not make meaning just anyhow (if you don't believe me, try it)' (CV,65). Criticism, however, is mediated by language as a social object, and must therefore be distinguished from reading, the immediate contact with the text which no critical pronouncement can ever replace. Akin to love, this relationship, this desire to merge with the work, ultimately with the experience which impelled the writer to write, in effect turns the reader into a writer.

Despite such precautions, Barthes's more recent pronouncements have appeared, in the eyes of some readers, as not merely un- but anti-scientific. Some professed themselves 'scandalized', others imitated his new found scepticism and praised this latest example of his fabled 'Protean-ness'. In fact, no one had found anything Protean about Barthes before: admiring his wide interests is quite another matter. But from then on this Gidean trait was incorporated into a new image, the nomadic thinker, forever on the move, taking theories as works of art and casting them aside once the exquisite novelty of their flavour had worn off, or perhaps just before. There is method in his Protean-ness however, although one can sympathize with the complaints of his early followers, inasmuch as the defence of his latest point of view does not seem to require the disparagement of his earlier ones — except perhaps in the protagonist himself, whose new internal economy makes this manoeuvre imperative, and tolerable. An additional irony comes from the fact that while the new values stressed by Barthes as an antidote to the tyranny of all systems were pleasure and the freedom of desire, those who followed him in his latest metamorphosis nevertheless rebuked those who did not feel so inclined and made other theoretical choices.

It is clear at any rate that Barthes was concerned that the 'proper' construction be put on his career. For recent special issues devoted to him by *Le Magazine littéraire* and *L'Arc*, he supplied two early texts (1942, 1974c) which seem to comment on this latest development. One is a review of the *Journals* of Gide, the master whose shifting allegiances long alienated the public and who enjoined his disciple, in *Fruits of the Earth*, to 'throw away this book'. The other is Barthes's only piece of fiction, a parody of the *Crito*, where Socrates, instead of setting an example of respect for the law, is tempted back to life by the sight of a plate of figs — a traditional emblem of sensuality — and decamps, trusting Plato, with his natural instinct for the flattering pose, to arrange matters with History. It is easy to imagine that some Gidean irony prompted Barthes to supply this text, both as a symbol of his accession to the Promised Land of fiction and of his indifference to the criticism levelled at him by some contributors to these review numbers.

This 'disappointing' attitude is another Gidean trait. As in a line by Donne to which Gide once gave a similar interpretation: 'Rob me, but bind me not and let me go', he escapes from his disciples' demands, leaving behind the mantle of the theorist in order to rejoice in the nudity of the hedonist. Literature is defined by Barthes, in a highly personal passage in *Critical Essays*, as that god who dares to take the motto 'I disappoint', and who forever eludes the grasp of definitive interpretation. The interpretations which adopt a teleological view where Barthes's earlier works are said to lead to the enlightenment of both Barthes and his reader (the lesson being that one should feel a permanent urge to displace problems) thus inevitably acquire the status of an authorized version, relentlessly promoted, confirmed by Barthes's own interpretation (1977, 1978, etc.) and indeed originating in him.[3] Perhaps one should conclude that critics who concur and congratulate each other for 'speaking barthesianese' and 'singing in tune' are happy to remain on what Lacan calls the imaginary plane.

Post hoc ergo propter hoc

In fact this stylized version repeatedly given by Barthes of his own career looks like a typical case of Freudian *après-coup*. It is also an example of the fallacy denounced by Barthes himself as the major prop of the illusionism of fiction: *post hoc ergo propter hoc*. Just as ignoring the development of his career results in a trite vulgate in which all principles are put on the same plane, a linear view of it removes all the tensions due to conflicts and antinomies, which are sometimes more enlightening than the doctrines themselves. But above all, if one wishes to add a teleological aspect, one should logically discard the major part of Barthes's work. It is worth noting that although enemies are delighted to do so, teleologically-minded friends draw the line there. What they call 'classical semiology' is somehow still said to be valid, in ways which are never made quite clear. Semiology is said to be both 'dead' and 'yet to come', from which one can only deduce that it is still-born; 'classical' semiologists did not fail to draw this conclusion, with some bitterness. Yet their methods are often used in practice. I shall argue in the last chapter that neither attitude makes sense in isolation and that they are structurally linked.

In fact, Barthes's stance is part of the general disillusionment about the possibility or even desirability of ever 'totalizing' or 'mastering' anything. This reaction has led back to the kind of academic-baiting which might have had some point at the time of the Quarrel but is less justified following the major changes in the organization and syllabus of universities since the events of 1968. But this reorganization is now often dismissed by means of the derogatory word *recuperation*. With its connotations of utilitarianism and normality, the word clearly stands as an antonym of gratuitous, inherently 'perverted' desire, and indicates a retreat from the orthodox Marxist worship of productivity.

Of course, the label of recuperation is justified in a way, since it is not only 1968 which followed the wide recognition of structuralism but also the critical reappraisal which resulted in a violent rejection of positivism, one that the 'new establishment' on the whole did not endorse. History was indeed going very fast then, and less informed well-wishers were understandably confused when their totalizing enthusiasm was openly scorned by trend-setters in the midst of the semiological triumphs of the Milan Conference. But there is yet another reason for all this. If Barthes, by his recantations, ends up, like literature, by disappointing, he has also ended up with a very different position on literature itself. In earlier days he stressed the continuity of all discourses, and especially the literary and the critical; but he came to defend, and so to justify, his change of heart by the intrinsic 'difference' of literature. Creative language was now seen as the only one to grapple with the 'otherness', the 'heterogeneity' of the world, of matter in short. All the 'positive' Marxist connotations could then be used again; the blurb of *Sade, Fourier, Loyola* (1971) alleges that this purely formal study of three authors is more truly 'materialist' than one which takes the content into account. There was equal room for the opposite notion, stemming from Georges Bataille, of reckless loss and one-sided expenditure.

Understandably, creative writers have been in the forefront of this move, and Barthes among them, since his recognition as such had at last brought him reassurance. Yet this new image carries its own dangers, epitomized by his phrase 'Culture recuperates everything', where the pejorative connotation spreads to any kind of durable and collectively recognized achievement. His final attitude can then be made intelligible not as yet the latest metamorphosis, or an attempt to silence dissenting voices, but as the expression of a life-long and typically modernist fight against reification. The striving after originality, which throngs of disciples may compromise, was not so much due to Barthes's intolerance to 'demand' as an example of the Darwinian struggle which exists supremely in matters of literary survival.

The fact that Barthes, the former mythologist of art and society, himself came to acquire a quasi-mythological status was thus as threatening as it was flattering. All this was of course accentuated by the merciless conditions obtaining in Paris where the thirst for novelty extends not only to style but to theory (thus exacerbating Barthes's twin obsessions), and recently caused one of the current masters, the philosopher Lyotard, to make a plea for more 'theoretical apathy'. Sects and coteries, political groups, institutions and the personalities of the pace-setters combine to produce a formal ballet of cultural terrorism which is the counterpart of the genuine wealth of choices offered by so many possible allegiances. There is under such conditions a very real danger that such a desperate flight from the *doxa* (the Platonic word for opinion, which Foucault re-launched as the opposite of *episteme* and which Barthes often uses) will result in not a few gratuitous *paradoxes*, a danger which Barthes himself points to in his autobiography. As Sartre once put it, just as there are commonplaces, there are common paradoxes. Let us note that even Derrida and Kristeva, whose work did so much to dispel the smugly scientistic mood of the sixties, recognize that the work of 'deconstruction', of negativity, must allow some positive moments so that the work of antithesis, and thus of synthesis, can take place, albeit provisionally. Such moments are also, of course, a psychological necessity, which can be descried behind some highly-coded statements by current masters, and which is in part catered to by the swings of fashion, a much-maligned reality.

Barthes's reaction was for a while a complete abandonment of mental life and its own logic, and a refuge in the apparently mindless yet meaningful depths of the body, with a mythical hope of translating them into words without the mediation of discourse. The fears he might have entertained about this primitivism — which is a classic feature of modernism — were to some extent exorcized by new psychoanalytical concepts. Ostensibly centred on the assessment of his self-image, his later work thus evinced a return to an earlier, 'utopian' attempt to grasp and express the essence of the world directly, through poetry, to be in touch with matter and nature, mostly symbolized by the mother, and thus to render not so much the body, as (in Barthes's terms) 'the body under the body'. This is a kind of realist ontology of language, in which the scientist and the poet reached a (perhaps ultimately fallacious) synthesis. It was bolstered by a resurgence of libertarian thought in all its forms and an awareness of marginality which can be traced from the earliest part of Barthes's career to, for instance, the late essay on Fourier. This withdrawal, on the part of both Barthes and our time, from many formerly established values may be interpreted either as a general disillusionment or perhaps as protective covering for values yet to come, whose appearance cannot be anticipated by anyone.

4

He is a writer, who wants to be one

Writer and critic

There is in Barthes, although not stressed either by him or his commentators, a strong, spontaneous and optimistic urge toward scientific enquiry. When he reflects about literature, however, he behaves like a typical 'modern', and never more so than when he defines the writer, not by any positive achievements (not even, following the surrealists, by the adoption of certain life styles), but so to speak negatively, by his questioning stance. According to a logic which can also be observed in exemplars of modernism like Duchamp or Borges, the crucial moment is not so much the finished product, the *oeuvre*, as the activity of writing, the idea of writing, and above all, the desire to write. And despite his widely admired performance as a stylist, it is *only* because Barthes shares this attitude that he claims recognition as a writer himself: 'He is a writer, who wants to be one' (E,146), 'for whom language is a problem, who experiences its depth, not its usefulness or its beauty' (CV,46). The religious connotations are unmistakable: 'Be comforted. You would not be seeking Me if you had not found Me.' What is thus marked is the foundation of a new order, based not only on the familiar replacement of 'the sacred' by art, but a recentring of art on the self-consciousness of its practitioners.

But there is yet another problem. What makes a poet is the fact that he knows himself to be a poet, as Hofmannsthal said, quoted approvingly by Maurice Blanchot. But what of the critic? His activity also involves, as Jean Roudaut once put it, 'a massacre of appearances and a poetic organization'. The question of social recognition looms even larger in his case, however, and when Barthes started to write, there were few people who were prepared to reconsider, as he was, the traditional opposition between categories like writer and critic, or artist and scientist. The formidable resistance such claims aroused would appear mysterious were it not for another major principle of contemporary thought — we learn a lot about a society once we know how it classifies, and which are the objects that function as guarantees of the order of things, the sacredness of the writer clearly being one of them. And indeed the distinctly religious language of Barthes's detractors during the Quarrel at least showed that the two sides saw eye to eye: the critic should show 'abnegation', he should 'humbly serve' the work and not yield to a narcissism which vainly tries to hide his true status, that of a priestly eunuch. Not everyone agrees with Mallarmé's view that all methods are fictions (see *C8*,53 and *L*,41); conversely, the critic's description of his calling in such terms can easily be turned against him and his findings dismissed as mere caprice. Both kinds of rejection cut deep with Barthes, an inspired methodologist for whom nevertheless fiction had always represented 'the original form of *wanting-to-write*' (*E*,xx).

The Quarrel had revealed the contrast between critic and writer to be a veritable myth, a morality play where the cardinal sins of the *nouveau critique* were listed as ignorance, obscurity, presumption and mendacity. The good critic instead was erudite, clear, modest and sincere. While no one denies that these qualities are indispensable in a certain type of communication, it became increasingly clear, at least to those not overwhelmed by their sense of being threatened, that the term 'critic' could denote other attitudes, which were also positive. However, the scholarly work carried out in universities purported to discover the meaning of a text once and for all, thanks to a sound knowledge of the history and language of the period and of the writer's psychology, which together would reveal his intentions. But the anamorphosis described by Barthes in *Critique et vérité* happens anyway in the course of history, especially when a socially powerful institution does not attempt artificially to immobilize the meaning of texts. A play may well have a fixed interpretation ascribed to it in universities, but it is impossible to legislate in quite the same way about its performance in the commercial theatre — although there was even an attempt on the part of some 'paleo-critics', carried away by their normative fantasies at the time of the Quarrel, to make an official protest about certain productions of plays in the classical repertory. In fact, even the most tradition-bound critics would be astonished if they saw these plays actually performed as they were when they were written. They certainly never object to better lighting and acoustics, more 'accurate' costumes, or more 'natural' acting: as with literary 'realism', what we deal with in fact is these critics' idea of the 'truth' improved by what 'progress' they consider has been made in the meantime.

The relativization thus accomplished by history without our permission may then be carried out by an individual critic as well. But there is no reason why he should have to be 'sincere' in doing so. If the 'natural' link between author and work can be argued to be irrelevant (in the 'intentional fallacy') so can the 'natural' link between the critic and what he writes. It is the coherence of the critical system he creates which matters; hence recent times have witnessed a rehabilitation of sophistry as a legitimate exploration of the functioning of meaning (see for instance Benoist, 1975 and Reichler, 1979). As for the 'clarity' which is taken as the test of the critic's modesty, it first assumes that a work and a reader's reaction can be clearly conceived: clarity of conception and expression were correctly linked by Boileau. But this makes short work of the problem of the relationship between a text and its meaning; it assumes that a summary is always possible and denies the choice one might make, of adopting a stylistic strategy to focus the immediacy of a text, its ultimate opacity and irreducibility. And the critic who can do this surely has every right to consider himself in turn as a 'subject of writing', whose text is at par with that which gave rise to it.

Above all, the Quarrel highlighted the power structure which is both cause and effect of the accepted hierarchy of topics and languages. Barthes was a Janus-like figure, half-innovator and half-popularizer, caught between the enthusiasm of followers all too eager to take his work 'further' and the attacks of the old guard. This may well have been one reason why he came to see the intellectual as fulfilling an indispensable but ambiguous part in society comparable to the witch as seen by Michelet or the witch-doctor as seen by Lévi-Strauss, 'included through his very exclusion' (*M*,212; *R*,162; *E*,154).

But does all this groundwork on the status of discourses make a mere intellectual into a writer in the eyes of his readers? 'One writes in order to be loved', Barthes states in *Critical Essays* (*E*,279); but as his cruel interpretation of Dumas's *Lady of the Camellias* proves (*M*,103), even the desire for love is not as strong as the desire for recognition. *Critical Essays*, and the whole of Barthes's work, can thus be read as an immense and varied development — or as some modern analysts of discourse would put it, an 'expansion' and a 'transformation' — of an appeal to be recognized as a writer, despite the critical disguise which the dialectics of modernity forced on him and on the galaxy of contemporaries he names in *Critique et vérité*. This appeal for a recognition, which alone would allow certain potentialities to develop, went unheard for a considerable period. Michel Butor was one of the few writers to appreciate that in terms of stylistic and architectonic quality, there was no real difference between Barthes's activity and his own. However, even though some of Barthes's most famous pronouncements hardly make sense if one forgets the creative meaning his work had for him from the start, his personal aspirations are just one factor in the coherence of his *oeuvre*. The other factor is the presence of an insistent thematic network, which has been noted, sometimes with puzzlement, by detractors and admirers alike. Still, a personal thematics is for him the *sine qua non* of the writer

(*SM*,232), and he certainly qualifies on that score (see on this Lavers, 1971). His study of Michelet, which presented a startling image of this idol of the Third Republic, twenty years before the publication of Michelet's *Journals* was to prove the accuracy of his guesses, shows his understanding of the thematic links between thought and style.

Classical and modern

We quoted Barthes's relegation to a subsidiary status of such important features of language as 'usefulness' and 'beauty' (*CV*,46). In fact this epitomizes the two-pronged attack made on the outlook of a previous period, broadly called *classical*, in the name of more recent values which characterize the period called *modern*.[1] These two words have already been used here, and must now be explained. The classical/modern opposition was not really established as a tenet in current French critical parlance until Barthes popularized it. It has now superseded the opposition, traditional in France, between Classical and Romantic — unless one sees modernism as itself a resurgence of Romantic tendencies, a point frequently made and which Barthes's recent interest in Romantic literature seems to confirm. (The polarity would then be a question of essences rather than one of chronology, ontological rather than historical, although based on history to some extent.)

Questions of periodization have much exercised contemporary thinkers. Scansion can alter the effect of a line of verse, and punctuation can change the meaning of a text; but how can the past be scanned or punctuated to reveal the meaning and implications of the present? Several contemporary thinkers seem to have concluded independently that the most revealing criterion is the way in which each period classifies its objects of knowledge, and, more generally, handles languages and signs. Barthes seems to have been the first, in the French context, to define the 'great trauma of classicism' as a period starting sometime after the sixteenth century (viewed as a kind of benign linguistic Nature), and lasting until the latter part of the nineteenth century, when we reach the modern period, whose specific traits are obvious to all but whose meaning is still enigmatic. It could hardly be otherwise since this is our own time, but we saw that Foucault, refining on this classification, thought he could detect intimations of a change of *episteme*, one of them being the new anti-humanist outlook. Kristeva, aware of the work of Barthes and Foucault but deriving her main inspiration from the work of the logician W. Van O. Quine's 1953 collection of essays, *From a Logical Point of View*, has sought to distinguish periods dominated by the sign from those dominated by the symbol (1969a). However hazardous the multiplicity of factors in historical structures and their uneven development renders such attempts to constitute what Nietzsche called a 'monumental history', the difference between the classical and the modern *epistemes* does seem to correspond to a genuine change in outlook, perhaps exaggerated for Barthes's propaedeutic or political purposes as semiologist and writer.

Bricolage

A strong framework such as the classical/modern dichotomy was perhaps necessary to Barthes because of his capacity to invest everything he touches with a problematic character. Just as some believe that the depressive's predicament simply makes manifest the essential contingency of life, so a basic failure in socialization in Barthes seems to have forced him to view all communication, whether social or scientific, as a dubious enterprise. He stands, as Forster wrote of Cavafy, 'at a slight angle to the universe', an attitude which has built-in creative potential (1923, 91). It is well known that untutored people often ask the most difficult, the most basic, questions, compared to those who have digested the established framework along with the content. In Barthes there co-exists an obvious refinement of perception and control of his material with the tentativeness and originality of the child or the savage.

This simile will not seem impertinent given the rehabilitation of the 'savage mind' by Lévi-Strauss. There are in fact striking similarities between the thought of these two men: the critical stance towards Western civilization, the tension between the belief that intelligibility is not given but constructed and a sensuous apprehension of nature. Despite appearances, neither is an epistemological sophisticate; what Lévi-Strauss said about his few 'rustic convictions' might equally apply to Barthes. But what Lévi-Strauss derived from a contact with primitive societies came to Barthes as a resentment at the restricted choices offered by language, and the nausea caused by what he calls the 'interpellation' of culture. This insight results in the choice of analogous objects of study: for Lévi-Strauss, the sign is 'between' the image and the concept; Barthes calls it a 'perceptible idea' and sees mythology as the study of 'ideas-in-form'. Both study the products of the symbolic function as new creations which take as elements existing fragments of earlier discourses. And the word *bricolage*, Lévi-Strauss's term for the operation of the savage mind in taking the first material thing to hand as a means to express its own classifications, had already been used by Barthes in one of the essays in *Mythologies*. There it was contrasted to the stifling effect of modern toys which impose the pre-formed image of the society children are meant to reproduce in adulthood.

There is indeed an element of *bricolage* in both Barthes and Lévi-Strauss who, like their common ancestor, Rousseau, tend to rely on home-made instruments. This Rousseauism does not stop there: an essay on 'Plastic' (M,97) reminds us that there is something crude about all natural substances, even the most luxurious, a richness which man's demiurgic chemistry cannot emulate. Throughout his career, Barthes spontaneously sought to supplement 'plastic' concepts by an apprehension of ideas as sensuous, a sort of guarantee of truth and a short-cut to the discovery of consequences. There is in his work, in the tendency to seek 'perceptible ideas', a pervasive reliance on what Kant called the *schema*, which mediates between images and concepts, and can in some ways be considered the ancestor of the contemporary 'structure'. Barthes also praised Bachelard for his conception of the image as a potential group of transformations, where the formal relationships are stressed rather than a presumed unity of substance. The reference to Bachelard allows science also to be part of 'the great adventure of desire' (1975d, 9) — as long as erudition is 'the living mask of a few obsessions' (R,171). Barthes has expressed a certain penchant for those scholars and savants 'in whom he could detect an excitement, a shiver, a craze, a delirium, an inflexion' (RB,160) — Chomsky, Michelet, Saussure and above all the linguist Benveniste.

Yet, despite a definite pugnacity, Barthes cannot speak except in the guise of theory, and even in his last writings, his loss of belief in signs merely results in mimickings or even parodies of Theory. There certainly is some vulnerability here. One is reminded of a humorous passage in his autobiography where he recalls his part in a performance of ancient drama with the Groupe de Théâtre Antique de la Sorbonne (which he founded): behind the mask of King Darius, he kept his eyes fixed on the high cornices of the courtyard. 'They, at least, were not frightened' (RB,33). Yet uttering gnomic statements from behind the mask of the universal generates its own fears, expressed, by another turn of the screw, in the third person:

> His unease which is sometimes acute — and even becomes, on certain evenings which follow a whole day's writing, a kind of fear — came from the fact that he felt he was producing a dual discourse, whose mode, so to speak, went beyond his purpose: for the purpose of his discourse is not truth, and this discourse is nevertheless assertive. This is an unease he has felt very early; he tries to dominate it — failing which he would have to stop writing — by bearing in mind that it is language which is assertive, not himself. (RB,48)

The absolutely terrorist character of language

Barthes's notion of the 'absolutely terrorist character of language', always maintained though rationalized at different times by different principles, understandably seemed rather obscure to the *Tel Quel* group of avant-garde writers and theorists when they interviewed him in 1963 (*E*,278).[2] It was hardly made less puzzling when associated with contradictory statements such as 'All works are dogmatic' and 'The writer is the opposite of dogmatic'. But language, for Barthes, cannot be dialectical, because it *records* hesitations or apologies instead of subsuming them under a transcendent synthesis; only the speaker can attempt such a synthesis in real life, by altering his behaviour to relativize and conciliate his own former utterances. Yet modality, which expresses the speaker's attitude in relation to the content of his message, is now seen as an integral part of linguistics. Wishes, doubts, intentions, as expressed in verbal moods, in words like *perhaps* or *doubtless*, or in terms conveying emotion and evaluation, are currently attracting attention as part of the new interest in *enunciation*, 'the presence of subjectivity in discourse', or better, 'the repeated act in which the speaker takes possession of his language (1974b). Needless to say, Barthes's refusal to acknowledge his assertiveness results in an intensive use of such modalizing devices (and never more so than in the passage from which these quotations are taken) — a typical case of what Freud called 'the return of the repressed'.

When, by contrast, Barthes speaks of language as a system, needing only to be valid, rather than true, to be complete, he is expressing his acute awareness of the *written* text. The writer does not know to whom he is talking; he is the person whom everybody can contradict. Anyone can oppose one of his 'complete' texts to the other in the absence of the context the living person could supply (*T*,95; *E*,xi). This can only have an unnerving effect on Barthes who has often referred to the 'aphasia' produced by contradiction and his dislike of that rhetorical figure of everyday life — 'making scenes'.

We shall see how he oscillated throughout between the Sartrean idea of a public whose image is built in every text, and a framework supplied by Lacan's concept of interlocution, of the effect within the therapeutic discourse of the patient's transference-relation to the analyst. Writing, in Barthes's version, is non-transferential, making it a special case among discourse, and giving it a 'congenital openness'. At first this appeared to be terroristic but eventually Barthes convinced himself that the writing subject, as opposed to the speaking subject, was dispersed throughout his writing and *irreperable* (*reperer* has no real English equivalent, and can mean 'to put a mark on' or 'to spot' or 'to keep an eye on' — all useful connotations for Barthes and our analysis of him). This is a better solution because Barthes was never satisfied with what would be the obvious answer for many people: encoding suitable marks of one's intentions so as to make them unmistakable even in a written text as described in Riffaterre (1971). The reason for rejecting this is fundamental to his outlook, and is to be found in his view of 'the life of signs in the midst of social life', to borrow Saussure's definition of semiology. As expressed unforgettably in *Mythologies*, everything in society which seems natural and eternal turns out to be cultural and historical. Since any communication must rest on a common code (whatever the degree of self-consciousness of its users) it is automatically turned into a gesture, a spectacle in the 'theatre of language' which cannot retain any trace of individuality.

The consequences of this postulate are far-reaching. An obvious one is the depreciation of content, which is never granted the ability to reach the reader by means of its own logic. It is always a prisoner of the form through which it has to be manifested. (This is all the more striking since, despite the modernist tenet of the fusion of content and form, Barthes had no qualms about their methodological separation.) Thus, there can never be a generous language — generosity is behaviour, not speech — because it can never do more than bear the *signs* of generosity (*E*,278). Barthes does not seem to realize that since behaviour itself can only be interpreted as generous thanks to signs of another kind (not only natural indices but largely conventional signs as well) there is no reason to deny language the authenticity he apparently grants to behaviour or vice versa.

Since nothing is eventually found to be safe from mythologizing, it is only at the level of utopia, or even 'atopia', that myth can be avoided, whether in art or the good society, finally the same problem. Barthes's books therefore often end on a despondent note, which contrasts not only with the programmatic statements they contain but with the achievement represented by the books themselves. His gifts never seem to have brought him reassurance, and this is only compounded by a vivid awareness of the obsolescence of disciplines.

Barthes was never totally unaware of the therapeutic function which his doctrine of language was meant to fulfil (for instance *T*,93). He often described his ambivalent response to demands made on him as a person, a teacher and a writer. He both resented and needed them, accepting this uncomfortable position as his 'truth', while still entertaining the symmetrical dreams of mastering a field of knowledge — where the collective law is at its most rigorous — and writing a text which would be completely free, both from any actual request and from the tyranny of avant-garde models (*T*,104). This would indeed be a new state of affairs, since Barthes, despite practically acknowledging that he sometimes engineered a demand for books he wanted to write, seemed to feel that the act of writing is so momentous that the responsibility must be shifted on to someone else's shoulders. Like Phaedra making her confidante utter the name of the loved Hippolytus in her place, Barthes thus tried to propitiate what he once curiously called in an article on Raymond Queneau, 'a rather terrifying Imago of Literature' (*E*,131).

Yet there was a Fall once. One single text was written by Barthes of his own accord. This 'zero-text' (*T*,103) was a short piece on the notion of 'colourless writing and the commitment of form'; never published, it was the nucleus of *Writing Degree Zero* and of Barthes's career. Such is his 'myth of origins': one where, not surprisingly, the exhibitionistic act of proffering a part of oneself is compensated by the actual content. For the 'zero degree of writing' is 'a style of absence which is almost an ideal absence of style'. The 'zero degree' can be characterized, in linguistic terms, by the indicative as opposed to the subjunctive and the imperative moods; similarly and ideally,

> the new neutral writing takes its place in the midst of all these
> ejaculations and judgments, without becoming involved in any of
> them; it consists precisely of their absence. But this absence is
> complete, it implies no refuge, no secret; one cannot therefore say
> that it is an impassive mode of writing; rather, that it is innocent.
> (*Z*,82-3)

This style was initiated, according to Barthes, by Camus in part of his *Outsider*, and there certainly are deep affinities between the two writers: in their pervasive guilt and yearning for innocence — *The Exile and the Kingdom*, as Camus put it — or in their general ambivalence towards Parisian cultural terrorism, which is denounced but nevertheless internalized.

Here is how Barthes describes his behaviour after this first move, presenting it (somewhat inaccurately) as an example of the current psychoanalytical version of man as a 'divided subject'. As the subject of a struggle to demonstrate the political and historical commitment of literary language, he could be sure of himself.

> But as the productive subject of an object publicly offered to the
> gaze of others, I was rather ashamed; I remember that one evening,
> after it became certain that *Degree Zero* would be published, I was
> walking on the Boulevard Saint-Michel and I blushed to myself at
> the idea that the book could no longer be retrieved. (*T*,92)

Barthes continued to feel this 'panic' whenever the power and responsibility of words appeared to him *insoutenable* — another example of his multivocal use of words. This adjective can mean 'impossible to look at' (because it is too dazzling or too terrible, for instance), while also evoking *soutenir*, which itself has a multiple meaning: to *prop up* (a heavy object), *to maintain* (an opinion perhaps *untenable*), and even *to sustain* (something in time): all of which, intertwined, perfectly define his feelings.

As for blushing, it is not devoid of erotic value, as is shown by the passage of *The Pleasure of the Text* (*PT*,31) which Barthes chose to read on the French radio. Commitment, in this late text, is reduced to ideology, that is to say an 'idiotic flush' which some people may find exciting. The early Barthes did not feel nearly so detached. To conclude, the relationship between Barthes and his own writing was in fact probably the cornerstone of his work. His gift for deciphering two messages at once (the primary meaning of an action or object and the second-order meaning which society attaches to the performance of this action, or the representation of this object), is not unconnected with his constant awareness of always sending a double message himself: a statement about the world and an appeal to this same world for recognition. Or to put it another way: a project of 'demystification', of removing the emperor's clothes, cannot be pursued without baring one's own motives at the same time.

Barthes and style

Barthes advocated 'the expression of subjectivity' in learned discourse and praised the 'great preciosity of the baroque era' as 'a knowledge of Nature which necessitate[d] a broadening of the language' (Z,69). He practised what he preached. His mastery of the obsolete noun and the unexpected adjective vividly conveys the excitement of pioneering intellectual adventure; at the same time, he gives an overall impression of simplicity because of a remarkably robust and straightforward syntax (as noted by van Dijk, 1972, 120).

Some features of Barthes's style result from his attempts to introduce new divisions in the social sciences while reconquering full freedom for the French language, whose capacity for coining words had been rendered rather anaemic by neo-classical academicism. In *Critique et vérité* he shows that what passes for clarity is often just jargon made familiar through decades of classical education (a common theme in Raymond Queneau). Instead of saying *Mr So-and-so writes French well*, one writes *We must praise Mr So-and-so's pen for caressing us so frequently with the unexpectedness of its felicitous style* (CV,32). Barthes always speaks disparagingly about tormented syntax, and indeed his inventiveness is mostly lexical. Poetry in *Degree Zero* is described as a 'Hunger for the Word' (Z,54). Even those late nineteenth century attempts to evolve a kind of expressionist writing, which may well have reflected in their own way the tremendous changes affecting French society and thought, must presumably be included in the devastating criticism of Naturalist writing made in *Degree Zero*. Yet some of their devices are not far from his: to start with, a full use of the available lexicon (Barthes lovingly uses words like *manducation* or *déshérence* when appropriate); and a deliberate effort to enlarge it in ways which are immediately understandable. If *bestiary* exists, why not create *gestuary* on the same pattern? *Tendresse* is so associated with the emotions that one must create another word, *tendreur*, for the human softness of wood as opposed to dehumanized plastic. Finally, there is a deliberate assault on the irrational gaps found in any language, and deplored by all classifiers, from Aristotle to Greimas. This rationalization of language is an indispensable scientific tool.

Neologisms, whether poetic or scientific, are in general motivated instead of being arbitrary like the majority of words in a language. The discussions in ancient Greece on the question of the natural or conventional character and origin of language are illustrated by Plato's dialogue *Cratylus* which figures prominently in structuralist discussions of language and text. Cratylus maintains that there is a natural appropriateness between the meaning of a word and its form; his opponent Hermogenes argues that the meaning of words is established by usage. Among the words coined by Barthes, some are transparently motivated since they are derived from a handful of Greek roots which are already found in many English and French words: *stereography*, *arthrology*, *semioclasm*. Others, which have become a feature of textual semiotics, advertise their content, which is the isolated essence of a thing, quality or event, a seme or 'atom of meaning', by the well-known ending *-ity* or *-icity*. As Greimas points out, this offers no cause for resentment, since such words are properly speaking not French or English but a metalanguage of the kind needed by all sciences. Barthes makes a slightly different point in the humorous plea we find in *Mythologies* in favour of such word formations. Myths are often transient forms, relevant only for limited periods; it might therefore happen that no word exists to denote them: 'The dictionary supplies me with a few: Goodness, Kindness, Wholeness, Humaneness, etc. But by definition, since it is the dictionary which gives them to me, these particular concepts are not historical.... Neologism is then inevitable' (*M*,121). Thus 'China is one thing, the idea that a French petit-bourgeois could have of it not so long ago is another: for this peculiar mixture of bells, rickshaws and opium-dens, no possible word except Sininess.' Such formations may be unlovely, but are never arbitrary, being constructed according to a sensible rule of analogy, of which Barthes had found the example in Saussure (*Course*,161). Thus if Latin/latinity = Basque/x, x = Basquity, a nice word to express the fraudulent use made of the most picturesque features of a Basque chalet by a petit-bourgeois dwelling which has no need of 'dark brown half-timbering, an asymmetrical roof and a wattle-and-daub front' (*M*,124).

Some people reject words they do not find in dictionaries; yet dictionaries themselves merely sanctify the most innovative phrases of the great authors. These 'classics' are simply successful revolutionaries who now occupy the centres of power, as Jakobson and Todorov pointed out. It is interesting to find the much-criticized Barthes now ensconced in the great

Robert dictionary, for the sake of the extra derogatory nuance his work has added to the word *mythology*. And there is, indeed, a classical quality about his work. He never engages in outright neology, like the poet Henri Michaux; even in the matter of spelling, his views are conservative, and the phonetic distortions of Queneau's *Zazie* are interpreted simply as polemical strategy. Nor does he seek meaning in poetic explorations like Michel Leiris's *Bagatelles végétales*, where the sound is made to reveal the sense as in *Rempart des parents.... Or de père hors de pair* or *Rhétorique rétorquée. Fosse si folle de la philosophie.* Such possibilities of linguistic productivity have struck writers at all times but were considered marginal until the surrealists rehabilitated them as examples of 'madness in language', madness here being not pathological but what Lacan called 'a phenomenon of thought'. In thus showing the deviant as typical of the normal, such examples have played a major part in recent textual theory and as a result generated a new kind of writing. Barthes, presenting some examples of this in *Communications 19*, devoted to first articles by 'young researchers', identified their plight as a conflict: on the one hand is the freedom of choosing a thesis 'subject' which at best corresponds to some of their fantasies and on the other are the restrictive prescriptions still ruling intellectual discourse in our society. What is denied them is the 'freedom of the signifier'. Yet he was driven to define this freedom as virtuosity, more, one feels, by current ideology than by the tastes his own practice reveals (1972b).

Needless to say, this new kind of prescription could be as crippling as the others, more so perhaps since virtuosity comes more easily to the phonetically than the semantically inclined, and the latter numbered Barthes himself.[3] Despite some half-hearted playing on words like *Adam* and *Eden* at that period, the 'hunger for the Word' he experienced was an etymological reverie, a kind of punning never purely decorative but pressed into service as the keystone of an argument, and received as a sign in a mystical quest. The deep significance of this etymological word play is that it offers a way out of the constraints of the linguistic system, and more specifically out of the synchrony which makes the system exist, since it calls on the resources of several language-states. Thus, although much of Barthes's work is devoted to a study of the social and aesthetic conventions which specify the meaning, finally this meaning is poetic, grounded in nature: 'Writers are on the side of Cratylus, not Hermogenes' (*CV*,52). It is above all, Barthes's fastidious handling of style which makes his work an exciting blend of theory and personal adventure; but in order to recapture this excitement, a diachronic view is indispensable. So the best thing is to start at the beginning, his first encounters with 'the life of signs in the midst of social life'.

Part II

Something beyond language

5

The network (synchrony)

Writing Degree Zero (1953) made up for Barthes's late start as a writer by the attention it aroused. Its originality of purpose was as startling as its extraordinary use of words, not least in its enigmatic title. The book is often regarded today merely as a first, and consequently rather dated, treatment of various topics Barthes was to deal with more competently later. But the stylistic handling of its themes makes it an existential as well as a theoretical statement, a veritable microcosm of Barthes's basic attitudes. The link between history and ethics and the corresponding identification of writing as the privileged index of this link, the sensuous, even sexual, nature of writing and the material force it exerts in the world, topics which Barthes tackled scientifically later, are here revealed in their poetic sources. *Degree Zero* therefore provides an excellent starting point for examining the whole of Barthes's early career. This must be done in two ways (which in fact correspond to the organization of the book): first synchronically, since Barthes takes the modern problematics of writing as a system whose elements must be reviewed; then diachronically, in order to trace the historical origins of the present situation. I shall call the synchronic part 'the network' (Chapter 5) and the diachronic part 'the voyage' (Chapter 6), following Barthes's plan in his essay on ancient rhetoric (*C*,16). Besides its organizational value, this schema has important symbolic implications in Barthes's first book. A return to a synchronic approach, in Chapter 7, will allow us to examine the stylistic and discursive solutions available to the members of society in their various roles as 'subjects': as writers, intellectuals, critics and teachers, roles which are of vital interest to Barthes. All these solutions are ways of coping with what he called the 'responsibility of forms'.

The text and its messages

The opening paragraph of *Degree Zero* was arresting:

> Hébert, the revolutionary, never began a number of his news-sheet
> *Le Père Duchêne* without introducing a few 'fucks' and a few
> 'buggers'. These improprieties meant nothing, but they signified.
> What? A whole revolutionary situation. Here is an example of a
> mode of writing whose function is no longer only communication or
> expression, but the imposition of something beyond language,
> which is both History and the stand we take in it. (Z,7)

This way of buttonholing the reader — statement, question, answer — is
an abiding feature in Barthes and conveys his gift for both diagnosis and
explanation. As for his choice of revolutionary imagery, it is, as he
would say, 'not innocent'. It was perhaps prompted by his contemporary
study of Michelet. But in any case, the French Revolution is not only 'this
mythical event which made History fruitful, along with all future ideas
on revolution' (Z,28); it is also a barometer of political feeling and
scholarly fashions.[1] This is precisely the way it functions here.

This iconoclastic image was to remain attached to Barthes for a good
many years. His complaint, so heartfelt in *The Pleasure of the Text*,
about 'the political policeman and the psychoanalytical policeman' must
have been voiced by many of his own victims in the 1950s. But when the
storm finally broke after the publication of *On Racine*, Barthes did not
seem altogether unhappy with this vulnerable prominence. *Must We
Burn Sade?* asked the title of a 1955 essay by Simone de Beauvoir; the
publicity campaign backing *Critique et vérité* echoed, *Must We Burn
Barthes?* In a particularly devastating article on the 'Diseases of the
Theatre Costume' (in *Critical Essays*) Barthes contrasted the 'aesthetic'
complacency of French directors with the meticulous practice of the
Berliner Ensemble which, on its visit to Paris in 1954 had struck him as a
revelation of an art both committed and artistically valid. He counter-
posed the methods Brecht's actors used to make costumes look properly
worn out with an allusion to a fashionable designer: 'One doesn't
imagine Léonor Fini applying a blow-torch to one of those beautiful red
gowns which make Parisian society dream' (E,48). No better metaphor
than this blow-torch could be found for Barthes's early activity.

In what was to become an established mode of dealing with an unsatisfactory state of affairs, Barthes's reaction was to suggest a new discipline
by positing a new object of investigation. This new object is the 'writing'
of the title, a specialized use of the word introduced as follows:

> It is impossible to write without labelling oneself: as with *Le Père
> Duchêne*, so equally with Literature. It too must signify something
> ... which defines its limits and imposes it as Literature. Whence a
> set of signs unrelated to the ideas, the language or the style, and
> setting out to give definition, within the body of every possible
> mode of expression, to the utter separateness of a ritual language

... it is therefore possible to trace a history of literary expression which is neither that of a particular language, nor that of the various styles, but simply that of the Signs of Literature. (Z,7-8)

It is clear that Barthes arrived at his central notion both positively and negatively. He noted the existence of a phenomenon which available concepts were unable to account for, and sought to make it tangible to his reader by differentiating it from each of the available concepts in turn. Thus, in the opening paragraph, Hébert was said to make use of 'a mode of writing whose function is no longer only communication or expression'. This new function was 'the imposition of something beyond language, which is both History and the stand we take in it'. Three 'messages' are thus 'sent' in every instance of literary expression, in addition to the content:

The text says: I am a literary text ('the Signs of Literature', Z,8).
It also says: I am a part of the literature of a particular period, and I came about owing to definite literary and historical events ('something beyond language, which is History', Z,7).
The author says: I am choosing this particular mode of writing in order to commit myself, since I know it to be recognized as having this particular value ('and the stand we take in it', Z,7).

Three different types of study follow from this. As far as the second, the 'history of the Signs of Literature' is concerned, Barthes never went beyond the brilliant outline given in the second part of *Degree Zero*. The first, the formal identification of literature, is one concern of his structuralist phase. As for the third approach, which studies form as the locus of commitment, it is the heart of the book. The 'message' is of course not always expressed so consciously. Writing can unwittingly reveal, as Barthes shows, bad faith or thoughtlessness. But in people of his own complexion the process is hyperconscious, to the point of inhibition, and this anguished casting about is apparent in many passages.

This despondency is understandable in view of Barthes's conception of the various elements of the structure which he identified through an approach which combines phenomenology with linguistics. At this point he has defined writing as 'a set of signs unrelated to the ideas, the language or the style' and in the synchronic part of *Degree Zero*, he therefore examines the relationships of these three components; and this is also what will be done here, paying particular attention to the formulation of basic attitudes which shape much of Barthes's later work.

Content

The 'ideas' or content are, as we have noted, generally dismissed by Barthes as irrelevant to a formal study. Thus he argues that Michelet's petit-bourgeois ideology would not lead one to suspect the extraordinary deployment of his thematic and stylistic imagination for which Sartre had hailed him as an 'authentic genius and prose-writer of greatness'.

The only case in which it is impossible to tell whether Barthes is speaking about form or content is the one in which this difference is immaterial, 'the commonplace'. Here the two planes merge, so to speak, robbing the speaker of all individuality and any desire to give his stamp to the 'language of the tribe'. The fixed image of man which underlies clichés is typical of bourgeois periods for Barthes as for Sartre before him (and before both, for Lukács in *History and Class Consciousness*). However, even the very façade of permanence of this image is shown as suffering gradual deterioration, until the acute seventeenth-century maxim becomes Flaubert's grotesque 'received idea'. Even when the form does not advertise it, Barthes can identify the stereotype under the surface with cruel lucidity.

Sartre too had, early in his career, mounted a full-scale attack against the still vigorous heirs of classical humanism, the 'professionals of experience', content to wallow in inauthenticity. But the significant differences between his analyses and Barthes's foreshadow the opposite stands they took at the height of the structuralist debate. Roquentin, the hero of *Nausea*, sees the stereotypes when he watches his fellow diners: 'they are not eating, they are restoring their strength in order to carry out the task which is incumbent on them.' Another character, nicknamed the Autodidact, cannot feel secure except in the hope of having one day learned a whole library by heart so as to guard against inadvertent innovation, and Derrida has interpreted this as a ferocious satire on the Hegelian idea of absolute knowledge. What Sartre later praised in writers like Dos Passos and Nathalie Sarraute was an attempt to render, by various means, the interplay between private and public experience.

Barthes, discussing an analogous attempt by the avant-garde playwright Adamov (the only one he praised, since he mostly levelled at the whole notion of avant-garde the same strictures as Brecht), does so with a perceptible nuance. Barthes's distrust of all 'depth' — whether because it seems spurious or threatening — makes him reject the very values on which existentialist criticism was founded. The relations between the characters Barthes finds 'not so much inauthentic as frozen by being compromised by a previously existing language'. And yet Barthes had just noted how 'the pressure of borrowed speech' prevented 'all invented speech from coming out', which would suggest that he placed some value on this possibility (*ET*,55-8). Once again we find the ambivalence between authenticity and spontaneity and the belief that the world is entirely coded. It is in trying to bridge these terms that Barthes evolved some of his most original theories.

Content having been dealt with in this ambiguous manner, the other two elements in the structure, 'the language and the style', are purely formal. But they are described in very different ways. Whereas the notion of style obviously derives from personal experience, that of language seems borrowed from the Saussurean concept of *langue*, which forms a seminal dichotomy when associated with *parole*, or speech (see Appendix, p. 228).

Langue

The fact that the dialectics of language and speech are the very foundation of *Degree Zero* has not been recognized. Much is made of the fact that the Thibaudeau interview and the second preface to *Mythologies* show that Barthes read Saussure only later, in the course of writing *Mythologies*, as is reflected in its afterword 'Myth Today'. But precisely because of Saussure's position as the founding father of modern linguistics his name did not actually have to be pronounced for his ideas to be assimilated. What better example could be cited than Merleau-Ponty, who in his *Phenomenology of Perception* (1945) only alludes to 'a famous distinction' without so much as mentioning Saussure's name (presumably too famous) in either text or bibliography. This is relevant because some of Barthes's metaphors seem to point to *Phenomenology of Perception* as an important source of inspiration; for instance, speech seen as a horizontal flow with language as a solid residue or deposit building up under it, which is the master schema in *Degree Zero*. The precariousness of mobility is of course a major theme of existentialism. Sartre was using words like *signifiant* and *signifié* in the early 1940s, as a matter of course, for instance in his *Sketch for a Theory of the Emotions* or his article on Maurice Blanchot's *Aminadab*. Even more to the point, Blanchot himself, the only theorist acknowledged in *Degree Zero*, not once but twice, shows in his review of Barthes's book not only that the concept of *langue* was perfectly understood but that Barthes's thesis made sense only in relation to it.

In the event, the definition of *langue* given in *Degree Zero* was technical enough to surprise the layman since, in good structuralist fashion, it did not stress elements but relationships: 'We know that a language is a corpus of prescriptions and habits common to all writers of a period' (Z,15). This recalls the strictly Saussurean definition of *langue* given by Viggo Brøndal (from whom Barthes took the notion of zero degree) which Barthes quotes a decade later in *Elements of Semiology* (S,15). The proximity of Brøndal's name to that of Merleau-Ponty in this later book suggests that Barthes had not basically changed his references but simply enriched his theoretical background: some of the main principles of modern linguistics were part of his thought from the start.

The insistent reference to Saussure by French structuralism (the Saussure of the *Course in General Linguistics*, for there is another one, that of the *Anagrams*) should however be taken with a pinch of salt.[2] It is important not to make Saussure synonymous with linguistics then or now, and especially in relation to Barthes, for two reasons. One is that the basic insights of the *Course* (notions like sign and value, *langue* and the primacy of synchrony) were all experienced ambivalently by Barthes whose criticisms were similar to those made today by an increasing number of linguists of a sociological bent. The other reason is that there is after all a genuine affinity between the intuitions of Barthes and Saussure, not only their tentativeness and originality, but a way of conceiving the components of meaning as distributed on two perpendicular axes, and a particular view of syntax (all of which will be examined later). Such specific affinities are obscured by a blanket assimilation of Saussure to linguistics.

There is another point. Barthes noted in *Elements of Semiology* that linguistics had chiefly developed the 'immanent analysis of the linguistic institution' and that 'this immanence is inimical to sociological research' (*S*,24). He added that the hypothesis concerning the sociological origin of Saussurean concepts had therefore lost some of its topicality. Needless to say the debate (if not the point of genealogy) had lost none of its topicality for Barthes, who was at this point trying to extend linguistic concepts in order to provide a foundation for semiology, whose first applications, as the examples in *Elements* show, were sociological. His initial research was on the vocabulary of politics during the French Restoration and on the language of fashion, and his preferences all seem to point to a field which has since then achieved recognition and a name: sociolinguistics. In *Elements* he therefore praised Merleau-Ponty for taking up at a more general level Saussure's distinction between language and speech (which can be traced back to Humboldt) and postulating (after Hjelmslev) that any *process* presupposes a *system*. This produced a new opposition between *event* and *structure*, a distinction classically posed with respect to the study of history by the *Annales* school with which Barthes was associated.[3]

On the other hand, it was never clear whether Barthes considered Hébert's 'revolutionary' linguistic strategy to be instinctive or conscious. Although the burden of *Degree Zero* is to show that 'it is when History is denied that it is most unmistakably at work' (*Z*,8), a writer's awareness is not entirely irrelevant. Barthes argues from such examples not that a historical stance is *less* historical for being denied but that it is *more so*. Yet in a work which we have seen shared Barthes's early concerns, *Elements of Semiology*, we find him applauding Merleau-Ponty for stressing the fact that language and speech make sense only in the dialectical exchange which united them and which is the real linguistic *praxis* (*S*,15). This mutual dependency is a philosophical fact, but also a methodological one, as appears in *Degree Zero* itself. For some structured notion of what literature is has to be postulated so as to make it recognizable before its fortunes can be followed as events. History is indeed dependent on structure. But for Barthes, as for Merleau-Ponty, structure is itself the result of history. This conviction is shown not only in relation to the problems posed by the sediment of *langue* but also in relation to the expression of an author's 'carnal structure' in his style: 'it must be remembered that structure is the residual deposit of duration' (Z,12).

Style

For language is not at first discussed in relation to *speech* but to *style*. This opposition is more evocative of stylistics than linguistics. Style in this perspective is conceived as an individual deviation from a collective norm, a conception which frequent onslaughts have only succeeded in reinterpreting and preserving, shorn of all prescriptive overtones. The notion of deviation tries to account for linguistic expressivity, which is the proper field of stylistics, but stylistics can be defined in several ways. Its founder, Charles Bally, one of the editors of Saussure's posthumously published *Course* and his successor at Geneva, saw stylistics as dealing with the expressivity, not of the individual but of the language, and the language as used in everyday speech, not in literature. By contrast — and despite his denials — Barthes's approach recalls the idealist reaction against positivist criticism earlier in this century, and is especially akin to Leo Spitzer's idea of style as a manifestation of the spiritual 'etymon', or principle of coherence, which informs all aspects of an individual author's production.

The theme of style is again introduced by means of the flow/deposit, horizontal/vertical schema: the 'abstract circle' of the language becomes a 'horizon' which 'outlines a familiar habitat for mankind', the acceptance of which is the writer's 'essential gesture as a social being' and which, despite its compelling nature, gives him the comfort of 'an ordered space', that of social intercourse. To this is opposed a 'vertical and lonely dimension of thought', which is that of style. Style therefore is not social at all; it is described even more lyrically and imaginatively than language: it is 'a germinative phenomenon, the transmutation of a Humour', 'a closed personal process', 'the product of a thrust, not an intention' (Z,16-17). One is struck by this passive and solipsistic conception of style, which the choice of metaphor and the incantatory repetitiveness render very well. Other writers might have chosen to stress the confrontation of style in its nascent state with the existing language of men. Despite a single reference to the formative role of the writer's early history, Barthes's contention is that language and style both constitute a necessity, or as he puts it, a Nature.

Writing

Yet an area for conscious and voluntary intervention does exist because 'every Form is also a Value'. This leaves room 'between' language and style for another formal reality: writing. Barthes's structural presentation shows that the notion of value, despite its dominant ethical connotation here, is also used in the Saussurean sense (see *M*,111, where the word is clearly used in both senses, and Appendix, p. 222). Writing is 'a general choice of tone, of ethos', thanks to which the writer, until then entirely shaped by forces beyond his control, acquires a formal identity; the undifferentiated 'written continuum' becomes 'a total sign, the affirmation of a certain Good'. But writing already pre-exists in contingent modes, and the choice of the writer between them is at most a negative value. Yet there can be no problematics of language prior to this 'act of historical solidarity'. Writing, in short, is 'the ethics of Form' (*Z*,19-21).

A language, then, is not quite the negative reality described at first. The writer finds existing linguistic formations which reflect social realities, relatively stable precipitates which act as signs by virtue of their plurality and which force him to commit himself. Barthes later realized that he had rediscovered on his own the necessity, recognized by several linguists, of inserting an intermediate level between language and speech. This is because speech must be already institutionalized to the extent that a group of language users produces and interprets all its elements in the same way. This stratum receives different names in different systems: in *Degree Zero* it is writing but Barthes later chose to call it *sociolect*. But in adopting such recognized linguistic terms in *Elements*, he was doing an injustice to his first work: the phenomenon which first drove Barthes to put pen to paper could, ten years later, still not be satisfactorily expressed in purely linguistic, or even broadly scientific terms (style and writing are *both* likened to idiolects in *Elements* — see Appendix, p. 227). It is to his credit that he felt that here was an uncharted area for research.

There are of course literary formations as well as linguistic ones: genres, registers, figures of speech, traditional subjects and themes, as well as institutions such as academic disciplines and literary periodicals. In *Degree Zero* Barthes considers the part played by these periodicals as well as the relation between classical rhetoric and of the novel. But it is clear that his reflections centre on *language*, not form, and thus the lack of structure in the Saussurean notions suits him very well. The linguistics which would deal with language as common property in usage as well as norms was 'hardly foreseen by Saussure' (*S*,20). This allows Barthes to feed in his own predispositions and envisage speech on the Saussurean model as everything that *langue* is not, that is, as wholly and perpetually creative as if it had no rules or patterns. Thus, curiously, an analytic operation of proven scientific fruitfulness, the language/speech dichotomy, ends up aiding and abetting a temperamental bias.

Yet when he tried, in *Elements of Semiology*, to transpose the distinctions elaborated in *Degree Zero*, to make them scientifically operative in the fields of sociology and literary analysis, he could not go beyond his early insights. He resorted to the same dialectics of hackneyed content and outright innovation, with systematicity envisaged only as fixed combinations of words or the stereotyped language of the mass media. As he put it in *Mythologies*: 'The opposite of *good writing* is not necessarily *bad writing*: today it is perhaps just *writing*. Literature has entered a situation which is difficult, restricted, mortal. It is no longer its ornaments that it is defining, but its skin' (*M*,83). All these contradictions can be discerned in the notion of writing in *Degree Zero*. For the modes of writing the author finds on offer, and which he must choose between to express his free commitment, are by definition tainted with sociolectal use. They *signify* both literature and a certain ethical attitude and must therefore be recognized as such by the receiver of the message. History thus 'forces him to signify literature in terms of possibilities outside his control' (*Z*,8). The modes which constitute writing as a 'system of values' are therefore not evoked by Barthes in any positive sense, either as a wealth of choices or malleable forms. Rather they are solidified languages defined 'by the immense pressure of all the men who don't speak them' (*Z*,93) and by their own coercive power.

One might have thought that some of these choices would be ethically neutral, but this is clearly out of the question. Barthes has chiefly in mind here the plight of the intellectual of fastidious literary tastes whose convictions nonetheless force him to endorse a type of political writing of a vehemence alien to his natural reserve: 'Writing here resembles the signature one affixes at the end of a proclamation one has not written oneself.' (*Z*,32-3). It is obvious that the main source in the discovery of the phenomenon called *writing* here was contemporary political writing; the description of this particular mode is the one Barthes tackles first, and he starts by describing the notion all over again, using the same metaphors for writing and for political power.[4] Another reason writing cannot be neutral is the reticence, verging on disgust, which overwhelms the true writer at the sight of hackneyed literary forms: but this is compounded by the realization that any creative effort becomes reified by attempts to exploit it, that is to say, that style relentlessly turns into writing (*M*,131ff). 'For language is never innocent: words have a second-order memory which mysteriously persists in the midst of new meanings. Writing ... is free only in the gesture of choice, but is no longer so within duration.' The unavoidable conclusion follows: 'Writing as Freedom is therefore a mere moment.' Understandably, Barthes exalts this brief and almost ideal stage: 'But this moment is one of the most explicit in History' (*Z*,22-3).

This is the crux of the matter. Originality is seen, in the modern perspective, as vital. Yet there is no theory of it in *Degree Zero*, where change is never explained. This view of freedom as existing only when exercised, and solidifying otherwise into inauthenticity, shows Barthes's affinities with the existentialists. Like them, he spontaneously borrows Pascal's dramatic language with its evocations of the wager for salvation or the image of being *embarqué* (finding oneself aboard the ship of commitment). And the essay in *Mythologies* on what Barthes calls 'neither-nor criticism', the would-be superior position claimed by the partisans of an unspecified 'culture', ends with a plea for explicitness — a principle of ethical integrity for the scientist and the artist as well as the critic: 'No salvation for the judges: they also are well and truly committed . . . So that freedom, for the critic, is not to refuse the wager (impossible!), it is to make his own wager obvious or not' (*M*,82).

The problematics of modern writing

So far, we have outlined the situation confronting the modern writer in Barthes's view. This view never was substantially altered so it is useful to spell out its implications: 1. Content is held to be irrelevant to the problem and, in any case, as the example of the commonplace showed, subject to the same dilemmas. This is serious in view of Barthes's belief that 'there is no thought without language' (*Z*,89). 2. A language is a reality both coercive and negative; it determines what the writer cannot do rather than offering guidance on matters of social belonging and artistic worth and existence. 3. Writing alone, through its various modes, can specify the writer's commitment; but these modes are historically determined by socio-economic factors upon which the writer's action can have no influence (*Z*,21). Such conviction of the determinant force of infrastructure is, to be sure, consistent with Marxist orthodoxy (as it was then conceived) but it is hardly encouraging and, like all denials of freedom or autonomy, probably even works as a self-fulfilling prophecy. 4. Even within the superstructure, there is little the writer can do to modify the existing modes of writing, owing to the dialectical contradictions of communication and innovation. Though style has built-in originality, its possible relevance for communication and action is not even considered. The story of *Degree Zero*, as indeed that of 'Myth Today', is told entirely from the point of view of the isolated writer or mythologist; it is he that the revolution would help by putting an end to his exile. This is because: 5. Style itself is not free at source, being almost biological, with no clear intervention of conscious preferences and orientated striving. 6. And in any case, style, like writing as freedom, is but a mere moment; soon the writer 'becomes the slavish imitator of his original creation, society demotes his writing to a mere manner, and returns him a prisoner to his own formal myths' (*Z*,84).

No wonder Barthes felt claustrophobic when he set out: he was caught in a classic double-bind, or rather sextuple-bind. From a desire to act on the world and a belief that it is not really possible through language, Barthes moved to the position exemplified in his Inaugural lecture: a denunciation of the 'fascism' of language, whose choices are always limited, contrasted with a celebration of literature for its 'permanent revolution'. As for the mechanism of the 'second-order memory which mysteriously persists in the midst of new meanings' (Z,22), it is the first appearance of what Barthes later identified with the phenomenon known as *connotation*, a notion he owed to Hjelmslev and used throughout his career despite various drawbacks. In *Degree Zero* it is introduced by means of the now familiar image of flow and deposit (Z,23). Barthes in *Elements of Semiology* was still under the impression that he had hit on a phenomenon to which linguistics could supply the key, although now the concept came as the crowning conclusion to the book, as the common space of all areas of social communicaton.

This persistent awareness can be read as a crushing superego, also observable in Sartre (one can imagine it exacerbating Barthes's own). One is not surprised to read that writing 'intimidates', that it is 'the weight of a gaze' — a celebrated Sartrean theme. But in Barthes it is more unexpected, since connotation is a recognition signal between the members of the same group, to read that it is 'in no way an instrument of communication' and even 'an anti-communication' (Z,25). Still, the absence of a theory of action in society goes a long way towards explaining the 'absolutely terrorist character of language'. In real life, the context would make things clearer; but it is never presented as helpful by Barthes, always as coercive. So that both types of communication, the context-bound and the context-free, are feared; the former because it is too revealing, and the latter because it is 'terroristic'. The symptom Barthes detects in the whole of modern literature, 'a negative momentum and an inability to maintain it within time's flow', also applies to him (Z,11). Here again, the schema remained but the attitude altered. Where in *Degree Zero* Barthes is fleeing forward and recaptured, in the later texts he is abandoning something, leaving it behind ('Writers, Intellectuals, Teachers', in *IMT; RB*, 108).

Speech

Since the writer is hemmed in on all sides, it is difficult at first to see why languages change, and how one can innovate or even make a statement at all. But such a factor of mobility is present after all, unseen at first because it is never formally introduced. It is speech (*parole*), the other part of the Saussurean dichotomy. It is brought in twice in *Degree Zero* (Z,17, 25) in the same unobtrusive way, as a foil to style and writing. Punctuation is always a valuable index in Barthes and in this case it is weirdly casual, speech being actually introduced in mid-sentence. Yet speech is the only safety-valve in the system, not only in its daily functioning but at the level of history. But — this is crucial — it is used without being theorized.

Style and writing were described by means of the same 'deep' metaphor, the gradual deposit and the developing seed; in contrast, the 'horizontal' flow of speech is the locus of social exchange. Style and writing were claustrophobic; speech is 'open', both because its secrets are dispelled by its own duration (Z,17), and because it is potentially the meeting-place of all men. The ever-renewed welling of speech was for the existentialists the very symbol of freedom and autonomy, and *Degree Zero* is about freedom as much as it is about writing. The title of Jacques Prévert's most famous collection of poems, *Paroles* (1949), is typical of a period when the supreme achievement of the writer was conceived as turning speech into art.

Paradoxically, if languages and modes of writing appear today more exposed to change than they do in Barthes's system, speech appears much more structured. This is because Barthes's linguistic framework, mostly Saussurean, supplied no model for what he had to call clumsily, in *Elements of Semiology*, 'extended speech', or discourse, which is ruled largely by syntax. Utterances are not random strings of words; one can reconstruct from them various types of arrangement which are grammatical sentences. The power of speech, as the neurologist Hughlings Jackson, quoted by Jakobson in his article on aphasia (see Appendix, p. 233) put it, is 'the power to propositionize'. Propositions are the logical equivalents of sentences, namely acts of predication, of stating something about something else. In his *Course*, Saussure repeatedly came to the verge of recognizing the importance of syntax; he did not do so, however, for reasons, it seems, which may have been also perceived by Barthes and have their counterpart in his own intuitions.

The first is technical: Saussure felt that much more than just syntax, that is, the knowledge of the function of words, was involved in the complex and still unknown operation which allows us to combine these words in an ordered statement. How he conceived the science of such linear arrangements or *syntagms* turns out to confirm Barthes's spontaneous vision — probably dependent on a broadly anthropological schema representing the human body and its action in the world — of a 'deep', 'vertical' fund of possibilities and of communication as 'horizontal', made up of successive choices from this fund. The second reason is Saussure's view of language as the passive accumulation of a storehouse of forms and patterns as well as words, a 'treasure', a deposit; when Chomsky's theories were introduced into France in the mid-1960s, it was his dynamic notion of how sentences were made and understood that was found most striking. But, interestingly, Barthes managed to read a dynamic aspect in Saussure too. What the latter called, in the ordinary sense, *signification*, is interpreted by Barthes as the active union of a signifier and a signified or, even more dynamically, the carving out of both with one gesture from the two unstructured masses of sound and thought. These images and expressions were indeed found in Saussure, but semiosis itself was clearly experienced by Barthes as a kind of predication.

The dynamic possibilities are even more apparent when we move from linguistics to semiology (of which *Degree Zero* is a first outline). The signs of linguistics are given, found in the dictionary (in the optimistic view of the layman, at least). But the units of other systems, those of myth, clothing, food, literature, although no doubt already existing and functioning since these systems function and produce meaning, have nevertheless to be discovered or hypothetically constructed. We clearly see here the common gesture shared by the scientist — the semiologist or the analyst of narrative — and the writer who also carves out and unites the disparate elements of the language and turns them, as Mallarmé said, into 'a new, total word, foreign to the language'. We can see also how the lack of a theory of discourse was crucial since, as appears later in an article Barthes wrote on Philippe Sollers's *Drame*, language use, in his view, compensates for the lacunae in the language system itself.

At the time of *Degree Zero* it was the theory of the poetic, creative word which was missing, so much so that Barthes, entitling a chapter 'Is there any Poetic Writing?' could not bring himself to subsume under the heading of a mode of writing the shattering creativity of René Char's poetry which 'questions Nature by virtue of its very structure' (Z,57-8). So that poetry, the creative core of literature, remained untheorized, outside the scope of the book, since it escaped all the ethical binds of existing modes of writing. The ominous implication is that there can be no salvation except in outright novelty: the pleasures of recognition are weighed down with the crushing burden of social responsibility, while the only alternative is a kind of astonishment caused by nature at its most awesome, before it becomes humanized. The first inkling of a change in Barthes was an acceptance of the literature of pleasure along-side that of *jouissance*, the ecstasy, not unmixed with terror, which comes with the loss of all notions of the self or culture.

Another reason for the lowly position assigned to the crucial notion of speech in *Degree Zero* is no doubt structural, an interference-pattern between several well-known oppositions. Saussure's distinction between language and speech must compete with language and style (stylistics) and speech and writing (the two main manifestations of the symbolic function, which are each given a technical meaning here). This does not agree with Barthes's fundamentally dualistic thinking, a trait that no doubt predisposed him also to the structuralist obsession with binary oppositions. Such a dualism has also been noted in Freud, and indeed Barthes might be diagnosed in terms of what psychoanalysts call a 'splitting of the object' into a good and a bad aspect, thus avoiding a depressing ambivalence, to which Barthes's obsessional temperament made him particularly prone. In *Degree Zero*, owing to these different possibilities of classification, speech and writing render each other structurally redundant, since they are each meant to represent individuality and freedom of choice, albeit in different ways. This structural equivalence also explains how it was possible for these two concepts to switch their connotations later in Barthes's career. It is only when writing fails to sustain its liberating value in time that it is replaced, though unofficially, by speech.

The two aetiologies of modernity: historical, structural

Any solution to the problem outlined in *Degree Zero* will therefore have to unite the necessary conditions of innocence and individuality, privacy without monadic loneliness, communication without alienation, commitment and freedom. Barthes here takes his place in a recognized problematic of twentieth-century French literature. It stretches from Gide who preferred, as Barthes puts it, the 'security of art' to the 'loneliness of style', yet recommended *disponibilité*, the availability of non-commitment, to Sartre whose hero Mathieu realizes that his uncommitted life has 'drunk' his freedom and robbed him of it. (As ever omitting context, Barthes never mentions Gide's lonely courage in his fight for sexual freedom, surely one source of a liberation which today allows new formal effects.) Barthes is well aware that the problem of commitment is the thread running through the whole of his work, but his originality is that he experiences this problem at the level of form, 'the first and last arbiter of literary responsibility' (Z,89). Some of the solutions have already been tried in the past, and this is one reason that Barthes gives a diachronic sketch of literary forms; the other reason is that past attitudes live on in the present. But the real solution, as appears eventually, would be a combination of past and present, of classical and modern attitudes to language, a possibility which, for the time being and perhaps for all time, can only be utopian.

There was a time when 'classical art could have no sense of being a language, for it *was* language, in other words it was transparent'. The ideological unity of the bourgeoisie was expressed in a single mode of writing: literary form could not be divided because consciousness was not (Z,9). The revolution of 1848 and the development of modern industry in the 1850s, which divided French society into three mutually hostile classes, changed all that (Z,66). Barthes does not name these classes but Marx's writings on the same period, Lukács's *History and*

Class Consciousness and Sartre's *What is Literature?* allow us to recognize the bourgeoisie, the petite-bourgeoisie and the proletariat, important dramatis personae in the whole of Barthes's work. We now understand whose gaze it was that created writing. Once the illusions of liberalism were destroyed, the writer 'ceased to be a witness to the universal to become an unhappy consciousness', and 'his first gesture was to choose the commitment of his form, either by adopting or by rejecting the writing of his past. Classical writing therefore disintegrated, and the whole of Literature ... became the problematics of language' (Z,9).

Yet writing at first appears as an internal phenomenon, a gradual seizing-up, a 'dramatic phenomenon of concretion' (Z,10). Classical art was transparent. It is only towards the end of the eighteenth century that 'this transparency becomes clouded', first in Chateaubriand where we detect self-awareness in a kind of narcissism, 'a light pressure of linguistic euphoria'. Flaubert 'finally' turns literature into an object by making ostensible labour an integral part of literature itself, its sign. Mallarmé 'finally' objectifies it by murdering language and reducing literature to its carcass. 'Finally' literature today reaches a 'last' metamorphosis, the zero degree (Z,10-11). The unconscious repetitions in this genealogy of modernity are only superficially contradictory, since what Barthes intends to show is that the plight of modern literature is insoluble at the formal level. The modern writer attempts to find purity in the absence of all signs, to realize, in a metaphor from Blanchot, 'this Orphean dream: a writer without Literature' (Z,11). Thus is explained the ontological structure of the modern work. Barthes sees literature as nowadays sending a dual message, a content and a meditation (which is the form itself) on its current problematic status. But he also sees that this meditation — and its masochistic forms, the 'murder', the 'Passion' whose stations of the cross were outlined above in the series of finalities — is also, so to speak, a way of keeping in business. Struck with a fatal self-consciousness by the gaze of all whom it excludes, literature, the descendant of bourgeois writing, has managed to turn self-consciousness into a new kind of subject-matter.

Despite a lack of theorizing, the metaphors used by Barthes to trace the birth of modernity testify to the rightness of his linguistic intuition. They describe the effect of what Jakobson called the poetic function of language (see Appendix, p. 227) in order to call attention to the structure of the message and the poem's appearance as a durable object. *Degree Zero* thus gives an imaginative rendering of the recognized evolution of literature, the relative disappearance of well-defined genres, which now merge under the general heading of poetry. As Mallarmé had put it: 'there is no prose; there is the alphabet, and then there is verse. Any effort towards style tends towards versification.' Cocteau and the surrealists concurred; and even Sartre, after taking up Mallarmé's sharp distinction between the 'raw' and the 'essential' use of language, ended up by blurring it in a definition of the writer as 'the poet who has chosen prose'. So the opposition between prose and poetry is just another facet of the opposition between classical and modern.

A brief comment will reveal other parallels as well as explain the 'Orphean' symbol taken from Blanchot and the epithet 'terrorist' taken from Paulhan (see Lavers, 1970). These two authors belong to a new breed of thinker who could be called literary anthropologists since they reflect on the human condition while ostensibly writing literary criticism or theory. Bachelard, Malraux in his writings on art, the surrealists, Queneau are obvious literary anthropologists, and so is Barthes. Art is taken as a short-cut to an understanding of man, and the artist as the archetype of human creativity. Paulhan, for a long time a director of the powerful Gallimard publishing firm, a quirky and independent thinker, used to be called the *éminence grise* of letters; Blanchot, a fascinating theorist, shunning all publicity and almost a myth himself, might well be called their superego. Paulhan originated a set of convenient terms to express the problematics of classicism and modernity and which, with Blanchot's rejoinders, came to serve as a framework French critical discussion: Rhetoric and Terror. Sartre used these terms constantly, from *What is Literature?* to his autobiography, *Words*, and Barthes would have encountered them there if nowhere else; he refers to the dialectics of 'terror or *vraisemblable*' (another name Paulhan gave to Rhetoric), in *Degree Zero* (Z,45).

Paulhan argued that during artistic reigns of terror, authenticity comes to be equalled with the purity of novelty or originality, so that new forms are worn out almost as soon as they appear. 'Showing signs of wear' or 'out of fashion' are great Barthean phrases to indicate words which have lost their operative, quasi-material, world-changing force. In criticism the counterpart of this state of affairs is uncertainty, and the replacement of genuine literary criteria by extra-literary values like naturalness, humanity or truth. Defects in form come to be valued as guarantees of authenticity. The chief victims of this romantic distaste for all constituted categories are the commonplaces, those maligned 'bourgeois' clichés, despite the fact that their power to render authenticity artificial derives from their accumulated wealth of human meaning. What is needed, in fact, is a new Rhetoric, and Paulhan uses the word metonymically to denote the period before the Terror struck. As we shall see, his wish was eventually granted; 'rhetoric' and '*vraisemblable*' have become crucial notions in the structural analysis of a literature no longer posed as terrorist. If language comes to be the condition of, not an obstacle to, thought, so, in another sense, are structures like genres, unities, and figures of speech. The reign of terror can only lead to subjectivity and ultimately to silence, the spectre of 'agraphia', or literary suicide, which haunts *Degree Zero*. As for the essence of poetry, it is a noted fact that the *practice* of poets of both persuasions, Terrorists and Rhetoricians, is the same whatever their theory. It evidences a belief in the equivalence of language and thought, the manifest and the immanent. This shows that the principle of identity, which is said to be the law of the mind, does not always apply; indeed, to be aware of it presupposes the experience of a diametrically opposed state of mind, which is the poetic state.

Blanchot was able to see clearly the pitfalls in an ideology like Paulhan's who, though describing correctly what poets actually do, stresses only the rules. The fact is that there is an asymmetry in the workings of constraint and freedom; conventions may make individual manifestations possible but no one has ever written *in order* to subject himself to rules. The very impulse to write is an intimation of absolute freedom; the Terror is literature itself, 'or at least its soul'. Thus the dispute about the respective importance of inspiration and work is based on false premises; *all* works have an accidental beginning, since literature is not of this world. 'How is literature possible?' Blanchot asks. It has a paradox at its very core. For the writer, who is different from other people only in that he questions the validity of language (in the wider sense that he finds fault with the existing state of meaning in the world), can ask his questions only by using language. Terror is therefore paradoxically creative. Moreover, its modern excesses are only too understandable in view of the symmetrical excesses of Rhetoric, so that there was nothing to do, as Paulhan agrees, but leave the latter to 'rot in its chains'. And how is criticism possible at the time of Terror? The critic's task has changed radically: 'Rather than explaining how one easily writes great books, [he] feels the duty to evoke, around books already written, all the problems which prove them impossible to write.' We can tell the great modern work by the fact that instead of opening new gates, it shuts a few of the remaining ones. It blazes a trail, since this is the condition of literary existence; but no one else can use it. Works are judged by the awareness they show of the contemporary plight of literature and its true essence. This stance is in fact resolutely normative, albeit of a very different kind from its Rhetorical analogue. It was also adopted by Barthes in *S/Z*, where he began by dividing texts into the *lisible* and the *scriptible* (readable and writeable), those which could still be understood but which he did not wish he had written, and those which he did, because they were truly modern, that is, they changed the linguistic or symbolic norms by introducing into them something irreducibly novel, *different*, and thus appeared as 'a force in [his] world, today' (*S/Z*,4). The book thus could not but appear as a recantation of the structuralist period which had preceded it, inasmuch as the latter had scientific ambitions, and science considers with equanimity all practices, it is *in-different* (S/Z,9-10).

But what is literature? Blanchot notes the trivialities with which this question is usually answered, and suggests a modern definition: literature is the 'question put to language by language become literature'. Barthes adds that although this question may one day epitomize our century (as the general symbol of the inner collapse of values), it has so far not even been raised in literary studies. Students, let alone schoolchildren, are thrown in at the deep end, on the assumption that all people of good background already know why there is some point in studying literature at all, what to study and how to do it.

Literature can perhaps be approached best of all through a myth. Blanchot proposes the figures of Orpheus and the Sirens, and Barthes adds a whole series in *Critical Essays*. The writer is like Orpheus in wishing to bring the dead Eurydice (or that 'inspiration' which comes from the beyond of literature) back to the world (to embody it in words). The condition is not to look at her (concentrate on technique). But, yielding to a higher temptation, he does compulsively look at and so loses her: he cannot achieve the literary death, the silence which would follow the exhaustion of the subject. Hence the urge for a new attempt, which must be similarly defeated. With Barthes's interpretation of the writer's 'Orphean dream' as a 'murder' is added a new twist which outdoes Blanchot for terrorism. While they share a scale of values, Blanchot was above all trying to suggest the dialectics of creation and rejoicing in the presence of an *oeuvre* as the outcome. But for Barthes the original descent into words is a Fall, for all that he was later in his career to value the materiality of discourse.

Barthes's tendency to stress the action rather than its results, or as he put it in his post-structuralist phase, structuration rather than structure, is made even clearer in the light of Blanchot's second myth. The Sirens exerted an irresistible attraction, 'but the strangeness came from the fact that all they did was to reproduce the usual song of mankind; but being only beasts, although beautiful, in doing so they aroused the suspicion that since they could sing like men, all human song was in fact inhuman.' The Sirens were vanquished by the power of technique, that is by Ulysses who, as technique always does, claimed to enjoy their song at no peril to himself. But he did not completely escape their power; he was drawn, via Homer, into a recital of his adventures, an Odyssey. The novel was born of a struggle between a song and a narration, it is an 'ode become episode'.

But why was Eurydice dead and the Sirens inhuman? Because for Blanchot, Sartre, Barthes and all followers of Mallarmé, language and therefore literature exist fundamentally as a relation with absence. The sign is at the same time a mark and a lack. If I pronounce the word 'flower', as Mallarmé remarked, I conjure up 'that which is absent' from all real bunches of flowers. Such words supply the framework for all Barthes's remarks on the novel during the whole of his career, from the essays on Robbe-Grillet in *Critical Essays* to the advent of the *scriptible* in *S/Z*. Barthes's articles on Robbe-Grillet are distinctly more sophisticated than Robbe-Grillet's own interpretation (and indeed were the acknowledged sources of these interpretations before Robbe-Grillet traded in his myth as district surveyor for that of explorer of the unconscious after *Last Year in Marienbad*) (see on this Genette, 1966a). Barthes sees these novels as an attempt to destroy all the basic elements which allow the idea of fiction to become manifest: the characters and the 'fable' or story. The fable is the more resistant of the two: while it provides the matter on which the destruction of convention can bear, its persistence cannot but 'rot' the purifying enterprises of the 'Orphean dream'. The fable lasts in time, and time is a vital element in the idea of fiction, the basis of what Barthes calls the 'realist illusion', or 'reality-effect'.

In *Degree Zero*, the order imposed on raw material by any kind of aesthetics is said to be a 'death' of which the preterite (a tense no longer used in conversation but reserved for the written text) is the sign in the French novel. This is because the nature of imagination, as explored phenomenologically by Sartre in *L'Imaginaire*, is to negate the world of perception in order to substitute its own constructs for it. Since mental life for Sartre is pervaded with self-consciousness, this provides the ontological foundation for the responsibility of the writer, and the necessity of commitment. Such a conclusion is very difficult for Barthes to refuse because he accepts Sartre's analysis of imagination, as many quotations make clear, in *Système de la Mode* and *Mythologies* (where it serves as an indictment of bourgeois mass-indoctrination with its impoverishment of the imaginative life of the masses). This 'death' imposed on the raw material of experience by artistic order substitutes logic for a true temporality. The time perceived by the reader in the novel's grammatical tenses is just such a fake, a part of the reality-effect. Barthes describes it in terms obviously inspired by Malraux's famous saying, often quoted by Sartre, that death turns life into destiny. To this can be added Barthes's further assimilation of human life and the work — which the structuralist analysts of narrative compare to a long sentence.

6

The voyage (diachrony)

In this chapter, I shall examine how Barthes tackles his problem diachronically, drawing out the implications of that very general polarity labelled 'classical' versus 'modern'. This will involve touching on differences like prose/poetry, bourgeois/petit-bourgeois, creator/ epigone, quantitative/qualitative, choice and communication/non-directive fullness, continuity/disruption, the resources of a rhetoric/the solitude of poetry, constraint/freedom or integration/loneliness. These aspects may well look disparate at first sight; but this is the point, for each feature of these clusters of meaning conjures up, when it is used, a memory of all the others. We are thus faced with a paradigmatic example of what Barthes means by *connotation*.

Sartre and Barthes

We have found Barthes at the beginning of his career locked in a problematic partly inherited but made by him immeasurably more con-strictive. Yet the 'negative' phraseology inherited from Mallarmé, Sartre and Blanchot could be exchanged for positive terms; it is Blanchot after all who quotes René Char's definition of the poem, which could equally render the 'utopian' character of the modern text: 'the poem is the fulfilled love of desire remaining desire.' Blanchot also protests against Mallarmé's image as a Stoic failure, insisting that the theme of impotence must be read against Mallarmé's actual achievements. But, before his displacement by Brecht in Barthes's pantheon, it was undoubtedly Sartre whose attempt to bridge the tragic modern gap between artist and society seemed most impressive. Sartre alone recognized both material and formal conditions and in *What is Literature?* had advanced a synthesis.

A Marxist view of society and consciousness is the backbone of Sartre's text, and it concludes that even though classless society implies the transparency of human relationships, literature will not disappear since it is the necessary self-consciousness of society itself. Sartre's handling of everyday speech in the novels making up *The Ways to Freedom* appeared to Barthes as a forerunner of this type of literature, despite the traditional framework of narration. At the same time Sartre was also the theorist of imagination as negativity, and had even characterized the artist's function, after the break-up of bourgeois consciousness, as the 'recuperation of failure' in a successful society, the 'black magic' which explores 'the black heart of things'. This ambiguous role was accepted by Barthes, and in *Critical Essays* he overlaid it with ideas found in Foucault and, as mentioned earlier, the image of witchcraft found in Michelet and Lévi-Strauss. The artist was henceforth seen by Barthes as included in society, but in the mode of exclusion (*E*,150). Most people, when they think of Sartre, think only of his diurnal side, turned towards commitment, forgetting his nocturnal side, possessed by a 'bittersweet madness', 'this myth of literature without which one cannot write'. There is some justice in this, and a difference from Barthes. For even though Sartre exonerates the poet, like the painter and the composer, from explicit commitment, and in terms which reveal in himself a 'murdered poet' (to borrow Apollinaire's phrase), he is still *speaking to us*. Whereas the corresponding section of *Degree Zero* sounds like a priestly incantation which we *overhear*. This striking difference between dialogue and soliloquy illustrates the passage from classicism to modernity.

The diachronic sketch in *Degree Zero* is not concerned to record the contingencies of literary history, and in this again it anticipates structuralist procedure. We must, Barthes says prophetically, 'put these linguistic problems in terms of structure and not in terms of art' (*Z*,61-2). The principle of relevance which determines the periodization consists in the unity of writing and the plurality of its modes after its modern disintegration.

Sartre's *What is Literature?* supplies the framework for the diachronic outline in *Degree Zero*, as indicated by many textual reminiscences.[1] But where Sartre attempts a genuine genetic explanation Barthes, who may well have started with the same end in view, shows rather how one or another of the various components of a permanent structure were dominant at certain periods of history, and can thus offer a commentary on their current analogues. Barthes later said that in these early days he was 'set on fire' by the writings of Sartre and Brecht, and has provided two comments on his relation to Sartre's work: in 1959 he declared that Sartre had answered the all-important question of his title 'from outside' (*E*,98); in 1971 that he himself had tried to 'Marxianize the Sartrean commitment' (*T*,92). These two statements not only seem to imply that Sartre failed on both counts but are somewhat at variance with each other. An examination of the intricacies of the relation between Sartre and Barthes may offer some illumination.

What is Literature? supplies some missing links which Barthes takes as read: why was the writer a witness to the universal? why did he embody the illusions of liberalism? Yet the historical outline it proposes diverges from the picture presented by Barthes in significant ways. It explains the otherwise mysterious relation between the two aetiologies of modernity, structure and history. The gaze of the Other for Sartre makes one conscious of one's body just as the gaze of the proletariat leads to the reification of writing.

One often reads reductionist versions of Sartre's famous essay which is in fact far more complete and subtle than many critics remember. It appeared in 1947, the year when Barthes published the first pieces born of his 'zero-text' and many of their preoccupations are identical. So why did Barthes say that Sartre had answered his own question from outside? Sartre begins by establishing the ontological purpose of the writer — to be essential in the world — in terms which are later taken up by Barthes (*E*,143). Sartre then specifies this by showing why literature is a special case; the choice of words, rather than other media for self-expression or action in the world, signifies a privilege granted to meaning. Even the post-structuralist conception of the speaking subject, so crucial in Barthes's later career, is found in Sartre's view of Leiris's play on words as an exploration of the subject working out his history through language. This is no accident: Sartre and Lacan (the immediate source of recent attention to the speaking subject) were both struck by the same surrealist sources. Of course Sartre adds the ethical meaning of literature, where it is a direct consequence of his ontological views and his conception of imagination. 'At the bottom of the aesthetic imperative, we find the moral imperative.' The metaphysical and political connotations of form in the novel and the essay are frequently remarked on in *What is Literature?* and in the articles collected in *Situations I*. Forms are seen as both consequences and causes of wider social practices.

As for Stalinist scholasticism, it had already been affronted by Sartre's declarations that the 'immense doctrine' of historical materialism should dissociate itself as soon as possible from the philosophical absurdity of dialectical materialism (he objected equally to the extension of dialectics to matter and to the application of material laws to man, who is conscious and free). In *Search for a Method*, he suggested that new disciplines like psychoanalysis or modern sociology should be utilized by Marxism when necessary; the habit of dialogue might cure the tetanic cramp which was holding Marxist orthodoxy in its grip. He was therefore not afraid of using Hegelian notions such as totality, negativity or the opposition between universal and particular; without wishing to engage here in the polemics with which Althusserians in particular have recently surrounded this Hegelian heritage, I will simply remark that such notions are, as the French say, 'mobilizing', and Barthes himself is not above using them freely.

The link between the ontological and the political in *What is Literature?*, and hence the cornerstone of the possibility of commitment, is the Marxist notion of the proletariat as universal class. Only the interests of the proletariat are not inimical to those of the rest of humanity, and therefore their emancipation is the emancipation of humanity itself. Literature, on the other hand, begins by postulating in essence a universal reader, but there is a distinction, which alters in the course of history, between this 'virtual' public and the 'real' public who actually read the books. This interplay between publics is Sartre's principle of relevance for his chronology.

Despite his use of 'idealist' Hegelian concepts, Sartre offered in *What is Literature?* a very novel framework for the creative process and its reception in terms of production and consumption. To many traditionalist humanist writers this innovation looked very undignified. Barthes, however, took it up, and it recurs throughout *Mythologies*, extended from literature to all cultural objects. Furthermore Sartre, by answering his own chapter headings clearly — For whom does one write? For a public. What is literature? Literature is communciation — supplied a matrix susceptible to reinterpretation in terms of information theory. The use of information theory by Barthes and Sartre is as one might expect very different. For Barthes it supplies a foundation first for a definition of originality (thanks to the notion of information), then later to that of the infinitely polysemic or plural text (thanks to the notion of noise, the random interference of individual readings — a polysemic word has multiple meanings, although finite in number in a given language-state). For Sartre, this same interference allows the writer to render the *vécu* in all its opacity.

Most striking of all is their difference of attitude to negativity. In *Degree Zero* and *Mythologies* uncertainty about the future is a dark night of the soul; even with the hope of a utopian future, Barthes despondently notes that revolution is forced to borrow from what it wants to abolish, the form of what it wants to create. In Sartre as in Marx, we find warnings against the idealism of planning too precisely for a future which is essentially unforeseeable. Negativity rather represents virgin possibilities, even if, like Sartre on his visit to China, the traveller, when enthusiastically shown the sites of future buildings, feels ruefully as if he were walking among the 'ruins of the future', all too aware of his own imminent supersession. These differences in attitude come out in the different ways Sartre and Barthes 'punctuate' the adventures of 'the French writer of bourgeois origins'. *What is Literature?* like *Degree Zero* is a kind of cautionary tale of which Sartre highlights the most representative moments. It is an image of progress where the paradise is in the future, a blueprint instead of Barthes's lost utopia.

Barthes starts with the Renaissance as a myth of nature explored through the 'mother' tongue. Sartre starts with the twelfth century, where he finds (very much like Barthes in the seventeenth) a real public although it is restricted to an élite. In Sartre's picture of the seventeenth century, repression is stressed more than conviviality; but literature still plays its ontologically critical part, and this is precisely what has ensured its enduring excellence. The eighteenth century is the high point in Sartre's chronology, a unique opportunity for French writers whose virtual and real publics for the first time coincided to some extent: the bourgeoisie, whose grievances these writers expressed, was genuinely oppressed. As a class it spoke the language of the universal tactically (even if without awareness), in order to claim its human rights; but this language was overheard where it was not meant to be. The proletariat in the nineteenth century naturally began to use the same principle as a lever for their own emancipation, claiming for themselves what the bourgeoisie had achieved during the Revolution. By then, of course, the writer as spokesman was no longer needed by his 'real' public, the bourgeoisie, and the split in society faced him with a dilemma: either keep the image and the role shaped by the struggles of the eighteenth century, transferring their object from the bourgeoisie to the proletariat; or keep his real public and begin an agonizing reappraisal of both image and role. The majority of writers chose the latter. From then on, Sartre's analysis and Barthes coincide, even down to viewing modernity as stylistic plurality: no writer can escape the choice and the self-deception of the second strategy calls forth much ingenuity.

So to answer the question asked above: why did Barthes, who took up and brilliantly sharpened so many of Sartre's analyses, go on to declare with manifest sincerity that Sartre had answered the question *What is Literature? from the outside?* Because his own vision commanded that he recentre every single consideration around language alone. This Copernican reversal is a metaphysical gesture. Blanchot, usually more lucid, in reviewing *Degree Zero*, expressed reservations about making form the universal criterion, adding 'unless everything begins to move from there' — but that, indeed, was the point. *Critical Essays* shows how every book read, every fact learnt is tested against the touchstone of literature, that is to say, for Barthes, language. The equation is justified, perhaps inadvertently, by the fact that he defines them both as that squaring of the circle, 'the institutionalization of subjectivity' (*R*,166; *E*,154). He was not incorrect to conclude a survey of his career with the remark that language represents for him the mythical 'lost object' of psychoanalysis, which starts the human subject on the quest for heart's desire (*T*,99).

The values revealed by Barthes's diachrony

Against such a background, Barthes undertakes to show diachronically which elements of a permanent structure are dominant at various times. He starts at the Renaissance, which is a mere evocation, a foil to the classical period. The latter, which spans 'the whole era of classic capitalism from the sixteenth to the nineteenth century' (E,143), is viewed as a very strong paradigm, based on a recent political and linguistic unity and bolstered up by an essentialist mythology of man which confers a natural status on this historical configuration. No wonder the bourgeoisie, after the Revolution had given it social and political power (it had held economic and intellectual power long before that), instilled in its newly-opened schools a worship of the classical age. The seventeenth century was an invention of the nineteenth, as someone said, and was indeed its 'myth of origins'.

It was only gradually that the price paid for this ideal image of classicism was revealed, and Barthes may have been helped by the appearance in the 1940s of a spate of books written from a Marxist standpoint on Descartes, Pascal, and the three main playwrights of the Grand Siècle. This was also the time of the re-discovery of pre-classical Baroque writers (see Bénichou 1948, Lefebvre 1947 and 1949-54, Rousset 1947, Tortel 1952). The great scholar Lanson (1912) had condescendingly bundled all these together, in his famous classification, as *attardés et égarés*: hence Barthes's remark (1971a) that the centrality of classicism to literary studies meant that the writers of other periods were presented as pre- or post-classical, or simply as deviant. Instead Barthes proposed to reverse this order for a change and teach everything from the point of view of modernity, not chronologically, of course, but normatively.

From Barthes's chosen standpoint, the eighteenth century appears merely as 'the moment when the class language becomes natural'. Voltaire was 'the last happy writer', who could enjoy his humanitarian fight with a clear conscience, without being forced by history, as the post-1848 writers were, to acknowledge that 'his happiness left a lot of people at the gate' (E,89). Besides Barthes, no doubt correctly, identifies him as an early example of those anti-intellectualist critics with whom he was himself having a running fight: 'He has no system except the hatred of system (and we know that there is nothing grimmer than this very system).' 'Poujade and intellectuals', 'Blind and dumb criticism', 'Neither-nor criticism', in *Mythologies*, show the skill and passion with which he defended what he most admired, the blend of theory and art which Brecht exemplified best of all.

Voltaire is another stock example of the use of 'clarity' (as well as 'taste') much in the manner of Boileau. But clarity is not a general attribute of language; Barthes argues that it characterizes a certain type of discourse which, like classical writing, is 'given over to a permanent intention to persuade'. In doing so, classical writing 'renounced all hesitancy in favour of a continuum in which every fragment was a *choice*, that is the radical elimination of all virtualities of language' (Z,64). In modern poetry, on the contrary, the Word is 'bereft of grammar', it 'can never be untrue because it is a whole; it shines with an infinite freedom and prepares to radiate towards innumerable uncertain and possible connections.' It is 'a sign erect'. In this description we already find all the features of the mythical *scriptible* text, a Text which would not be merely polysemic.

Classical ornaments were taken unself-consciously from tradition, from the treasure-house of rhetoric, conceived as a means of persuasion. There was, so to speak, only a quantitative difference between prose and poetry, which was conceived as prose plus ornaments. It is the point at which rhetoric aroused no more interest (it ceased to be taught in France towards the middle of the nineteenth century) that classical writing began to disintegrate. All the attributes of rhetoric, good or bad, can be traced to its origin as the art of public speaking. It presupposes an audience and is therefore basically sociable, even if the homogeneous public it needs is achieved by means of pitiless exclusion, and language is impoverished and reduced to a pure algebra for communication. Thus the description Barthes gives of the society from which it stems is not an unmitigatedly hostile environment for the writer after all, since this instrumental and persuasive language had not yet become 'conscious of solitude'. It is left to style, which has replaced this common writing in modernity, to introduce 'a vertical and lonely dimension of thought'. The play between rhetoric and style haunts the chapter on poetry, which is written as a kind of lyric sung by alternate characters. No sooner has Barthes praised modernity which, unlike classicism, gives one 'the respite afforded by wonder' and satisfies one's hunger for the Word like Mother Nature, than through the sheer momentum of his incantation this 'discourse full of gaps and full of lights', this 'sign erect' begins to look more like a phallic mother. Sartre's words, 'terrible' and 'freshness', attributes of the world as it appears in poetry, without social mediation, recur obsessively, and the charms of classicism reassert themselves. The 'infinite freedom' of the poetic word even begins to look like 'coercion' beside the merits of classical 'choice'. This ambivalence of the poet in society cannot really be solved under present conditions. The classical age at least had the advantage that rhetoric taught one not only to comment and criticize but also to *write*. It led gradually, through an imitation of the various styles, registers and genres, to a mastery of the verbal palette from which creation might flow. Genette (1969a) traces the gradual elimination of this approach in literary studies to the benefit of metalanguage, whose main function may well be to provide a convenient yardstick for examination.[2]

The new rhetoric which Valéry and Paulhan had demanded was eventually undertaken by structuralism. Milestones include the work of the Groupe μ, Genette, Kuentz and Gritti but Jakobson's article on aphasia was particularly suggestive in its mapping of the two functional axes of language onto forms of neurological speech distubances, via the two major rhetorical figures of metaphor and metonymy. Barthes was among those who extended these tentative applications to literature and the visual arts. Not quite symmetrically, Lacan applied rhetoric to psychoanalysis, identifying the Freudian mechanisms of condensation and displacement with, respectively, metaphor and metonymy.

Barthes had also spontaneously arranged his impressions on 'the life of signs in the midst of social life' in *Mythologies* not only by reference to models derived from Saussurean linguistics and various types of psychoanalysis (Freudian or Sartrean), but as rhetorical 'figures', a loose codification of the various patterns he noticed in current discourses or customs. He continued to do this as *A Lover's Discourse* (1977) shows: lover and beloved alike are compelled to submit to the configurations forced on them by the laws of society, desire and language. The reference to rhetoric became obligatory, and despite its enlightening virtues not always without a certain terrorism, facilitated by the bizarre names of its figures, accismus, catachresis, ellipsis, antiphrasis, etc.

The three divisions of rhetoric, *inventio*, which teaches what to say, *dispositio*, how to arrange one's arguments, and *elocutio*, how to put them in words, also sum up three problematic areas for Barthes. Verbal manifestations (*elocutio*) function more as an ontological than a practical problem, but *inventio* is forced to pass through the defiles of history imposing a critical metalanguage on those unable either to submit to the hackneyed form of contemporary fiction or to find alternatives for the genre. Barthes's own fear of that literary aphasia which struck dumb so many twentieth-century writers (chiefly among surrealists) in the event proved unfounded since he managed to harmonize scholarly and literary interests in a unique and very modern genre. As for *dispositio*, on it Barthes has fixated his distrust of all that seems to 'go without saying'. The smooth coating of sauce which characterized French *cuisine bourgeoise* until the recent mutation of the *nouvelle cuisine*, is in *Mythologies* a humorous symbol of the universal effort of bourgeois society to persuade everyone that its rules are the very laws of nature (*M*,78). At the stylistic and logical level, this produces a smooth linking of arguments which ancient orators called the *flumen orationis*, the flow of speech, which Barthes considers one of the most objectionable forms of *vraisemblable*. He is helped in this by psychological theories which identify ellipsis, the rhetorical figure which pushes the elimination of syntactic elements to the limit of intelligibility, as a more natural state of language, found for instance in dreams and in the language of children (*C16*,220).

His conception of poetry naturally leads him to favour turns of speech which maximize disruption, and to adopt information theory as the key to originality, which he experiences (somewhat guiltily, as the preface to *Critical Essays* shows) as the single remaining value in modernity. The statistical 'distance' between two words or two arguments becomes the index of the force of a text. In an essay on Chateaubriand's last book (*NEC*), Barthes presents even metaphor purely as a factor of disruption, not assimilation. As is well known, information theory is in fact very slippery to handle in semantic matters, if only because messages which are expected (that is, redundant) still signify something. However it offered Barthes a way out of his theoretical *impasse* with respect to poetry since the lessons of statistical linguistics seemed to confirm and explain some of the intuitions of ancient rhetoric. This is a view even better suited to a reader than to a writer. The latter writes, in principle, what he likes, whereas the reader has to put up with many so-called *lisible* texts which are in fact pretty well unreadable to a modern. *The Pleasure of the Text* therefore mischievously — in view of Barthes's professorial status — but with undoubted seriousness, advocates a kind of reading which artificially re-establishes the ellipses which the old authors (except the most wilful) did their best to avoid (*PT*,18-24). A leisurely, attentive kind of reading, which closely 'grazes' on the text, is on the other hand indispensable for modern texts, where the only adventures happen to the language.

Such views on the relation between rhetoric and writing also led Barthes to an aesthetics of the fragment. All his books after *The Pleasure of the Text* were collections of fragments; and in order to forestall any unconscious organization, these fragments are arranged in alphabetical order by title. Praised by Barthes in connection with Butor's book on the United States, *Mobile*, the alphabetical listing is presented in *Système de la Mode* as an 'adult' and 'emancipated' type of order which escapes the bounds of analogy and manages to institutionalize what is neutral and insubstantial. It is thus favourably compared with motivated classifications, whether semantic ('natural') or structural ('rational') (*SM*,111-12). But, by a final turn of the screw, this often turns out to be a *faked* alphabetical order, engineered by the simple device of assigning the titles afterwards.

Rhetoric, which for centuries dominated all ideas of language and literature, showed the same 'taxonomic mania' which Barthes recognized in Sade, Fourier and Loyola (not to speak of himself), such a passion for classification and denomination that it must finally cause incredulity, especially when carried out in the face of widespread mockery. There comes a moment in all treatises of rhetoric when the classifier has to stop, still unconvinced, one suspects, but simply because, as Du Marsais put it, 'one finds the infinite everywhere'. What made the rhetoricians run? The supreme mirage: the codification of speech, a linguistics of speech necessarily impossible since speech is by definition what the code is not. Saussure wisely renounced this chimera in his *Course*, Barthes says; but he does not add that this was in order to write out in full more than a hundred exercise books devoted to the phonetic structure of ancient poetry (the *Anagrams*) where he hoped to tackle the organization of language at a still more basic level.

Introducing his text on rhetoric (*C16*) six years after it was written, Barthes kept his distance not only from his subject-matter but from the new rhetoric which structuralists hoped to build. He begins with a denial of its existence and condemns the very project of a scientific study, based on linguistics, logic and psychoanalysis, of the mental operations necessary to read a text as not so much chimerical but misguided and perhaps harmful. For already, 'the world is incredibly full of ancient rhetoric' (*C16*,172). Could it ever be otherwise? This is doubtful if we believe Barthes's concluding words, which ascribe this Aristotelian survival to mass culture, to the norm imposed by majority rule, and in fact, to democracy. *The Pleasure of the Text* exhorts us to 'graze' on modern texts at the leisurely pace of days gone by, and thus behave as '*aristocratic* readers' (Barthes's emphasis, *PT*,24).

Such passages from the later works shed even more light on the picture of classical society in *Degree Zero*. For, however ruthless and myth-ridden, this was a community for which one could feel nostalgia (assuming of course that one was among the leisurely readers and not outside the gates). It was a kind of cultural nature, an oxymoron which occurs practically at the end of the book. Linguistic sociability was only one aspect of its charm. The Grand Tour derived from a curiosity for human realities quite different from the ethos of those guide-books based on the nineteenth-century accumulative idea of 'culture' (*M*,76). And *Barthes by Barthes* laments the fact that only a combination of socialism and the charms of bourgeois life would provide real satisfaction. Although these bourgeois charms seem to be of a relatively modest kind, this combination is presented as outrageously utopian. It all depends of course on how one conceives socialism; for Barthes, it is essentially puritanical.

Diachrony as the genealogy of our time

Barthes's choice of criterion in *Degree Zero* makes it clear that he sees no rupture occurring at the Revolution, since writing did not perceptibly alter from Fénelon in the seventeenth century to Mérimée in the nineteenth. As for Romanticism, it gets short shrift. While making a few showy concessions, like the mixing of the genres, it ensured the continuation of the main objective: the integrity of instrumental writing. Barthes is probably helped here by the fact that the French are on the whole not very impressed by their own Romanticism, which seems too bombastic and lacking in visionary force. German Romanticism has had to do duty for it. Barthes, along with many others, finds myth 'incurably petit-bourgeois' in France, but a seminar on Goethe's *Sorrows of Young Werther* supplied the basis of his *A Lover's Discourse*. In a sense, symbolism and surrealism are the real French Romanticism, which thus merges with the modern period.

The ambivalence in the characterization of both classical and modern does not carry over to Naturalism, an approach to art which is neither avowed convention nor the successful reinvention of nature. It is savagely attacked both in *Degree Zero* and in essays like 'The Romans in Films' in *Mythologies*. In Mankiewicz's film, *Julius Caesar*, all the characters wear fringes as a sign of Roman-ness; they are all sweating because this is a tragedy and everyone must be seen to debate within himself 'questions of universal import'. These signs are 'bad' according to Barthes because though they are conventional they pretend to be natural and reinvented. This surplus of motivation has a name — Naturalism — and the treatment of this nineteenth-century movement in *Degree Zero* is the first inkling of the satirical vein of *Mythologies*, which lambasts its modern representatives.

For we can interpret the new dualism between Classicism and Naturalism as the difference between bourgeoisie and petite-bourgeoisie. There is at first some uncertainty about the target of Barthes's criticism in *Mythologies*. The first preface of the book speaks about 'this general semiology of our bourgeois world'; but the second speaks about 'the mystification which transforms petit-bourgeois culture into a universal nature'. The bourgeoisie is identified, more and more, in later texts, with its inventive core, for which Marx and Sartre praised its once progressive role. The petite-bourgeoisie, on the contrary, is now for Barthes a kind of mythical monster and the living proof of Marx's remark that what occurs the first time as tragedy appears the second time as farce (*T*,96). The petite-bourgeoisie is a kind of substance which is an ideal foil for the infinitely free modern Text; and indeed a partitive expression could be used for both, so that in a literary work one can detect the parts where there is '*some* Text' and '*some* petite-bourgeoisie'. Once again, the conditions of mass culture and mass production seem to make the degradation of prototypes inevitable, although one would never guess, reading Barthes, that some people are aware of the dangers by now. Despite his Luddite tendencies, he never seems to have found any appeal in ideas of an alternative society or counter-culture, perceiving in them only effects of coercion, degradation or futile contradiction.[3]

But besides its association with mass culture in general, the prosperity of Naturalism is seen in *Degree Zero* to have its roots in the Stalinist establishment. The 'well-behaved writing of revolutionaries' seems to have been an eye-opener, confirmed by later disappointments when Sartre's *Les Temps modernes*, and perhaps the left-wing Catholic monthly *Esprit*, also mentioned here (Z,32), left a more and more restricted place for literature and textual research.

Naturalist writing naively hopes to 'set off' words (in populist writers, mostly collages of slang) by means of syntactic 'expressive' rhythms. These devices again are obvious conventions which are mythically presented as Nature. Such stylistic manipulations, however, are clearly the product of time and labour, and this convenient yardstick for merit is welcome in the schools where the petite-bourgeoisie is trained. And indeed it looks more productive than an intelligentsia where literature itself is questioned and a proletariat cut-off from all culture (Z,75). For the same reason, this 'Literature which can be seen from afar' is taken up by Communist writers, and Barthes mercilessly exposes their preciosity: '"to type", "to throb", or "to be happy for the first time" is real, not Realist language; for Literature to come into existence, one must write: "to strum on the linotype", "his arteries hammered" or "he was clutching the first happy moment of his life".'

Barthes's first-hand experience of the Stalinist 'terror before all problematics' (Z,79) could only have been underlined by the story of the elimination of the Russian formalists to the benefit of Zhdanov's 'engineers of the soul' (an expression conceived by Stalin), as told by Victor Erlich shortly after *Degree Zero* appeared. But concepts evolved during his structuralist period also shed retrospective light on this pasage and the one in 'Myth Today' where he notes that Krushchev, although he devalued the Stalin myth, did not explain, that is, repoliticize it (a point also made later by Althusser). As Krushchev's own testimony makes clear, he and his friends essentially reproached Stalin with getting rid of their old comrades, namely the Stalinists themselves. Now *Mythologies* shows that naturalization is a powerful device of conservatism, both in the political and literal senses. But Barthes's later article on the 'reality-effect' shows that this effect establishes credibility. It is an aspect of the 'referential illusion', a set of devices which collude in the belief that it is possible to ignore all codes, to simply by-pass the signified and introduce the referent directly into the representation (see Appendix, p. 220).

Socialist Realists claim to supply an unanswerable slice of life. But literature of that kind can be used to legitimize any sort of power, the bureaucratic East (since the repoliticization of the Stalin myth would of course have consisted in showing how it contributed to the constitution of a new bourgeoisie), or the technocratic West (since, whatever Barthes's passage seems to suggest, mimetic art is not only found among

Communist writers). It can therefore be viewed as what Althusser (1976) described, after Gramsci, as an Ideological State Apparatus (ISA).

Gramsci thought that the state could not be reduced just to its Repressive Apparatus (or politico-legal aspect) but also included a certain number of institutions from 'civil society' (a term which covers the personal and economic relations between citizens; see Descombes, 1977). Althusser gives an empirical list of these other elements of the superstructure: the system of the different churches, that of schools, the family, the system of political parties and trade unions, the media and the cultural institutions — a list which practically sums up the subject-matter of *Mythologies*. Thus whereas the repressive part of the state apparatus is a unity, the plurality of ISAs means that their unity is not immediatley visible; also, while the other part of the superstructure belongs to the public domain, these are part of the private domain. They belong to the system of state apparatuses all the same because the distinction between public and private depends on the content of the state law in the first place. The function of the ISAs is essentially for Althusser the reproduction of the relations of production, and this tallies with Barthes's constant link between literary realism and educational methods. But Barthes's apparent belief that it might be possible to live without an ideology of any kind, *à ciel ouvert*, as he puts it, in the open, under a godless sky, is as different from Althusser's theory of ideology as it is from Sartre's belief in the permanence of literature. For Barthes, ideology may reflect but it does not produce anything.

Communist writers use the petit-bourgeois writing of Naturalism because for the time being the artistic norms of the proletariat cannot be different from those of the petite-bourgeoisie, a fact which is said to agree with Marxist doctrine. Marx did indeed say that the ruling ideas of a period are always the ideas of the ruling class. But this does not mean that there are no other ideas to be 'ruled'; even a tyrant needs subjects to tyrannize. Indeed the demonstration that there are also dominated ideologies, from the most inarticulate to the fully-fledged though vanquished, is invariably put forward in books which intend to 'raise consciousness'. A well-known example in France is Baudelot and Establet's *L'Ecole capitaliste en France*, which addresses the same subject as the chapter of *Degree Zero* on Naturalism, namely the type of culture propagated in secondary schools.[4] The Marxian dictum, however, is interpreted quite differently by Barthes, no doubt a reaction to the atmosphere in Marxist circles at the beginning of his career, which subsequent events did nothing to invalidate. Ideology, we read in *The Pleasure of the Text*, is simply that which dominates (*PT*,32). The same Barthes who had enumerated the 'figures' of bourgeois tactics in *Mythologies*, now finds that, in contrast with all the discourses he has come to regard as tyrants — the Marxist, the psychoanalytical and the

Christian — there is in capitalism no 'figure of system' (as rhetoric distinguishes 'figures of speech' and 'figures of thought') (*PT*,29).

Throughout Barthes's career, the proletariat is completely excluded from the problematics of literature (*M*,139). This lacuna in Barthes, Sartre, Gide and a whole galaxy of left-wing writers was recently underlined with bitterness by the author of an anthology of proletarian writers and equated with cultural genocide (Ragon, 1973). This is where a first-hand acquaintance with sources is indispensable before interpretation: history being written by the victors, one runs a risk of seeing only what the powers that be let one see. Even the sources might be obliterated: it is so easy not to reprint! The proletariat is nowhere in sight in *Mythologies*, although Charlie Chaplin is accused of confusing it with 'the poor', from an amiably anarchic point of view. A note even tells us that one has to go to migrant workers to get an idea of what Marx meant by 'proletariat'. Presumably, even in the mid-1950s, Barthes already found the proletariat *embourgeoisé*. There is certainly a lack of what Gramsci called 'organic intellectuals', capable of creating and expressing its own ideology. The only trade unions mentioned are American ones, an easy target. The 'people', Michelet's word often used by Barthes, is represented as the 'voyeur of its gods', the stars of the Tour de France. 'He has always been a worrier, politically', we read in *Barthes by Barthes*. 'Writers, Intellectuals, Teachers' gives a Lacanian version of this: the proletariat 'may well be mute, but it still speaks in the discourse of the intellectual ... as unconscious; explicit reference by the intellectual to the proletariat in no way prevents the latter from occupying the place of the unconscious in our discourses: the unconscious is not the absence of consciousness' (*IMT*,212).

Barthes suggests that neo-realist writing may have been adopted because of a feeling of powerlessness to create a new writing on the spot. This gives us a sense of how he conceives the interaction between history and forms, and is important in view of his frequent returns to this question of a new writing in relation to the doctrine of literature conceived shortly after *Mythologies* and whose evolution can be traced throughout *Critical Essays*. Barthes rejects immediacy with its claim to by-pass the logic of forms, which are relatively autonomous and develop at their own rate, as the formalists insisted. Surrealism is condemned by him for being a 'technique for immediacy' although he notes with puzzlement that the surrealists (who at first appeared in his work only as literary suicides), experienced the crisis of language as a liberation. For the same reason Barthes was in the 1960s against the 'happening' as a form of art, arguing that its open structure allowed effects in fact less powerful than those of combinative play on a finite set of elements. *Sade, Fourier, Loyola* clearly shows the link between the aesthetic and the socio-political.[5]

The quantification of quality

It is very important, Sartre said, that the bourgeoisie was able to speak for itself without realizing its own nature as a class. Its adoption of the analytic spirit is typified by the institution of money as universal means of exchange: analysis purports to deal with all realities by decomposing them into homogeneous parts instead of properly accounting for their individuality and situation. So typical as to be practically constitutive; it is enough to adopt analytic reason to become bourgeois. But, despite its success in the natural sciences, analytic reason cannot account for the human sciences; dialectical reason alone can do that. Hence Sartre's later efforts to construct it, taking Marxist dialectics as a starting-point.

Barthes also adopted this aspect of the Marxist-Sartrean framework in the first part of his career. The 'quantification of quality' is one of the 'figures' of bourgeois myth identified in the rhetoric sketched at the end of 'Myth Today' (M,150ff). Barthes stated later that his chief asset from Marxism was dialectics (T,92) and indeed it is dialectics which he identifies in *Mythologies* as the antidote to the bourgeois view of the world summed up in the 'figures' of its myths. Sartre's definition can therefore serve equally for Barthes: 'Dialectics is not the opposite of analysis; it is the control of analysis in the name of a totality' (the notion of totality is commented on further in ET,100).

Structuralism, on the other hand, was viewed initially by its proponents as the first science of the qualitative. Thus Barthes objects, in *Critique et vérité*, to the notion of average as irrelevant in a structural study. Whether a certain feature in Racine's plays is important or not does not depend on the number of times it occurs but on its place in the structure — provided of course that the latter is a well-thought out coherent hypothesis and not one of those loose common sense views which can accommodate any number of contradictions (CV,66). Certain practitioners of structuralism even went so far as to consider all statistical considerations irrelevant, but this mistake was never made by Barthes. Statistical factors cannot be ignored by any analyst concerned with the study of actual languages or literary works rather than with a tabulation of abstract possibilities, although some would prefer to keep the name *poetics* only in connection with the search for universals.

However, the awareness that every fact of social life must be explained not only quantitatively but qualitatively within a structure must, therefore, be credited, before structuralism came on the scene, to what Barthes loosely calls 'dialectics' in *Mythologies*, and which has both a Marxist and a Sartrean source. Like structuralism, it opposes the mixture of positivism and essentialism characteristic of the bourgeois approach.

The flight from the name 'bourgeois'

In bourgeois myth, 'nothing is produced, nothing is chosen'; all the multifarious realities of the world are reduced to fixed essences whose sole origin or purpose are those of the myth-makers they reflect, in a universe reduced to tautology (*M*,151-2). So dialectics is the core, the active principle in this 'intellectualism' in art which Barthes so skilfully defended during the first part of his career, against the attacks of both petit-bourgeois rabble-rousers like Poujade (the spokesman of small shopkeepers, crusading against fiscal reforms and economic moderniza- tion) and distinguished bourgeois critics, the true heirs of Aristophanes when he ridiculed Socrates in *The Clouds* (*M*,206).

Such an alliance between petite-bourgeoisie and bourgeoisie is not as unlikely as might appear at first. The pivotal role of the petite- bourgeoisie, with its capacity to produce massive swings either to the Right or the Left, is notorious. The bourgeoisie depends, economically and politically, on the stability of the petite-bourgeoisie; and one way of ensuring this stability is to bind them in a state of ideological depend- ence. An essential condition is the concealment of the real nature of the bourgeoisie, namely, its capitalist foundation. This spiriting away of its proper name is done in three stages. Economically, capitalism is openly professed. Politically, the connection becomes more problematic: there are no 'bourgeois' parties in the Chamber, although there are 'national' ones: conflict may thus be defused by covering a divided society under a name which assumes a mythical unity, the 'national interest'. Ideologically, this operation has become complete, and the connection is no longer seen (*M*,137). The whole of civil society, 'our press, our films, our theatre, our pulp literature, our rituals, our justice, our diplomacy, our conversations, our remarks about the weather, a murder trial, a touching wedding, the cooking we dream of, the gar- ments we wear', become 'normalized forms'which are in fact elaborated by the bourgeoisie but, being neglected both by intellectuals and militants, 'gravitate towards the enormous mass of the undifferentiated, of the insignificant, in short, of nature' (*M*,140).

The alienation of the petite-bourgeoisie is therefore profound: it is used for purposes it does not suspect. Certainly the bourgeoisie is itself alienated when it believes in its own universality and is scandalized by the revelation that there are other cultures to be neutralized by the 'figure' of *exoticism*. But its self-assured caricature of other mores at least expresses an awareness of real power which is a far cry from the infantil- ization, 'privatization' (the dejected withdrawal from all great political issues) and the claustrophobic view of the human couple generated in the petite-bourgeoisie, and which Barthes expresses so well in essays like 'Conjugales'. Theirs is a life lived entirely vicariously, commiserating with the troubles of ex-Queen Soraya, reading about dishes meant to be only photographed, or about fashions for an unlikely 'weekend in Tahiti'. Some modern thinkers, following the 'Freudo-Marxists' (who, like Wilhelm Reich tried to conjugate the findings of Marxism and psychoanalysis) have compared this phenomenon to the 'latency period', an apparent arrest in sexual development taking place between the Oedipal phase and puberty which, they say, is not innate but engineered by social repression in order to regulate the labour-market and the reproduction of the labour-force. (Political disillusionment, however, conferred on the private sphere a progressive connotation welcomed by the later Barthes).

The obscure awareness in the proletariat and the petite-bourgeoisie that they are not in control of their own fate explains the role played by the idea of luck. A world view meant to ensure conformism is carefully programmed into the pronouncement of the stars, which do not differ perceptibly from those emanating from more recognizably human agents in the agony columns .(*ET*,91, and 'Astrologie' in the French *Mythologies*; see also Sartre's *Respectable Prostitute* and Parkin, 1971).

At the time of writing *Mythologies* Barthes saw the petite-bourgeoisie as particularly prone to fascist tendencies, a temptation epitomized by the Poujadist movement. 'Too weak for either pure reason or powerful myth', no longer even in possession of its famous 'common sense', it was 'poised for political adventure'. This diagnosis implies that myth might not always be alienating but could at certain periods be an inspiring agent of social cohesion (just as the French Revolution is 'this mythical event which made History fruitful', *Z*,28). The content of Barthes's diagnosis, however, is all too easily explained by the political and economic upheavals which followed the Second World War, both inside and outside France and which have left a trace in the book. The French Pretender, the Comte de Paris, was leaving the 'Blue-Blood Cruise' organized by Queen Frederika of Greece in order to 'keep close watch' on the fortunes of the European Defence Community; in Indo-China, Dien-Bien-Phu fell and General de Castries countered by asking for the national dish of steak and chips for his first meal, a symbolic gesture signifying that he was still proud to be a Frenchman; 'exotic' films such as *The Lost Continent* were still being made while those lost continents, henceforth known as the 'Third World', found themselves at the Afro-Asian Conference of Bandoeng; the big settlers in Algeria still had tee-total Muslims tending their vineyards while the Algerian war, which would put an end to the Fourth Republic, had already begun; the first tours to the USSR were taking place after the death of Stalin, but Billy Graham was coming like a knight in armour to fight the dragon of atheism in its French lair as a prelude to a world-wide crusade against Communism. Poujade equated culture with illness, a typical symptom of fascism, and encouraged in the petite-bourgeoisie a 'mythical imperialism'. He appealed to notions like 'race' which recent events had made sinister, and launched against intellectuals the familiar accusation that they lacked virility (*ET*,127).

7

The responsibility
of forms

No literature without an ethic of language

We have now seen the problematics of writing and of society as Barthes sees them. What possible solutions are there to the problem of literature as social language, and what solutions does Barthes envisage? Barthes's first instinct is to stress ruptures rather than continuity or possible articulations. Yet the attitude of other theorists shows that one does not have to see the modern break as totally without precedent or incapable of integration into a wider historical perspective. Starting from premises similar to Barthes's ('Governments pass, prosody remains'), Mallarmé already saw his age as witnessing 'a really extraordinary sight, unique in the whole history of poetry: each poet going off on his own to play, upon his own flute, the tune he fancies'. Evocative of the libertarianism of the Age of Aquarius (and its typical phrase, 'doing one's own thing') it shows Mallarmé's relaxed appreciation of plurality and optimism about a possible harmony. For Barthes there is only the scorched earth policy of modernity. Believing in such a rupture, what can be done? Writing is a dual reality, inward and outward looking; the magniloquent writing of the Revolution was suited to a society which required theatrical amplification. A comparable harmony can therefore be regained theoretically either by bringing society nearer to the writer's concerns or bringing the writer nearer to society's needs.

Despite his social pessimism, Barthes is a natural *Aufklärer*. The first part of his career especially shows his skill in explaining the best of modern research in the human sciences and literary practice. If we now consider the same problem from the writer's angle, we can extract from *Degree Zero* several solutions which form a hierarchy which he was never really to alter, although the drastic reassessment in *Critical Essays* forced some of its components underground.

We find six types of practice or modes of writing outlined in *Degree Zero*. Two are definitely 'bad'. The highly-wrought and traditional mode of classicism, by definition, cannot be of use because it is not adjusted to modern realities. Even worse, the populist is a disingenuous compromise, clinging to tradition yet making gestures towards colloquial speech. Two other modes of writing, the zero degree and poetry, are, so to speak, noble but misguided, 'recuperated' without difficulty by an alienated society. The bid for innocence represented by the zero degree was important enough in Barthes's first book to give it its title; by the time Barthes wrote 'Myth Today' (where the section 'Myth as stolen language' gives an updated version of *Degree Zero*) he had come to believe that 'nothing can be safe from myth, myth can develop its second-order schema from any meaning ... and start from the very lack of meaning' (M,131) which it then interprets as 'disorder', 'the absurd' or 'surrealism'. Yet this passage shows that the ideal of 'colourless writing' was too dear to Barthes for him to abandon it completely, and it remains on the horizon of his work as a kind of utopia of language.

As for poetry, which in *Degree Zero* could escape ethical considerations because it is born of a violence done to social language, it has become in 'Myth Today' as ineffectual as the zero degree. Trying to reach the natural, not the social meaning of things, poetic language is an ideal prey for myth which uses it to signify ... 'poetry' itself. The same thing happens even to mathematical language despite its enormous precautions against interpretation. Myth is not vanquished for all that and carries it away bodily. A formula like $E=mc^2$, part of a transitive, operational language, can be made to signify 'mathematicity' when photographed on a blackboard with Einstein next to it, as if it had just sprung fully-armed from his mythical brain. But here again, poetry conceived as an ontological realism, that is, as a means of reaching reality itself (M,134), is a solution so tempting to Barthes that it is merely submerged, and makes a triumphant return in his later works.

But perhaps the next way to tackle the problem of writing could answer this objection. It is casually mentioned in the introduction to *Degree Zero* when Barthes, identifying the significance of colourless writing, couples it with the conversational mode and at the end it is one of the two solutions which remain viable. It is based on the concept of speech (Z,85). For instance, instead of using the preterite tense, the mark of Literature, this type of writing uses the present perfect, a fresher, oral form. Being close to the actual everyday use of language, which is constantly altered by history, it is better able to resist kidnapping by mythology.

The first writer to hit on this felicitous solution, if one excepts Proust, was probably Louis-Ferdinand Céline, who impressed Sartre deeply and probably suggested to him the style of the conversations in *The Ways to Freedom* which, as we saw, Barthes had in mind in this chapter of *Degree Zero* (although he could see that with Sartre these conversations are more like arias caught in traditional recitative). And its best modern exponenent was Raymond Queneau. This solution seemed all the more urgent at the time of *Degree Zero* because of the opportunity of leaning on the new humanism of existentialism, which had at last integrated history instead of being based on class essentialism. At the same time the writer could become a desired member of this humanist movement which, in for instance Sartre's early articles in *Les Temps modernes*, had explicitly requested the co-operation of literature. Hence the 'speech' solution. Speech expresses freedom by its form, and union with the community by its content.

This solution merges with Barthes's other efforts to spread enlightenment — in *Mythologies*, in his articles on Brecht in the periodical *Théâtre Populaire* and, later, on structuralism. The nostalgia it expresses is also recognizable in the ending of 'Myth Today' and especially the Thibaudeau interview where Barthes states that if the relations between the subject and the world must change one day, language will be deeply altered and some words will disappear. The examples he gives are possessive pronouns, or the word *death*, since the utopia of 'revolution' can evoke a community of a kind unknown even in the dream of religion, one in which the terrible loneliness of death would be abolished (*T*,106). This is a familiar theme in atheist eschatology, explicit in Malraux's novels, where the saga of human fraternity supersedes Christian transcendence as another Golden Legend.

Yet this 'speech' solution disappears, fairly quickly from Barthes's texts on literature, and is replaced by the last solution, which could be called that of the 'mask'. This is a mode of writing described chiefly in terms of Flaubert's practice (*Z*,70-2; *M*,135-6) and it is totally unconnected with the official favourites, speech or the zero degree. This is very important. It shows that from the start Barthes had in mind, besides the admittedly utopian zero degree, two serious rival solutions to the problem of writing. The counterpoint between them is often responsible for what appear as sudden shifts or inconsistencies in his thinking.

While some writers still tried to achieve actual union with society or nature, Flaubert stressed the inevitable distance between life and art and played along with literary conventions instead of meeting them head-on. Though nothing is safe from myth, we read in *Mythologies*, not all languages are equally susceptible. An art like Flaubert's which 'points to its mask as it moves forward' may not make the writer a universal spokesman again, but at least it achieves responsibility for its form. Flaubert experienced the bourgeois state as 'an incurable ill which sticks to the writer' and thus donned his mask clear-sightedly (which, as Barthes notes, is the essence of tragic feeling). Further, he could even conceive what came to appear to Barthes as the only possible way out: a counter-myth like *Bouvard et Pécuchet* gives to the insoluble problem of realism a frankly semiological solution. By this Barthes means that as language cannot *represent* reality but only *signify* it, the writer might as well consciously endorse this state of affairs.

It is important to note that this solution is not adopted by Barthes straight away and light-heartedly. It is unsatisfactory to a certain extent (each reader will decide just how much) because it appears to grant ethical salvation only to a rather specialized type of work, limited by its very project, which is that of transcending the bounds of unself-conscious literature. Beyond this narrow circle, there remains only a resigned acceptance of the conventions of writing, a realization which finally redeems *all* writers to the extent that what makes them writers is their use of convention (Z,72, 41). This echoed Sartre's remark that the surrealists' slogan of 'an end to language' led to books which were 'voluminous capsules of silence', a strategy not really different from *Bouvard et Pécuchet*.

The two sexes of the mind

Although the solutions to the problem of writing and history concern the writer in general, Barthes is clearly speaking in his own name. Now there is, in the gallery of literary types depicted in *Degree Zero* one which occupies a very depressed position: the intellectual (Z,32-4). He appears simply as the practitioner of a sub-type of political writing. But political writing, as we saw, is in fact the archetype of writing, for it poses the whole problem of the writer and society. Thus the intellectual, hovering as he does between impotence and complicity and reduced to 'a para-literature which dares not speak its name', is in fact the truest representative of the modern writer. He is geared to history and terrorized by what he believes in his heart of hearts to be the more adequate response to it: action, or at least the kind of axiological political writing which enlightens and judges at one stroke. Yet the process of intimidation is never quite successful; literature, for the intellectual, is never completely 'liquidated' (Z,33). This curious word speaks volumes about both Barthes's view of the reductive effect of action upon language, and his guilt at not being able to condone it.

We saw that Barthes has adopted the Mallarmean/Sartrean dichotomy between the 'raw' and the 'essential' use of language. His most famous restatement of this distinction is an article reprinted in *Critical Essays*, whose title calls for careful translation: 'Ecrivains et écrivants'. *Ecrivain* is the traditional term for *writer*. For the mere user of language, the person who — as Barthes was later to put it — simply writes down what he could otherwise say orally, he has always tried to find less hallowed names: *scripteur* (scriptor) in *Degree Zero* (Z,34), and here *écrivant*. This seems to relegate the intellectual (or *écrivain-écrivant*) to a realm outside literature; yet we now observe a phoenix-like resurgence. To start with, the position of the adjective (*écrivant*) after the noun in French clearly places the emphasis on the *writer* (*écrivain*). *He* is the hero of the whole article even when, like a god in disguise, he uses language as a mere scriptor, so that the writer-scriptor has, to borrow Michelet's phrase, 'the two sexes of the mind' (on this Gnostic cluster, see *MI*,153-61). The genealogy of the intellectual differs in this article from that given in *Degree Zero* inasmuch as more importance is given to the content; the term 'intellectual' seems to have originated with the Dreyfus affair, applied to the Dreyfusists by the anti-Dreyfusists. The distinction also involves the time element. While the intellectual's duty is to state what he thinks immediately and unequivocally, the writer is to comply with the timing determined by the development of forms, a law unto itself.

The real, though tentative, answer to the question of the intellectual's relation to history and society appears only in a later article, an interview given to *Tel Quel* where Barthes, after stressing the incompatibility of a writer's preoccupations with the day-to-day material of newspapers and periodicals, stated that he could see a way out: taking current topics as 'the material of a secret work' (*E*,157). It is easy to see this as self-advice when we remember that he several times mentioned his inability to write without at least an idea of who he is writing for, for example friends on the editorial committee of a periodical (*T*,95). This also sheds more light on his insistence about writing only to fulfil commissions. As he declared in the Thibaudeau interview, it is only during the 'very short reprieve' between an assigned task and the return of the awesome responsibility of literature that he can write (*T*,104).

The tortuous rhetoric of 'Writers and scriptors' was presumably a means of coping with the kinds of guilt generated in turn by both a direct, transitive made of address and, differently, by an intransitive use of language, but the argument is so convoluted that it is easily misread. The same applies to the preface to *Critical Essays* which, baffling many French critics, is often dismissed as so much pretentious nonsense. In fact, its extremely involved argument is simply a faithful transcription of the critic's plight as Barthes sees it: if the essence of the writer, as symbolized by his ability to objectify himself in the third person, as a 'he', is his ability to speak intransitively (indirectly, in mediate fashion), then the critic who disdains or is unable to put himself in the same position, to 'turn the "I" into a sign' is condemned to the immediacy of pronouncements in his own name. He can only manifest his true nature as a writer by somehow considering this condition as itself the very distance, the mediation which constitutes the writer. Through the figure of the intellectual, the critic's position comes to define the writer, rather than the other way round. 'There is, then, a certain misapprehension attached by its very structure to the critic's work, but to point to it would be to put this distance at risk. The critic is 'condemned to error — to truth', even if he keeps wishing, through 'a last silent ruse' that readers will find their way through this maze (E,xviii-xxii). Very few seem to have done so, understandably perhaps. For here is a true antinomy, worthy of the sophists' famous conundrums. And as Barthes sees these conundrums as constitutive of modern views on language, we are once more brought back to the central place of self-consciousness in modernity.

Committed/compromised

Barthes has a favourite theme, that of an irony which exists in the text without being textually marked (CV,74). And the assimilation of writer and critic under the figure of the intellectual shows that solving the problematics of writing involve not only the form of literary works but also, from a wider point of view, the writer-scriptor's chosen attitude towards the link between himself, his work, reality and his readers. He may or may not think truth is his concern; that it can be reached or not; and that it is his business to communicate this truth to his public or not.

In order to characterize the changes in Barthes's attitude toward this complex topic, it is useful to resort to a simile of the turnstile which Barthes borrowed from Sartre's analysis of bad faith and used to good effect in *Mythologies*, in revolving it now this side and now that. The various positions of the turnstile form a kind of 'figure' or pattern with three available positions where Barthes successively occupies: 1. The self-assured fight for progressive ideas and 'intellectualism' in art. 2. The equal attention given, chiefly after the turning-point in the middle of *Critical Essays*, to the strategies of what he called 'derision' and 'serious-ness', broadly to the two viable solutions of 'mask' and 'speech' in *Degree Zero*. 3. The tendency to interpret Flaubert's dictum, 'stupidity consists in concluding', which he often quotes, as if it itself expressed a conclu-sion. Despite its 'terroristic' effect on opponents, it is open to the classic retort to absolute scepticism, namely that doubting everything is at least evidence of a belief in absolute doubt. As this position concerns the last phase in Barthes's career, I shall leave it aside for the time being (we shall see later in Chapter 15 that a new kind of poetic certainty had by then replaced earlier models of truth). Let us examine briefly, the first two attitudes.

Mythologies was to establish for many years Barthes's image as a committed writer, even though *Critical Essays* shows how quickly he abandoned this assertive stance, apparently because of doubts about the status of literature in a committed life. Existentialist literature had spent its force by the late 1950s, although the problem would arise again in 1968 (when, incidentally, Sartre's faith in the permanence of literature in all social epochs was perhaps borne out by his lack of support for those *gauchistes* who advocated working in a factory instead of writing — see already on this Z,33-4). The timing of Barthes's change has been obscured as has the split in his mind in *Degree Zero*, on the one hand simply by the excellence of *Mythologies* and, on the other, by the fact that Barthes was involved in a series of struggles for different progressive causes.

Barthes's early assertiveness had to rest on a firm standpoint. This was implicitly supplied in *Mythologies* by the Marxist 'class position', that is, the representation one has of one's objective 'class situation' (defined by one's place in the process of production) and the decision not to be determined by it, and if need be, to oppose it. It is a little paradoxical to call the position adopted in *Mythologies* Lukács's 'point of view of the proletariat' since Barthes precisely believes, as we saw, that in a bourgeois society there is no proletarian culture, art or morality (M,139), but it is at least a stand against the bourgeoisie. This type of knowledge born of struggle is the only case where what is necessary to arrive at the truth is not 'impartiality', which can only mystify, but taking sides. As the preface puts it, our time 'may well make sarcasm the condition of truth'. This is why an essay like 'Blind and dumb criticism' is such a skilful parry; for the critics attacked by Barthes who, 'as luck would have it', always find themselves unable to understand existentialist or Marxist plays, cannot decently refuse enlightenment which is the rationale of their calling (M,35). Whatever the generosity of the intentions, this is what would be called today the 'discourse of mastery'.

A similar 'masterful' attitude is discerned in the comic quality of *Mythologies*; it is significant that no hostile reviewer ever mentions this notable aspect of the book which greatly increases its efficacy, while making nonsense of the reproach of humourlessness traditionally levelled at left-wingers. Every reader will treasure his own anthology but a few features are particularly notable. Barthes excels at picturing an object and making its mythological meaning explicit at one stroke. We need only think of his characterization of bourgeois vocal art, with its needless stress on syllables already highlighted by the meaning, by his vignette of a lieder-singer 'ejecting the word *bonheur* from his mouth like a [fruit] stone' (ET,120); or of Billy Graham holding up the Bible, the answer to every problem, as a street-seller holds up a universal tin-opener (M,114). Barthes is a master of the smear-word even when, as in his later career, he turns this art against himself. He makes the reader squirm on behalf of the victim when he quotes a particularly jejune passage from a popular magazine, relentlessly spelling out all the unethical considerations which were meant to work subliminally. Often the victim condemns himself out of his own mouth and Barthes makes devastating collages of singularly feeble remarks. As might be expected,

Système de la mode finds a particularly good quarry for this device. But the high spirits, the intellectual fun, in *Mythologies* convey an unmistakable derision of the petit-bourgeois world, which sees nothing unlikely in attempting to understand Einstein's genius by placing electrodes on his skull, or representing the labour of thought by profuse sweating. The nimbleness of the style, the art of the delayed punch-line, emphasize an Ariel-like superiority over Caliban, even if the mythologist is thereby cut off from the communal pleasure, which 'is no small matter'.

This attitude carries over into the first part of *Critical Essays*. Barthes divided this book into two parts, significantly characterizing the first by its content (the defence of Brecht and the New Novel) and the second by its language (structuralism). The turning-point occurs with a series of meditative articles written in 1959-60. They explore, whatever the ostensible subject, the status of various types of discourse, and lead to a new doctrine of literature which Barthes held to the end of his life.

The process seems to start with his preface to *The Witch*, his favourite of Michelet's writings. It is followed by three crucial articles, on Queneau's *Zazie*, on the novelist Yves Velan and on Kafka. The first opens a general interrogation on the possibility of an absolute discursive weapon. The second is one of the very few texts where Barthes, who, as we saw, defines the critic as stricken with an aphasia for the word 'I', does for once speak in the first person. And he can do so because Velan's novel — precisely entitled *I* — both expresses a subjectivity which seems torn by many of the conflicts also found in *Barthes by Barthes* and suggests an aesthetic solution for them. This solution is confirmed by the third article which, as its title, 'Kafka's answer', suggests, is also a resolution to Barthes's crisis. The Queneau of *Critical Essays* is radically different from the one in *Degree Zero*, who there seemed to offer a means of bridging the gap between writer and society through the use of everyday speech. Now, on the contrary, what is found remarkable is Queneau's control of the grand tradition of French literature which allows him to mock it at every level. Yet Queneau manages to do this without labelling his irony, by a play within language itself, a move which is profoundly opposed to the clear conscience of classicism (see also on this *CV*,74-5). He is not standing outside what he criticizes, he is not *committed* but consciously *compromised*. So that whereas 'metalanguage [like sarcasm] is always terrorist' (*E*,170), the anti-language invented by Queneau 'is never peremptory' (*E*,122).

It is difficult to say why Barthes should have suddenly felt that admonitions were a sign of bad faith, or rather why his own admonitions to his contemporaries no longer seemed able to redress the balance of his own accusations. But when he surmised that Queneau, in psychoanalysing literature had probably psychoanalysed himself as well, purged himself of a 'rather terrifying Imago of Literature', it is easy to believe that Barthes was carrying out a similar psychoanalysis on himself. For derision is bad faith too, just as much as seriousness (a *serious* or *committed* use of language is here to be understood both in the Sartrean sense and in the sense used by philosophers of language like John Searle). And if 'derision empties seriousness', 'seriousness *understands* derision', as we saw in 'Blind and dumb criticism'. This is why there cannot be about language a reassuring synthesis subsuming the opposites, and why the model of dialectics is finally insufficient to account for it. Another proof of this is that Queneau's *Zazie* achieved the Flaubertian feat of thoroughly stultifying the language of criticism: some commentators thought that it was a serious work to be deciphered by exegetes, others thought the very idea of doing this grotesque.

We are all part of Robbe-Grillet

Yet Barthes did not think of explicitly asking the question, 'what is Literature?' until after the appearance of *Mythologies*, and his somewhat mysterious change. As is shown by the existence of two parallel solutions to the problem of writing and society, that of speech and that of the mask, his new doctrine was not entirely new, but it could look so because it was now unilaterally propounded. Until then Barthes had believed equally in what Blanchot called 'the writer's twin myths', that of Orpheus and that of Prometheus, who could be represented by Blanchot himself and by Sartre. Perhaps Barthes could now afford to ask the 'Oedipean', the 'tragic' question, 'who am I?' in relation to himself and to literature because of a general disillusionment due to the *embourgeoisement* of the proletariat (as we saw in *Mythologies*). This was the period associated with the phrase 'the end of ideology' (see on this Leenhardt, 1981), an atmosphere which can be compared to the recent revulsion against Marxism which resulted, in the words of Sartre's follower André Gorz, in an 'adieu au prolétariat'. The world was henceforth to be taken 'tel quel', as it is, and the advent of a new periodical precisely entitled *Tel Quel* in 1960 probably also encouraged Barthes, ever dependent on the existence of an identifiable addressee for his discourse, by offering an alternative to committed periodicals. All this gives a new meaning to the myth of Orpheus which informed *Degree Zero*. The idea then had been to write without 'Literature'; now the problem has become one of guaranteeing the existence of literature without tying it to a topical content, however pressing.

This solution both to the urge to write and to the entailed ethical problems is confirmed in the article on Kafka, which besides integrates the reader to the life of the work. 'The work of Kafka lends itself to everybody but answers nobody.' The 'meaning' of his work is not

'Kafkaism', that is, the sum of its themes; it is, quite simply, his technique. Literature is means without cause or end, and for the first time Barthes uses words and images which will remain with him to the end: 'the writer is like a craftsman who might make in all seriousness a complicated object without knowing after what model or for what purpose, rather like Ashby's Homeostat' (*E*,134). Obviously, the search for meaning cannot but be *déçu*[1] (*E*,135) by this kind of homeostatic system. But in these early formulations Barthes was constantly anxious to show that literature is not divorced from the world, even if their connection exists in ways which vary to the point of contradiction. Sometimes the reader interrogates the world by means of literature, sometimes literature itself does this, and sometimes it is the world which interrogates. Besides, while the work is without cause or end because it is without social sanction, it is not disengaged since the idea is to commit the forms as well as the contents. This, however, was a slippery slope to the increasing depreciation of content. It was as if the awareness of language as practice came to involve a reduction of the whole praxis to form.

Barthes seems at this point to have found just the reference he needed in order to specify this cluster of relationships, in Hegel's *Lectures on the Philosophy of History*: the Greek world is presented as a youthful age for humanity, a time when activity, not yet relentlessly transitive, was disinterested and autonomous, half-way between the concrete and the intellectual. The Greeks, marvelling at the *naturalness* of nature, responded by an intellectual activity which conferred meaning on the world which had given the original stimulus. We now realize that the complicated expression of Barthes's doctrine on the relations between the world, the literary work, its author and its reader, comes in fact from Hegel, although it is difficult to imagine that Barthes's own divided mind did not find such ambiguities welcome. What the Greeks perceived in nature was an immense shiver of meaning, to which they gave the name Pan. This image is often taken up by Barthes in order to convey a significance which is still diffuse, reducible neither to one meaning (*un sens*) or even to meaning (*le sens*) but is simply some meaning (*du sens*). He realizes however, that the 'exemption from meaning' (a term he compares to the exemption from National Service in *Barthes by Barthes* (*RB*,87), non-meaning, is only a kind of philosopher's stone, an intellectual utopia, another version of the zero degree. For the work needs some meaning, just as it needs some plot, even if only to stage its own destruction. Here are some of the better known formulations of Barthes's new doctrine: 'the writer can bring to light only signs without signifieds' (*E*,135); 'literature does not permit one to walk, but it permits one to breathe' (*E*,267); 'literature is both meaning affirmed and meaning disappointed' (*R*,ix; see also *E*, blurb and *CV*,50).

At a time when clearly everything Barthes wrote was poured into the melting-pot of his doctrine, Bruce Morrissette's book on Robbe-Grillet (whose work Barthes felt included his own interpretations, see *E*,204) appeared. Morrissette's discovery of an Oedipal framework in Robbe-Grillet can only have reinforced Barthes's feeling of a fundamental elusiveness of literary works. The Oedipus complex, which Barthes equates with fiction, was now revealed at the heart of the work of this archetypal anti-novelist. It is clear that this unexpected discovery, reinforcing Barthes's conclusions at the multiplicity of interpretations of Racine and followed by the attack on his own attempted synthesis of all the 'deep' interpretations that could be used on his subject, played a part in the final formulations of the doctrine. Barthes's position is epitomized by the memorable phrase in this article on Morrissette's book: 'we are all part of Robbe-Grillet'. Barthes's new doctrine of literature now seemed indeed 'ultrastable' since it could cope with the two main problems which had burdened his early work: it allowed at last a solution to the nagging question of commitment and it brought about the integration of the reader/critic with both the life-cycle of the work and the creative process.

Literature is thus itself a world we interrogate and onto which we project our responses. With what images does Barthes seek to convey his new doctrine? We find a host of them in *Critical Essays*. The definition of literature is a kind of *ostinato* running through the book. Orpheus, the patron-saint of *Degree Zero*, is equally omnipresent in *Critical Essays*, as is Mallarmé, for real persons can be mythical as well. Proust is another mythical example for the writer since he made his work out of his very preparation for writing, as is Proust's character Brichot, who failed to hide his self under the third person, the '*je*' under the '*on*'. Or again, also developing the ideas contained in the Orpheus myth, the writer is seen as Moses, but a Moses who cannot even see the Promised Land; or Eriphile, the only character invented by Racine and the only tragic one in his work *Iphigénie*. As Barthes puts it in Marxist terms, 'Eriphile is nothing, Iphigénie has everything'. As a Trojan carried away by Achilles (in a way which recalls the dolorist descriptions of the Passion of literature in *Degree Zero*) Eriphile asks the 'Oedipean' question which is that of literature itself: 'who am I?' Like Eurydice dying when Orpheus turns back to look at her, like the sculptor Sarrasine in *S/Z*, she dies when she at last knows the answer. This is symbolic of literature: there is a meaning, but literature dies if this meaning is stated explicitly.

We have already found Barthes comparing the writer to Michelet's *Witch* and to the witch-doctor as seen by Lévi-Strauss. Yet structurally this role is no different from the vaccine which Barthes had accused the bourgeois world of using so as to inoculate itself against dialectics, history, innovation. It is this realization which prepares his final characterization of literature as a fundamentally unrealist and conservative activity. The entities to which he compares literature are similarly ambiguous, oscillating between an infinity of meanings and a mere combination of a finite set of elements: Ashby's homeostat, fashion (as we shall see shortly) and the ship *Argo* 'whose long history admitted of no creation, nothing but combinations' (since each of its pieces was replaced one at a time while the whole ship could still be called the same one). Objects of the kind one finds in Robbe-Grillet's work, for instance, are naturally polysemic: their meaning always flickers and is never definite. Like the statue of Charles III in *Last Year in Marienbad*, which smilingly and enigmatically points to an unknown object or person (which might be in the story or in the real world), literature is perhaps 'in this anaphoric suspension which at one and the same time designates and keeps silent' (*E*,204).[2] Like Gide's Oedipe who did not fear the Sphinx because the understood that 'man' was the answer to all questions, Barthes had found a universal answer, but one which, according to the structuralists, is the exact opposite of 'man': language. What remains is the question of a suitable discourse for speaking *about* literature. It is not enough to assert that there is 'a responsibility of forms'; the link between these forms and the society to which they are *answerable* (since this is another meaning of *responsable* in French) must be thought out. Do we observe the same evolution in Barthes's ideas on this topic as on the nature of literature itself? We do in one of his best early essays, 'History or literature?', which is included in *On Racine* and was an immediate cause of the Quarrel.

History or literature?

This review of existing critical and educational practices starts in a very Saussurean manner by noting that there are in literature two aspects: 'one historical, to the degree that literature is an institution; the other psychological, to the degree that it is a creation' (*R*,155). The methods of all the available discourses which attempt to deal with these two aspects can then be discussed. The historical aspect means that one should model one's approach on the best of current historiography, the *Annales* school which has reduced the gap between history and anthropology. This makes the positivist pattern of literary history, a sequence of eclectic monographs, as irrelevant as *histoire événementielle*. Barthes's new approach to writing about literature does away with the individual, the author, just as modern history superseded royal chronicles. It is, finally, the 'history of the Signs of Literature' Barthes had suggested in *Degree Zero*. But, ruled out from the point of view of the institution of language, the individual comes back from another angle. 'It is virtually impossible to deal with literary creation without postulating the existence of a relationship between the work and something besides the work' (R,163). For a long time, this relationship was taken to be causal: hence the talk of *sources, genesis, reflection*, etc. This representation of the creative relation now seems far too simplistic.

Hence the necessity of passing from the notion of the work as product to the notion of the work as sign. The sign consists of a signifier and a signified which together make up the signification. In relating this to literature, we shall see that Barthes tackles in his article the question of how to transpose the units of the plane of expression and the plane of content. But before we come to this point, let us remember that the sign in its totality has a link to a referent. Although Barthes never mentions the word in this connection, the problem looms large in his article, not only because the link between text and referent was the main preoccupation of standard academic practice at the time, but because the more sophisticated distinction between signified and referent does not entirely solve the question of the 'responsibility of forms' Barthes wants to demonstrate. But the difficulty involved in differentiating signified and referent in such an untested area becomes crucial when one attempts to make positive suggestions. This makes the neat distinction of poetics and criticism, in *Critique et vérité*, look rather utopian: the critic who wholeheartedly projects himself into his interpretation, as Barthes recommends, can no more see it from the outside and announce it than a psychoanalyst's patient enmeshed in transference. He is making a bid for the truth, as does Barthes in this early article.

Right from the start, in *Degree Zero*, a link between forms and infrastructure had been postulated although even there Barthes had specified that it was not narrowly deterministic (Z,8). In 'History or literature?' he asserts the futility and artificiality of attempts to relate art to history either mechanically through chronological coincidence, or by analogy between cause and effect. Barthes here endorses the critique of positivism carried out by Bloch and Mannheim (R,155n, 162n). The Leninist notion of consciousness as mere reflection of the external world is of course no better; as in *Degree Zero*, we find bourgeois and orthodox Marxist practices dismissed in the same gesture. Sophisticated Marxist attempts like Lucien Goldmann's, who tried to connect a form (tragedy) with a content (the world view of a political class) in his study of Racine, or the work of the psychoanalyst Charles Mauron at first impressed Barthes because they were the most profound and literally the 'deepest' (R,167). Soon, however, they came to seem unsatisfactory since the link between signifier and signified was 'not thought out' (E,153, 271), and remained analogical.

One can understand such reservations about analogical explanations, whose deceptively 'natural' look makes them the staple of historical and biographical criticism. In 'History or literature?' Barthes had already loosened the bonds of analogy as far as the link between characters and their purported biographical 'sources' was concerned, using instead psychoanalysis, rhetoric or Lévi-Straussian analyses for their non-analogical models, such as denial, antiphrasis or compensation.

A simplification of outlines is an indispensable preliminary to synthesizing these models. Barthes, in his pioneering essay 'Racinian man' (R) tries to draw together everything he found most exciting in contemporary anthropology, mythology or linguistics. The slightly chaotic effect produced by such *embarras de richesses* is compensated for by Barthes's reading of the plays, which clearly favours characters who, whether or not the focus of critical attention, were seen by Barthes as champions of emancipation against the crushing weight of the law — often embodied in castrating females: Pyrrhus in *Andromaque*, Néron in *Britannicus* or Titus in *Bérénice*. No doubt a psychological bias, this image has a theoretical import as well: the defence of infidelity as a condition of freedom prefigures Barthes's reaction (which came just after he had written 'Racinian Man') against any kind of determinant for literature, whose essence is more and more identified with radically new language. Simultaneously engaged in a study of fashion, Barthes came to see it as the perfect metaphor for literature; indeed the essence of fashion is the 'infidelity' which establishes it absolutely over nature and last year's fashion alike.

There is another reason for this metaphor of fashion and it has a direct bearing on the problem of forms and history. Barthes was very impressed by the fact that Kroeber's study of fashion over three centuries (briefly summarized as an appendix to *Système de la Mode*) recognized two discoveries which accorded with the methods both of long-term history in the *Annales* school and the intuitions of structuralist writers like Lévi-Strauss. One was that history does not intervene as content in the shaping of a form: there is no analogical link between high-waisted dresses and the post-Revolutionary period. History can at most speed up slightly the endogenous turnover of forms. The other discovery is that this turnover is not haphazard but a rational alternation of possible shapes: skirts are always narrow when waists are wide and vice versa. This striking phenomenon seemed to Barthes to prove conclusively that history, or at least the history of forms, was beyond the grasp both of conscious intervention and analogical explanation. This is why both fashion and literature — and perhaps human history itself — could be compared to Ashby's homeostat.

And yet, does analogical change never occur? It may well be that the popularity of analogical explanations is due not only to their inherent plausibility but because of an actual statistical primacy. It would be a bold historian who deliberately ignored analogy as a possible principle of explanation of the concurrence of an event and a form. This refusal may even be an implicit limitation of the otherwise exciting modern approaches to the sociology and history of art and literature. The causes of the modern crisis in *Degree Zero* were certainly presented as analogically related to it: the break-up of writing follows the break-up of society and Barthes states explicitly that writing's way back to unity, should it ever happen, will not stem from anything but a transformation analogous to that of the social base.

All this was renounced by Barthes's new doctrine of literature. He was henceforth simply to assert the absence of any knowable link between history and human artefacts and to concern himself only with the exploration of semantic techniques which would show how *any* meaning could be imposed, even an 'empty' one. As we saw, this preoccupation with what he called *la cuisine du sens* (*E*,154), a derogatory phrase which suggests underhand manipulation (thus *la cuisine électorale* hints at gerrymandering — cf. 'cooking the books') clearly has subjective causes.

Yet he was never to tackle the problem of forms and history again. In *Critique et vérité*, for instance, we find history mentioned as a prerequisite before the three approaches congruent with literature, poetics, criticism and reading; but its link with them is 'not thought out' there either. This explains why Barthes did not avail himself of the more sophisticated models evolved during the structuralist period: structuralism for him had already come to mean the reliance on the systematic character of the interpretation, on sense rather than reference. One of these new models was proposed by Althusser in order to think out the autonomy many contemporary Marxists wanted to grant superstructure while retaining the economic base as the ultimate determinant. This model of the 'structure in dominance' makes use of the psychoanalytic notion of overdetermination. As defined in Ben Brewster's Glossary appended to *For Marx* (1969, 255, given here in abbreviated form) it states that the elements of a structure are asymmetrically related but autonomous, one or other being dominant depending on the overdetermination of the contradictions and their uneven development.

Even such a supple interpretation would look too restrictive to Barthes after 1960, like all attempts to establish a connection, let alone a hierarchy, between the elements as a whole, whether this concerns the components of society, the various psychic processes involved in language and literary production, the terms of a paradigm or the elements of a metaphoric series. But this is a typical case of personal motivations generating results which are of general value. For Barthes's partiality calls attention to the forms themselves and to the kind of discourse most suitable for dealing with them. Criticism of creation is a semiology that dares not speak its name. It should instead tackle its objective in proper semiological fashion, that is, by first identifying a signifier and a signified. If the work is a sign then, what counts as the components of its units? And what is one to make of the fact that they can be subsumed under one another, as a whole book may be signified and thus summed up by a single signifier (often its title)?[3] The conclusion seemed obvious to Barthes, and in line with his new doctrine: in identifying the components of literary signifiers and signifieds, we always choose a level less in terms of the work than in terms of our preconceived ideas about the structuration of content and expression. Objectivity is therefore impossible and both the language of literature and the language which speaks about it are arbitrary, like all languages. They are based on a contract of some kind and their only 'proof' is their coherence and systematic character. As for the ethics of the critic, they can only consist in his stating his point of view openly.

The problems discussed in 'History or literature?' (as well as the articles in *Critical Essays* on Queneau and rhetoric, *E*,117) and of course the tentative use of figures and functions, as well as the layout on the axes of syntagm and paradigm in 'Racinian man' were in fact the first formulations of modern structural poetics and analysis of narrative. As the Quarrel proved, Barthes was certainly premature. Many of these points had to be re-stated six years later in *Critique et vérité*, but by then his ambivalence about structuralism in literature had become as great as his distrust of psychoanalysis. All types of meaning which *name* the meanings they discover seemed to him to threaten the integrity of the forms with which they were associated. As this process of naming is precisely that of *semiosis* and even of cognition, the far-reaching consequences of Barthes's later position can be imagined; their full extent will be seen in *S/Z*. According to Barthes, the work of literature in Goldmann seemed to be reduced to a *product* of the social situation and in Mauron to an *expression* of the author's psyche, because these authors named their findings. Thematic criticism, as practised by Georges Poulet, Jean Starobinski or Jean-Pierre Richard seemed preferable since the meaning was coextensive with the forms analysed, immanent in them. Barthes's strictures nonetheless seem unfair to Mauron and Goldmann, and Sartre before them, since they all tackle the study of forms, thus attempting in the literary field what iconology was doing in the realm of art. Barthes's own earlier theory of theme (*MI*,177ff) shows that he saw it as a prototype of the semiological idea, since it spans the abstract and the concrete, as well as the diverse 'substances' in different sign systems. His constant evocation of 'very ancient' themes, as well as his inordinate fondness for capital letters, show a yearning for essences and origins, a view of theme as unity in diversity, which he was later to disperse as 'biographeme' and 'anamneses' (see Chapter 15). (For a critique of the subjectivism often found in the thematic approach see Mauron 1962, Genette 1966b, Derrida 1972c.)

But the low spirits evident in the essays written around 1960 lifted towards the end, when Barthes experienced the promptings of 'the euphoric dream of scientificity'. Yet it is worth noting that this optimism is not reflected in the preface of *Critical Essays* (1964). The reason for this is that, when Barthes is considering writing itself, science spells constraint rather than freedom except at those rare moments of miraculous equilibrium, as in the two articles on 'The Imagination of the Sign' and 'Structuralist Activity' (discussed here in Chapter 9). It is probably through the problems of semantics, encountered in his structuralist studies, that Barthes came to realize the part played by the reader in the constitution of meaning for the writer as much as the critic. We can see, at any rate, that all the major tenets of the later Barthes are already present in *Critical Essays*. No doubt he was himself terrorized by failing to recognize, in the ontological and logico-mathematical approach favoured by later thinkers, his own ideas writ large.

Part III

A euphoric dream of scientificity

8

Everything, then, can be a myth?

Having seen how the elements of Barthes's intellectual framework were reorganized into a new pattern during the course of *Critical Essays* (1964), now is the time for the most important flashback: we must return for a while to 'Myth Today' (1957) which initiated semiological analysis.

What is myth?

It is as a semiologist perhaps even more than as a literary theorist that Barthes is known abroad; but in France the reverse was true for a long time in the eyes of his public and, it seems, in his too. Thus in the first preface to *Mythologies*, we find Barthes anxious to stress the continuity of his work; and *Elements of Semiology*, as the footnotes reveal, is a compendium of what he considered his discoveries to date. As for *Writing Degree Zero*, he updated it twice (M,131ff, E,97ff), using the tools he had acquired in the meantime, not a difficult task considering that the chapter on 'Writing and the Novel' in *Degree Zero* contains in embryo the whole of *Mythologies*. Barthes had identified as the major 'Signs of Literature' in the novel two forms which happened to have a deep significance for him: the use of the past historic (particularly striking in French since the preterite is obsolete in the spoken language) and a specific use of the third person singular. However depressing its content, the novel can offer, thanks to such clear labelling as fiction, as an institution, an image of security and order. Such signs are thus 'a part of a security system for Belles-Lettres', 'one of those numerous formal pacts made by the writer and society for the justification of the former and the serenity of the latter' (Z,38).

But Barthes also thinks he can see *how* this effect is produced and uncovers a complicated 'machinery aimed at both destruction and resurrection' in the relationship between the work and society. As the discussion of the 'mask' solution showed, the formal marks of literature are the end products of 'a dialectic which clothes an unreal fact in the garb first of a truth, then of a lie denounced as such' (Z,39). This strange contradiction shows the structural kinship between literature and myth: both, paradoxically, buttonhole us while announcing at the same time (in our society at least) that what they draw attention to is perfectly normal and natural. This contradiction explains why Barthes tried to account for myth by a two-tiered structure, as we shall see. In *Degree Zero* he already attributes the peculiar ambiguity of signs, like the use of the preterite (both tense and sign, existence and meaning), to a fraudulent notion of universality: what is true of one section of society is not necessarily true of all the others, but in bourgeois ideology 'the true is supposed to contain a germ of the universal' (Z,39). This is how the values of the triumphant bourgeoisie were extended to other classes and cultures. Decolonization, which was under way when Barthes was writing these words, started the process of disillusionment, and various liberation struggles have since then completed it. Such manipulations are 'strictly how myth functions', he concluded (Z,39), although he noted in passing the existence of a radically different artistic tradition in the East, suggesting the possibility of doing without myth altogether. In a certain Chinese tradition a wooden walnut is meant to convey simply the image of a walnut, and not at the same time 'the intention of conveying to me the art which gave birth to it' (Z,40).[1]

Whatever the truth about the mimetic element in Eastern art, Barthes's theoretical essay is emphatically called 'Myth Today'; it is 'a synchronic study of myth' (M,137) which does not, in principle at least, claim to describe other periods. It was easy to take *Degree Zero* in its entirety as an example of myth; vice versa, *Mythologies* was presented by Barthes as a kind of monograph on a particular mode of writing, the bourgeois one; its peculiar characteristic is that although historically determined like any other, it always presents itself as 'what goes without saying'. This kind of semantic overkill, which superimposes a 'natural' layer onto what is already justified culturally, produces in turn the nausea and irritation which first alerted Barthes, as he tells us in the preface, to the presence of a significant social phenomenon, and even gave the first clue to its mechanism. As the essays in *Mythologies* make clear, the manifestations of society is myth-making activity are not random but occur in a regulated manner. There is more to drinking wine in France than meets the eye — whoever does not do so encounters minor but definite problems of integration; having to justify abstention to start with. The intuitive efforts of the former Prime Minister Mendès-France to transfer some of the mythical quality of wine to milk by ostentatiously drinking it in the Chamber in order to combat alcoholism show that it is possible to 'speak' the culture one 'understands' more or less consciously.

The theories proposed in 'Myth Today' were generated from just such experiences, Barthes tells us, and this is verified by the parallel structures of the essays themselves. They are, like Barthes's and Sartre's versions of the development of modern writing, cautionary tales for the modern citizen. Starting with the detail which 'interpellated' Barthes and indicated the presence of a myth, they follow with a supple mimetic description, the seductive aspects of which make myth attractive and thus credible; slowly, description turns to analysis and the last sentences wake us up from this hypnotic spell with an ethical denunciation of the sleight-of-hand perpetrated. As one goes on reading, the essays begin to refer to each other and, under the surface variety due to Barthes's interests and obvious zest for living, they begin to show the homogeneity of a corpus for research.

Within this corpus, Barthes and his reader progressively discover regularities. This 'repetition' seemed significant to him, as he explains (*M*,120) as is the pleasure he took in his exploration too, although this is a classifying principle which he would dare to confess only in the latter part of his career.[2] But regularities indicate only the presence of an object of knowledge, not its structure, even if there are vague intimations of the latter. In order to study myth *in detail* — Barthes underlines this aim in his second preface — it is necessary to borrow from existing models. 'Right from the start, the notion of myth seemed to me to explain these examples of the falsely obvious. At that time, I still used the word "myth" in its traditional sense' (*M*,11). But what *is* this traditional sense? The recent controversy about *The Myth of God Incarnate* showed that the word can be interpreted in various and even opposite ways. For some people, a myth is a story which gives a poetic form to an unsayable truth while for others it has an essentially fictitious character. It is significant that this ambiguity (duly recorded by dictionaries) also affects two other words expressing realities highly relevant for the study of myth, *ideology* and *the Imaginary*, taken from two of the main models used to study it: Marxism and psychoanalysis.

Essays like 'The Face of Garbo' seem best suited to the definition of myth as a 'fabulous and rare thing' (as the Larousse dictionary puts it) conveying no particular lesson, although one can recognize at the end a discreet and amused echo of the opposition between structure and process which Barthes praised in *Elements of Semiology* for having renovated the social sciences: 'The face of Garbo is an Idea, that of [Audrey] Hepburn, an Event' (*M*,57). In other myths, the lesson is more pointed; this calls for a deciphering, which explains Barthes's second step after resorting to the notion of myth itself: the assimilation of myth to a language, and the effort to draw all the consequences from this premise.[3] The slight variations in terminology at this very early stage (myth being successively called a *language*, a type of *speech* and a *message*, which all have very different technical definitions) does not obscure the meaning: myth is a message sent in a certain code, it is the *parole* of a *langue*. From such messages, which are immediately understood — how consciously will be discussed shortly — the code (or *langue*) has to be reconstituted. This hypothesis unifies what could at first appear heterogeneous: the media which prompted Barthes's reflections (newspaper articles, photographs, films, exhibitions) and, secondly, the objects or events which are taken up by society to 'speak' its messages, such as, in various cultures, the arrow one sends to signify a challenge, the black pebble which means a death sentence, the bunch of roses sent to convey one's love. To this list Barthes adds many others, to which we respond without their being traditionally identified as signs: a wrestling match, an elaborate dish photographed in the glossies, the 'miracle' of plastic, the euphoric foam of detergents, the conventions of striptease.

All these heterogeneous manifestations of social communication are to be reduced to their *meaning*, and henceforth the only operation which they call for is a *lexis*, 'a reading or deciphering'. Barthes's hesitation here is significant; having taken the legitimate first step of classifying all these phenomena as means for social communication where meaning is the only thing which matters, he takes the second step of assuming that this meaning can be verbalized. The vocabulary he chooses to convey this tends to make the inference acceptable: any object, he says, can become a myth provided that it is 'conveyed by a discourse', since there is 'no law which forbids speaking about things'. This is because he is less interested at first in the semiological structure than in the ideological use of signs; he wants to show that 'it is human history which converts reality into speech' (M,109-10). Yet this way of presenting semiological facts is begging the most important question: if meaning is to be verbalized, *who* is to verbalize it? This makes it crucial to specify whether myth is 'deciphered' or 'read', or even, as Barthes also says, just unilaterally 'received'.

This important point will be discussed later; let us simply assume for the time being that myth is a general form, a mode of signification. The consequence is that everything can be a myth (M,109). There are no privileged objects which are either mythical in themselves or impossible to mythologize. But not all objects are mythologized at the same time. Before they become suitable for mythical use, they must already be recognized as part of social usage; they must produce what the structural analysts of narrative later called 'meaning-effects'. Semiology is therefore a science of *forms*. It concerns itself with the way in which messages are constituted and transmitted, not in principle with their medium or even their content (it now in fact includes a study of these).

A certain degree of consciousness is necessary for myth to function, for it to be deciphered or read. Thus it is not surprising to read that it is only after having started his exploration of current myths that Barthes conceived the project of understanding their mechanism *in detail* (M,9,

11). These words, which could not be overstressed, indicate that he had in mind an explicit account. But the fact that 'Myth Today' is placed at the end of the book also shows that the essays can be perfectly well understood without a formal semiological analysis, and this is part of the lesson. The lack of a self-conscious theory serves very well in the first essays, corresponding to the protagonists' lack of awareness of their role in society. For although it would be naive to ignore the presence of actual conspiracies left, right and centre, a conspiracy theory of society would still fail to explain the mysterious cohesion of the social machine. A proper theory of myth which purports to be a contribution to the theory of ideology must therefore account for both lucidity and blindness.

The essay on 'The world of wrestling' which opens *Mythologies* is a good example of a transitional stage between being taken in by appearances and fully understanding what produced them. This is evident in Barthes's playful use of linguistic terms, and one is a little startled to find that this essay has been taken at face value (whether in praise or blame) by some critics. Such a 'deafness to connotations', as Barthes calls it, is unfortunate in connection with a book devoted to their study. In the essay, wrestling, as opposed to boxing or judo, is shown to be more of a spectacle than a sport; cheating does not seem to matter and takes place in full view of the audience. There is no real or great suffering, yet the opponents make a lavish display of it, etc. Barthes recognizes here the trace, debased in our era of mass culture, of the needs of tragic catharsis once satisfied by ancient religious or magic rituals. Those who go to see wrestling both know and don't know why they go and what they seek, and need this ambiguity. They are not able to think clearly (for cultural or psychological reasons): I pretend to go to a sporting event, but in fact I go because this is the next best thing to a Greek tragedy in our secular world. What they feel is perfectly expressed by a common phrase which the psychoanalyst Octave Mannoni (1969) saw as epitomizing the structure of fantasy: *I know, but all the same.*[4] Although the behaviour of both wrestlers and spectators is regulated by socialized behaviour and thus conventional or institutionalized up to a point, this unconscious element casts doubt on the Saussurean image of *langue* as a 'social contract', also used by Barthes in *Elements of Semiology*. This is important when one comes to choose the models suitable for semiology.

The very idea of semiology, as well as the mention of Saussure alone in the second preface to *Mythologies* (at a time when Barthes already had a somewhat mythical and stylized view of his own career), has given an undue emphasis to the role of linguistics in *Mythologies*. It must be remembered that what has been established so far is only the *principle* of semiology, namely, the assimilation of social facts to signs, with the structure this entails in Saussurean thought: the union of a signifier with a signified. What is striking, on the contrary, both in *Mythologies* and even in the more linguistically inclined *Elements of Semiology*, is how anxious Barthes is to synthesize the results of many contemporary disciplines. In selecting models for semiology, he has to bear in mind the two aspects he wants to account for: on the one hand, the dual aspect of myth due to the peculiar interplay between nature and culture and the exploitative use to which it consequently lends itself; and on the other hand, the degree of consciousness involved in the functioning of myth. Or to put it another way, on the one hand the presumed *structure* of myth, and on the other the *purpose* of myth and its *use*.

It is fair to assume for a start that the sciences and theories listed at the beginning of 'Myth Today' do function as implicit models, and this is in fact justified by an examination of the text. Semiology is thus seen as having already started by the time Barthes rediscovers it; it was the implicit denominator of all these sciences and theories. Developing it will help *them* to develop, and this includes linguistics itself. What then are these theories which are presented by him as having, without realizing it, partly filled out the space reserved by Saussure for semiology? 'Psycho-analysis, structuralism, eidetic psychology, some new types of literary criticism of which Bachelard has given the first examples' (M,111). In other words, as a later passage makes clear (M,114), the theories of Freud, Lévi-Strauss (and probably Jakobson as well), and Sartre, and finally thematic criticism which as we saw was not only practised by Barthes (in *Michelet*) but accepted by the early structuralists as a forerunner, before they saw it as an enemy. *Elements of Semiology* is also explicitly presented as a synthesis: not only of the 'quadrivium of pilot-sciences' (history, economics, linguistics, ethnology, S,55, 101-2) analysed by Merleau-Ponty and based on the opposition of system and process, but also of all the other fields tapped in the Notes, especially, as the exploration of the notion of *sign* makes clear (S,37), psychology (represented by Jung and Wallon) as well as logic and philosophy (represented by the Stoics, Peirce, and Hegel).

Barthes thus claimed that since Saussure, both inspired by and indepen-dent of him, 'a whole section of research has constantly been referred to the problem of meaning'; the mark of this is that the sciences mentioned 'are no longer concerned with facts except inasmuch as they are endowed with significance' (M,111), as 'tokens of something else' (M,111). In fact of course, these sciences deal not only with the tokens but with the 'something else', just as 'mythology' includes both a study of forms, semiology, and a study of contents, ideology.

The structure of myth

Saussure's model of the sign is very useful to Barthes, who is at pains to stress that it is made up of *three* elements, not two: the signifier, the signified, and the sign itself, a new entity born of the union of the other two. This tripartite schema is the constant form from one medium to another, whether linguistic, iconic, gestural, etc. We remember that the linguistic sign is seen by Saussure as carved out in one gesture from the two shapeless and labile masses of sound and thought. Let us see how this works for each of the sciences cited. For Freud, slips of the tongue and neuroses are the correlation of manifest behaviour, the signifier, and latent meaning, a form and intention. Sartre's biographical and literary studies present an author's work as a relation between the original crisis of a subject (the separation from his mother in the case of Baudelaire or the naming of the theft in the case of Genet) as signified, and the discourse of literature (its signs, like Hébert's obscenities or the use of the past historic) as signifier.

But this structure also has an explanatory value when Barthes transposes it to myth, following his hypothesis that 'myth is a type of speech'. Myth does not depend on the specific material of its support; its raw material is a pre-existing signifying system. So myth is a *second-order semiological system*: what was a *sign* (namely the associative total of a concept and an image) in the first semiological chain becomes a *signifier* in the second.[5]

He gives two examples to make all this more concrete. A pupil who reads in his Latin grammar a sentence borrowed from Aesop or Phaedrus *quia ego nominor leo*, receives at the same time two messages, just as the reader of Hébert's news-sheet read some of his words both as swear-words and as the author's profession of faith: *I am a revolutionary*. The first message is literal: *because my name is lion*. This is a general message, accessible to all those who understand the language in which it is expressed. The second message is much more specific and is addressed to the reader as pupil in the second form of a French lycée. It is functional; it says: *I am a grammatical example meant to illustrate the rule about the agreement of the predicate*. Furthermore, the second message is experienced as more important than the first. It is obvious that many other examples could have been found to illustrate this particular rule. To underline his point that the nature of the substance chosen does not matter, since semiology as the science of signs is not limited to language and myth deals only with the final signification, requiring only a reading operation, Barthes chooses a pictorial support for his second example which is iconic. If I am handed a magazine while waiting to have my hair cut and I see a photograph of a black soldier in French uniform saluting, with eyes fixed on the tricolour, I again receive two messages at once. The first is again literal: the shapes and colours are correctly 'read' by me as a black soldier, in French uniform, etc. The second message is again one which is meant to be correctly read or decoded by the right person: it is a praising — if need be a defence — of the French Empire, all of whose sons serve faithfully without any colour discrimination, a complex meaning which Barthes for convenience calls by the rational neologism, French imperiality (M,116).

We see that in these two examples the global signification of the first system, the *sign* proper, is somehow emptied of its substance in order to be used as a mere signifier of the second system which, while tremendously reducing its general scope, nevertheless derives from it a considerable part of its own force. Such mechanics seem to Barthes to explain the affinity of myth for exploitative purposes since it benefits from the interplay between the cultural meaning which caused it to be used and the reserve of natural plenitude belonging to the first system. Whether this alteration of the contents is viewed as an impoverishment or a transfiguration must depend of course on one's view of imagination; we saw that Barthes subscribed to the Sartrean conception of the image as schematic and impoverished. Thus it is the fabricated quality of colonialism which disappears, to be replaced by an essence which is felt to be justified in itself. But is myth always bad, even myth *today*? In order to understand Barthes's answer, we need to examine separately the two questions mentioned earlier: the structure of myth, and its purpose and use.

Let us return to Barthes's second example of myth, that of the black soldier. There are at least three layers here: the functional, *connoted* meaning, the defence of 'French imperiality' and which is 'appropriated' to a certain type of reader; the *denoted*, general meaning which Barthes verbalizes as 'A black soldier is saluting'; and finally a *perceptual* meaning since it requires a certain training to recognize photographed objects (although Barthes conflates this layer with the previous one). But on reflection, what he says about the connoted meaning — 'Truth to tell, what is invested in the concept [of myth] is less reality than a certain knowledge of reality' (M,119) — applies also to the denoted meaning. Even to understand this denoted meaning, we need a certain amount and type of knowledge: what is a soldier? a black soldier? a uniform? a flag? France? an empire? the French Empire? a photograph even, since the dangers of this reportedly 'objective' medium are well-known.[6]

It is true that the vast majority of readers will not ask such questions; and the mass media of modern society are guaranteed to tire even the most dedicated questioner. But then we must know more about Barthes's anonymous person who, speaking in many voices, tells us 'whether naively or not, I see very well what [this photograph] signifies to me' (M,116). We may say that he is a theoretical construct, like Chomsky's speaker/hearer although, here in relation to social language, this concept creates more problems than it solves. Here again, as in the case of the meaning of wrestling, we are confronted with the problem of knowing whether there is in a community a unitary *langue*. Words and photographs are different things when uttered or reproduced by different people or newspapers; and furthermore, the fact that some things are within what Chomsky would term the *competence* of a social speaker, yet would never be actually uttered by him, drives home the unilateral, intimidating character of myth. Though Barthes is well aware of this, he, in his turn, seems to be its victim as well as its theorist.

Such questions are today being rediscovered by linguistics itself; but the problem lies deeper still. It would be very difficult to answer the qeustions suggested by the photograph of the black soldier in a totally neutral fashion, and above all it would not be clear whether one did so on the plane of denotation or connotation. We saw earlier how Barthes came to the conclusion that neologism was necessary, since mythical meanings change very rapidly with socio-historical conditions, while dictionary definitions only give information on conventionally agreed notions. But such objections must naturally apply with even greater force to semiology's attempts to formalize social languages; in other words, the problem does not lie so much with connotation as with denotation itself. As Pascal put it, if custom is a second nature, perhaps nature is nothing but a first custom. The most accessible and famous lesson of *Mythologies* is the realization that all social usages, as soon as they are recognized, turn into signs of themselves, so that it is almost impossible to do anything without self-consciousness.[7] But this is perhaps not so giddying as the problem about denotation, a slide backwards from what one assumed was the bedrock of all assumptions. Barthes came to realize that denotation itself is ideological, like the corresponding concept of 'object-language'. But both correspond to a social reality nevertheless; we understand Barthes's examples in *Mythologies*, and they have an undoubted didactic value. We may have an ideology different from that of the national press; but we know what it means — we are all multilingual in that sense. So perhaps Barthes's solution in *S/Z* was justified; after criticizing the dichotomy of denotation and connotation, he decided to make use of it nevertheless, to 'keep denotation, the old deity, watchful, cunning, theatrical, foreordained to *represent* the collective innocence of language' (*SZ*,9).[8]

There is some evidence in the text of 'Myth Today' that Barthes was not entirely happy with the way he cut loose the Gordian knot of natural language. By making the meaning of a semiological sign (that is, one whose signifier is made of objects and events instead of words) equivalent to verbalization, some of the old problems of natural language remained. The same signifier might mean, to different 'readers' of social signs in different circumstances, 'wealth', or 'waste', or 'conspicuous waste', for instance. This is why he stresses at the beginning of 'Myth Today' that there is no 'identification' between a signifier and a signified in semiology, as there is in language, but only 'equivalence' (*M*,112). The difference is that while the linguistic sign is arbitrary, the semiological sign is always in part motivated (M,126).[9] Linguistic motivation means analogy. Examples like the lion or the black soldier must present some analogy with the situation they are meant to illustrate. It is this motivation which is necessary to the duplicity of myth, which alternates between the empty form which serves as its signifier and the full meaning which gives it verisimilitude and allows it to hide in the bosom of innocent nature (M,118, 126). As we saw earlier, a society built on the myth of 'order' (and is there any society which is not 'a social order'?) can even confer meaning on an ostensible lack of order, mythologizing it as surrealism or the absurd, for instance. But Barthes finds that this motivation is always fragmentary, and it is these 'scattered' manifestations of mythical intent that he later called, borrowing a term from Hjelmslev, *connotators.*

The question of arbitrariness and motivation depends on what one considers to be language and linguistics; here Barthes obviously has taken only the idea of the sign as a two-sided entity, rather than the sentence or the discourse. At this point, when he speaks about literature (M,120) he calls it myth. In other words in 'Myth Today' what has not yet been clarified is the difference between myth and the semiological sign. Despite Barthes's reputation as the pioneer of semiology, he came to it through mythology and never quite reconciled himself to the idea of an autonomous structuration of a sign system, that is, to a genuine semiological denotation, independent of the interpretation he had already placed on the rules of the social game. This will be quite apparent in *Elements of Semiology* and *Système de la Mode.*

It seems therefore that Barthes's remark on the partial motivation of semiological signs should be rephrased. What makes them different from linguistic signs is not so much the fact that they always contain some analogy, since linguistic signs often do, either at the level of the sign or part of the sign, or at the level of discourse. It is the fact that because semiological signs are the products of multiple causality, they can be viewed from an almost infinite number of points of view, they can lend themselves to *multiple* motivations. Among these, there is one which is the equivalent of the myth of object-language, or denotation: it is the motivation based on use-value, the satisfaction of needs; and Barthes identifies with this the technological motivation, the fabricated quality of an object which according to him reveals the same integrity as its proper use, in that it excludes interpretation.

Yet this direct connection with nature and work remains a kind of utopia, a horizon like the poetic solution in *Degree Zero*; in practice, society makes this unmediated contact almost impossible. Thus I can always maintain that I wear mink for warmth and that I eat caviar for nourishment, not for social display; or that I wear tattered and faded jeans for the sake of economy and not 'cheap chic'. It is very difficult to prove — and still more difficult to make someone admit — that he is speaking on the connotative and not the denotative level. Again, we find that Barthes's sensitiveness to aggression (and his intellectual intrepidity provided ample occasions) helped him to discover the universal sway of connotation in social life. This was still the case in a text written some fifteen years after 'Myth Today', 'Writers, intellectuals, teachers', in which he shows how in many intellectual debates the laws of the game dictate that the speaker reply to the content of questions and not the manner in which they are asked, whose message may be quite different: 'If I am asked in a certain tone of voice *What's the use of linguistics?*, thereby signifying to me that it is of no use whatsoever, I must pretend to reply naively *It helps you to do this and that* and not, in accordance with the truth of the dialogue *Why are you attacking me?'* (*IMT*,202). But the same problem occurs in psychoanalysis, where the analyst is constantly faced with wrong interpretations and rationalizations on the part of his patient. Here we see at one stroke Barthes's perspicacity and his feeling of social impotence. It is one thing to defend oneself from the impregnable position of bad faith — this is the whole foundation of the *vraisemblable* (e.g. in sophistry) to which *Communications* 11 devoted a special issue. But although an interlocutor who speaks in good faith is still bound by the same rules, it is assumed in practice that committed speech in social life is possible. But Barthes eventually seemed to have moved (for reasons perhaps not 'innocent') on the turnstile separating commitment and irony to a position which excludes serious language altogether (see 1975g).

Given what I have argued so far, it is impossible to subscribe to Barthes's conclusion, after he examined the tri-dimensional signifying pattern of myth, that 'when he reflects on a metalanguage, the semiologist no longer needs to ask himself questions about the composition of the object-language' (*M*,115). On the contrary, the structure of what is taken as the first layer, or denotation, *is* important and in fact Barthes acknowledges this almost in the same breath when he says that the semiologist needs to know what, in the global sign, 'lends itself to myth'. This cannot be possible without reflecting on the structure of the objects or events which come to be taken as signs. The two examples chosen by Barthes demonstrate this since they both illustrate the theme of domination: of colonized peoples in the case of the black soldier, and of the heifer and the cow in Aesop's fable about the lion who claims more than his share *because his name is lion*. Barthes rediscovers only later in the text (*M*,144) the political character he had built into his examples. This again comes from not sufficiently separating the structure of myth from its use. In the case of the pupil reading the story of the lion as a grammatical example, Barthes notes that when this story is told not for its intrinsic interest but for a particular social use, 'into the naming of the lion, first drained of its contingency, the grammatical example will attract my whole existence'. But this is *not* part of the myth, as Barthes seems to imply; on the contrary, this is the meaning which the mythologist alone can read, it is what enables me to read the story as a quotation, not what the story conveys to me, unless I am a mythologist as well.

Models to study myth

The conflation of the two meanings, the mythologist's and the non-mythologist's, may have been due to Barthes's disgust and the resentment over the tactics of myth, which he invariably speaks of in metaphors of rape, prostitution, criminality, sacrilege, corruption, vampirism, slavery and parasitism. But another factor in this conflation may be Lévi-Strauss's methodology for breaking the mythical code, one which yields a meaning comprehensible only from the point of view of an all-knowing God, mythologist or psychoanalyst. The various subjects are condemned to live out the episodes of a story which they cannot understand from their limited point of view. Later, in *S/Z*, Barthes claimed the right to read the story as if the ending were already known to him, in order to highlight the text's structural articulations. It cannot be denied that this way of reading, which structural analysts call *tabular*, is as indispensable to a full understanding as the *linear* reading of a story. But it cannot replace it. It is this question of the *use* of myth, that is, of its *reading*, which Barthes tackles next.

In order to illustrate the play, the 'turnstile' between the empty and full aspects of the mythical signifier and the various readings which can be made of myth, Barthes uses another metaphor: 'If I am in a car and I look at the scenery through the window, I can at will focus on the scenery or on the window-pane,' alternately stressing either the presence yet emptiness of the glass or the fullness yet unreality of the landscape (M,123). In the same way, I can produce three different types of reading: if I focus on the empty signifier I read the photograph of the black soldier as an *example* of French imperiality; if I focus on the full signifier, I read it as an *alibi* of this same French imperiality; if I focus on both at the same time I receive this myth according to the very logic of its dual structure, both as an intention or value and as a 'fact' which makes the value look necessary, natural, innocent. But the problem just identified above in terms of a specific difficulty in identifying what can be safely recognized as *the* language or as *one* of the languages recognized at a given moment by a specific community as denotation, is specifically discounted by Barthes as not being a *linguistic* problem: 'the freedom to choose what one focuses on is a problem which does not belong to the province of semiology: it depends on the concrete situation of the subject' (*M*,128*n*). Few linguists, and least of all Barthes, would today accept this Sartrean solution, nor would Sartre himself, since ultimately he understood that language can also be part of what he calls the practico-inert (see on this Pateman 1980a).

When Barthes implies in the preface of *Mythologies* that he came to see more in myth than just its traditional sense, it is safe to assume that what he understood later was the *extent* of the politicization of social life. He cites Marx's example of the cherry tree in *The German Ideology* to show that the most natural object contains a political trace, 'however faint and diluted, the more or less memorable presence of the human act which has produced, fitted up, used, subjected it or rejected it'. Even an innocuous grammatical example like Aesop's fable, revived in the imagination of a child, for instance, can reveal its political content — unless, Barthes adds, we are dealing with a bourgeois lion who would not fail to assert his rights as natural, not political! (*M*,144). Of course, it takes more effort on the part of society to produce an apparent depoliticization of a Senegalese than of a lion. But Barthes does not draw the obvious conclusion for connotation: if everything in society is political, everything is *already* connoted, and mythologizing is not the politicization of an object, but on the contrary, *depoliticizes objects when needed*. This might seem to amount to the same thing but it is heuristically more fertile. Otherwise one might just concentrate on the obviously 'marked' elements and reject the rest as nature, as the normal denotative language of a community. Whereas if one assumes that it is the other way round, one can start looking for the meaning of every single social usage, a meaning which has become deeply internalized and therefore invisible. What we need in other words is a social psychoanalysis which assumes that everything is significant.

But in order to carry out a psychoanalysis, one again needs some idea of a norm or at least a principle of reading. We saw that 'sarcasm' here is another name for taking sides, class position as a cognitive instrument, since it is only in struggle, with its requirement of choice, that some aspects of social reality become visible. Myth constantly oscillates between fact and value (*M*,123, 131); it has 'the physique of the *alibi*', a word Barthes elsewhere speaks of as 'an elsewhere and a justification' (*Z*,26). Hence the only way to cope with it is to adopt a language which itself conflates fact and value, a language which claims to be scientific, whether that of psychoanalysis or of Marxism. When in *Degree Zero* when Barthes described the sort of political axiological writing which presents a theory as a fact, he clearly spoke as one oppressed by it: he views it with more lightness of heart in 'Myth Today' because there he is using it himself and believes in its necessity.

Such considerations should qualify Barthes's apparent rejection the idea of an unconscious in social psychoanalysis. He says: 'Myth hides *nothing*. . . . There is no latency of the concept in relation to the form: there is no need of an Unconscious in order to explain myth' (*M*,121). As always, we should decide by looking not at what Barthes says but at what he does. His preference for marginal kinds of psychoanalysis, those of Bachelard or Sartre, is stated explicitly in *Mythologies* (*M*,67); but in 'Myth Today' he resorts to Freudianism whenever he wants to clinch an argument (*M*,119). The principle of reading he chooses could be summed up in Sartre's well-known saying, 'The truth of oppression is the oppressed'; but not merely for its political side. It also makes one think of psychoanalysis, of the side of what is repressed in society which cannot find a voice in any of society's accepted discourses, and to which the mythologist must give speech. In *Elements of Semiology*, Freud is replaced by Lacan as a model for semiology. But many aspects of 'Myth Today' would tend to suggest that Lacan's early undertaking to spell out and connect all the implications of the linguistic elements in Freudianism played a greater part in the first elaboration of semiology than was earlier assumed.

Considering that various notions taken from the 'materialist tradition' (including Hegelian concepts divested of what Marx called their 'mystical matrix') are constantly used by Barthes in *Mythologies*, it is at first surprising not to find Marxism among the models given at the beginning of 'Myth Today'. In *Degree Zero* (*Z*,68-71) and *Mythologies* (*M*,141) Barthes makes use of the Marxist theory of ideology, the image of bourgeois consciousness as a camera obscura which yields an inverted view of reality, turning culture into nature (from *The German Ideology*), or the fetishism of commodities (in *Capital*), by which the products of human labour, in capitalist society, are fetishized to the extent that they become alienated from those who made them while human labour itself becomes a thing. Thus *Degree Zero* shows how, in the cult of highly-wrought form which develops in the second part of the nineteenth century, the writer's work becomes part of the notion of literature, fixed in picturesque detail by complacent working recipes. Despite such assimilations, by which writers clearly advertise themselves as members of a guild, the economic position of the writer is not immediately evident. This serves to condone to some extent the writer's adoption of alienated values. As Sartre put it, he feels more like a student on a grant than a worker with a wage: 'On the one hand he sings and sighs, on the other he is given money.' The fetishism of form as an unquestionable value comes from the fact that the writer is unable or unwilling to see his connection to the economy of society as a whole. But payment is always for services rendered, as Sartre and Paul Nizan stated with some brutality, for being either a jester or a watch-dog.

Such unease about the value of literary and critical labour is an abiding feature of Barthes's thought. Its roots lie not only in an awareness of recuperation by society and the affinity of language for sophistry but in the uncertainty about its basic nature. This explains why the Marxist opposition between use- and exchange-value, that is, between the usefulness of an object in satisfying human needs, and the value of an object for exchange, underpins the whole of Barthes's work. Although the distinction in fact belongs to classical economics, what is specifically Marxist is the exposure of exchange-value as ultimately resting on the human labour it represents, when this labour is in turn treated as a commodity in a situation of exploitation. This is not discussed in detail by Barthes, who is concerned with symbolic practices and not with economics, but the hierarchy implicit in the opposition between use- and exchange-value has a structuring force in his thought. During the whole of his career, at first spontaneously and poetically then more self-consciously when the theme was taken up and amplified by the *Tel Quel* group, Barthes opposed the honesty, integrity and thoroughness of work which bears directly on nature, without residue or make-believe, to work which uses signs, that is, means of exchange. Within language itself, the two types of production become what he then calls object-language and metalanguage. For instance, the woodcutter *'acts the tree'*, he cuts, he does not speak *about* it (*M*,145). Proverbs, however gnomic, are grounded in practical experience, in the countryman's knowledge of the weather, and are quite different from the maxims which the bourgeoisie use to express an essentialized human nature (*M*,154). Thus it is that in 'Writers and scriptors' work on form is seen as a factor of alienation, unlike the authentic work of the woodcutter. This is because literature is *already* seen as conservative and unrealistic. Any distance from nature, any mediation, introduces the possibility of interpretation and thus deception.

Thus Barthes, despite his denials, responded from the start to the affinities of Marxism and structuralism inasmuch as they both deal with the interplay of the manifest and the latent. Besides, the Marxist models for ideology are undoubted *forms*, which is what Barthes is interested in. In order to understand why the synthesis between these disciplines remains only latent in 'Myth Today' it is necessary to remember Barthes's hope of analysing myth *in detail*. It is a Marxist tenet that every situation should be analysed in concrete terms; such precepts can be found in Zhdanov's critique of Alexandrov's *A History of Philosophy*, part of which is quoted in 'Myth Today' (*M*,111). But this is the point: there was in contemporary Marxism a taboo on formalism (the movement of Russian formalism was stamped out), which was in fact a smear-word for anything not stolidly 'realist'. In consequence, semiology is presented at the outset not simply as a Marxist project, but one which has to be affirmed in the teeth of current Marxist orthodoxy (*M*,111-12). Barthes first uses Zhdanov's own words to defend the legitimate use of the notion of form. Then he shows that the sacred injunction to reach a synthesis cannot always make one materialize, so that as a result many Marxist studies are dogmatic and sterile. Finally he turns the tables on Zhdanov by showing that it is socialist realism, not formalism, which is a hybrid; it does not really level its criticism at form, which is relational, but at a reified idea of form.

The fact remains that Marxism is used in 'Myth Today' to explain the purpose of myth and not its structure, despite the project of the book. Marxism functions as a framework, but it is not an explicit model, despite the fact that many of its concepts, like *work, need, demand,* and *fetish,* also bear a psychoanalytic interpretation, since psychoanalysis is also concerned with production and exchange of a kind. Thus although all the components are there, the synthesis between psychological, economic and symbolic exchange, which was to be widely used in the 1960s (not without some glibness) by many theorists, and which supplies the basis of *S/Z,* is not explicitly worked out in 'Myth Today'.

Using and reading myth: a typology of discourses

The scale of values implicit in Barthes's ideas on the production of various discourses blurs the picture he gives of how myth is received. The three types of reading he lists (*M*,128) are obtained by taking into account, but not sufficiently distinguishing, on one hand, the structure of myth and, on the other, the motives of myth producers and the attitudes of myth receivers: 1. When the photograph of the black soldier, for example, is taken as an example or a symbol of French imperiality, we have myth as seen by the producer of myths, for instance the journalist who starts with a concept and seeks a form for it. 2. When myth is seen as an *alibi* of French imperiality, we have myth seen by the mythologist, who deciphers it and understands its distortion. 3. When myth is received as an inextricable whole made of concrete and abstract elements, a very *presence* which naturalizes the concept, we have myth as it should properly be read in order to function at all. But as Barthes notices, the first two ways of focusing on myth are static and analytical and in fact destroy the myth; whether the attitude of the onlooker is cynical or demystifying is irrelevant. Only the third attitude does justice to myth, since it is a dynamic way of looking at it and experiencing its built-in turnstile between the true and the unreal. There are therefore only two alternatives and not three: in Jakobson's words, that of the decoder and the cryptanalyst or code-breaker. And the code here means of course two things: the content, that is, the interpretation one puts on the very existence and production of myths in society (and we saw that this meaning was known to Barthes at the outset); and the technical aspect of the code, the *how* and not the *why*, which is exactly what Barthes set out to discover in 'Myth Today'. It is important to realize this, as otherwise a work like *Système de la Mode* might seem disappointing: the 'system' turns out at the end to be The System, and it is then not quite clear why such an arduous path had to be taken to reach this obvious conclusion. In fact, of course, as Barthes stated in an interview about this latter book 'it is the path which makes the work' (*E*,216).

Let us note that for Barthes as cryptanalyst, *sending* is assimilated to deceiving; it is *receiving* which is demystifying. This goes a long way towards explaining his tormented relationship with his own writing; in the latter part of his career the notion of the active reader will be the answer to this particular contradiction. But for the time being as the diagrams in *Elements of Semiology* make clear, what we are dealing with are two competing ways of receiving, rival interpretations of the same content, two structures which are the mirror-images of each other, connotation and metalanguage. Besides, as Barthes himself realized in *Elements*, these two structures can be combined, although he does not make it clear that this again can happen in symmetrical ways. The example he gives is that of the fashion writing which 'speaks' the significations of garments, just as one speaks a language. In relation to the garment system, it is therefore a metalanguage. But of course the language of fashion magazines is itself heavy with connotations, the vehicle of many definite ideological elements which Barthes unearths and classifies in the second part of *Système de la Mode*. We therefore have a further connotative language on top of the language of the garments and the fashion writing taken as metalanguage. And of course we also have Barthes's own metalanguage, and hence a series of languages stacked one on the other.[10]

Let us however stay for the moment with the simplified view which I have suggested above, namely that of connotation and metalanguage as symmetrical 'ways of speaking' the same social objects or events. This view is justified in terms of the linguistic fact that a sign is defined not only by the nature of its signifier and signified but by the relations which it has with other signs both in the text and in the mind of the speaker. At first sight, the symmetrical structure of connotation and metalanguage seems to suggest a simple division of labour in the production of social languages which makes taking sides easy. As *Elements* puts it, society speaks the signifiers of the system while the semiologist speaks its signifieds (*S*,94). But there is an assymmetry in this way of 'speaking': society, that is bourgeois society, hides its true nature while the semiologist *names* its signifieds, a revolutionary activity. However, as soon as he has offered this obvious interpretation Barthes qualifies the image of a semiologist overconfident in the face of connotation. The reason is that any science bears the seed of its own supersession by a later theory, or rather by the language of the latter. The semiologist's objectivity is therefore made provisional by history's capacity to renew metalanguages (*S*,93-4).

Taking value into account qualifies this image even further. The new signs formed by the addition of either a signified or a signifier to the system taken as denotation are themselves related to a whole system in each case, so that really the semiologist is caught in the middle of this process of *semiosis*. He is less *committed* than *compromised*. Connotations can be named, but no metalanguage can be used without carrying at least the connotation of 'scientificity'. Each new sign thus formed poses afresh for the receiver the question of belonging to a (speaking) community. Barthes shows that statistically myth is on the Right (*M*,148). But as he had already shown in *Degree Zero*, the Left has Terror instead, and Terror is a connotation. What is more, it is possible to terrorize by means of names on the Right as well, as Barthes also shows in *Mythologies* (in 'Grammaire Africaine', 'Poujade et les Intellectuels', etc.). The conclusion must be that *both* connotation and metalanguage can alienate. The question is, if metalanguage can have a liberating value as well as a terror-effect, can connotation ever be liberating? In other words, we now return, better-equipped, to our previous question: is myth always bad?

Barthes shows that in most cases, and especially in a society dominated by mass media, myth is less read than *received*; it impresses immediately, even when the receiver is a mythologist well able to cope with its wiles. Reading a headline in an evening paper which trumpets that there is a FALL IN PRICES, he cannot but receive a signified to be named by a barbarous but unavoidable neologism: *governmentality*, the government presented by the national press as the 'essence of efficacy', an effect which persists even alongside what is printed in much smaller type, that 'the fall in prices is helped by the return of seasonal abundance' (*M*,130).

Literature, which uses the objects and events of the world as signifiers to speak its own meanings, is technically a connotation, a myth; and there is evidence to show that it acts with the immediacy of myth. Interviewed by some journalists somewhat intimidated by the display of critical technology in *S/Z* and expressing the traditional fear that the literary work would be swamped by the new critical methods, Barthes exclaimed that this did not prevent him from responding to the story as much as the next man and perhaps more (a fact borne out by an examination of the text). This immediacy is produced by a subject's linear reading, the path or route (*parcours*) through the tabulaton which represents the structure of the work. The singularity of a point of view is an essential element of the *vécu*, the immediacy of personal experience.

But it is impossible to distinguish between 'good' literature and 'bad' myth solely on the strength of their structures, which are identical; it can only be done as a consequence of taking sides. Whatever the motivations of the active partners in the consumer society, one might have thought that there was something admirable about their ceaseless manufacturing of significations, what Barthes later described as the hum of the immense meaning machine of humanity, thinking out its projects by applying to all the objects offered to its gaze the impressions derived from self, world and society (*E*,219). Social myths are bad not only because of their content but because, in becoming 'received ideas', they impoverish the objects they fasten on and the imagination of those who receive them. Yet any concept needs a certain stability over time, and those myths which stay alive do so because of the ceaseless interplay between a constant core and topical variations. Barthes solves this difficult question by saying that myth is not at home on the Left, where it exists only in an impoverished form (*M*,145). This resistance to myth is seen as a mark of integrity: people who are destitute cannot afford the luxury of lies. Such a solution is a kind of political zero degree, but has as its consequences the relegation of literature to the conservatives and the failure to take account of the genuine action of myth on the Left. Barthes's answer is that 'the Left' is itself a myth, where it is not revolution. For revolution is antithetical to myth; insofar as it is a 'cathartic act meant to reveal the political load of the world, it *makes* the world. Then its language, all of it, is functionally absorbed in this making' (*M*,146).

But Barthes goes even further. Not only myth, which is the nucleus of a story, but articulated language itself, is seen as containing some mythical dispositions, owing to its expressiveness (*M*,131). If myth is so ingrained, the only way to get rid of it would be to imitate Sartre's hero in *Nausea*, who tries to bring people to tear out their eyes and tongues. Would it not be better to consider myth a neutral structure, which could then be described in the words of René Char as 'the fulfilled love of desire remaining desire', the union of the concrete and the abstract, as miraculous as that of sound and sense?

By such a route we thus end up in Barthes's second, semiological, period ('Myth Today', *Elements of Semiology, Système de la Mode*) with a typology of discourses which confirms the scale of values identified in *Degree Zero*. The two poles are, at one end, language directly geared to action, that is, changing the real, and at the other, language which in itself constitutes an act through the creation of something novel. And between them we find, first, the language of work and revolution, then metalanguage (the language of myth and literature) and finally poetry, which 'attempts to regain an infra-signification, a pre-semiological state of language' (*M*,133). It is impossible to reach the unattainables which lie at either end of this spectrum, either the a state of permanent revolution or the natural quality of things outside all semiological systems, Thus if we object to both connotation and metalanguage, we have the choice only between two extreme methods: 'either to posit a reality which is entirely permeable to history, and ideologize; or, conversely, to posit a reality which is *ultimately* impenetrable, irreducible, and in this case, poetize' (M,158).

Barthes characterizes this as a difficulty of our times but an analysis of the structure and conditions of the production of discourses makes it look rather like an ontological barrier. For this typology of discourses has to be replaced in or within its proper eschatological perspective. As Barthes shows in the preface to *Critical Essays*, if I wished to convey to a friend that I condole with him the last thing I should do is to write only the word 'condolences'. Paradoxically, I must not use the word if I wish to convey what its meaning expresses. Barthes sees deep language as essentially banal; the art of the writer is therefore a combinatory one, that of variations on a theme. The new in literature, then, is 'the amorous dimension of writing', the only way the writer has to reach out to communion with his fellow men. This combinatory aspect of writing is of course also part of the the scientific endeavour, and as Barthes realizes, was part of the euphoria generated by his 'dream of scientificity'. Signification, as we have stressed, can be seen as an active process of uniting a signifier and a signified, both of which have a formal nature, and can thus be seen as both active and 'empty'; signification is itself formal. Thus fashion and literature both signify, with force and subtlety, but what they signify is 'nothing' (E,156). This notion is found from beginning to end in Barthes's work, the most enduring of his theories (or rationalizations), from the early praise of Brecht's theatrical practice to the later images of Oriental attitudes.

It is interesting to find Brecht embodying Barthes's two successive views of literature: that of the adequation of all elements of the artistic message to the central meaning, in the notion of the social *Gestus* (E,41), and later that of the responsible writer who lucidly commits himself by *deciding* to unite a certain content with certain material elements of the spectacle, thus proving that forms were politically responsible (E,262). But Brecht's intention in adopting these theories and techniques — and Barthes's — are somewhat different from those of the poets and philosophers who have universally identified as the aim of true art the stripping of the layers of habit off the pristine face of nature. For both Brecht and Barthes, this destruction of pseudo-physis does not reveal anything which already exists: only an anti-physis which is the world to be made. But even then, the politicizing effect is not guaranteed. The effect of demythologizing might be that the members of the audience, instead of being galvanized by the spectacle of a blindness similar to their own, simply despair and give up. Sartre has argued that Brecht's methods were not sufficient, and that it is necessary to fight myth with a counter-myth.[11] The widespread tendency to defuse Brecht's political dimension by praising his 'broadly human' qualities shows that Sartre had a point. The irony of course is that exactly the same thing happened to Barthes in his last period although, unlike Brecht, he connived in this recuperation.

The code of myth

To come back now to the starting point of 'Myth Today', if myth is a message sent in a certain code, did Barthes crack that code? We saw the two-tiered structure he proposed, and how it is not in fact specific to myth but covers much more: the languages of literature, science and action. But there are three additional elements in a code, not explicitly connected to the two-tiered structure: 1. the units themselves; 2. a rhetoric formed by some particular figures; 3. the general figure formed by all these. During the structuralist period, it became fashionable to call such analyses the 'grammar' of this or that. But here the word would be inappropriate, since what we find is rather a semantics and a rhetoric. These form the metalanguage of Barthes in 'Myth Today'.

Right from the beginning, Barthes shows his determination to deal with things and not accepted words (M,109, 113). He not only redefines many notions already labelled but decomposes reality into semes and regroups them differently, finally giving a neologistic name to the meaning-effect thus identified: 'Meaning is above all a cutting out of shapes' (S,57). He also pays attention, in the identification of such units, to the arbitrary or motivated characters of the signifiers whose signifieds have thus been named and tackles the question of who sends and who receives, although both problems get a more precise answer in *Elements of Semiology*.

Finally, in the discourses of society, Barthes identifies figures which he lists at the end as in a treatise of rhetoric. This gives rise to the question, as in the case of Marxism, why rhetoric, which clearly corresponds to Barthes's spontaneous way of looking at things, is not presented as an explicit model in 'Myth Today'. Actually, the two problems partly overlap: Marxism and its Hegelian sources (for instance *The Pheno-menology of Mind*, frequently used by Lacan) have often of late been viewed as systems of figures. All of Barthes's spontaneous objects of study, themes in Michelet, myths in *Mythologies*, functions and patterns in *On Racine*, and even the signifieds of the various fragments which make up so many of his works, are all figures in a wider sense. His use of figures as a category is therefore heavily overdetermined.

Since myths have been identified as compromise formations and since the figures they form give a general representation of bourgeois pseudo-physis, it is not surprising that the figures Barthes lists, somewhat unsystematically, recall the list of psychoanalytic defences: society ensures its own permanence just as the ego defends its integrity. Since everything is political, what is represented as natural, that is, mythical, could properly be said to be *repressed*, a view which would be analogous to Althusser's views on ideology, which make use of psychoanalytical concepts. A rhetoric is defined as 'a set of fixed, regulated, insistent figures, according to which the varied forms of the mythical signifier arrange themselves' (M,150). These figures are 'transparent' and thus do not affect the form of the signifier; yet, not totally empty, they are sufficiently conceptualized to carry their own ideological implications while still being adaptable to the historical specifications of the concept. Barthes lists the following figures: *inoculation*, which preserves the social order by acknowledging a few of its faults; *the privation of History*; *identification*, which consists in assimilating anything foreign to oneself and conceiving the Other only under the harmless category of 'exoticism'; *tautology*, which is magical behaviour mimicking the rights of brute fact over language which explains and defines, as in 'Racine is Racine'; *neither-norism*, which pretends to ponder the two sides of a question only to dismiss them both at the end; *the statement of fact* as in proverbs, which are often used to eschew boldness in both thought and action. Each of those could be likened to psychological defences such as regression, reaction-formation, isolation, denial or projection. Barthes himself subsumes them under two super-figures, the *Essences* and the *Scales*, which express the basic mechanisms of the bourgeois world, naturalization and homogenization through quantification.

Thus is the multiplicity and originality of the world reduced to tautology; language is suspect because it relativizes, classifies and situates, never resting in the argument of authority; the 'because I say so' which mimics rationality, gestures towards it without fulfilling it. We saw that what was invoked against such tactics is a true science of the qualitative; on the face of it, it would not seem to be very different from what Barthes calls liberalism, that is, 'a sort of intellectual equilibrium based on recognized 'places' (M,152). Barthes normally heaps contempt on liberalism, probably when he feels himself under its gaze, included through exclusion. Yet, once this nuance of contempt is discarded, the idea of a universally recognized right to particularity becomes very attractive, and can be used to characterize Barthes's evolution since *Mythologies*, whatever name one wishes to give to this new outlook. There are more forms and mechanisms for the production and transmission of bourgeois representations than those which Barthes attempts to formalize, since *Mythologies* is full of concrete studies of everyday situations. Finally, Barthes is also doing what he later explicitly recommended in *Elements of Semiology* (S,47, 56), searching for common forms taken by systems of signs, myths or connotations across all the domains studied, ending eventually with the basic unit which could be called, using the word launched by Julia Kristeva, an *ideologeme*, oppositions between Nature and Culture, or Essence and History (an ideologeme is the function which connects the various social practices by condensing the dominant mode of thought).

As I said earlier, Barthes makes it clear that the structural study of myth can supply only one half of the truth; the other half must be supplied by empirical means, by sociology which deals with the quantitative aspect. Only a sociology of the press, for instance, could chart the 'isoglosses of myths' (the lines which connect the places where a myth is spoken) as they ripen from inventive culture into duly 'run-in' mythical material, sufficiently familiar to look like eternal nature. A myth can start its life in the glossy monthly publications for the upper middle class, then reach petit-bourgeois weeklies and finally the tabloids read in the tube (*M*,150). Barthes had not changed his mind by the time he was interviewed by Thibaudeau, although in the meantime he had come to stress a 'socio-logic' inspired by Lévi-Strauss and explained in his review of the latter's *Totemism* and *The Savage Mind* (1962). For example, the fact that all the holiday camps organized by a certain firm show the same organization of space (allotting places to sleep, eat, dance, play games), whether the camp is set up on the shores of the civilized Mediterranean or in the midst of 'primitive' Australia, shows that nature in no way impinges upon what has been predetermined by culture. This is another aspect of the 'responsibility of forms'; it highlights the necessity of a purely relational study between the terms of a structure, paying no attention to the contents and substance, but taking into account the fact that needs have to be thematicized in order to become values. This difference between the human and the animal is equally important in Lacan, where the notion of *desire* is defined as the discrepancy between an inarticulate *need* and the *demand* which articulates it in a socially recognized language or code.

The review of Lévi-Strauss shows one reason why Barthes, despite his lively curiosity for all dimensions of reality, eventually came to stress the qualitative more than the quantitative: objects, rituals, arts, institutions never come to be consumed in the full human sense of the term without being subjected by society to the mediation of the intellect, to a conceptual scheme. What matters then, more than the discrepancy between the number of Rolls Royces and Minis owned by the citizens of a community, is the difference in the structures of these cars; once the latter is reduced to a system of relations — which are here conceived, as in Lévi-Strauss, as a pattern of binary oppositions — we may hope to understand how a society 'makes the world intelligible to itself by means of its cars and its literatures'. For cars too are representations or fictions (in that sense), since they are 'written'; they are language reified. Barthes was still at this stage unclear about the relationship between the denotation of these socialized objects and practices and the language in which they are expressed. It was only in *Système de la Mode* that he 'solved' this problem. The principle of this solution is simply to assimilate the meaning of these practices to language again, as he had done in the beginning, in 'Myth Today'. However, in interviews he claimed that the mini-skirt would hardly have been noticed if journalists had not abundantly reported the phenomenon (*GV*,46, 62); this makes one suspect that the answer is not so simple. Whether the similarity in the forms observed in various social practices within a given society or between several is due to the contagion of a mode of classification to several objects or to a homological correspondence remains to be determined from concrete studies. There is some evidence to show that some categories, such as that represented by the English adjective *crisp* or the Greek *genos*, apply within a given community to objects classified in ways other than the expected ones since they can apply to flavours, sounds, colours, etc. The logic of perception expounded in *The Savage Mind* contains similar observations; as Lévi-Strauss said, in such cases it is not the resemblances but the differences which are resembling each other.

A problem remains, that of the formal nature of this logic. The pattern of binary opposition, based on phonology (especially Jakobson's brand) is an attractive hypothesis (see Appendix); all the more since this 'digitalism' has allowed the development of cybernetics and computers, and is perhaps found in physiology itself, which would explain its universality. Barthes, however, unlike Lévi-Strauss, is anxious to limit this principle. He is comforted by the fact that Saussure made no use of binary oppositions (since for him each term was like the centre of a constellation from which associations of all kinds could diverge) and that Martinet, another one of Barthes's major sources, also questions the universality of binarism. Barthes suggests that while binary logic may exist in the primitive societies studied by Lévi-Strauss, modern societies make use of more complicated alternatives, such as complex terms (*this and that*) and neutral terms (*neither this nor that*), in addition to the two polarized terms (*this or that*). He thinks this solution can account for the strategies described in *Mythologies*: as they progress from nature to culture, primitive societies adopt a more sophisticated logic, while mature societies regress, for reasons not innocent, from culture to a pseudo-nature. Perhaps then what looks like logical confusion is in reality a historical process of reification. Nothing is insignificant, futile or unavoidable, a dynamic view that reveals the ethics of signs and its own underlying generosity. This is undoubtedly how Barthes viewed his own project, as he expressed it in *Elements of Semiology*: to discover the structure of 'intellectual imagination in our time' (*S*,12) and later,

through a consideration of semiology and taxonomy together, 'to redis-
cover the articulations which men impose on reality ... namely, the
science of apportionment' (*S*,57).

The immediate success of *Mythologies* was due to its stylistic brilliance
and didactic force. Barthes remained identified with it for a long time,
and it determined his image as 'intelligent' (an adjective more ambivalent
than it sounds), a 'lean Cassius', a dangerous man. Yet, despite the
recognition it brought him *Mythologies* was twice explicitly disavowed
by him, or at least firmly relegated to the past. The first time was in the
second preface written in 1970, and the second in an article written for
Esprit (and translated in *Image-Music-Text*). The title of the latter is
'Change the Object Itself' and refers to what had become for Barthes the
proper object of intellectual activity applied to society. But he wanted to
call it 'Mythology Today', a title which cannot but be an ironic echo of
'Myth Today'.

This time lapse of fifteen years certainly justified a qualified end-
orsement by Barthes of his former work, especially in one so sensitive
to theoretical innovation and matters of timing. But there was more at
stake. What was now needed, he said, was no longer a semiology (a
science of signs) but a *semioclasm*, a breaking-up of the sign and
ultimately of the whole culture which fantasizes the sign (seen as a closed
unit) as the basis of its mental operations. How Barthes came to conceive
such an ideal will be traced through an analysis of the works he produced
in the next stage of his career. The models he chose for semiology in
'Myth Today' already contained potentialities for opening out the notion
of sign; but the main impetus derived not so much from such technical
consideratons as, it seems, from two more important sources: on the one
hand, the withdrawal from activism anticipated in *Critical Essays* and
the theory of literature founded on it; and on the other, the drive of
Barthes's terrorist ideology, which always made him choose the more
radical interpretation. But it is not necessary to depreciate the content in
order to stress the reality and responsibility of the form; nor is it
necessary to reject the analysis and demystification of signs, which
certainly still pervade mass culture. There may well be today, as Barthes
says, a mythology fo demystification; but we need have no elitist fears of
seeing this healthy activity appropriated by the *hoi polloi*: without
having to undergo the mutation of semanalysis, and the purge of semioclasm, straight 'mythological' analysis is difficult enough to practise, and
like psychoanalysis, since it deals with the social unconscious, it is
'interminable'.

9

Homo significans

Structuralism at last allowed Barthes to theorize his taste for thematic criticism and the stress he had always put on technique and activity in artistic and intellectual creation; this is shown by the two articles he wrote to present its basic concepts, 'The Imagination of the Sign' (1962) and 'Structuralist Activity' (1963) and published in *Critical Essays*. In an interview given to *Tel Quel* just before he wrote these two articles, he alludes for the first time to his current attempts to extend to all cultural objects the analysis sketched in 'Myth Today'; he also sums up his new doctrine of literature and thus shows how his twin interests were merged for one brief euphoric moment when language became 'at once a problem and a model' (*E*,151, 276).

In 'The Imagination of the Sign' Barthes completes his understanding of the linguistic sign by a description of its relational nature. He does so in three stages, which show his concern with a theory of creation and its confirmation in the actual development of linguistic science. The various relations of the signs (which Barthes makes a point of taking from several substances and media) are first explained in linguistic terms, then in terms of types of consciousness, then as the core of a vision which can generate symbolic artefacts. In other words, this article and the one on 'Structuralist Activity' are Barthes's answer to Jakobson's essay on aspects of language and types of aphasia (see Appendix, p. 233). Jakobson had listed examples of preferences for metaphor and metonymy in individuals, genres, cultural patterns and artistic media; these preferences could be found at all the linguistic levels: phonemic, lexical, syntactic and phraseological. His typology deeply impressed Barthes, who suggested further examples (*S*,60-1). The fact that Jakobson placed Romanticism and Symbolism in the category of metaphor, and Realist literature in the category of metonymy confirms the picture of Barthes as one who thinks rather on metaphoric lines. (This probably also applies to Saussure and to Jakobson himself, for whom the word — not the sentence, which is seen as totally free — is the highest coded unit of linguistics.) Jakobson, quoted by Barthes, had remarked that his observations also had a bearing on the metalanguage which deals with these phenomena: since similarity in meaning connects the symbols of a metalanguage to those of the object-language, the researcher possesses a more homogeneous means of handling metaphor than metonymy. Jakobson then extended his observations to the whole of human behaviour, to all symbolic processes whether intrapersonal or social: for instance, to the two types of magic ritual described by Frazer, 'metaphorical' homoeopathic magic based on similarity or 'metonymic' contagious magic association by contiguity; and to the two mechanisms Freud identified in the 'primary process', or unconscious mental activity as observed in dreams: metonymic displacement and condensation, and metaphorical symbols (we saw how Lacan adapted this later).

The three types of consciousness of the sign

Barthes's existential involvement with the material he is expounding in 'The Imagination of the Sign' gives his successive 'mythologies' of the three types of consciousness a peculiar fascination. The first relation in the sign, that which unites signifier and signified, he calls 'symbolic' because it appears most clearly in the motivated sign such as a cross to symbolize Christianity. The description of the symbol, erect, lonely, 'anarchic', communicating only with myth-laden depths, is practically the same as that of style or that of the poetic Word in *Degree Zero*, and also probably owes something to Baudelaire's image of nature as a 'forest of symbols' watching over man. Of course this internal relation is also found in the conventional sign, but clearly Barthes's point in choosing motivated signs is to admonish himself for the 'imperfectly liquidated determinism' that he finds at play. Luckily, he says, the word 'symbol' is 'now beginning to show signs of wear'; but when we remember his predilection for psychoanalysis and Marxism as the 'deepest' interpretations, we realize what love-hate relationship binds him to motivation, a magic participation which by-passes all codes.

The second type of consciousness is paradigmatic. Access to a form of consciousness less imprisoned in its origins is made possible through the comparison of partly similar forms. When the symbol of the Red Cross is opposed to the Red Crescent, cross and crescent no longer have a solitary relationship with their own signifieds, Christianity and Islam. A relationship comes into being and a paradigm is born. This always involves the four-term proportion we encountered in what Saussure called *analogy*, by which rational neologisms can be constructed. Lévi-Strauss's renovation of the concept of totemism was made possible by this same notion which he called *homology*, a term which has had an extraordinary fortune in recent years. Homology seeks to express not an analogical resemblance between substances, but a relation between forms and functions. Thus, there is no 'full' analogical link between a totem animal as signifier and the clan it signifies, but only the 'ratios' between totem animals and clans. 'Paradigmatic consciousness' has both allowed and profited from the success of phonology, and through its application we see that the idea of the differential unit is, so to speak, a spare dialectics: it serves the same intellectual purpose of relativization. Paradigmatic consciousness may look as if it 'emptied' the signified; but Barthes trusts that after this ascetic withdrawal, the world and human society will be given back to him, having in the meantime been made intelligible.

'Syntagmatic consciousness' is able to view signs in terms of the relationship they acquire within the discourse itself. The existential role of Barthes's ideology is again obvious at this point: just as the first internal relation characterized both sign and symbol but was described only in terms of the latter, combination and selection are complementary processes; yet Barthes evidently experiences his passing from one type of consciousness to the other as a progress outwards, accomplished in time, both for him and for linguistics (before semantics and pragmatics came to spoil the symmetry). The distributionalist school, the researches of the Russian formalists on the folktale which Lévi-Strauss applied to myth, and the work soon to appear in *Communications* on the structural analysis of narratives produced by mass culture are all products of syntagmatic consciousness.

The three types of vision

Barthes then tries to outline the types of vision which both in science and art centre on sign relations; 'vision' here conveys both a *Weltanschauung* and a visionary experience. The 'symbolic vision' experiences the world as the relation between a superficial figure and a massive background whose inner developments ceaselessly shift the relation itself. This is the vision we easily recognize as phenomenological and Marxist, and considering that this article appeared in *Arguments*, it reads like a valediction. Under the heading of 'deep' imagination, Barthes here bundles biographical and historical criticism together with Goldmann's work, to which he had so recently paid homage, and for which its author always claimed he title of 'genetic structuralism'. Nonetheless Barthes convicts all these approaches of postulating a 'sovereign signified', full and in existence prior to the work: here we already see, clearly expressed, the gist of Derrida's critique of logocentrism (see below, p. 170). Throughout the period spanned by *Critical Essays*, while Barthes was elaborating his doctrine of literature and of a discourse suitable to it, he had no doubt been encouraged by the dialogue conducted by Sartre and

Lévi-Strauss on the question of whether there were any societies without history, or at least whether the 'cold history' of primitive peoples could be distinguished from the feverish history of the industrialized West. And sure enough when, in 'Structuralist Activity', Barthes updated the picture of contemporary thought he had given a year earlier, he no longer started from the level of the sign or its relations, but from the notion of synchrony. He argued that this concept, which is purely operational in linguistics, was being extended to set up a certain immobilization of historical time. Further, the representation of the historical process as a pure succession of forms, necessarily demoted the subject, whether individual or collective.

The world revealed by this type of imagination is not the inhuman face of nature confronting the poet. It is 'the imagination of the surveyor, the geometer, the owner of the world who finds himself at ease in it' or, to take up a distinction made in *Mythologies*, the vision which created Jules Verne's *Nautilus* rather than Rimbaud's *Drunken Boat* (*M*,65). The lure of structuralism was its offer of the best of both worlds: the freedom to view everything from all angles and to roam in the world at will, secure in the belief that there is a kinship between man and nature (binary coding being not only man's system of thought but also found in the human brain), and at the same time the secure belief that man retains his powers of control. It is as if the wish at the end of *Degree Zero* and *Mythologies* were coming true: 'the reconciliation between reality and men, between description and explanation, between object and knowledge' (*M*,159).

Structuralist activity

In 'Structuralist Activity', Barthes's way of putting things is again more didactic and confessional than strictly linguistic. Explaining how the 'text without end', the continuum of fashion or narrative, is segmented to yield the units, which are then combined into a system which accounts for the actual structure, he uses this framework to show the unity of the modern intellectual imagination. The syntagmatic imagination represents for Barthes a kind of promised land of mobility and activity. This perhaps accounts for the terseness of his description of it: as is well known, paradise is difficult to describe. The same examples recur significantly under the 'paradigm' classification and that of the 'syntagm'. The title is obviously modelled on 'Surrealist activity' a phrase due to the surrealists themselves, and which Barthes had just applied to Robbe-Grillet (*E*,200). Further, the blurring of the boundary between science and art, and among the arts themselves, is itself reminiscent of surrealism. Writers, painters and composers, but also linguists, mythographers, economists and historians, are shown to have not only a practice or a concept but an experience of structure. Their 'activity' consists in dismantling an object and reconstructing a simulacrum of it, thus making nature more intelligible and reaffirming man's power. For Barthes this is essentially the power to impose form on the raw material of experience, a battle against blind chance, very much in the manner of Sartre and before him Malraux, who defined art as a 'counter-destiny' and made it the paradigm of human activity. But here this theme combines with the linguistic assimilation of information theory to produce a notion of originality, which Barthes sees, like Lévi-Strauss in *Tristes tropiques*, as a frail human defence against increasing inertia or disorder.

This intuition of the nature of art is universal according to Barthes; hence the respect artistic achievement excites in all cultures. But its specifically *modern* forms, namely abstract art, atonal music and non-figurative fiction, even though they show the essence of art and even human activity in their purest forms, are for this reason misunderstood; without 'fable', those very forms or shapes appear shapeless. Such a characterization of the modern gap between creator and public recalls Goldmann's claim that the dehumanization of 'organization capitalism' (which follows nascent, liberal and monopoly capitalism) was at once the source of the best of modern art since its creators were acutely aware of form, yet also the cause of the public's inability to understand this art. Goldmann gives the example of Godard's film *Contempt*, where ninety-nine people out of a hundred perceive only the anecdote (a couple is breaking up because the wife is beginning to despise her husband) and not the real theme, which a representation of an attempt to film the Odyssey should have made clear, namely, the impossibility of tackling such a subject now that the gods are dead, and the contempt for someone who, like the husband, is unable to perceive this. Goldmann's analysis tallies with many analyses on the decay of the sacred in *Mythologies*, where the cosmonaut or *jet-man* 'is a reified hero, as if even today man could conceive the heavens only as populated with semi-objects' (M,73).[1]

Man then is no longer seen as rich with meaning but as meaning-maker, *homo significans* — a term which connotes an anthropological mutation. But structuralist activity, whether artistic or intellectual, is essentially anaphoric; it hints at meaning and provokes a yearning for it which it is not its function to assuage. The artist, the analyst, re-create the course taken by meaning, they do not designate it; in the terms later used by Barthes about his *Système de la Mode*, 'it is the path which makes the work'.

10

Both diffident and rash

Barthes and structuralism in literature

1964 saw the appearance of *Communications* 4, entitled 'Recherches sémiologiques', the first of several special issues this periodical was to devote to semiology and structural analysis. In it was contained Barthes's epoch-making *Elements of Semiology*. At the same time as such pioneering pursuits, Barthes was engaged in the rearguard action with literary criticism, since 1964 is also the date of the first attack on him by R. Picard.

One senses in Barthes's answers to his opponents an appeal to a whole background unsuspected by them, and in particular the knowledge that there existed a team of researchers bound by a common ideal and united in their methods. *Communications* 4 contained, in addition to Barthes's essay, articles by Christian Metz on cinema, Claude Bremond and Tzvetan Todorov on literature and a semiological analysis of a poster by Barthes himself. The second special issue, *Communications* 8, on the structural analysis of narrative, came out in 1966, the year of *Critique et vérité* and Doubrovsky's book, and almost completed the team, with articles by Greimas, Genette, Jules Gritti, Violette Morin and others, all more or less specializing in literature or sociology, with Barthes firmly in the latter category.

Barthes does not present any hiatus between his previous output and *Elements of Semiology* whose footnotes contain many references to his previous books and articles, including those on literary subjects. Nonetheless it is obvious that he was very anxious, even in the most fashionable period of structuralism, not to be identified with it entirely as far as literature was concerned. The scientific and clinical treatment of structuralism could not satisfy his existential aspirations to the status of writer; at the same time, the Quarrel exacerbated the schism between writer and critic, and quashed all hopes of recognition for anyone identified with the new structuralist approach.

The preface to *Elements* does not mention literature at all, only rituals, conventions and the products of mass communication. Narrative, in the specialized sense used in *Communications*, means only the layer of the 'story', that which literature has in common with other media such as film, strip-cartoons, oral folktales, pantomime, etc., and whose units must be detected, so to speak, 'under' the verbal art which is the *sine qua non* of literature.[1] It thus acknowledges the fact that literature is not only 'made of words' but also of representational elements, although the latter can of course only be conveyed in words. The essay on 'Racinian Man' was no more than a forerunner of structuralism, despite an attempt to arrange it on the axes of paradigm and syntagm, synchrony and diachrony, and to express the basic relationships between the 'figures' by means of a single formula:

A has complete power over B.
A loves B, who does not love A.

Doubrovsky, despite his sympathetic account of this work in 1966, still found this formula 'needlessly mathematical', little suspecting the explosion of logico-mathematical symbols which were soon to be strewn all over studies in literary semiotics.

With some exaggeration, one might say that the only structural analysis of literature Barthes ever gave, that is to say an exhaustive and methodical study rather than a programmatic statement like his 'Introduction to the Structural Analysis of Narratives' (*IMT*), is *Système de la Mode*, since fashion is for him a kind of literature. And fashion is suitable for structural analysis, not only because it is entirely ruled by convention, but also because Barthes falls victim to a kind of romantic intentional fallacy and reserves as true literature only what springs from 'an intention of being' which constitutes the writer (*CV*,46). It is interesting to find how this conception, rightly rejected by Christine Brooke-Rose in her *Grammar of Metaphor*, was still prevalent at a time when in principle an immanent consideration of the verbal object ought to have made it untenable. This has again been shown recently by the modern students of metaphor, the Group μ based in Liège, who naturally also reject it in their *Rhétorique de la poésie*.

Although the examples Barthes gives of fashion writing do make one squirm, one feels that fashion's intrinsic unworthiness rules out from the start the chances of finding an inadvertently worthy metaphor; and this is indeed explicitly stated: the fashion utterance 'can advertise literature [by copying its tone] but precisely because it *signifies* it, it cannot fulfil it' (*SM*,232) — a surprising statement, since Flaubert or Queneau are praised for a strategy which involves precisely this. Difference in talent and awareness ought not to be relevant and the results should be judged strictly at face value. Although this discrepancy is hardly surprising in view of the doctrine of literature in *Critical Essays*, the implications are very far-reaching since, as we shall see, they bear on the whole problem of the possibility of an individual *parole* in mass culture. So just as we saw that the elements of the third phase of Barthes's career were assembled even before the second began, now we see that as far as literature is concerned, the latter never really took place. Semiology is defined in the preface of *Elements* as working on 'non-linguistic substances', including what Barthes calls the 'great significant units of discourse', since the units (the 'words', so to speak) of the story are not necessarily verbal but can be expressed in many other substances; this even applies, according to Barthes, to the inner language of fantasies. Thus despite the complaints one began to hear in the mid-1960s about the 'imperialism of linguistics', the preface of *Elements* makes it clear that what was in the making was rather a 'translinguistics' which would tackle any system of signs, whatever their substance and limits; images, gestures, musical sounds, objects, and the complex associations among them which form the content of ritual, conventions or public entertainment — an investigation 'both diffident and rash'.

Confronted with so many substances, the prospective semiologist must feel like Saussure facing 'the "multiform and heterogeneous" nature of language, at first sight as an unclassifiable reality since it "partakes at the same time of the physical, the physiological, the mental, the individual and the social"' (*S*,13). But the semiologist is in an even worse plight, since Saussure's inaugural gesture must be repeated not once but as many times as there are substances. At the same time one must show what these have in common, since what we might call the 'semiological hypothesis' postulates that all the regions of experience listed by Barthes are sign systems. This postulate is reached in two stages: first the intuition (which we saw actively at work in *Mythologies* but already present in *Degree Zero*) that objects and habits, once social, become signs of themselves (*S*,41); thus food gives nourishment, but it is also used to signify status, circumstances, tastes, relationships, etc. Second, that where we perceive a sign, a system exists. This liberating motif of 'The Imagination of the Sign' was formulated by an enthusiastic disciple of Saussure, Karčevski (quote in Pierssens, 1977), when he wrote that 'one could argue that it is impossible to create a word in isolation, and that one can only create at least two words at the same time' because of the differential character of the sign, whose value depends on its relations with its 'brothers' and 'neighbours'.

Following Saussure's founding gesture as it does, it is appropriate that the headings in *Elements* mostly come from his famous dichotomies: Language and Speech, Signifier and Signified, Syntagm and System (or Paradigm). The dichotomy between Synchrony and Diachrony is found in the chapter on language and speech in connection with the notion of linguistic value and also in the conclusion, in connection with methodological hints about the formation of a corpus for research. Each of these sections first establishes why some particular linguistic concepts and operations are suitable for extension to semiology, then gives some examples of applications, which often result in modifications to the linguistic concepts. The fourth chapter is on Denotation and Connotation; these notions, as well as that of metalanguage, are based on Hjelmslev's work but are interpreted in the way discussed earlier in connection with 'Myth Today'.

Linguistics and semiology

We saw that Saussure conceived semiology as a science which, once constituted, would subsume linguistics and perhaps solve some of its difficulties. The obvious thing therefore was to try and create semiology independently, and it seemed simplest to start from non-linguistic structures explicitly designed both as signs and as systems, such as the Highway Code. This enterprise did not get very far since the concepts involved, although useful, did not seem likely ever to be capable of dealing with the highly complex systems involved even in the slightest act of human communication. Where Saussure and other linguists in the first part of the century cited ritual or clothing as examples of sign systems, writers like E. Buyssens (1943) and L. Prieto (1964, 1966) restricted the meaning of semiology to the study of messages sent voluntarily by conventional signals to an identifiable receiver who understands the code and is aware of the intention to communicate. Semiology thus studied such things as military and maritime signals, deaf and dumb alphabets as well as road and railway signs — a somewhat restrictive interpretation of Saussure's definition of the object of semiology as 'the life of signs in the midst of social life', and one which needs a similarly restricted definition of the sign. Far from denying that such relatively simple systems can help to throw light on the mechanism of communication (and thus be very useful from a practical point of view in computer science, automatic translation, etc.), Barthes used the Highway Code several times, in *Système de la Mode* for instance, but he warned against the danger of conceiving *semiosis* as an unduly simple and mechanistic process. However the question of the legitimate scope of semiology, interesting as it was, was allowed to bedevil much of the work done in the field, all the more so when the extended and restricted meanings of the word were specified respectively as *semiology of signification* and *semiology of communication*.[2] There certainly are two levels, rather than two kinds, but the frontier between them is difficult to determine. Many critics have been too interested in literature, sociology and linguistics to ignore the more challenging semiology of signification;

but they often continue to think that the semiology of communication is its scientific kernel.

That the opposite is true has been convincingly demonstrated by L.J. Calvet (1973) from the socio-political point of view, making the point that the semiology of communication typified in the Highway Code rests on a restrictive, positivistic and compartmentalized conception of science, whose aim is to keep the discussion from spreading to areas of concern more urgent than semaphore. Similar points have been made by J.M. Klinkenberg (1979) from the point of view of the analytical foundations of semiology. He argues that it is on the contrary from the semiology of signification that we must start if we want to understand what is going on in the semiology of communication. The seemingly impartial division of labour between signification and communication in fact gives a privilege to the latter, since it rests on a postulate which excludes from the sign all the signifying practices in the arts and in everyday life, as well as the facts of simple manifestation, that is, natural and social indices (an *index* is a sign whose signifier is linked by contiguity, not resemblance, to its signified, but after the discoveries of modern psychology, it would be very rash to treat classical examples of indices such as clothing or bodily symptoms as devoid of an analogical dimension). In effect, the separation between signification and communication rests on philosophical or psychological criteria which are very difficult to apply, such as the difference between conscious and unconscious. Finally and above all, one must note that the most fundamental schemata of the semiology of communication make use of considerations which can only be classified by the semiology of signification: the attribution of a precise signification to a message, for instance, can only result from a consideration of the class of possible significations within a certain context, and this in turn can only be done if one takes indices into consideration. It is therefore legitimate to assume that there is a unity of semiology and that it spans the full spectrum from the simplest codes to all indicial facts, including on the one hand connoted systems and on the other the systems studied by zoosemiotics, cybernetics, etc.

Language as foundation

When Barthes uses the word *translinguistics*, he does not mean merely that semiology extends over a wider field than that of linguistics; he is chiefly thinking of the nature of its conceptual models. Whereas in 'Myth Today' he had been anxious to provide semiology with models other than linguistics, notably psychoanalysis, he seems at first sight to have changed his position radically in *Elements*. In the introduction he attributes the relative sterility of semiology so far to the fact that in all sign systems where the sociological significance is more than superficial we are once more confronted with language itself. This is how Barthes 'solves' the problem of non-verbal denotation which we discussed in Chapter 8. Taking his cue from another part of Saussure's *Course* which stated that linguistics could serve as a model for semiology (*Course*,16) he suggests that 'we must now face the possibility of inverting Saussure's declaration: linguistics is not a part of the general science of signs, even a privileged part, it is semiology which is a part of linguistics' (*S*,11; *SM*,9). This is going much further than Saussure: language is not taken as the model of all science systems but as their foundation.

The contemporary expansion of linguistics into cybernetics, computers, and machine translation probably played its part in Barthes's evolution on this subject; but the true reason is no doubt to be found in the metaphysical change in outlook which resulted in his new literary doctrine. Barthes was henceforth to attempt to reduce all meaning to verbal meaning, and this is practically stated in the introduction to *Elements* (*S*,11); the essential feature of verbal meaning is that it is both strong and empty, or at least uncertain and subject to interpretation. Barthes was in later years to attempt to ground this affirmation more firmly in Derrida's theses and their commentary by Julia Kristeva. Barthes's description of language was thus restricted to written language, with the curious consequence that, since writing was thereby exonerated from commitment by its very structure, his resentment against the unavoidable commitment demanded by life in society was displaced onto speech, so that *speech* and *writing* came to assume meanings and overtones diametrically opposed to those they had in the early part of his career (as he realizes, *T*,103). The succession of justifications Barthes offered for what is basically an unchanging theory of language and writing make one suspect that more than a little rationalization is involved. But as his explanation for the stagnation of semiology and his proposed remedy have been productive as well as controversial, it is worthwhile to try and disentangle them.

The privilege granted to verbal meaning is overdetermined in Barthes's structuralist works by at least four lines of reasoning. The first is Barthes's own inclination and evolution; when he writes in *Système de la Mode* that 'it is not the dream, it is the meaning that sells' (*SM*,10), he not only means that the language of fashion artificially promotes buying by making distinctions which have a purely verbal existence (the fashion for *hairy* cloth being said to succeed that for *shaggy* cloth (*SM*,60), he also hints that, as in the case of mini-skirts, fashion phenomena have no other existence than customers' responses to them. The denunciation of a Society of the Spectacle (as the Situationists later put it) in *Mythologies*, where cooking recipes were seen as just a pretext for a petit-bourgeois reader to dream over their photographed representation, has yielded to a doctrine which presents the whole of experience as ruled by signs.

The second reason is Barthes's belief that when dealing with mixed systems it is better to separate signs according to the substances of their signifiers, thus obtaining the concept of the *typical sign* (S,47). It is partly because of such considerations of structural purity that he chose to write only on fashion *writing* in *Système de la Mode*. His choice of this particular 'typical sign' was of course, as he would have said, 'not innocent'.

The third reason is socio-historical. Barthes makes it clear that he purports to speak only about what he can observe in our own society (S,9; SM,9); just as we had 'myth today', we are dealing here with 'semiology today'. What then is so different about our society? According to Barthes, the fact that it is a civilization of the word, and even of the written word: 'In a society like ours, where myths and rituals have taken the form of a *reason*, that is, in the last analysis, of articulated language, the latter is not only the model of meaning, but also its foundation' (SM,9). A *reason* is here a rationalization, the false causality which mass culture and industrialized society impose as natural, and of which fashion is an outstanding example.[3]

The fourth reason given by Barthes for concentrating on the verbal element is his belief that in all systems of real social significance language re-appears, under one of three aspects: as *component, relay* or *signified*. Let us first see language as component. Objects, images or patterns of behaviour almost never appear in isolation, without some admixture of language to make their meaning more explicit. There is a fundamental openness in the sign, as Peirce had already observed; no sign can mean by itself without some other sign to confirm its meaning (and so, in theory, ad infinitum). Of course, the other signs need not be verbal but language tends to intervene because of its unique properties, chiefly that of producing meaning, which enables it to deal with all unexpected situations (so that in principle nothing is unsayable). It is thus the universal interpretant. Naturally, this way of putting things privileges the cognitive dimension, against which should be weighed the advantages of other substances such as music or painting in conveying notions like sadness, rage or bliss with a directness which reduces prose to the level of a flat-footed paraphrase.[4]

When language is not simply redundant, it plays an even more important part. Sets of objects like food or clothes really become systems, according to Barthes, only because they are *relayed* by language at both levels of the sign. The signifiers are, to start with, given in the form of nomenclature. For instance, on p. 63 of *Elements*, taking his cue from Saussure's illustrations of the syntagm as a column made of different parts which have their analogues in the various architectural styles, Barthes tentatively reconstructed Garment-, Food-, Furniture- and Architecture-systems according to the perpendicular axes of paradigm and syntagm, selection and combination. Thus, designations like 'entrée', 'roast' or 'sweet' are, so to speak, the 'parts of speech' which form the 'syntax' of the food-system in our culture. As *Mythologies* showed, the fact that there is a norm for a 'well-formed meal' is discovered when one breaks the rule, either inadvertently like Coty, the President of the Republic who shocked the whole nation when a photograph revealed that he drank mineral water instead of wine at a main meal, or consciously and mythically, like Mendès-France, the Prime Minister who made a point of being seen drinking milk at a time other than at breakfast. A similar problem of grammatical correctness arises in Anglo-French households when one has to decide, in view of the nationality of the guests, whether serving cheese before or after the sweet would be experienced as a solecism.

Once the rules are grasped, rhetorical considerations arise, and the 'sociosemiotics' of food (to coin a word after sociolinguistics) indicate which type of food is appropriate according to the various 'registers' one chooses to speak in. Finally, personal invention or *parole* comes into its own, rising to the challenge of these often tacit but constricting rules. Guillaume Apollinaire (1947) tells the story of a deceived husband who thought culinary art should satisfy not only hunger but intelligence, and who, after regaling his guests with tragic, comic, pastoral, epic and philosophical meals in turn, ended up with a satirical meal including toadstools, dispatching himself and all his wife's lovers at one go. He had succeeded in each case in producing what was clearly comprehensible as a meal while respecting the laws of a rhetoric of genres which, though it had evolved historically in relation to literature (with parallel developments in music, painting and ritual), might well have unsuspected equivalents in everyday practices. Barthes suggests that a formal study of each of these systems might lead to the discovery of general forms, such as the great opposition of work and leisure; ancient as it is, this opposition may not necessarily involve the same components now as it did in the past, just as the opposition of prose and poetry is universal but not always recognized by the same signs. The revelation that one has been following some personal or cultural pattern completely unconsciously often causes embarrassed laughter; one feels foolish and somehow subhuman because what is revealed as totally predictable behaviour puts one on a level with automata or animals — as Bergson put it, the mechanical replaces the living.[5] The possibility of exploring levels of consciousness had in part stimulated Barthes's interest in such systems, as he explained in an interview: after completing *Mythologies* and conceiving the idea of an immanent study of sign systems other than language, he felt 'the desire to reconstitute step by step one of these systems, a language at the same time spoken by everybody and known to none of its users' (*GV*,45).

The fact that we need to know pragmatically what in our society is recognizable as a main course, for instance (as in Mary Douglas's study of the structure of British meals, 1974), should have made Barthes realize that there might be perceptual categories at work as well as a nomenclature. But Barthes's answer would be that in practice such categories merge with the *signifieds* of these systems. Language reappears at the level of signifieds not in the sense that within each system we find some admixture of language, but more fundamentally in the sense that thought for Barthes does not seem possible without language. Echoing *Degree Zero*, we find in *Elements* 'there is no meaning that is not designated' (*S*,10). This Whorfian view is obviously true to some extent as is shown in the case of sound symbolism, where the perceptual patterns can come to the fore only if the cultural ones allow them to do so; it is an unusual strength of feeling which can break through them. Thus *flow* sounds fluid but flannel does not because the meaning interferes; an advertisement can work on the association of coffee with a pause in work to state that 'coffee relaxes you', advice which some customers would be unwise to believe. Such messages call for a social decoding, not a simple reading of nature.[6]

The problematics of semiology

Social signs are therefore either of an explicitly conventional nature like the Highway Code, telephone numbers, semaphore, the numbers of hotel rooms, etc.; or they take as signifiers objects which already have a function and use them to signify something else. For this reason Barthes then prefers to use the term *sign-functions*. In sign-functions, we find the double movement described in *Mythologies*: first some rare foodstuff or a fur coat is 'semanticized' and made to signify status, for instance, then it is re-functionalized, or naturalized, in order to disguise this connotation (*S*,41-2). We therefore face the two problems which were already present, but less explicitly, in 'Myth Today': the dialectics of language and speech and the arbitrary or motivated character of a significant unit.

Langue and parole

In verbal language, *langue* and *parole* are strictly contemporaneous and cannot exist or be fully defined except in relation to each other: one cannot handle speech except by drawing on a language, and a language does not exist fully except in the 'speaking mass'. As we saw earlier apropos of *Degree Zero*, Barthes's observations lead him to borrow the concept of various intermediary strata between language and speech from thinkers other than Saussure (since stereotypes and sociolects cannot be freely chosen). It would have been highly relevant here for Barthes to have drawn further on his experience as a critic and writer in order to recognize the normative aspect of language over and above a deposit of linguistic practice. Grammars, treatises of rhetoric, dictionaries and other institutions dispensing and enforcing this kind of knowledge also curtail the freedom of the language user and hence limit praxis, the dialectical relationship between language and speech. This is the reason why Saussure found it impossible to give a linguistic account of speech, since as soon as an element is grasped in communication, it is *already* part of the language.

When one comes to apply linguistic concepts to other sign systems it is thus impossible to sort out *a priori* what belongs to language and what belongs to speech, since this is precisely what semiological investigation is all about. Taking his inspiration partly from Lévi-Strauss, Barthes therefore postulates language/speech as a general category, to which are assimilated other dichotomies like system/process and code/message (*S*,24-5). He then examines how this works out in several semiological systems: the garment system, the food system, the car system and the furniture system; in each case what is part of the language (what Barthes calls 'glottic', after *glotta*, the Greek word for *langue*, which also means a *tongue*, in French) are the contrasts which can be observed on the two axes of language, syntagm and paradigm, in accordance with Saussure's dictum: 'In a language (*langue*) there are only differences without any positive terms.' It is also important to determine within each system the relative 'volumes' of language and speech. Barthes begins by dividing the garment system according to the substance of the signifier, since very different conditions obtain in each case. In fashion as *written* about, there is practically no speech because fashion is a language which is elaborated consciously by a pressure group; it is therefore paradoxically a language without any speech, what Barthes calls a 'logo-technique', established by a unilateral decision (*S*,31). But since a language without speech is impossible by definition Barthes has to acknowledge that in fact this language is spoken by the deciding group itself, just as, incidentally, ad men devise slogans and posters before semiologists decode them!

There is here an ambiguity in the use of 'arbitrary', an all-important epithet in discussing language, and this is found throughout *Elements;* structural freedom merges with social freedom, linked by the concept of the 'contract', since language is a convention. The fact that it is also very constrictive and that the 'contract' is established over a long period of time shows how unsatisfactory this way of posing the problem is, since Barthes is led (perhaps under the influence of his theory of literature) to praise those languages which, like fashion, flaunt their structural freedom from analogy even if they are socially coercive. Furthermore, the speaker of the garment system bears two yokes: not only the language of fashion but that of *costume*, which is also social in origin but is the product of the long diachronic evolution studied by Kroeber. The sole freedom the wearer has, what corresponds to speech, is found in *clothing* (his individual way of wearing garments, size, degree of a cleanliness or wear, personal quirks, free association of pieces).

The same situation obtains in the car and furniture systems. The language of the car system is made up of the contrasts between proto-types; the scope of speech is very narrow since choice is restricted by buying power, although speech reappears in the use the buyer makes of the object, in driving. This analysis indicates that in his pioneering work, Barthes may not always have selected his object in the most fruitful manner; he tended to concentrate on commodities rather than practices, which is perhaps inevitable in the consumer society. In finding analogues of the axes of paradigm and syntagm in the menu of a meal, the consti-tuents of costume or a bedroom suite he has picked on combinations prescribed socially; although the styles can vary, it is language, not speech, which predominates. But one could equally find these axes at the level of the use made of these objects, just as Mary Douglas took as her unit not the meal but the food event. Speech could, of course, also be found in all the phenomena of anomic fabrication (that is, those which do not conform to social rules (*S*,27); few of these remain in our culture although the alternative society has relaunched the idea since Barthes wrote.

The problem which in 'Myth Today' took the form of the degree of consciousness attached to socially significant phenomena is therefore expressed here in terms of the dialectics of languages and speech; who sends, who reads and how? As Barthes recognizes (*S*,46), a corpus of practices and techniques corresponds, in the mind of each reader, to the lexicons supplied by society. Each *lexia* or unit of reading (corresponding to those 'large units of discourse' which are the object of semiology, *S*,11) can be read more or less deeply, even by the same reader, depending on the context and circumstances. We begin to see how Barthes was led to those areas of linguistics in need of development by his effort to extend linguistic concepts and by virtue of the knowledge obtained through his own practice. What he rediscovered is what was missing in the Saus-surean theory and was soon to be introduced by Chomsky: the speaking subject (the speaker/hearer) and the mechanics of syntax.

Arbitrary and motivated

After having established what counts as language (*langue*) in each system, the units of this language have to be determined, using techni-ques borrowed from linguistics and which will be discussed shortly. But first one must consider the second focus of Barthes's reflection through-out *Elements*: the dialectics of the arbitrary and the motivated in linguis-tics and semiology. It is another aspect of the question of the relation between language and speech, for Barthes's use of 'analogy' is as ambiguous as his use of 'arbitrary'. This is again probably due to a failure to distinguish at the outset the various sources of meaning, a distinction which is even more important in semiology than in linguistics. If we take the minimal definition of the sign as a relation between two *relata* (S,35), what could any object taken as signifier be related to in order to produce a meaning? And if the relation is motivated and not arbitrary, what could the object resemble? Either the expressive qualities of matter which Barthes designated as the object of poetry at the end of 'Myth Today', or social usage, or existing words, which furthermore are sometimes already classified in series (S,80, 95). Influenced by the then prevalent ideology of language as discrete and non-analogical, Barthes was very anxious to dismiss analogy of all kinds, onomatopoeia for instance, as somehow infralinguistic because it is devoid of the second articulaton. Barthes even denies that certain abstract shapes can express a certain mood; the trade mark of the Berliet lorries (a circle with a thick arrow across it) therefore puzzles him because it produces an impression of power analogically. Obviously, such phenomena have to be explored rather than dismissed, and indeed elsewhere Barthes acknowledges the general ignorance about the mechanism of expressivity in images or paintings, an ignorance which semiological studies have to some extent repaired (S,53).

When he comes to the consideration of the classification of units Barthes again thinks that he can find an essential difference between linguistics and semiotics; some variations which are not significant differentially must however still be present, they belong to the language. All the more when we pass from denotation to connotation: the rolled *r* is a mere variant in denoted language, but in the speech of the theatre it signals a country accent and is therefore part of a code (S,20). Barthes's study of fashion established (in contradiction to Saussure's differential view of language) the effective importance of a non-signifying *support* of the variant which makes signification obvious; in the phrase a *short/long dress*, the vestimentary meaning pervades all the elements — which proves that we are really dealing with a unit of meaning — but the qualifying element is purely in *long/short* while the *dress*, which is the support, keeps its positive value (S,73). Since for Barthes the whole field of semiology, which includes all socially significant systems, is connoted, he concludes that the elements in which the meaning is concentrated, which he calls *connotators*, are scattered and discontinuous, and borne by the denoted language which at the same time naturalizes them. Barthes even thought that he could locate the naturalizing role in the syntagm and the differentiations or meaning proper in the paradigm ('Rhetoric of the Image', *IMT*,32). Naturalization thus functioned by neutralizing the oppositions previously established between the units. He chooses two semiological systems to show how this works, the Highway Code and the fashion system (S,79). Naturally enough, he finds that in the former, where the legibility of the meaning is crucial for safety, few of these neutralizations occur; fashion, on the other hand, largely achieves its persuasive power by managing to suggest an infinite number of distinctions where there really are none. The tenacious semiological sleuth can put his finger on quite a few of the neutralizations which help to produce this effect.

The second problem therefore centres on the question of that of the materiality of the signifier and that of the purely relational and differential conception of language as opposed to the necessity of a positive element. Barthes consistently excludes language from this problematic, but perhaps this results from his having concentrated on the wrong object within the broad phenomenon of language, namely the sign. As Ducrot and Todorov judiciously observe in their encyclopaedia, the thesis of the arbitrary character of language can be maintained at four levels at least: that of the relation between sound and sense, that of the relation between signifier and signified, that of the syntactic organization, and that of the relation between the language as a whole and its own units (1972, 170ff). The semiological problem should be re-examined at each of these levels.

Technical problems: 1. finding the units

When the semiologist tackles a sign system, either the meaning of objects, images, gestures is already indicated in verbal language, or it is not. If it is not, the meaning, so to speak adheres to the objects, the signified to the signifiers, thus recalling the way they are stuck together in verbal language. Barthes needs a name to designate this phenomenon, in order to distinguish between systems where it occurs and those where it does not; he calls it *isology* (S,43). If signifier and signified are not stuck together, that is, if the meaning is indicated in another substance — usually verbal language — the system is said to be non-isological. Let us first take the case of one such non-isological system. If a reader is advised by a fashion magazine to wear a certain sweater (which is the signifier) for *long autumn walks in the woods,* he is thereby given the signified and knows 'the meaning' of the sweater within the code of fashion in that particular year. Thus verbal language considerably helps the semiologist in one way but there is a corresponding danger — a constant temptation to mix the signifieds of the explanatory verbal language with those of the system studied. For instance *long autumn walks in the woods* might simply be expressed as *week-end*, that is, by a word instead of a phrase (S,45). To make matters worse, a proper semantic theory, which would tell us the structure of the verbal signified, is as yet non-existent.

If a meaning is not indicated, the system is isological. All that the semiologist has to go by then are the signifiers (verbal, graphic, iconic, gestural, *S*,47) which materialize the signifieds. In these isological systems, the analyst has to impose his own metalanguage on the system.[7] The units are discovered through the segmentation of the syntagm or 'text without end' by means of the commutation test (*S*,65). This consists of artificially introducing a change in the plane of expression (signifiers) and observing whether it leads to a correlative modification on the plane of content (signifieds). The commutation test allows one in principle to spot, by degrees, the significant units, which will then be classified into paradigms. This is possible in linguistics because the analyst has some knowledge of the meaning of the language he is analysing; some linguists have maintained, however, that this recourse to meaning is not necessary since it is only a short cut for the lengthy distributional process of replacing words by other words in all the different slots, patiently observing how consistently certain changes and certain recurrences are produced. This laborious definition of the units is of course the only one available when the linguist is confronted with an unknown language, which is often the case in semiology.

Technical problems: 2. articulation

Another problem that plagued the early development of semiology, was that of the double articulation (see Appendix, p. 231). Were all articulated phenomena to be considered as languages, or did they have to present a double articulation to be worthy of that name? On p. 39 of *Elements*, the double articulation principle is presented as enriching the Saussurean theory of the sign. Its importance was stressed by Martinet, who made it the criterion that defines language (the theory has in fact deeper implications in Martinet's theory, and follows from his functional notion of language as a series of choices; hence his defence of the idea of the unique character of this double articulation). It seems therefore normal to try and find correspondences for semiology. But then we come across the fact that double articulation concerns only the plane of expression while the plane of content can also be divided into atoms of meaning. Would this not in fact be more relevant for semiology? Besides, the problem is complicated by the fact that the two planes of language are non-conformal. More interesting therefore than the double articulation is the question of syntax; something like syntax has been found in both spatial (visual) and temporal codes like dancing. A vigorous refutation of this would-be dominance of the double articulation is found in *Communications* 15, on the analysis of the image, in essays by both Christian Metz and Umberto Eco, and researches of this kind have finally given the lie to Barthes's early assertion in 'Myth Today' that, once the connoted meaning of the social sign is found, we need no longer trouble with the structure of the underlying denoted message (*M*,115).

Metz's essay is concerned above all with establishing the legitimacy of the transposition to the iconic field of conceptual instruments elaborated apropos of language. The field of images also had its Quarrel of the Critics, in which the final line of resistance to semiology was the claimed specificity of the image or, in Peircian terms, its 'iconicity'. Metz points out that, just as the concepts used in semiology do not come only from linguistics, so the conceptual apparatus of linguistics itself is not limited or solely appropriate to language; some of these much more general concepts were expressly elaborated by, for instance, Saussure, Peirce and Hjelmslev, as having potentially a much wider expression. While concepts like *word* or *suffix* make sense only within linguistics, oppositions like expression/content, form/substance, and syntagm/ paradigm can be extended to other sign systems, not only the iconic systems but the study of certain types of writing, or the structures of narrative, for example. Just because a *message* is visual does not mean that all its *codes* are. Besides, even a visual code is never visible; it is a network of logical relations. The image must be situated within all the other discursive manifestations.

What has to be reconsidered is the notion of 'field' or 'domain', such as film. These are powerful institutional entities, but alternative, more logical forms of apportionment may be preferable. Significantly, there are as yet few university departments of semiology or narratology. Domains, like genres, are prescientific units, although it makes sense sociologically to specialize in, say, cinema or advertising. For Metz and several other theorists, semiology must not be content with either consciously adhered to institutional entities like genres, or units derived from technical and sensory conditions of production and reception. It must aim for structural configurations, 'forms' in Hjelmslev's sense, in which content and expression come together to form systems. Analytical labour alone can reconstitute these configurations, since they do not exist in a free state and are not present in the social consciousness like the genre 'advertising' or the channel 'cinema'. On the other hand, theorists like Louis Marin or Jean-Louis Schefer maintained that, up to a point, a painting is nothing but the reading which is made of it: narration, description, *mise-en-scène*. Schefer questions the very notion of image, and displaces its definition so that it is no longer an object but the image of the labour of production of the image. (Barthes's commentary on Schefer's work is an important part of his own later theories, as will be seen in Part IV.) As for the problem of unwelcome analogical relations, Metz concludes that 'analogy is itself coded', thus hoping to mitigate the 'intellectual trauma' brought about by the imaginary tenet of the absolute separation of arbitrary and motivated.

Meaning therefore results from the conjoined effects of a whole hierarchy of codes; this has been noted by theorists like Panofsky, Francastel and Bourdieu as well as Barthes. In the same issue of *Communications*, Eco tentatively lists ten such codes. But he does so only after establishing very general methodological starting-points in preference to a slavish modelling on verbal language. These principles are: 1. Any communicative act is based on a code. 2. Codes do not necessarily have two fixed articulations; they may well have two, like language, but equally they may have none, or only the first articulation, or only the second; and when they do have articulations, the latter may be mobile and not fixed.

The components Eco finds the most useful are *figurae* (which have only a differential value and correspond to linguistic phonemes), *signs* (which correspond to linguistic morphemes), and *syntagms*. The last are viewed as freely combined into *discourses*, but it is only more recently that attempts have been made to build discursive grammars.[8] Since the word 'code' is, like so many linguistic terms, not precise enough unless it is specified by each user (thus it sometimes means a repertory of terms, or the rules for using these terms, or both), Eco specifies that he is concerned with simple lists of signs which are not in most cases structured as a system of oppositions. The question of how codes are structured was also a concern of Barthes, who was very sensitive to one aspect of the phonological ideology, the discrete character of language (the pun on *discrete* and *discreet* is even easier in French, and Barthes did not like being crowded in any way). He came to the conclusion in *Système de la Mode* that what matters for the production of meaning is not so much a strict system of oppositions in a semantic paradigm, as in phonology, but a sense of closure, of firmly established extremes in a spectrum of meaning, which can then be divided into almost infinite nuances (*SM*,174). This was the principle he applied in the codes used to study Balzac's text in *S/Z* and Edgar Allan Poe's 'The Case of Mr Valdemar' (1973f).

Such studies are very enlightening for a transposition to what may eventually seem the most difficult of all fields, that of literature, where the substance through which the meaning is *manifested* (Level I) is the same as that through which the meaning is *expressed* (for instance, summarized, Level II), and that through which it is *studied*, by metalanguages like criticism or semiology which name its components (Level III) — not to speak of the substance in which these metalanguages are *established* (Level IV), that is, metatheories. The building blocks of narratives, like characters, events, descriptions, are not 'made of words' as such but are manifested through them, and to get at them we must reconstitute their signifiers and signifieds from the discontinuous state in which they appear. If words can function on at least four levels, we can understand all too easily variations in interpretation. A reader sorts out in his mind, as he goes along, what words or rather what in each word or group of words belongs to each of these four levels. In *S/Z*, Barthes has projected elements belonging to all four levels onto a linear sequence, interspersed with the fragments of Balzac's text. This is not intended to be an accurate rendition of the reading process, although in fact Barthes introduces typographical distinctions to differentiate Levels III and IV from Level II, and sums up the findings of Level II in tables at the end.[9]

But even before *S/Z*, strictly structural studies already showed the roots of what would develop into a crisis of the sign. This two-sided entity is simply not the best unit to study many systems of meaning. One needs elements of both smaller and greater size and, on the plane of meaning in particular, the process at work is obviously more complicated than the double articulation which characterizes the plane of expression of verbal language. It is interesting to watch Barthes rediscovering this question of the size of unit and the synthesis between semantic elements in the course of his own practice as semiologist in *Système de la Mode*, and this in spite of rather than with the help of the linguistic equipment he started with, which, as one commentator put it, was labouring 'under the crushing weight of the phonological model' (*SM*,199). In addition to the notion of units and their possible articulations, what all semiologists have preserved is the basic Saussurean conception of the distribution on the two axes of syntagm and paradigm. Today the most glaring absences in *Elements* are no doubt recent ideas about syntax and semantics, although the absence of a proper and explicit theory does not of course mean that the concept of syntax is absent from the book (see *S*,70). The first translations of Chomsky appeared in the mid-1960s and we see the turning point in 1966, in *Critique et vérité* and the 'Introduction to the Structural Analysis of Narratives', making use of the Chomskyan notion of 'kernel'. But the latter text also indicates that Harris's notion of *transformation* and Martinet's notion of *expansion* had, to some extent, generated comparable insights. But, since it is rule-governed, Chomsky's idea of linguistic creativity could offer no solution for Barthes's anxieties about freedom since what is coded is automatically commonplace in his view. As the preface of *Critical Essays* shows, he already conceived language as essentially combinative.

Luckily, it is in the nature of things that semiology suffers less than linguistics from the absence of a theory of syntax, since between its units, whether they are objects, or stretches of discourse as in written fashion or narrative, there is only a 'pseudo-syntax' (*SM*,57). This 'syntax of semantics' (in Greimas's words) can be found only after the surface syntax, that of verbal language, has been discounted as well as such rhetorical effects as triplication of episodes in folktale, which similarly obscure the bare bones of meaning.

The development of structural semantics in France followed on Greimas's seminal book *Sémantique structurale* (1966). The question of whether it is developed or superseded by approaches like Kristeva's, based on another theory of signification (which will be discussed in Part IV) is a moot point although one which seems to inflame the passions of quite a few semiologists. But the whole notion of structural semantics can be criticized from another angle, one that is crucial to textual analysis. Rules for discourses may not be possible without, on the one hand, some sort of semantic universals and, on the other, some socio-linguistic or pragmatic restrictions. As we saw above, Barthes is well aware that society can be 'read' at various levels by its members. Yet in real life the meanings of words depend on the position of those who utter them, so that, as modern theorists of discourse have pointed out, there are difficulties of translation even within a single language. While not completely rejecting the notion of *langue*, these theorists say that it should be supplemented by a semantics of discourses. This is also the criticism they level at sociolinguistics which, in dealing only with phonological, syntactic and morphological phenomena, still makes the social element secondary to the linguistic. It cannot serve as a model for semantics, where such factors are on the contrary central, and constitutive of the meaning.

The same theorists also criticize conceptual couples like constraint/freedom, system/creativity, even when they are politically well intentioned, as they are in Chomsky; for here they find reflected the naive model of Saussure and his sociological sources, the notion of a totally free individual, with the state as his defender. Discursive semantics bears not only on the words but even more on the notion of what can and must be said in certain situations and 'positions'. Barthes's study of fashion can be read as a comment on this problem.

11

It is the path that makes the work, or, Between things and words

Elements of Semiology contained some practical indications on how to go about describing a semiological system, starting from the general conception of language as distributed on the axes of syntagm and paradigm. These consisted chiefly of instructions on how to select a synchronous and homogeneous corpus of elements (*S*,95-9) and on the operations of segmentation and classification. However there are no automatic discovery procedures for units in linguistics, let alone semiology: in every case, description is linked to the theoretical premises chosen. Structuralism certainly helped in making analysts conscious of their presuppositions and of the necessity of making them explicit at each stage. This is very obvious, for instance, in *Système de la Mode*, a book about method as well as a description of a given system. It stands in relation to *Elements* as Lévi-Strauss said his four-volume *Mythologiques* stood to his *Structural Anthropology*: despite its greater length, it is only the description of a single system. This caution must be borne in mind when reading the *Système*, since the lexicon, the syntax and the rhetoric of fashion are found to be very peculiar indeed; showing this specificity is the point of describing the system, and anchors the thematic and socio-political interpretation Barthes gives of it.

There are three reasons for which reading this difficult book is important and rewarding: the method, the system of fashion itself, and the asides, comments and digressions which Barthes makes on his 'path' of discovery. As innovative in its way as *Elements* and *S/Z*, *Système de la Mode* is a very clear and detailed example of how the singularity of a system can be discovered by patient and meticulous examination. Once a system is fully described, it becomes possible to make a detailed comparison with other systems, which opens the way to a comparison, not only of the objects of a single discipline (here semiology), but of the taxonomies of various sciences and eventually perhaps to what Barthes called 'the science of apportionment', how our society and perhaps any society organizes the world and represents itself to itself. From this point of view, the meaning of *Système de la Mode* is, so to speak, its use, the use we make of it when we read it; we see how meaning is produced, *la cuisine du sens*. One is saddened to find that it has had to be defended as a playful exercise. An awareness of the comic effects produced by the clash of languages that one finds in *Système de la Mode* is one thing, the appreciation of a fundamentally serious project is another. Barthes came to view the book as 'a kind of naive stained-glass window' (*SM*,7) after the advent of the new Chomskyan approach and semanalysis; but the act of publishing it can be taken performatively as a recognition of its merits by its author. It will be contested here from yet a different angle, focusing on the implications Barthes wished to draw from his theories for the study of literature and society.

The object

The first quarter of the book, some seventy pages, is on method; it explains the choice of first principles. Barthes's great care in justifying them can perhaps be attributed to his perennial duality of purpose. This methodological prelude has two aims: to define his chosen object and to explain how it can best be described. The choice of object is the most ideological part. Not that Barthes is confused as to what he has selected or still less because he wants to confuse us; he is, on the contrary, very honest, open and consistent about it. But we need to read him very attentively to perceive what he actually says, not what we think he said or ought to have said. His object might then perhaps seem stranger and more restricted than one would have thought was advisable; but it will still be legitimate, and, if properly used, its study will appear useful for the philosophy of literature and generally for all problems of transcription and expression. The use of linguistics in the book is 'assuredly frequent but always elementary' (*SM*,8). This again in keeping with broadly-based projects like those of Saussure, Peirce or Hjelmslev.

The first important decision, then, concerns the choice of object (*SM*,8-29). Barthes started out with the idea of making a sociological study of actual feminine garments; he ended up making a semiological study of 'garments as written', or rather, 'fashion as written', and it is the latter which from then on Barthes denotes simply as Fashion (capital F). Very soon, the essence of fashion seemed to him to be a written phenomenon, so much so that it was hardly worth indicating this in the title — one can imagine the disappointment of imprudent buyers (*SM*,9). We know Barthes's conviction that semiology should, at least at first, work only on 'typical signs', that is, signs whose signifiers are supported by a single substance, and this is obviously one reason for his choice. This argument, which bears on the question of structural purity, was, it seems, presented to him by Lévi-Strauss in conversation, and one would like to know the exact point at which Barthes was finally persuaded, for this covers the same period (1957-63) during which he also elaborated his new doctrine of literature and of the relations between language and reality.

Another argument in favour of selecting the descriptions of fashion garments read in fashion magazines is that this makes the rule concerning a synchronous corpus extremely easy to follow: the whole point of fashion is, or used to be, to engineer a complete change from year to year. Barthes therefore selected as his corpus the descriptions found in two fashion journals from June 1958 to June 1959 (*SM*,21); needless to say, his investigation does not bear on that year's particular fashion since what he is interested in is the pure language (*langue*) of Fashion, seen as a function (which can only be persuasion) and constructed accordingly. His object is therefore neither *real* or *photographed* garments, nor a subset of verbal language, but those 'great significant units of discourse' which *Elements* had designated as the object of semiology (*S*,11), an object' between things and words' (*SM*,8, 38, 203). That is where Barthes hopes to find the play of language, the production of meaning in all its purity; for a 'represented' garment does not have to fulfil the ends ascribed to real garments (protection, modesty, display); nor is it essentially ambiguous like an image, which always has to be specified in a caption by a verbal adjunct (*SM*,17-19).

So far, so good. Or is it? As always, specious lines of arguments in Barthes leave stylistic marks. His descriptions of the object he selected with such care and which he himself called an 'ambiguous object' (*SM*,8) are not as precise as one might expect. He wavered on two crucial points: he did not describe women's *garments* as stated on p. 7, nor did he deal with *written* Fashion as stated on p. 8. He did not work on *articles* found in fashion journals, but on fashion *captions* accompanying fashion photographs, not on *written* Fashion but on *described* Fashion. This word '*described*', which at first appears simply in brackets, introduces a crucial restriction, and allows Barthes's ostensible project (how new fashions are propagated, and how promoters make such sudden and radical changes palatable and even attractive to the buyers) to be invaded by his real project, his life project, which as always can be summed up as 'what is literature?' Thus specified by Barthes, Fashion appears an activity which encapsulates what literature is trying to do, epitomized by the technique of description which is common to both: 'What happens when a real or imaginary object is converted into language?'

We have already come across fashion as an image of literature for Barthes; or rather as two images, just as there are two fashions: one is the slow movement described by Kroeber, which Barthes suggested was perhaps like literature, a homeostatic system; the other is the yearly crisis, engineered by Haute Couture, dominated by the new and resembling an original turn of speech in literature in the context of the long-term history of costume.[1] The interesting thing is that Barthes managed to use both notions to bolster the same philosophy; the first helped him to combat the idea of an activity controlled by the human subject and the second to prove that literature is constitutively unrealistic because it depends on language, which is not analogical but digital and proceeds by cutting 'furiously' into the continuum of experience (*E*,151, 261). Literature cannot but attempt to copy the real, but for this reason it is essentially 'a delusion', as Barthes put it in his Inaugural Lecture.

There is, however, an essential difference between literary description and the descriptions which make up Barthes's corpus in *Système de la Mode*. In the latter, the object described is actualized, represented in a different code; it could also accompany a real garment at a fashion show for instance (*SM*,17, 23). Because of this, the Fashion description can be allusive, since the reader can also see the photograph or object. What could, therefore, Barthes's purpose be in choosing such a restricted object? His aim is to work his way back to literature by means of this special case, as is shown in the text as well as in the comments he later made on his book (*GV*,48). For him even literary descriptions, which do not have a real but an imaginary object, are purely intelligible, they do not make one 'see'. While this might be true of Balzac's hyperrealist descriptions, it is not true of the most successful ones, some of which conjure up visions more vivid than reality. By selecting a kind of text which by definition does not attempt to do this, since it simply describes an image, Barthes hopes to extrapolate from his remarks on such descriptions to the whole of literature and demonstrate its unrealistic character. But by pointing out that the fashion texts chosen by Barthes *do* gesture towards an object, we could reverse his argument and stress the fact, so unfashionable nowadays, that literature also has something to do with reality. On this condition, we can then accept the very general significance Barthes attached to his work in the blurb: 'how do men make meaning with their garments and their language?'

Fashion, like literature, is pure in that it never condescends to materialize what it contradicts. Fashion has only two values: *in fashion, out of fashion*. But the infamous mark of what is out of fashion is expressed only by absence; what is mentioned by Fashion is automatically *in fashion*; the 'noted' is by definition not(e)able. We might say that Fashion is essentially 'performative'. Myth already had this character, and descriptions of Fashion are like connotations scattered over a stretch of insignificant material. Taken by themselves, Fashion utterances are pure meaning, 'speech without noise' (*SM*,29). Can we therefore take *Système de la Mode* as a guide for the study of other systems, especially those conveyed by a verbal support like literature? Our object would similarly be 'between words and things', it would be a real code like that of the fashion garments themselves (*SM*,14), 'borne by language, but also resisting it, and making itself through this interplay'. This object would in the case of literature be the referent, real or imaginary; at present its status is far from being clearly established by semiologists of literature. It is true that many modern texts are organized so as to destroy any impression of a referent, and have used a wide variety of techniques to achieve that effect; but in order to destroy, one must first have established something. Whether this is done schematically by modern texts or whether they assume the previous existence of stereotyped referents established by literature itself or by the commonplaces of everyday life is precisely what literary semiology must determine.

Must we refuse the name semiology to the study of such a 'translation' (*traduction*) or 'displacement' (*translation*) of verbal and object-codes into one another? Barthes says so unambiguously (*SM*,8), since linguistics is only the science of verbal signs and semiology that of object-signs. But here again, Barthes's object is to reverse the Saussurean proposal, and to make semiology a part of linguistics (*SM*,9). This reversal would obviously give credence to his views about the fracture between literature and even language and reality. The responsibility for this is projected onto mass culture: it is because of the place occupied today by persuasion, that is to say rationalizations, which are also a function of language, that language now pervades our most intimate experiences. Thus paradoxically the society which Barthes still professes to criticize also seems to be the source of his own hope of seeing linguistics reborn as 'the science of all imagined universes' (*SM*,10). And yet, as he acknowledges, the study of obsessions involves a quantitative element which only sociology can cope with; and even while defending his structural study, Barthes managed to introduce a sociological dimension in selecting his corpus (*SM*,19, 21), thus undermining the very attempt to reduce fashion to literature and literature to language.

The method

Barthes begins *Système de la Mode* with two kinds of instruments at his disposal. First, the general linguistic operations of commutation and the comparison of partially similar utterances, as described in *Elements* (*S*,65-6). Second, the schema from Hjelmslev similar to that used in 'Myth Today' and specified as connotation and metalanguage in *Elements*, that is, the two types of 'staggered systems'. This allows Barthes to differentiate the levels of meaning contained in Fashion utterances, and to decide whether it is feasible and worthwhile to study them.

Using the commutation test to break up the 'communication without end' of an unknown system, Barthes notes some privileged cases in which the fashion magazine itself performs this task of 'code-breaking' for us (*SM*,31). If we read, for instance, that 'this long cardigan looks demure when it is not lined and amusing when it is reversible', we are given two concomitant variations: a variation in the garment described brings about a variation in its character, and vice versa; other simple utterances can easily be reduced to this kind of concomitant variation. Thus he postulates two great commutative classes: one contains all the vestimentary features (forms, materials, colours), the other all the expressions denoting the characteristics of the garment (demure, amusing, etc.) or the circumstances (evenings, week-end, shopping, etc.) in which it is worn. In other words, these classes are 'garment' and 'world', but it is important to remember that these are not the terms mentioned in the magazines; they are part of the analyst's metalanguage. One could call them X and Y (*SM*,32) (which some people wish Lévi-Strauss had done instead of using terms like Culture and Nature — although surely the analyst's recompense is to engage in a little interpretation at the end of his labours, provided he makes it clear that this is what he is doing).

But some utterances never mention any characters or circumstances; they just describe the garment. Commutation would then be impossible if we did not know that the aim of *any* description of a garment is to transmit the idea of fashion. In the only existing variation 'in fashion/out of fashion', the second term is almost never manifested; it is implicit, like the signified of a word, and this will be found to have important consequences.

So we now know that any fashion utterance comprises two terms; garment/world in set A, and garment/fashion in set B (*SM*,34). What is the nature of the signifying relation between the two terms? It looks quite varied at first, but careful examination reveals that it is in fact no more than a vague relation of equivalence. The seductive art of the fashion writer will consist in providing this wide but superficial variety, when the sole point is in fact to make the two terms appear together. What is signified at bottom is always fashion in both cases, directly in set B, indirectly in set A, where the dictates of fashion are disguised via mythical naturalization as detailed advice on how to dress on all possible occasions. Every Fashion utterance implies therefore at least two systems of information: linguistic and vestimentary. At this point Barthes therefore uses the Hjelmslevian schema, having first explained it by means of the example of the Highway Code *as taught*, that is, when it is *spoken* (*SM*,42). First I associate the different colours of the traffic lights (signifiers) with different situations (signifieds); in principle this does not necessitate language. This is a real, non-linguistic code. But as taught by the instructor, the meaning of the association between 'red' and 'forbidden to cross' is expressed by a *proposition* voiced by a *sentence*: 'red means crossing is forbidden'. At the same time, the instructor probably cannot help revealing his character, his notion of his role, etc., by his phraseology, which Barthes calls, as in 'Myth Today', the rhetorical level. What we are in contact with is of course always this top level, the *vécu* — indeed, the threatening tone of the instructor can obscure the informative meaning to the point that it is not perceived at all, and it is left to the analyst to dissociate the levels clinically. Once more Barthes's choice of authoritative modes as examples seems itself connoted, and we are reminded of his original source, the political writing described in *Degree Zero*. Meaning is associated with domination — indeed it is identified with it in *S/Z* (*S/Z*,154).

The system

The middle level, which is the meaning proper, is accessible only to man; a dog could understand only the rhetorical connotations and the signals. Barthes excludes from the book any analysis of the first level, the real code, and he also excludes the extra layer which in the diagram on p. 47 of *Système de la Mode* adds the connotation 'Fashion' to the mere fact of a garment's being mentioned at all. So he is left with the two components of Fashion meaning, the *vestimentary code* (the building blocks used to transmit a certain representation of garments) and the *rhetorical system* (the phraseology through which the magazines strive to persuade). Barthes studies these in turn, tackling in each case the signifier, the signified and the sign.

The vestimentary code

The signifier of the vestimentary code is the syntagm without end which must be divided in order to get the units, again by commutation. It should be noted that the planes of the code are no more conformal than those of verbal language, which means that there can be no stable correspondence between the units distinguished in both planes; the meaning can appear only globally. Commutations gradually allow Barthes to whittle down utterances to the smallest significant unit, which he calls a *matrix*. It is important to realize that this matrix is not obtained mechanically; its actual form has to be postulated. This 'canonic form' is composed of the object O to which signification is aimed, the support S which is the part of the object on which the signification will bear, and the variant V, the actual difference which allows the significations to occur. The object and the support are material, the variant is immaterial, and it is such findings that led Barthes to suggest in *Elements* that in all systems other than language we must accept the idea of a non-signifying support.

These three elements are syntagmatically inseparable; Barthes compares them to a sentence, and indeed they represent a kind of predication, although the syntax is only a pseudo-syntax, as in all semiological systems where elements can only be juxtaposed, but never truly synthesized as they are in verbal language (by what Benveniste called *signifiance*). Just as the matrix is not obtained automatically, its application is by no means mechanical. In complex sentences, the analyst has to sort out what belongs to the object, the support and the variant, to conflate and reduce matrices, an operation requiring a high level of analytic skill. The recompense is that 'one finds oneself attending the delicate and patient birth of a signification' (*SM*,95). Barthes is especially interested in showing how meaning is whittled down to a fine point in complex utterances which can be decomposed into many matrices, which moreover are often discontinuous and embedded within each other. He also shows how the matrix is transformed, and this is of obvious importance for the study of comparable literary codes. Here again, what the analyst does laboriously is done in an instant and unconsciously by the reader.

The study of the vestimentary signifier is completed by a classification of the species Barthes finds in his corpus in order to designate garments, and by the grouping of these species into genera, followed by a classification of the variants. All these classifications are based on different criteria, which the researcher has to decide and make explicit at each stage. The vestimentary code is an example of the systems contained in language, whose units are grosser and whose 'syntax' is coarser; it is in fact only a 'pseudo-syntax' (*SM*,57), so that Barthes simply uses two very general symbols to express combination (' • ') and equivalence (' ≡ ') without deciding exactly what the relations between the units are. The rules or logic expressing these structural relationships are taken from Hjelmslev: solidarity or double implication, simple implication, combination (*S*,69, *SM*,58). This is found by Barthes to be sufficiently general.

He tries to develop the philosophy of each finding and decision as he goes along, and this is of the greatest methodological interest in addition to providing much of the richness of *Système de la Mode*. For instance, he finds two types of relationship among signifieds: *ET*, typical of the case where the garment described is euphorically presented as suitable for all possible occasions, able magically to reconcile extremes: clothes can thus be 'audacious and discreet', or the line of a dress have a 'rigorous suppleness'. This type of relationship also serves to make between words conjunctions which would be unlikely in real life for a certain class of reader: a dress is said to be appropriate for 'a week-end in Tahiti'. The second type of relationship between signifieds is expressed by *VEL*, which is disjunctive and inclusive, and in fact means a real possibility of combination: a pullover is described as suitable 'for the seaside or the mountains', which means that the sentence designates a realistic proposition (*SM*,205). Once more, what is discussed here is not the literal verbal language but what has been called earlier the 'syntax of semantics'. It must also be stressed that such discoveries can only be made from a corpus; they cannot be anticipated about any system, and it is only from the accumulation of comparable studies that a general configuration of the production of meaning in a given society emerges. In other words, Barthes had by then forged the instrument to study society *in detail*.

The comparison of the units discovered yields surprising results. Meaning is found to exist only at the global level. In some texts a sweater made of coarse wool is the equivalent of 'an autumn week-end in the country'; but elsewhere the same type of wool will mean 'spring on the Riviera'. It is impossible to establish a proper structuration of oppositions between such signifieds. These pages on the relations of semantic units with each other (*SM*,197-214) are among the most interesting in the book and they also hold the key to it, since they connect the study of the vestimentary code to the study of the rhetorical system. It would be difficult otherwise to understand why it was necessary to go through what some people would view as such an arid stretch of desert in order to reach thematic reflections which anyone, and Barthes supremely, could have reached without them. It would then be as if the mountain gave birth to a mouse, even if it was a lively mouse, since Barthes's reflections are sharp and amusing.

What Barthes discovers, when he studies the oppositions and neutralization of semantic units, is that there is no lexicon of Fashion; the same signifieds can have sometimes distinct and sometimes common signifiers. It appears as if the lexicon of Fashion is in fact composed of a single series of synonyms or perhaps one immense metaphor. Again taking some terms from Hjelmslev, he finds that every 'function' (a function is composed of terms or 'functives') can become a functive in its turn: an opposition between terms like *morning* and *afternoon* can be neutralized and become a function, which is the *day*; but as 'all meaning is generated from oppositions' (*SM*,210), for the day to have a vestimentary meaning it has itself to be a functive, a term of a virtual function, for instance the opposition between *day* and *night*. Barthes finds that meaning in Fashion eventually arranges itself as a pyramid, the upper reaches of which comprise only very large categories like time, place, climate, ending with a summit, a final function which is 'on all occasions'. Let us stress once more that these are not truisms or part of a rationally arranged lexicon like Roget's *Thesaurus* but attested phrases Barthes found in magazines. One even finds a garment which is expressly described as a universal: *tout-aller* and also *passe-partout* (for all occasions). This universal garment, which means everything, at first resembles what is indeed the only garment worn in underdeveloped countries; but Barthes points out that here, on the contrary, it is a kind of culmination of all the previous orgy of differentiation so that it is made to appear quasi-miraculous.

And yet the lexicon of Fashion *seems* to exist; this is the paradox. When read syntagmatically and not from a reconstituted tabulation, Fashion seems to refer to institutionalized meanings, even naturalized ones. It is therefore a conjuring trick and one must now see what is at stake. Fashion suffers from a continuing loss of memory; its meaning is strong in the instant, but comes undone as time unfolds. Fashion represents but does not really signify. This can only mean that the final signification is not to be found in the vestimentary code but at the level of the rhetorical system. In set B, garment/fashion, it matters little whether 'flannel' means morning or evening since its real meaning is fashion; in set A this ultimate meaning is the same, but mediated by naturalizations which Barthes now analyses. The parallel with literature so far is clear; both in relation to literary studies which include the systematic analysis of basic significations under the obvious lexical ones — which can show very similar phenomena of instability in the lexicon — and in relation to literature as defined by Barthes, which like the utterances in set A seems full of meaning but on closer examination is found to deceive or disappoint.

The rhetorical system

The analysis of the rhetorical system, although simple in its themes, may seem even more complicated than that of the vestimentary code in its structure. Barthes first analyses the rhetoric of the verbal system which conveys the system of Fashion proper; as usual, this is divided into a study of the signifier, Fashion writing, and a signified, Fashion ideology, which is always implicit, attached to the signs which manifest it. If this ideological value is missed, there still remains a meaning, but, as we saw, it is unfinished. As in myth, therefore, these connotations are received rather than read (*SM*,235). In order to characterize these latent messages Barthes uses the distinction, drawn from social psychology, and before it, biology, between *phenotype* (manifest behaviour) and *genotype* (latent, hypothetical and inferred behaviour). (These are given a new meaning by Julia Kristeva in her theory of the text, which is the basis of Barthes's later theories.) The analyst of Fashion here is in the position of the mythologist faced with the 'nebulous' mythological concept which is in essence imprecise, yielding itself to all readers.

Barthes then tackles the rhetorical element in each of the components of the sign of the vestimentary code. The rhetoric of the signifier is the 'poetics of the garment', since for Barthes 'the meeting of a matter and a language' is a situation that is inherently poetic. The mystery of matter is a topic that appears throughout his work, for instance in essays like that on 'Plastic' or the Citroen DS-19 in *Mythologies*; it is the intransitive, non-functional attitude that generates poetry. But what 'imaginary' do we find behind fashion poetry? Only one which is sparse, banal and poor. It is shared among three broad semantic fields. First culture (the dress which Manet would have 'loved to paint'), where all the stereotypes of Nature, Geography, History and Art are ransacked. These are not really cultural, they only signify culture. The second field covers the infantilization we already noted in *Mythologies*. Garments are often described as 'nice', 'good', 'warm', 'pretty', 'small'. These two fields reflect the position of woman in modern society, at least before the recent feminist movements: woman is being educated and at the same time kept in an infantile position. The third field refers to a vitalist model, which stresses 'details', the 'little something' which magically transforms an outfit. This is a kind of symbol of the power of Fashion itself: it makes something out of nothing. The review of these three fields cannot but evoke for Barthes his illustrious predecessor, Mallarmé, who also deconstructed language and was for a while the sole writer of an entire fashion magazine.

The signified of the vestimentary code reveals how Fashion sees the world. Fashion, like a novel, builds a cosmogony. Paradoxically, fashion writing, which is so often concerned with leisure, is in fact organized around the notion of work; it is its negative counterpart. One always specifies what the woman is doing, when and where. In fact the activities described, such as dancing, shooting, shopping, are here taken not as techniques but as social behaviour. In the world of Fashion you must always be seen doing something; even doing nothing is itself presented as an activity for which you need appropriate clothes. But Fashion also reflects the universal aspiration of the modern world, the lung which allows it to breathe, in its three moments of spring, the week-end, holidays — which designate it as primarily a fantasy. Even a chore has to be presented by Fashion no longer as a bind but as a sign, in the course of which it loses all the aspects which made it tiring, cumbersome and disappointing. Another aspect of Fashion which belongs to fantasy is that it flatters the universal desire for identity together with the no less universal desire to be a multiplicity of persons. Since each one of the latter is *named*, this is an exorcism of the anguish behind the tragic question, who am I? which Barthes still asks in *Barthes by Barthes*.

The semiology of society

The Fashion sign is, as always, the union of signifier and signified, of a certain view of clothes and of a certain view of the world. It is what Fashion presents as its *raison d'être*. This is where Barthes becomes bound by his ambiguous definition of what is 'arbitrary', and paradoxically excuses fashion when it is at its most dictatorial, in the utterances of set B, garment/fashion, which do not try, like those of set A, to hide their finality under a false nature. Barthes has to remain ambivalent towards Fashion, because he has already defined it by criteria which it has in common with literature; the aggression of Fashion, which is rhythmically organized like a vendetta (*SM*,274), is that of art, which exists only by murdering its father. Fashion and literature, which are among the 'least natural' values, that is the most human, thus thrive on guilt — a conclusion of Freudian pessimism.

As far as short-term movements are concerned, Barthes has what James Laver has called a 'conspiracy theory of fashion', which attributes it to obvious social manipulation; but a long-term view reveals the consumer society as the supreme meaning-maker even if the subconscious knowledge that this activity, signifying strongly yet signifying 'nothing', generates guilt. Barthes wrote before the boutique craze of the late sixties, which, together with permitting greater eclecticism in clothes, for the first time allowed customers to talk back. The decline of the aristocracy of Haute Couture may of course be replaced by the iron rule of middle-class ready-to-wear. At any rate, the groundswell of anarchism which both prepared and followed the events of 1968 coincided with the period when Barthes obsessively stressed not freedom but combinative rules and ritualized behaviour. Whatever is the case with costume, it has become clear that Fashion is not a *langue* without speech and that it can be and is spoken by individuals: fashionable clothes are not all alike and individual innovation stands out against the backcloth of fashion just as fashion stands out against the background of costume. Fashion, costume and clothing are one more proof that we are all multilingual; pressed by the consumer society to use the courtly language of fashion, we may well choose to reply in the demotic language of clothing. Or, if provoked enough, actually undertake to revolutionize costume, which many women would say happened in the 1960s.

In keeping with his new philosophy, Barthes alleges that although he concentrates on written fashion, the latter has no priority over the photograph or the real garment. He ignores the fact that in the magazine the photograph comes first, and that it is only afterwards specified by verbal language. Besides, for him both photograph or sketch and verbal description are only the traces of an original fabrication (*SM*,15), which supplies the real structure. We find here again the ideology of the use-value, or what Derrida calls (as we shall see shortly) a 'metaphysics of presence', which holds out the illusion of being able to get at an original meaning or transcendental signified, of which all other signs would be only secondary expressions. In fact it is likely that the photograph or sketch came *after* verbal language, which is precisely the speech of the original fashion group; and people who do not belong to that group but are fashion-conscious have internalized a language which they did not create originally and which is not, whatever Barthes says, a real social contract; they are alienated since they speak with other people's words in their mouths. Although Barthes denounces this when he makes the consumer society solely responsible for it, he is himself alienated when he does not realize that the fabrication is not the original structure, as his fantasy of matter as Mother Nature makes him say; what happens very often is that couturiers conceive a 'line', the epitome of fashion, which Barthes analyses very well (*SM*,116-17), an image specified in words, which they attempt afterwards to materialize, sometimes in spite of the natural properties of the material chosen. Barthes has internalized, probably because of his parallel analysis of modern literature, the perpetual motion of modern society which, while perpetuating the myth of use-value, is in fact totally dominated by economic exchange values and even more by the symbolic value of display. The latter is an empty form, filled at will by the upper stratum who alter it whenever the lower strata look as if they might achieve it in their turn. Economic and symbolic causality are thus inextricably intertwined; inequality is built into the system and cannot be eradicated since its economy, based on growth, and its scale of values, based on display, depend on it.

Such ideas, which remain disconnected in Barthes's oeuvre, have been developed systematically by the sociologist Jean Baudrillard, who supplements Barthes's ideas with those of Georges Bataille. Barthes has written on Bataille, a thinker of whom Philippe Sollers has said that he may well one say be more influential than Nietzsche, and whose synoptic thought has become more and more seminal since the war. He attempted to develop a theory of generalized exchange, concerning not only society but the whole cosmos. Although Barthes never attempted a true 'dialectic of nature', the tendency to think in similar terms is unmistakable in him, not only in his poetic view of matter as holding the ultimate key of the universe and of human creation, but in his attempts to dismantle the mechanism of meaning, and especially that of poetic meaning, which is one aspect of the cosmic law. But the ambivalence which marks Barthes's treatment of matter and which is epitomized in his treatment of objects as themes derives from the fundamental split in his thinking, which is directed both at society and at literature, as he pointed out at the end of 'Myth Today'. We can only talk about the world in the language of *excess* (a word especially associated with Bataille, and used by Barthes in the essay on wrestling to provide the key to its religious meaning); we can either 'poetize' or 'ideologize'.

The emergence of the economic crisis, following on the anarchist wave of the 1960s and the wild competiton between outlandish theories which has been remarked on by every observer of the French intellectual scene in recent years, exacerbated this late development in Barthes's thought and that of Baudrillard. The generalized floating of currency and of values was presented — by those who did not view it as a desperate form of nihilism — as a modern answer to the simultaneous loss of belief in the gold standard and the unitary sign (see on this in particular Barthes 1973b). Baudrillard has argued that since (as Barthes also pointed out) our present culture recuperates everything, there is no more room for any transcendence or symbols; the consumer society is totally immanent, it is itself its own sign. Whether it can subsist without the fetish of use-value — the equivalent of the naive classical theories Marx called 'robinsonnades' — remains to be seen; the self-image of the intellectual depends ultimately on his continued faith in the demystifying powers of his own metalanguage; in other words, on a belief in the autonomy, or comparative autonomy, of superstructures. Baudrillard has refused this, pointing out the desperate verbal gymnastics which have been engaged in to account for the relations of infra- and superstructures (words like *superstructural, dialectical, structure in dominance, determinant instance, relative autonomy, overdetermination*). Barthes redefined the task of the contemporary intellectual as essentially a negative one, in Brecht's words, 'to liquidate and theorize'; his positions were in many ways comparable to those of the Frankfurt school, which has been enjoying an unprecedented success in France.

But perhaps these theories have all fallen victim to the mechanism they denounce; to counterbalance their symbolic terrorism, we have to resort to such arguments as those used by J. Rée in his perceptive review of the recent translation of Sartre's *Critique of Dialectical Reason* (Rée, 1976a). Rée points out that Sartre wanted to specify the condition for under-standing *any* praxis (or purposive action), regardless of its content, but shifted imperceptibly to the assumption that the content of human praxis simply *is* its form (namely, the preservation of its own purposiveness, which is what makes it human, against 'otherness'), thus providing a very one-sided view of human experience. The whole span of the latter is reduced to a single dimension, the fight between dominion and subjection. Thus

> it involves the same kind of abstraction as an economic theory which operates purely in terms of value, and never in terms of use value. It makes Sartre rule out the possibility that, say, the water and the sunshine, the wine and the conversation, could simply be enjoyed because — for some contingent material reason, and as a matter of brute fact — they satisfy your needs and desires.

Add to this a purely differential view of language as a relation between signs rather than one between language and reality, and a view of the whole of literature reduced to the mechanics of originality, and you have the Barthesian view of art and society.

Part IV

The science of literature is literature

12

In those days, intellectual history was going very fast

Subversion in semiology

We saw that in *Degree Zero*, although Barthes had specific proposals to make about the attitude the writer should adopt toward society, there is no actual theory of the poetic word except one important pointer to his later theories: poetry is linked to what Barthes called the 'pace' or 'delivery', the rhythm an individual imprints on his discourse. In his later career, it was mainly on rhythm that he pinned his faith in the ability of the writer to coincide with the cosmic heartbeat, the 'proof' being *jouissance*. Barthes's next acquisition was the revelation of information theory, which continued to loom large in his theory of originality. It is only with *Elements of Semiology* that he arrived at decisive specifications. We can actually reconstitute from this book, whose layout is arranged for another end (the development of semiology), the outline of a theory of poetic creation. The key idea is that of transgression, which is found in each of the chapters which bear Saussurean headings.

The chapter on 'Language and Speech' contains a section on what Jakobson calls 'duplex structures'. These are special cases of the general relation between code and message and include two cases of circularity and two cases of overlapping: reported speech, proper names, autonymy, and shifters (which Barthes codes as follows: M/M, C/C, M/C, C/M). The case of the shifter, the personal pronoun, is particularly significant. Here, it no longer appears, as it did in Humboldt, as the most primitive layer of language but, as Barthes revealingly puts it, as 'a complex and adult relationship' between the code and the message with which it struggles, a process taking place on the very frontiers of language.

The chapter on 'Syntagm and Paradigm' outlines a poetic zone of speech which again makes poetry depend on 'the smallest degree of probability'. Barthes quotes Valle Inclan: 'Woe betide him who does not have the courage to join two words which have never been united'

(S,70). This is again taken up in Barthes's article on Chateaubriand, where, as we saw, metaphor is actually presented as a factor in disruption, not assimilation; this fractured speech is seen as the mythical language of the gods, as in *Degree Zero*, where the words stood 'erect' without grammatical connections. The key word is 'distance', which can be applied to all aspects of language. There is distance of a kind between syntagm and paradigm, and in *Elements* the transgressions which can give rise to literary effects are enumerated (S,86-8), chiefly the extension of a paradigm onto the syntagmatic plane, as Jakobson suggested.

The chapter on 'Signifier and Signified' has two topics. Ostensibly it is a discussion of the arbitrary character of the sign and the methodological advisability of keeping a neutral support in the case of semiological systems. But we saw that Barthes made an exception for fashion and literature since their *raison d'être* is to be wholly significant, that is, *different*. This is the underlying topic of the chapter; it announces the crisis of the sign and shows one of its causes, which is psychoanalytical, specifically Lacanian. Rejecting various representations of semiosis as unsatisfactory, Barthes praises Lacan's representation S/s.[1] He also quotes from an influential 1963 article on the unconscious by two of Lacan's disciples, J. Laplanche and S. Leclaire, who refer to 'the paradox of the dictionary', already known to logicians: 'The dictionary seems to give a positive definition of a word; but as this definition is itself made up of words which must themselves be explained, the positivity is endlessly referred further' (S,103n78). Barthes had already analysed Bataille's *Histoire de l'œil* as a metaphorical chain where each term acts as a sign for the next (E,239) and used this in *Elements* (S,104n91).

The two time-bombs which would eventually explode under the closed sign were thus already set to go off in 'Myth Today', and even more so in *Elements*; one is the question of the speaking subject and the other is connotation. This shows Barthes's acumen in selecting not only areas which were shortly to undergo profound changes but also issues which would revolutionize the status of linguistics itself, as had been predicted by some linguists: Jakobson, perhaps because of his exceptional sensitiveness to literature, or Hjelmslev because he conceived the extension of linguistics from the start into a science of pure form, an algebra. The other models found in 'Myth Today' do not appear in *Elements* or *Système de la Mode* because from then on Barthes made a sharp distinction between literature and society. He argued that there was no longer anything to be said about the latter, which he now viewed as a gigantic battle of stereotypes leaving no possibility for *parole*, whether at the level of the individual or that of the group. The only remaining creative possibilities lie within literature, which does not admit of any scientific approach since science must ultimately be based on some *langue*; so that one can talk about texts only by means of other texts.

Thus the semiological project, when put into practice, was shown to be inherently subversive. It shows how discourse compensates for lacunae in *langue*, essentially by transgressing its rules, not only well-known grammatical and rhetorical prescriptions, but the very arrangement which makes language exist: the distinction between code and message or signifier and signified, and the axes of syntagm and paradigm. But the theory explaining this process of subversion was to develop dramatically thanks to new concepts which, emerging at the very apogee of structuralism in 1966-7, eventually resulted in a complete re-reading of the past. These theories were to cleave a sharp division between semiology and the new theory of signifying practices, called *semanalysis*, a word which seeks to embody the fusion of semantics and psychoanalysis.

A new theory of signification

Let us then briefly examine this new theory of signification, the precondition of an understanding of Barthes's later work. Here Hjelmslev's theory was probably most important at first. Greimas, who introduced Barthes to linguistics, was crucially influenced by Hjelmslev, who thus like Saussure may be said to have fathered the two complementary semiologies. Hjelmslev went further than Saussure in combatting the 'natural' primacy of sound over other substances of expression, particularly writing. This theme has been taken up by Derrida, who was better equipped to give a philosophical account of Hjelmslev's argument that *langue* should be regarded as an abstract form, independent not only of the substance of expression but also of its use as language. The attractions of philosophy can be seen in the works of Peirce, who was interested in signs from an extremely wide perspective (as Leibniz had been), comprehending the very configuration of human thought and its constitution of what we call objects or 'things'. Derrida, who edited Husserl's writings, is well aware of all the pitfalls open to philosophical reflection if it does not take into account the distinctions, stressed by phenomenology, between empirical realities used as examples and the essences which they help us grasp. Derrida thinks that the basic concepts of linguistics rest on a metaphysical foundation which Husserl explored and developed best of all. But he is even more aware of the other traps offered by phenomenology since his own work is a critique of the phenomenological tradition.

Derrida's train of thought was started by a meditation on *Le geste et la parole* by A. Leroi-Gourhan, an anthropologist concerned with pre-history and human evolution and whose original classifications may have been a spur to a consideration of the abstract matrix of concrete practices. The science of writing, or grammatology, Derrida notes, has always taken the form of history, not theory, and this is part of the consistent disparagement of writing in the work of theologians, metaphysicians and even linguists. In Western thought, language has always suffered from being considered a 'representation', with writing, conceived as a sequel to speech, made secondary, only the image of an image. Derrida gives examples of this from Plato to Jaspers, some of surprising vehemence. Any attempt to reverse the order of precedence is interpreted as a rebellion of body against soul, and experienced as a threat to the laws of logic, which determine dual categories like inside/outside, more/less, original/derivative.

Like Foucault, Derrida concentrates less on a history of opinions than on the assumptions which made them possible. Such a synchronic 'reading' of our time reveals that the West is on the point of imposing its phonetic writing on the rest of the world (wiping out equally or perhaps more interesting forms such as ideographs) because of its superiority in the sciences, whose 'languages', paradoxically, are more graphic than verbal. Exploring the relations between speech and writing, Derrida is led to realize that the concept of *difference*, on which linguistics is founded, cannot be primary; there must pre-exist a notion of a *trace*, a simultaneous intimation of sameness and difference. This trace is no longer derivative, as phonetic writing was; it is a kind of 'arche-writing', of which oral language itself is only one kind. In order to stress that this trace is anterior to the categories of experience or sensibility like space and time, he calls it by a neologism, *différance*, a homophonous pun which conveys the spatio-temporal relation of *differing* and *deferring*, and which, symbolically, cannot be heard but must be seen on the printed page. Derrida suggests that only the subordination of our ideas on oral and 'natural' languages to this enlarged notion of writing can save us from logo- or phonocentrism, the primacy erroneously assigned to an ultimate meaning or signified conceived in its immediacy, without imprint or trace, and in a mode of presence which only the idea of a God can fully contain — this basic idea supports the whole of Western rationality. Reflection on non-European practices, on non-verbal practices, on the language of the unconscious (which Freud himself compared to a hieroglyphic writing) can help us 'deconstruct' these basic concepts of metaphysics and thus free us from their unwanted implications. A major part can also be played by a new conception of the dual activity of writing and reading, which views texts as an infinite play of traces, where the signified is 'always already' in the position of a signifier (as the paradox of the dictionary had shown). The activities of the subjects are then seen as a basic reorganization of these traces, relying indeed on *langue* but transforming it according to their desires and thereby producing meaning-effects.

Can such notions have a practical application, however? Can they lead to a positive science of either the text or the social *vécu*? We certainly find in Derrida many warnings against what phenomenologists would call the 'mundane' view of the vistas he opened. A concept, and before that the object, of a science can only be obtained by a foreclosure of the endless cross-references between the terms of the signifying chain. Derrida's *Writing and Difference* is a collection of essays in which the choice of topics functions as part of his demonstration. The works he chooses exemplify an unease in our ideological system; they show the final impossibility of escaping metaphysics, although they also show that greatness and originality are reached only at the limit of an attempt to do so. Beside, many statements in which Derrida exposes metaphysical assumptions have nevertheless proved true and fruitful at the scientific level. Is grammatology destined not to be a science but rather a wariness of metaphysical presuppositions and a glimpse of what the original divided trace conveys, a contact with whatever is not 'the living', with exteriority, with otherness?

The difference between signifier and signified cannot be purely and simply erased, Derrida says; but we must be aware at the same time of its (limited) usefulness and of its ultimate lack of real foundation. For instance, it is only by allowing this difference that translations, or the structural analysis of narrative, are possible. Both rest on the recognition of an autonomous stratum which can be 'translated' from substance to substance. Moreover, it is in a way unnecessary to resist expressivity at all costs, since the meaning one wishes to 'express' is already constituted by a text woven with differences. One cannot very well see, therefore, why the project of a structural semantics, within its proper limits, should be illegitimate. In short, grammatology offers no short-cuts to science, to the painstaking labour of describing a (somewhat arbitrarily) defined object. But it shows that a full awareness of the 'differing' can only be reached by means of literary practices. Reality is now seen as a sum of all texts in various media, including action and thought, and getting to know it consists, as Sollers put it, in a *traversée des écritures*, a voyage through writing.

On the other hand, any reader of Barthes must realize that Barthes's thought is particularly sign-bound despite his pre-Derridean discoveries and his later search for strategies to postpone meaning indefinitely. This appears clearly in his predilection for the 'etymological proof'. Perhaps a later period, less bent on making a one-sided and tactical use of scientific discoveries, will be better able to appreciate Barthes's quest as the very embodiment of the semantic process: a twin labour of denomination and deconstruction, identification and diversification, discovery of hierarchies and equivalences (see on this Greimas, 1970a on 'L'écriture cruciverbiste' and Le Ny, 1979).

Derrida's theory supplied the missing link between concepts born of applied linguistics and their counterparts in Marxism and psychoanalysis, made their synthesis, which already had a *de facto* existence, operational, and gave it an ontological grounding. By the time Kristeva's review of *Système de la Mode* appeared (1967) the new vulgate had been established.[2] It supplied the background to *S/Z* and to much literary theory for the following decade, although meanwhile the reader was kept on his toes by the constant supply of neologistic catchwords which, together with logico-mathematical notations, changed the look of critical writing overnight.

Kristeva's critique of Western thought concentrates on what she calls its *ideologeme* (a term of Medvedev's) or main ideological 'figure'. This is the sign, which, as sociology shows, was an exchange of ready-made objects between, so to speak, ready-made persons. These objects are meanings, and Kristeva praises Barthes who, by showing that Fashion is a meaning, had introduced the idea that meaning is a fashion, which need not exist in a culture based on a different ideologeme. It is thus relevant that Barthes saw her uninhibited use of neologism as an index of conceptual intrepidity; this 'freedom of the signifier', which he also admired in Fourier, may well have played a part in guiding Barthes towards a conception of textual handling to bring it even nearer a writer's practice. A selective sketch of Kristeva's theories is therefore indispensable at this point since Barthes, over the last ten years, came increasingly to depend on them theoretically and even, as we shall see, existentially (the best article on Kristeva's early work is Houdebine, 1971).

Her reading of monumental history outlines three stages in the coming of modernity. The first is illustrated in the arts and sciences by the names Freud, Marx, Nietzsche, Lautréamont and Mallarmé (this pantheon could no doubt be added to); the second occurs between 1920 and 1930 with surrealism and Russian formalism; the third is the present period, when a new object has been defined, the text, which requires a new theory in order to understand it.

Actually, the new object of study is not so much the text as its *signifiance*, a word already encountered in Benveniste's characterization of the synthesizing power which makes human language unique among other sign systems. In order to account for *signifiance*, it is essential not to assume that the sign is the main unit of what Saussure called 'the object at once integral and concrete of linguistics'. Despite his life-long attempts to delineate this object, Saussure finally had to limit himself to *langue*, an ambiguous gesture which is that of all science, indispensable but unsatisfactory. But, further, it is a move which has obscured the full scope of his research. It is only by returning to the manuscript sources of the *Course*, as well as what Kristeva calls 'the immense mass of the

Anagrams whose weight contests the *Course'*, that Saussure's full project can be reconstructed. We then see that Saussure did realize that there was a problem of the subject, which Chomsky was later to introduce as the intuition of the speaking subject. Kristeva shows that this speaking subject occupies several positions in the various areas of Saussure's research: as the subject of a scientific metalanguage, that of linguistics; as the absent subject of *langue* (which is only an unconscious classifying activity) in the *Anagrams*; and as an explicit subject in the notion of *parole*. Unfortunately Saussure's inability to theorize speech resulted in a gap, syntax. It was left to Chomsky to theorize this subject (however inadequately) into the system. Ideally, this notion would articulate competence and performance.

Kristeva again identifies three stages in the genesis of a language to describe the text: Saussure's total reflection on language at the turn of the century, phonology as elaborated in Prague in the 1920s, and Lacan nowadays. The school of Prague did not stop at the sign but atomized even sound, analysing it into distinctive features. This was done only at the empirical level; it was left to others to aim at a theory of signification and was later extended mechanically in 'structuralism'. Jakobson, however, pointed out the relation between the phoneme and other notions, such as that of the *sphota* of Indian grammarians, conceived as a conceptual overdeterminant of the phoneme, the merging of sound and meaning at the very heart of language. Lacan's theory is a major breakthrough precisely because it asserts that the signifier is in part in the signified, and in a form which is in some sense material. This poses the question of its place in reality, while conceptualizing the relation between signifier and meaning as a relation of *insistence* and thus not relapsing into anything like the consistency of a positive substance.[3]

The third breakthrough (which is chronologically the first) is found in Saussure's *Anagrams*. It is also a theory which looks for signification through a dismantled signifier, and sees it as meaning insistent in action.[4] Thus, whereas in *langue* the signified is only due to the interplay of the terms among themselves, or value, in the anagrams the signifier produces a value which exceeds the total meaning of the individual elements. *Langue*, the repository of the signs, then seems to be, as Saussure put it, 'the last compromise that the mind accepts with certain symbols; otherwise, there would be no language', only the infinite play of *signifiance*, or difference.

This theory suggests the idea of a subversive and creative way of reading. We can choose to liberate the text from *langue* and ideological constraints, reconstructing from what Kristeva calls the *phenotext*, that is, the text as we see it, the *genotext* which preceded it. These terms must not be equated with Chomsky's surface and deep structures: the genotext, or signifying productivity, should be viewed as what Freud calls 'another stage', on which the unconscious drama is continuously unfolding. The appropriate way to approach a text is therefore not the description of a structure (thematicism, the description of a corpus, structural semantics or anything based on the idea of a secure communication between a sender and an addressee), but the restitution of the structur*ation* or structuring movement preceding the text. Nor must the difference between pheno- and genotext be reduced to the difference between *énoncé* and *énonciation*, since this attempt by Benveniste to introduce the subject into linguistics is still conceived on a phenomenological model: to the extent that it thus postulates a full subject, it cannot account for the modifications discernible in the subject's discourse, which only make sense by reference to unconscious processes and to socio-historic constraints.

Kristeva therefore brings together psycholinguistic findings and Benveniste's distinction between the *semiotic* and the *symbolic*, the two modalities which are inseparable in the process of *signifiance*. Their varying articulation determines a typology of discourses on a spectrum ranging from music to artificial languages via narrative, metalanguage, theory and poetry (see also on this Klinkenberg, 1973, which draws on the ideas of the Romanian linguist, S. Marcus). For Kristeva, the genotext does not generate a sentence based on a logical form following the subject-predicate pattern, but a signifier seen at different stages of the signifying process: a word, a syntagm, a nominal sentence, a paragraph, a nonsensical effect, etc. Barthes has often mentioned those mysterious units of meaning (in his articles on Chateaubriand or La Rochefoucauld for instance — see *NEC*) which may consist of ideas, sounds or rhythms and do not correspond to typographical, grammatical or logical divisions — and he acted on this realization in *S/Z*.

Language, Kristeva says, is the imposition of an articulated language onto a mode of *signifiance* logically anterior to it and akin to rhythm, whose specificity can never be grasped by any metalinguistic description; only one practice can do that, poetic language. From social structuring, there will emerge the notions of subject and object, and finally the act of predication expressed by propositions. This structuring of the subject cannot but be experienced as antagonistic to him, since it breaks into his continuity. It is due to displacement and condensation in the unconscious, and to relations which can be represented by topological figures. These figures indicate the connections between, on the one hand, the zones of the 'fragmented body' among themselves and, on the other, these same zones with external subjects and objects: the subject's own sphincters, for instance (which gave their names to the Freudian oral and anal stages), the modulations he can produce with his voice, and the protagonists of the family structure (for a background to this aspect of Kristeva's theory, see Fónagy, 1970 and 1971).

The 'dual corridor of reminiscence' which the phenotext opens to us, thus leads towards the symbolico-mathematical processes at work in semantics (and far from elucidated at present), and also towards the ideological corpus which saturates each block of monumental history. It is this ideology which has rendered modern texts unreadable until now, making them look obscene, pathological or meaningless (Sollers, 1968a). No wonder that reconstituting the genotext is described by Kristeva as 'an immense task'.

Barthes and the text

We can now ask what bearing this new theory of signification, which so often harks back to Barthes's pioneering work, had on his own work and attitudes. As we have noted, Barthes never really was a structuralist in the field of literary analysis. In deprecating those who account for all the world's stories by a single structure, just as the ascetic practices of certain Buddhists 'enabled them to see a whole landscape in a bean', he did not include himself among them (*S/Z*,3). Yet he had made a major contribution to the elaboration of a machinery for the study of those larger units of discourse which are obviously relevant in literature. Indeed his reputation as semiologist-in-chief was so well established that those who had interpreted *S/Z* as part of the same attempt were quite mystified by an apparently sudden conversion to something he called 'textual analysis', a practice said to be the exact opposite of structural analysis. There was indeed a gap in the theory of literature, which neither the old normative rhetoric nor linguistics (even extended from sentence to discourse) could fill. We saw early on that the apparent neatness of the schema for literary studies proposed in *Critique et vérité* in fact hid quite a few ambiguities: not only was the status of poetics not easily distinguishable in practice from criticism, but the criticism itself could be defined either in relation to *a* critic or to *a* system (this was solved in practice by the critic unfailingly plumping for the 'deepest' doctrines). Finally, the methodological problems raised by the question of the single work had not been solved either. All these ambiguities culminated in a recentring of literary theory on the notion of *text*. The work was now seen not so much as a sign (made up of the signifier and signified) but as a signifying practice, and one which moreover was said to be more suitable than all metalanguages for its own study and for action in the world.

The question of how Barthes's work and attitudes were affected by this new theory therefore needs to be answered on several levels: theoretical, ideological and practical. It is obvious that, subjectively, Barthes felt there was a great change. Just as we found that around 1960 there was an overlap between his earlier committed attitude, still apparent in his articles on the theatre, and his new doctrine, which applied to the novel, we now find some transitional texts at this point. We shall see that his 'Introduction to the structural analysis of narratives', (*IMT*) is in fact deconstructed by him from the inside. But the most interesting transitional text is probably the reprint, in *Théorie d'ensemble* (1968, also in *SE*) of his earlier article on Sollers's *Drame* (1965), now peppered with footnotes where Barthes seeks to convey his dramatic change of outlook. The problem is that the Text (openly mythologized by its capital letter) is still somewhat elusive, if not actually impossible to grasp. The plethora of distinctions which seek to render the difference between *text* and *work*, as well as between textual analysis and structural analysis, often look more like modalizing symptoms than referential pointers. The 1960 change had involved an obvious switch from the 'speech' to the 'mask' solution, previously rival strategies. Now the text is defined in the same way as, in 1960, the relation of the work to meaning was specified, and with the same uncertainty between *a, the* or *some* meaning. Sometimes Barthes states that the modern text is not an object at all, sometimes that it is an object which does not yet exist, sometimes an object existing in partitive fashion (so that we can find *some* text) and sometimes that it exists as a network of relationships found best of all in life, rather than art (see for instance 'The death of the author', *IMT*, 'The struggle with the angel', *IMT*, 'From work to text', *IMT*, and 1973f). One certainly can see no 'mutation' here.

Textual analysis is best defined negatively, in contradistinction to practices which Barthes disapproved of and which turn out to be all the disciplines available in literary studies: stylistics, lexicology and grammar, thematics and any approach which stresses a plan, exhaustive *explications de texte*, history, sociology, the psychology of characters or the biography of authors. The clearest definition which can be found of textual analysis focuses on the notion of corpus. Where structural analysis hoped to extract a universal scheme for narrative from such a corpus, textual analysis seeks to 'infinitize' a single text by treating each of its elements as the point of departure for an infinite 'drift' of meanings.

Yet in practice this distinction is not so clear-cut: structural analyses often bear on a single text (witness Barthes's study of the biblical episode of Jacob's struggle with the angel, *IMT*) and the background one draws on has perforce a certain universality — as we shall see in *S/Z* where the symbolic field contrasted with the codes of the text turns out simply to be the *vraisemblable* of either our time or perhaps, despite his hopes of dispersing the subject, of Barthes's in particular. The symbolic field rests chiefly on Lacanian psychoanalysis, or perhaps even more on a favouring of the pre-Oedipal in the 1970s, seen particularly in Kristeva, as a reaction against Lacan's oppressive phallicism and stress on law and castration. But these seductive attempts to remotivate the language and turn it into a supportive maternal figure, however suggestive, are not sufficient to establish a clear distinction between a textual analysis and a naive structural analysis. In other words we are here once again dealing with a veritable myth; one just imagines the Barthes of *Mythologies* let loose on all this, if things had turned out differently! In the circumstances, one can only admire the forbearance of some structural analysts who, like Claude Chabrol (1973), chose to concentrate on the genuine glimpse of new horizons which is afforded by such an imaginary theory.

As for Barthes's practice, apart from the special case of *S/Z*, whatever ideological justifications he gave, he (fortunately) went on doing what he had always done: giving very sensitive commentaries on individual literary texts, which somehow renew and refurbish them, as every poetic approach should do. We therefore find oracular pronouncements or sensuous descriptions of a somewhat problematic Text coexisting with extremely valuable and enjoyable pieces on individual works or authors. Other critics, however, have practised something that looks more like textual analysis as defined by Barthes. The results are interesting and should lead one to accept this practical pluralism at the theoretical level. There was thus no need for Barthes to describe himself as working 'in the rearguard of the vanguard' (*T*,102), unless vanguard means doctrinal irresponsibility. But perhaps his fate lay in being the 'uncertain subject' of his Inaugural Lecture, a subject into which the quickening of intellectual history after 1965-6, the events of May 1968, the take-over of critical language and the teaching establishment by structuralism, and the mystical radicalism of the *Tel Quel* group turned the defiant structuralist of the early 1960s. This uncertain subject was also, as it turned out, the subject of writing, and ultimately one which achieved the supreme synthesis of theory and narrative. But to see how this came to pass, we need a second flashback which will examine the beginnings of structuralism in literature.

13

A whole landscape
in a bean

Characters, actions, authors[1]

When Barthes published his pioneering 'Racinian man' (1960, now in *R*), it looked as if he would forever endorse an approach to literary texts which — whether this was his intention or not — amounted to a 'deconstruction' of the traditional notion of character. Character was now seen as either a 'figure' or a 'function'. This is a nuance which still persists in some analysts of narrative who, following the mythographer Dumézil — one of Greimas's named sources — define an agent as the sum of his qualities or the support of his actions. More radical theorists maintain that, in the generation of a text, the same initial arrangement can be eventually manifested by either qualities or actions and so, for them, keeping the distinction between qualities and action is therefore a humanist residue. Conceiving character as the representation of a human person, having a consciousness and an identity manifested in its actions is an ideological, not a scientific concept; François Rastier for one urges all theorists worthy of the name to get rid of it, since, as Althusser says, 'one has always gained something when one has lost an inadequate concept'. From a certain angle, no doubt he is right; from another angle, the case is far from proved.

We shall find this opposition at every level, reflecting the clash between the two conceptions of the subject we are now forced — unless we are very strong-minded — to think of as rivals. Moreover such a quarrel makes sense only if literature is a proper object of science which, as even Rastier acknowledges, is far from clear. But if literature is only an ideological phenomenon, then a science of ideology must surely take careful stock of such phenomena as the attribution of consciousness and a permanent identity to characters rather than sweeping them under the carpet or discouraging them — unless, that is, one means to bring about a large-scale change in the perception of reality, of which literature is a part. In any case, recent work presents a more balanced distribution of interest between agent and action.

Certainly the hypertrophy of psychological analysis which culminated in the nineteenth-century novel was still providing the staple fare in twentieth-century France until the committed literature of the 1940s and early 1950s confirmed the metaphysical twist of writers like Malraux. By contrast it is the story which provides most of the interest in works like Boccaccio's *Decameron* or the *Arabian Nights*, the favourite texts of structural analysts of narrative still practising their scales. Sensible as it may have been, this emphasis on the story provided opponents of the whole approach with a ready-made weapon (which we saw Barthes using in the introduction to *Elements of Semiology*): alleging that 'great' literature is outside the scope of structuralism. After that initial stage it became imperative to tackle more complex works, however tentatively, just as the 'semiology of signification' turned out to be the real basis of semiology, and not the simpler 'semiology of communication.

Besides, it is clear that one could not readily classify works of literature, or even narratives, or even plots, without some sort of simplification of outline, based on the judicious choice of a principle of relevance advocated in *Elements*. One could not even properly understand them, if meaning is the result of a *parcours*, a linear path through a complex semantic universe. This step was taken independently by all the theorists who, working in very different fields, must be regarded as the founding fathers of the modern structural analysis of literature. As Rastier (1974) observes, considering the humanist attachment to the primacy of the character and what is ideologically at stake, the impetus for renovation had to come from a different field, and it was the studies of mythography. Myths and folktales exist in colossal numbers; their authors and the cultural context of their creation are uncertain. Often, the sheer complexity and incongruity of their story lines force an approach totally different from that which was (still is?) used for literature. For, where a structural analysis seeks meaning in a matrix consisting of a few basic oppositions, traditional literary criticism depends upon forms of the *vraisemblable* in order to produce readable texts for a given public.

There is another point. The shift of interest away from characters is mirrored by a refusal to treat authors of texts as a substratum of consciousness, permanence and identity behind the characters, holding them together for the reader through whatever transformations, transpositions or inversions are involved. There again, Barthes was ready to follow suit; although his essay on Racine makes occasional use of biographical detail, closer examination shows that this occurs only when Barthes identifies with either Racine or some of his characters. This is still out of keeping with his declared intentions at the time, but perhaps it fits in with the attitude adopted later in *S/Z*. In this work, Barthes thought for a while of adopting as one of his 'codes' (or general headings under which he classifies his observations as his reading of Balzac progresses) a 'code of schools and universities', under which irreverent name would be classified all the facts or notations which can in some way be associated with what we know of Balzac's life and times. The author is then seen as a figure of the text, a 'paper being' on the same level as his own characters. And there is nothing to prevent the reader from playing the game of connotations and metalanguages in his turn, reading Barthes's works with the help of a code which would locate the identification marks he left in them!

The Thibaudeau interview is the first of the series of texts where Barthes started making 'admissions' which have proved very damaging in the hands of those who cannot read them structurally. For instance, he declared that he did not like Racine, and had written about him only because he was asked and presumably needed the money. Those who cannot read this as a typical denial provoked by an unpleasant experience — the statement is characteristically couched almost in Picard's own terms — should perhaps think again before they go on teaching or reviewing literature, which is full of such subtle metamorphoses. Barthes may not like Racine, but Racine, so to speak, likes him, there is an affinity between them. Barthes's analysis of 'amorous alienation' in Racine, its sado-masochism and spiteful attention to detail, and the broad schema of the struggle to break free from compulsive passion and the feminization which results from being placed in the structural position of the dependent partly: all this prefigures *S/Z* and *A Lover's Discourse* to a remarkable degree. Moreover, his prescriptions on how Theseus should speak, as one who has seen the gods, and the general connection between the violence of the passions and the small scale of the Greek landscape with its constricting effects on the lives of the characters, are obviously reminiscent of Hegel's *Lectures on the Philosophy of History*, which in the same year had been a source for Barthes's new doctrine of literature.

The different plots of Racine's tragedies are reduced, in Barthes's analysis, to a matrix based on oppositions in love and power relationships for which the work done by Goldmann and especially by Mauron had already prepared the way. These are also connected with a general anthropological story (a theoretical one, since, as with Lévi-Strauss and Rousseau, this kind of speculation may be safer when the period is too distant for any fragments of empirical knowledge to be reliable), that of the primal horde. Freud had used the notion of the primal horde in *Totem and Taboo* to account for the prohibition of incest as the cornerstone of society. Initially the father is the most powerful of all the males in the horde, keeping all the females for himself and thus depriving his sons of them. The sons band together and kill him, agreeing subsequently among themselves on a fairer arrangement of the women, to which they are bound by contract. Barthes presents this myth to polarize the tensions between male/female and power/subjection; with it he is able to tackle works previously treated from the psychological angle, and to do it in a way which not only suggests a matrix for each tragedy, but a development throughout the whole of Racine's career. Barthes begins by listing the elements or units of his interpretation, then organizes them in a paradigm of oppositions, then treats them syntagmatically. Mauron's interpretation of this syntagmatic development showed how Racine, encouraged by successive identifications with ideal fathers, chose his Oedipal love-object (literature and especially the stage), and abandoned his cruel archaic mother-figure (the world of piety and scholarship represented by the austere gentlemen of Port-Royal, the devout Jansenists), only to fall back into her clutches because of his guilt and the relative inadequacy of the king as father-figure. We shall need to remember all this when we come to the period which immediately preceded *S/Z*, and even more when we come to Barthes's later career.

The structural analysis of narrative

Apart from Lévi-Strauss's work and Barthes's 'Racinian Man', the main source of structural analysis as it is currently practised is Greimas's work, starting with the models suggested in *Sémantique structurale*.[2] In view of their similarity to Barthes's own, his sources of inspiration must be briefly listed. An outline of his main concepts will follow, since they provide the basis for Barthes's article on the structural analysis of narratives in *Communications* 8 and a foil for Barthes's subsequent practice, especially *S/Z*. Special attention must be paid to such topics as the relation between the structure of a text and the nature of narrativity, the dialectics of agent and action, the different levels of narrative, the distribution of meaning throughout a text, and the relation between logical schemata and their anthropomorphic or figurative forms (as Ricoeur pointed out (Ricoeur, 1980), this distinction is subtle and sometimes difficult to apply).

It is very important to realize that Greimas's structures are not a mechanical application of phonology, or even of its first processing by Lévi-Strauss, but were reached as a synthesis of work done in different fields. He found his inspiration in mythography (in the work of Dumézil and Lévi-Strauss, in Vladimir Propp's *Morphology of the Folktale* — which has often been compared, in its own field, to Saussure's *Course* in linguistics — as well as Propp's predecessors like Veselovsky and the French medievalist Joseph Bédier and successors in the American continent and the Soviet Union); in an original study by the aesthetician Etienne Souriau of a corpus of French plays; and in the 'psychocriticism' of Mauron and two different collections of case-histories by the psychoanalysts M. Safouan and L. Irigaray. A major source was the syntactic model of L. Tesnière who, in his *Eléments de syntaxe structurale*, like the linguist Bréal, argued that the sentence could be seen as the plot of a drama; this was neatly inverted by Greimas, the agents of the plot being seen as the components of a predicative sentence. Another source was a psycholinguistic datum; the Copenhagen linguist Brøndal had maintained that the mind can absorb only six lexical units at a time, and this gave Greimas the idea of a six-unit structure of signification. He combined this with a matrix proposed by the logician Blanché, which uses the opposite and the negation of a given element to produce the form A:B: : − A: − B (A is opposed to B as − A is opposed to − B) or *semiotic square*. Greimas, like Barthes, also drew on his own experience in semantics, which led him to realize that the word or lexeme is not a proper semantic unit and that one has to resort to semes, and then postulate different levels of coherence in a text, to ensure its cohesion on a level beyond that of syntactic links. Finally he also derived inspiration from thematic criticism, and from Barthes's models for the study of myth in modern society. This formidable array indicates that opponents of the structural analysis of narrative or, more generally, literary semiotics, cannot proceed simply by rejecting the linguistic model, itself reduced to phonology, which in turn has been reduced to the Jakobsonian brand. One has to deal with a considerable mass of evidence originating in many fields.

Just as we find the opposition between structure and process as a basic schema at the beginning of *Elements of Semiology*, we also find in Greimas an awareness of the stress put by the *Annales* school on long-term historical movements. This, together with his interest in both syntax and semantics, convinced him that 'all texts are at once *permanence* and *diachrony*', that 'all is diachronic in the manifestation of meaning, except meaning itself (1966, 149). Greimas applied this principle to both the nature of narrative and the dual way in which every reader tackles a text. Thus, just as several kinds of time are involved in history, a text is a hierarchy of temporal structures (long-, middle- and short-term). Greimas starts from Tesnière's comparison of the proposition to a little drama, or *énoncé-spectacle*, which man as *homo loquens* performs continuously in infinitely varied situations. To the main 'roles' of Subject and Object, he adds the two poles of communication theory, the Sender and the Receiver. (The Sender is now interpreted as the originator of the values which determine the Object.) He finds rough equivalents in Propp's list of seven basic roles abstracted from the infinite variety of concrete characters in 100 Russian folktales, as well as in Souriau's list of six similar roles drawn from his corpus of French plays. He calls these *actants* (after Tesnière) and completes his own list by two subsidiary ones, the Helper and the Opponent.

Such general classes of characters are not tied to character in the traditional sense, that is, what we, in a given work (through an illusion which may be structural or historical) tend to constitute as persons conceived as adequate supports for all our emotions and projections.[3] An actant can be manifested in an actual story by several characters (who all oppose, help or are sought by the subject, for instance) and similarly, the same character can represent, say, two actants.[4]

No sooner had Greimas decided on his list of six actants than, in a way which recalls the whole atmosphere of Barthes's early career, he applied it to the 'drama' of the intellectual in society, as seen by a classical philosopher and by a Marxist:

	Classical philosopher	*Marxist*
Subject	Philosopher	Man
Object	World	Classless society
Sender	God	History
Receiver	Mankind	Mankind
Opponent	Matter	Bourgeoisie
Helper	Spirit	Working class

It would be interesting to rewrite the latter thematization, in which, significantly, the role of the party apparatus is the 'unsaid' or 'unthought', first with the specifications brought by Althusser, then as it now appears after the wave of disillusionment which has led practically every Communist French intellectual to write an explanatory autobiography in the last few years. The two applications to philosophy and politics show that the model is very general and can be centred on various 'thematic forces', in Souriau's own terms; the main force in the first one is the desire to know, and in the second, the desire to help mankind.

Greimas has applied his narrative structures to discourses which few people before him had thought of taking as narratives. In *Sémantique structurale*, he considers interviews, showing how the answers, freely worded by the subjects, can easily be analysed in terms of his 'actantial model' since they are already moulded, so to speak, in mythical form in spite — or because — of the fact that the topic discussed in this case was company investments. The Subject-Hero is the investor, whose Object is the salvation of the firm (often described as a child protected against the threats of the external world); the Opponent is scientific and technical progress which destroys the existing equilibrium; the Helper's role is played by preparatory studies, and above all by the flair and the intuition of the tycoon. The Sender is the economic system, which entrusts the hero, by an implicit contract, with the mission of saving the future of the enterprise; and the Receiver is the enterprise itself or rather, its ability to make a profit, since, unlike what happens in folktales, such a hero is disinterested and never seeks any rewards for himself.

The same model has since been applied to cooking recipes and to Destutt de Tracy's theory of intellectual faculties in *Eléments d'idéologie*, an early nineteenth-century text on signs and languages analysed by Rastier. Objects and abstract entities can be actants too; Don Juan's fiancée or her convent can both play the part of opponent, and the same applies, for instance, to the timidity of a character.[5] These roles are not always explicit, and their identification is not mechanical, just as the interpretation of a Fashion utterance was not always easily cast in terms of the general matrix suggested by Barthes. This is the answer to those who allege that this sort of study fails to be 'interesting' in that it reduces the infinitely varied human drama to the basic plot of the *énoncé-spectacle*. This complaint, which used to be so often made about psycho-analysis, misses the point that one does not *start* from this basic story. One (sometimes) *arrives* there, if the tale full of sound and fury, told by the symptoms and reported by an uncomprehending patient, ends by making sense; this will have occurred with the aid of the interpretations offered by the analyst who, at every stage, tries to supply a level of *vraisemblable* acceptable to the analysand, clothing the same structure in various 'realizations' or 'manifestations' until the analysand can hear the voice of his own desire (see Boons, 1968). Greimas often alludes to Barthes's work, and retrospectively one can hear in *Mythologies* the nuance of heroic-comic mockery produced by discrepancy between the homely character of the 'heroes' and the mythical tone adopted by ad men, as in the epic of Dirt attacked by Detergents or the tale of how the Pores were saved from Grease by Tonic Lotion.

From sentence to text

Propp found that in his corpus of 100 folktales the seven roles took on thirty-one 'functions', or typical actions, such as 'departure' or 'villainy'. These appeared in the actual text as a variety of variants and motifs; for instance, a 'kidnapping' could be materialized by a dragon abducting the king's daughter. Moreover, these functions always appeared in the same order, although they were not always present in the same tale. What Propp thereby lost in combinative power he gained in accuracy by adopting the sequence instead of relying, as earlier theorists had done, on atomistic conceptions of the folktale, where motifs and subjects were taken as primary indecomposable elements. When Barthes wrote 'Racinian Man', narrative analysis thus had to proceed by induction from a corpus if it wished to simplify the outline of plots in order to understand and classify them. However, Barthes's study already contains something like the 'homological hypothesis' he explains in his 1966 'Introduction to the structural analysis of narratives', which postulates the 'homological' relationship already mentioned between the grammar of the sentence and that of the discourse, since both, at different levels, are more than the sum of their components. This hypothesis may well be grounded on the fact that perception, action and language are structured by a common experience. After Greimas, the way was paved for a systematic application of syntactic theories to narrative. One can recognize in discourse the categories of the verb (tense, aspects, modes, persons) and of the subject (agent, patient), and Jakobson had pointed out (as Barthes notes), that the co-ordination within a discourse already implied relations between sentences. Barthes's article in *Communcations* 8 shows how Chomsky's 'standard theory' was integrated into this existing framework. The idea of a deep and a surface structure for a sentence lent itself readily to explaining the difference between actants and characters; and even though Barthes later dissociated himself from the whole enterprise, many attempts have been made to constitute text-grammars. Obviously, the problems which occupy linguists at present tend to reappear at the discursive level; this applies in particular to the most momentous, the articulation of semantics and syntax. (As discussion can become very confused when one projects one model onto another — as in the case of *sign* and *myth structure* in 'Myth Today' — one wishes theorists would adopt a clear terminology.) The main question which confronts narrative grammar is the number of the levels one must postulate 'below' the apparent surface, which is language in the case of literature but could be iconic, gestural, etc. Whether a single 'discursive manifestation' can be postulated for all substances (which means that one must supply a theory of how they become specified in a given work of art), or whether the mechanism is different in all of them, can only be settled by concrete research, since the arguments on both sides are inconclusive or contradictory.

The articulation between semantics and syntax is fundamental for the grammar of both sentence and discourse, requiring an elucidation of their articulation with logic and pragmatics. This issue also affects the decision as to which model to borrow from linguistics; the main criticism of Chomsky's theory (even in its latest state) concerns the absoluteness of the disjuncture between a deep structure which is a purely syntactic skeleton (generated by base rules) and the semantic aspect or component of the grammar which is purely interpretative. The partisans of the theory known as 'generative semantics', on the contrary, would do without the syntactic deep structure and go straight from the base to the semantic component. *Their* deep structure is both syntactic and semantic; but this semantic element is not made of words (or lexemes), but of semantic primitives which are perhaps universal and whose transformations explain the different meanings a surface item can have. Unlike Chomsky's, this deep structure also contains logical aspects — suited to natural not artificial languages. All those who, more or less intuitively, tackled the grammar of narrative came upon this problem.

When Lévi-Strauss reviewed Propp's book, he reproached him with neglecting the 'surface' of the text, pointing out that we never come into direct contact with the fundamental roles or functions — they remain 'immanent' — but with manifest characters. This desire to account for the whole of the text is the reason that Lévi-Strauss's own analyses are purely semantic, although Greimas has tried to give them a syntactic component, just as he tried to give mobility to Propp's 'actions' by reducing them to a small, finite number of oppositions which can then be combined to produce individual situations. But Propp, only a few years after his first book, was already trying to specify the main roles and to connect them to their surface manifestation by taking into account the historical and literary expectations of readers. Greimas, in order to cope with this problem, has suggested an intermediate level between that of the actants and that of the characters or actors: the level of the roles, which are anonymous and social (e.g. the godmother in folktales). An actor, by contrast, is a unit of both the syntax and the semantics of narrative, and is the locus of the manifestation of discursive and narrative structures.

Claude Bremond, one of the first analysts of narrative, has objected to this idea, showing that in some cases one can make do with only two levels, characters and roles (1973). He has, however, joined others in trying to supply something which also seems to be indispensable in linguistics: some 'meaning postulates' which are to be located in the deep structure, alongside the logical form of the sentence. These postulates would make explicit links of inference or truth between the atomic elements of meaning. Where are these postulates to be found? A priori universals are one possibility, and Bremond has accordingly tried to decompose each action into an occasion, a performance and a consequence for instance. This may seem to lead to an infinite regress, since what is an action for one person — say, writing a book — may be only a preparation for action for another, as in the case of Proust's narrator. The point is that different works do not share out experience in the same way, and one learns only by comparing works (as one compares words in semantics) or by comparing them to the reader's expectations.

Alternatively, Bremond and others have also tried to specify the meaning of a work by taking into account restrictions due to the ideology specific to a period or group of readers. A rule which says that merit calls for recompense and demerit for punishment can be a component of the 'moral tale', although the content of 'merit' can naturally vary. Thus, components which at first seem of very limited scope may very well be suited to the particular corpus chosen. The kind of theoretical problem involved here has to be grasped before one makes the commonsensical objections which, presumably, must have occurred to those who proposed such distinctions. To repeat it again: it is the problem of universals of meaning, and of the way in which a link between the deep and surface structures of the text *and* between these and the actualization of the latter as words, pictures, etc. can be conceived. A typology of genres and a 'discursive dictionary' which would be an inventory of configurations and motifs must be envisaged, but is a very complex task. So far, there have been many interesting suggestions, but these do not have the finality of proofs.

Isotopies: the production of meaning

Greimas has also proposed a notion which plays a part in accounting for the organization of meaning in the text: that of isotopy, or level of coherence, which gives the text cohesion at the semantic level in addition to its syntactic links. An isotopy regroups all the semes which are related (and remain immanent) in the manifest words (or lexemes). Barthes mentions this notion in his article on narrative and had already used it in *Critique et vérité* in order to show that literary texts can bear several meanings simultaneously; everyday communication, which mostly aims at being univocal and unambiguous, sometimes cannot avoid misinterpretations and misunderstandings, resulting from the hearer's having selected the wrong isotopy, until the context straightens out the meaning. Jokes rely on this sort of occurrence and Freud extended it to dreams, slips of the tongue, etc. It is therefore an inevitable consequence of the loose structure of human language, which is the source of its ability to cope with any meaning. Ethnomethodology has shown that meaning and communication are the result of labour in all cases, and not only in that of the modern text (as Barthes said, citing Greimas, in answer to Picard's mythical ideas on 'clarity', *CV*,54).

The reader, if he is to make sense of his reading, must perform operations both from the linear, left-to-right point of view — where suspense is generated and resolved — and from the tabular point of view which reconstitutes the underlying structure, by sifting and assessing the units of information as he goes along. Of course Barthes came, especially after 1960, to value strategies which prevented meaning from reaching what he calls 'idyllic communication', occurring without irrelevant 'noise'. This disruptive interference is actually treated as information by him in *S/Z*. The result is called by him a 'cacography' (on the model of cacophony) because he realizes how frustrating such an uncertain text is to the lazy reader, who is patronizingly presented as a lover of beautiful stories, but one who loves these stories once and discards them afterwards in favour of a newer one. Only an enduring structural relationship with the text, a reading which must be at once the 'first' and the 'last' or 'latest' reading, can save this Don Juan from monotony and the text from banality (*S/Z*,15-16). Semantic ambiguity was still assumed to generate insecurity in *Système de la Mode* (286), although the euphoric effects of Fashion rhetoric, which reconciles the twin aspirations of identity and freedom in choice of personality were duly noted. Fashion is in this akin to poetry, which also sublimates differences, although poetry achieves this effect through a genuine synthesis whereas Fashion can only do it through a 'loss of memory' which, in the last analysis, makes its lexicon a mere illusion. This syncretism, in Barthes's later career, of two very different ways of handling meaning may be an index of what is finally unsatisfactory in his stance, to the reader and perhaps to himself.

Let us see the concept of isotopy in use by means of an example borrowed from the Groupe μ (1977, 230-46). They take a couplet by P.J. Toulet, which may not be poetry of the first order but at least shows how complex the play of isotopies can be:

> Etranger, je sens bon. Cueille moi sans remords:
> Les violettes sont le sourire des morts.
> (Stranger, I smell sweetly. Pick me without remorse:
> Violets are the smile of the dead.)

Sixteen pages and several diagrams are needed to deal with the meaning. A broad philological knowledge is assumed (considerations on epigrams or traditional images of death); the rhythm and punctuation as well as phonetic aspects all yield information. The meaning of the couplet is ambiguous because we do not know the circumstances or the identity of the speaker, and because of a causal structure whose elliptic character permits several interpretations. The authors find four isotopies, each of which they designate by a single substantive. The first is 'Flower' and is built from words like *smell sweetly, pick, violets*. The second isotopy, 'Death', comes into being owing to the single word *morts* and it proves to be the most productive one in the poem. The connotations it generates do not destroy the first isotopy, and one reason for this is that it coexists with the third, 'Love'.[6] The fourth isotopy, designated as 'Logos', includes everything which can be construed as communication, signal or message. It has become more and more explicit in modern literature — outstandingly in some poems of Mallarmé or Valéry, which are metaphors of the writing act — and would include here all the marks of the process of enunciation, or speech act, left in the text. We note that the constitution of these successive isotopies requires more and more complex operations on the part of the reader. The important thing to remember is that ambiguities are not dispelled by analysis. It is therefore polemical to assert, as the semanalysts do, that other approaches differ from theirs in aiming to reduce all tensions and ensure the iron rule of a norm. Quite the reverse is the case; this type of structural analysis has revealed ambiguities where literary ideologies, disguised as scholarship and the expert's intuition, used to brush them aside. It is true that one has to choose a meaning for a moment in order to make it exist; but such decisions do not erase the trace of other rival interpretations, and although these are limited in number at any given moment and in some readers' intentions, any text disposes in principle of the infinity of the code in a 'productive' reading.

System and deconstruction

Barthes's article on the structural analysis of narratives is a case in point; it will be read here through our two usual cipher-grids, his scientific urge and his existential quest. From the first point of view, it still has considerable epistemological interest, although it is necessary to complete it with the recent conclusions of other workers in the field. Starting with his by now familiar 'Saussurean' gesture, which accepts the limitations of the scientific attitude and thereby hopes to achieve a manageable object, Barthes shows how the 'homological hypothesis' offers a many-sided model. In particular, linguistics suggests not simply that narrative should also be studied at different levels, but that meaning can only be grasped as the product of them all. The controversy as to the number of levels under the linguistic surface had not yet occurred, and perhaps Barthes does not sufficiently distinguish the top level of the narrative structure from its linguistic realization. Other indications in the text, however, suggest how he might have resolved it: a later section (*IMT*,119) shows how the linguistic substance seems to be incomparably freer than any other as to what distortions, expansions and omissions can be introduced at the final stage: time is stretched out in suspense, or a lengthy episode is collapsed into a few words.

The difference, originally derived from Benveniste's observations, between the *story* (*histoire* or *diegesis*, a Platonic and Aristotelian term suggested by Souriau and now adopted) and the *discourse*, where such distortions occur, is indispensable here, although each term has to be characterized with care. Todorov shows that even the story is not the faithful, 'denoted' sequence of events most people *think* they give when asked to summarize a film or novel. Like a police report, it is in fact a kind of projection (which, for instance, does not respect an accurate chronology) embodying a kind of logic we find *vraisemblable*.[7]

The units of the story have to be found according to a semantic criterion, and Barthes uses the concept of *function*, defined by the Russian formalists (especially Tomashevski) as a correlation: buying a revolver has as its correlate the moment when one uses it. If this does not take place, the information against the context of this expectation has to be reclassified, to become an index of the characters or atmosphere, rather than what he calls a *kernel* or *cardinal function*, which indicate the two poles of an action. We see here that the word *function* has two genealogies (added here, no doubt, to Chomsky's *kernel sentences*); the second comes from Hjelmslev, and had been used by Barthes in *Système de la Mode* in connection with the problem which modern semantics has as yet failed to solve — of giving a strict structuration of paradigms. Yet this is not so crippling because all that is necessary to suggest a meaningful order is the notion of two definite poles, between which an indeterminate number of intermediary terms can be interpolated.

This process is called by Hjelmslev *catalysis*; it makes the cohesion between the terms more or less explicit. (Barthes also used this notion in *S/Z*.) For instance, a string of narrative actions which together can be called 'kidnapping' (since 'to read, is to name', *S/Z*,29) can be decomposed into the elements which each author chooses to make explicit (as against Bremond's a priori classification). Balzac in *Sarrasine* (the text analysed in *S/Z*) chooses the following (here expressed in Barthes's metalanguage): 1. decision and plans; 2. preliminary information; 3. recruiting accomplices; 4. arrangements made; 5. rapid means of escape; 6. gathering of the accomplices; 7. ambush; 8. the victim's innocent departure; 9. the act itself; 10. journey; 11. arrival at the hide-out. Some of these elements are essential; if they were lacking, one would not be speaking about a kidnapping at all. The others simply indicate that an episode is unfolding — although the wealth of such indications is also a tell-tale index of Balzac's classic Realism and they are called by Barthes *catalysers*, following Hjelmslev.

Kernels, catalysers, indices and informants (minor indications which also reinforce the reality-effect) account for the whole surface of the text; there is no noise. Another admired accomplishment, for realist novelists, used to be the ability to make the same unit of information perform several duties. Barthes, who admires the theory of the four meanings (*CV*,51 and above, Chapter 6, *n* 2), is very scathing about its modern equivalent. The reason is no doubt because it reinforces the realist illusion instead of pluralizing the meaning so that this phenomenon, now described as a tyrannical force, cannot take place or is indefinitely postponed (*S/Z*,154).

For this is the crux. We find a second meaning in the 'Introduction to the structural study of narratives', and one which deconstructs the first. It affirms the kinship of literature and language, not structurally this time, but ontologically: they both negate reality. We have seen how fashion was reduced to written fashion, and the latter to comments on an image (which therefore do not have to make one 'see'), and how finally this conclusion was extrapolated even to texts which are not adjuncts to images or objects. In the same way Barthes is at pains here to stress that suspense, for instance, is an experience for the mind, not a gut-reaction (*IMT*,119) even, it seems, when it causes 'anguish and pleasure'. The world ends up in a beautiful book, as Mallarmé wanted; but he is made to say that what happens in that book is 'nothing' (*IMT*,124).

Such affirmations were widely interpreted, even at the time, as expressions of Barthes's personal myth. He needed to prove this emptiness of meaning, yet to affirm at the same time that this is superior to an enjoyment of life pure and simple. Such are the consolations of having invested all one's emotions in language (*T*,99), achieved, according to Freud's *Beyond the Pleasure Principle* through the hard apprenticeship of loneliness. Once this second meaning is grasped, the plan of the text assumes a new importance. Barthes is determined at all cost to show that each of the levels of the structural analysis of narrative is incomplete; the level of the functions leads to that of the actants or characters (who are further demoted by *not* giving their name to the section, entitled 'The Actions'); the level of the characters leads to that of narration (in complete contradiction with the main hypothesis, which states that the stratum of the story is what remains permanent whatever the substance and its handling). The latter in turn leads to a consideration of the whole system of narrative, which then retrospectively spreads its meaning over all its components, so that the meaning is not 'at the end', as the law of suspense suggests, but pervades the whole system (*IMT*,87).

But does it? Barthes uses all the means at his disposal in *S/Z* to diffuse meaning and make it 'reversible'; but the other tendency is visible here in 'Introduction to the structural analysis of narratives' when he discusses Poe's *Purloined Letter* (*IMT*,87), a text which Lacan had found to exemplify the directionality of meaning. The conception of narrative suggested by Bremond was a series of choices, an arrow oriented from left to right as in the model information theory calls a Markov chain (where what happens is determined by what has happened before), and this is the very model adopted by Lacan. Appealing to Barthes's awareness of responsibility, it was adopted by him, christened with an Aristotelian term, *proairesis*, and used again in *S/Z*. This is fundamentally the model of structural linguistics, which Chomsky demonstrated could not, taken by itself, account for embedded sentences. One cannot help feeling that this earlier ideology was more dramatic, Pascalian and existentialist, more attuned to Barthes's representation of the formation of meaning and the responsibility it carries. Two observations follow from this.

The first concerns the sheer fact of actualizing meaning through a medium, writing, which is 'fatally definite'. The other concerns the consequent ethical questions. As *Degree Zero* had already stated, 'the novel is a death'. And the second meaning of the article on narrative does come 'at the end'. Barthes tells us that the genesis of narrative is shrouded in as much obscurity as that of language; but a hypothesis about both can reasonably be made: narrative developed at the same time as monologue, which succeeds dialogue. It is at the same age, when he is about three, that the child — significantly called *le petit de l'homme*, the male offspring of man, so to speak — 'invents' simultaneously the sentence, narrative and the Oedipus complex (*IMT*,124). A curious article on 'Flaubert and the sentence' (*NEC*), written just after his summary of structural research on the narrative, offers a comment on the link between the Oedipal crisis and the sentence, while shedding light on the thought processes of a Saussure or a Mallarmé, who shared a similar inhibition before the blank sheet of paper. Barthes also has his inhibitions, but they are expressed through his theories and discourse. He first observes that, of the two French writers who are famous for sequestering themselves for the sake of their art, one, Proust, locked himself up because he had a lot to say, while the other, Flaubert, did the same thing because he had a lot to cross out. As shown by his correspondence, Flaubert did not mind the mountainous difficulties of organizing the episodes of major novels (this was just 'tedious') but suffered from a mysterious unease due to a peculiar experience of language. In order to explain it, Barthes first sketches a typology of the corrections authors can bring to their texts.

They can either substitute (vertically) one word for another, or they can suppress, condense and expand (horizontally). But the axes of paper are also those of language. The first type of correction is metaphorical, paradigmatic (metaphors here include contrast, as in the psychology of associations); the second is metonymic, since it affects the whole chain, and includes either ellipsis or catalysis. These three types of alteration have neither the same structural possibilities nor the same status in the traditional idea of writing. There substitution is limited to terms which have affinities; ellipsis must eventually stop at the cell of the sentence, the group subject-predicate. But augmentations have no limit, as shown by Martinet's notion of *expansion*, and the Chomskyan view of the sentence. The sentence can multiply embedded parts, be expanded *ad infinitum*, and forced to stop only because of physical or literary constraints, that is, at the level of performance. The writer, when he writes a sentence — and this is the unit constantly mentioned by Flaubert — thus experiences the infinite freedom of speech.

And indeed classical treatises on style recommended only substitutions and ellipses (the latter, mysteriously, being supposed to make language clearer); augmentative corrections are found only in Rousseau or Stendhal, classical writers in Barthes's definition, but in another sense, Romantic rebels. As for Flaubert, he bore two crosses. The first concerned the repetition of words. He often substituted one word for another in order to avoid the recurrence of a phonic shape. Although this operation is limited in principle, he gave it the sense of a dizzily infinite correcting; the difficulty was to find the *place* where the correction had to be inserted. Repetitions that were not perceived one day were perceived the next. This insecurity fixated on *hearing* reminds one of Saussure hearing in his anagrams a 'language within language'. Barthes himself was taken with *Les mots sous 'les mots*, Starobinski's title for his edition of Saussure's *Anagrams*. Barthes often paraphrases it as 'hearing voices within voices' or 'the body under the body'. We can understand why: he too started out by hearing messages within messages.

Flaubert's second problem concerned the articulations and transitions of discourse. For a writer who hoped to reabsorb the content into the form, it was natural enough that logical transitions should be experienced as stylistic problems. What had to be obtained was fluidity, an optimal rhythm of speech, in fact the *flumen orationis*. He was here again 'caught in the infinity of the syntagm'; the 'good' syntagm achieved a balance between excessive constriction and dilatation, between ellipsis and 'unscrewing' (as he said) its results. What makes one reel is that there is no conceivable sanction; though the corrective protocols are coded, their application is uncertain. We saw Barthes's emphasis on 'the pace', 'the delivery', where he located, in *Degree Zero*, both maximal individuality and maximal success. Michelet similarly complained about the demands of what for him was the mark of the writer, namely 'the ear', the internal representation of the point of coincidence with what one seeks to render, something far more extensive than the *mot juste*. Rhythm and number are the best approximations, and the joint theories of Kristeva and Benveniste supplied a substratum to this intuition, as is shown by the article on Schumann's obsessive scansion ('Rasch', 1975e) which Barthes contributed to the Festschrift for the eminent linguist.

By making the sentence at once a 'unit of style, a unit of work and a unit of life', Flaubert conferred a metaphysical meaning on it. The reassuring rhetoric of the classical age had just expired, confronting the writer with the anguish of law-making and the assumption of freedom. Yet Mallarmé's *Coup de dés* (Dice-Throw) would soon be explicitly founded on this freedom of phrastic expansion, thus pointing to the meaning, strong but empty, of the *livre à venir*, the utopian idea of the Book. Mallarmé thus acts as guide towards the utopian fusion of method and fiction, of the 'I' and the 'he', under the aegis of language.

The second observation is suggested by Barthes's similar conflation of meanings between the sentence and human life, considered in its three relations, for-itself, for-others, for-death. This is exemplified in the hiatus between what we conceive of as persons and the grammatical person in language. As Barthes points out, the traditional construction of character involves projecting a person behind the linguistic surface, but this can never be reduced to the kind of 'point of view' by which some modern writers let the reader in on things which only that character can know and see. This technique actually functions not as a deepening but as a limitation, even more so in the case of the still more recent technique of the first person narrative in the *caméra-je* or *caméra-stylo* which shows on the screen only what a certain character can see. Instead we need a mixture of personal and apersonal elements. If this is a construct, so is what we experience as an objective '*histoire*'.

Barthes has shown on the other hand how the level of narration can take extreme liberties with this underlying level of the story, by lengthening or shortening events, by hiding or revealing them. Yet there are limits: when, say, Agatha Christie uses this freedom to hide the murderer behind a first person narrator, Barthes sternly accuses her of 'cheating', and contrasts her lack of integrity with the ethical rigour of the modernists. This again gives the game away. Barthes *still* thinks in terms of the problematics of freedom and responsibility, and this is shown by his final remarks — the Oedipal genesis of story-telling is linked to a responsibility towards the reader whose faith in the writer's truth makes the story possible.

Valéry notes that novels and dreams have a formal similarity: all their deviations are part of the genre. This is exactly what Barthes thinks is wrong with structural analysis, as he told R. Bellour just after completing his article on the structural analysis of narrative. In place of these norms and deviations, Barthes instead dreams of a theory for which this distinction would be simply irrelevant. Barthes (at the same time as Foucault and Sollers) wrote a preface to Pierre Guyotat's *Eden, Eden, Eden*, a book which consists of one single sentence. He claimed the book reduced criticism to mute complicity because it turned the sentence into a substance, and representation into an unrelenting, inextricable mixture of flesh and language (1970c). Not all critics were struck dumb though; Sollers himself said about a later work by Guyotat that only psychoanalysis can deal with this type of text, which makes us realize how threatening this approach could become for the later Barthes. In *The Pleasure of the Text* the sentence, instead of representing the maximal point of freedom between the strictly coded lower units of the language and the code of narrative which structural analysis was fast erecting around the hounded writer, has become the enemy.

In a way which must have disconcerted not a few readers, Barthes's reaction against the sentence often takes the form of an unspecified attack on Chomsky, the joint causes being his stress on the sentence and perhaps his political stance (since we saw that Barthes was in fact no libertarian). Benveniste's opposition between symbolic and semiotic also permitted a rejection of Lacan's oppressive phallicism and his ambiguous use of the notion of castration. The latter denotes the symbolic renunciation of immediate pleasure which is the price paid for admission into society, but often sounds like a barely disguised wish directed at Lacan's opponents or even all interlocutors. The hypostasized sentence, a reified object which cannot be tampered with, and the law of social exchange based on castration provoke in *The Pleasure of the Text* a sullen yet aggressive withdrawal into the inarticulate inner speech of Jakobson's aphasiacs, who could no longer handle connections and regressed to a 'word-heap'. But we know from *Degree Zero* that the Word is truly poetic only when by its own lexematic richness it abolishes all dependency on its brothers and neighbours and shines forth as a promise of infinite possibilities, a 'word erect'. Whoever misses the significance of this challenge of the father's erection, which is ridiculed, by the son leaning triumphantly on the theories of a woman, has not yet learnt to use the Nietzchean 'third ear' to which Lacan often refers, and should read more of the latter for practice. This reading is better, at any rate, than the uncomprehending dismissal which this enigmatic chain of associations has evoked from some critics.

But what is really wanted is not only theory, not only a new way of reading, but a practice which, uniting both, would make the distinctions between sending and receiving, form and meaning, writing and criticism irrelevant, as in the symbol chosen by Lacan, the Moebius strip, which is at once inside and outside. What is wanted is dislocation of the text and of oneself in the same movement: what Barthes attempted to do in *S/Z* and what the experience of writing it did to him. As in the case of the shock he received from Japan, on which he wrote the delightful *L'Empire des signes*, he was put *en situation d'écriture*. This phrase does not so much require translation as a similar dislocating commentary, for it seeks to convey the disorientation which creativity implies, and the pleasure which is its indicator. Mallarmé's own version of this, *Coup de dés*, was described by Valéry, when he saw its typography for the first time, as the sky full of stars. The starting point of this cosmogony is therefore called, in *S/Z*, the 'starred text' (*S/Z*,13) — an apt simile since the constellations we 'read' in the sky are purely a product of a selection due to the perceptual laws of vision at a given point in the universe and the psychological disposition to seek meaningful shapes.

14

The starred text

Despite the mythological atmosphere which envelops the later part of Barthes's career, we can see that there was no 'mutation' as far as his theories are concerned. What he essentially sought after 1960, in his own research and the ideas of other thinkers, was a theory which would effectively underpin his doctrine of literature; he switched allegiances quite a few times in order to ensure this. The importance of what is metaphysically at stake in *S/Z* can be gauged by the many occasions on which it has been invoked here as an explanation of much earlier aspects of Barthes's work. This is an example of what Lacan calls the life in the future anterior, the tense which (in Kristeva's words) marks the passage of the subject in his discourse. The criticisms which follow, therefore, apply more to the *doxa* of epigones who consider *S/Z* in isolation rather than within the wider context of Barthes's work. It is my belief that the full meaning of *S/Z*, the philosophy which underpins it, was in fact developed only later, in *The Pleasure of the Text*. The latter work, incidentally, was also interpreted superficially, as a new variation on the theme of classical versus modern. I will argue that *The Pleasure of the Text* does indeed rest on a dual foundation, but one which is both deeper and more subtle than its updated versions, the opposition between *lisible* and *scriptible*, or *work* and *text*.

Is *S/Z*, as we sometimes read, a book whose form supersedes earlier approaches to literature, surpassing in particular the structural analysis of narratives and the use of models taken mostly from linguistics, that is, from science? Barthes certainly intended it to be so; but his reasons may not be ours. Just as the defence of structural analysis involved an attack on traditional approaches to texts, the emphasis on the reading experience, to which *S/Z* is all too often reduced, involves an attack on structural analysis. One wonders how far Barthes realized that this reduction to a new New Criticism, should it win the day, would not only stamp out structuralism but even more surely the notions Barthes wished to defend — plurality, intertextuality, productive reading, the infinity of codes.

S/Z is like Descartes's *Cogito*. It *is* in fact Barthes's own *Cogito: I think, therefore I am* acquires a meaning only when each of us pronounces it for himself. Barthes's solution is an answer to a problem which may not be universal; we cannot simply take it on lock, stock and barrel. As a theoretical gesture, it can never be repeated, even by its own author. It is in any case imperative not to treat *S/Z*'s mode of analysis as an unchangeable form: Barthes himself shows the way in his later study of Poe's *Case of Mr Valdemar*, where the reading is organized by different codes from the reading of Balzac's *Sarrasine*. *S/Z* came out in 1970, the same year as *L'Empire des signes*, and these two texts, which each in its own way exemplified the sensuous and systematic sides of their author, also represented two of the many strategies he used in his assault on univocal meaning, or perhaps meaning altogether.

Bataille (1970) had praised *Sarrasine* as 'one of the summits' of the Balzacian oeuvre despite being only a little-known short story. We can understand why when we compare it to Bataille's own stories, which are full of what Barthes praised as 'impossible' situations, transgressions of sexual and textual taboos. Bataille attempted to connect mysticism with a theory of the universe, of generalized exchange. *Sarrasine* has something to offer on both planes, if one is willing to ignore its novelettish nuance in order to apprehend its force, the 'symbolic extra-vagance' which Barthes appreciated (*GV*,71) but which has put off some commentators. It describes an eighteenth-century sculptor, Sarrasine, who is wholly absorbed in his art but never satisfied by it for reasons similar to Flaubert's obsession with the organic unity of the *flumen orationis*: the parts do not coalesce into a living whole. He goes to Rome, sees and hears a prima donna, la Zambinella, whose voice has those very qualities. Ignorant of the existence of castrati, he falls in love with what he assumes is a beautiful woman. The statue he makes of her satisfies him at last and allows him to reach the summit of his art. When told the truth, he seeks a confrontation with the castrato (whose name, 'the little leg', is an ironic allusion to what he has lost, in a Lacanian reading) in order to kill him but is himself killed by the henchmen of Zambinella's protector, a jealous cardinal. This story is itself recounted — within the story *Sarrasine* — at a party given by the wealthy Lanty family, to a young woman mystified by the sight of a repulsive elderly man she sees there. The narrator is a man who hopes to exchange the pleasure thus given for a night of love. But the old man is none other than the beautiful Zambinella. The portrait which the young woman noticed at the Lantys' was copied from Sarrasine's statue, and the origin of the family's wealth is the immense fortune of their relative, the former castrato. This revelation produces an effect opposite to what was intended; the young woman is 'contaminated' by castration, and does not fulfil her part of the bargain.

Sarrasine had first been analysed by one of Lacan's disciples, J. Reboul, and thus came to Barthes already overdetermined. But it is in addition almost embarrassingly appropriate for someone who, while purporting to deconstruct meaning, in fact leans on a synthesis of economics, psychoanalysis and linguistically-inspired literary theory ('Marx, Freud and Aristotle', *GV*,77) which, as we saw above, is much stronger as a field than any of its components would have been in isolation. Balzac's thematic and structural coherence testifies to an uncommon symbolic intuition on the part of an author who stands for Realism, and who could not have read in his own text all the implications available to a modern reader in touch with the contemporary human sciences. But perhaps realism in literature is 'imaginary', in the Lacanian sense, corresponding to an ideal of what reality is like and what realism should be, rather than to what so-called Realist writers actually did, which is a good deal more complicated and subtle. (Greimas has recently carried out a similar demonstration on a short story by Maupassant — Naturalism here revealing the same symbolic depth as Realism).

What are these critical *topoi*, these 'places' which many critics today take as starting-points for their demonstrations? In *S/Z* they include the action of discourse upon itself (the familiar structure of 'the tale within the tale') and upon life (since a story influences the fate of both teller and listener); the erotic dimension of writing (a story exchanged for sexual favours); the nature of classical representation, which refers to cultural prototypes in the name of nature; the genesis of myth-making in a refusal to face the truth, especially that of castration; the structure of capitalism, for Balzac, in revealing that the family's wealth rests not on feudal land ownership but on the fabulous wealth of a castrato, ultimately on absence, can thus be seen as indicting French Restoration society, propped on the universal floating of currencies, languages and contracts; finally, the possibility that a text can transcend the boundaries of nature, since the moment of recognition of the right gender to designate Zambinella can be postponed and the reader who savours a 'first' and 'last' reading at the same time can experience the 'impossible' coincidence of inner and outer truth when Sarrasine kisses Zambinella.

This moment is treated by Barthes as one of the summits of the story, and reminds one of a similar effect in an eighteenth-century novella, Cazotte's *Le Diable amoureux*. The hero of the story is asked by the woman he loves — who is really the devil in disguise — to kiss her while saying, 'My dear Beelzebub, I adore you.' For the devil is actually in love, and nothing but such a declaration can satisfy lovers. This strange case of performative utterance is pondered by Barthes with all the respect its mystery deserves in *A Lover's Discourse* (175, see also *RB*,112, 140); Lacan's notion of *jouissance*, or orgasmic ecstasy, as that which precisely cannot be voiced, since the loss of the archetypal love object is the founding moment of language, only increases the darkness in which the subject is shrouded. The lover in Cazotte pronounces the fatal sentence, whereupon the devil resumes his 'real' shape only to find that this particular contract, under such new conditions, is no more respected than the two love contracts in *Sarrasine*.[1]

How do such *topoi* emerge in *S/Z*? Here lies the originality of the book. It seeks not to yield a structure of the object text, but to produce a structuration in which text and metatext tend to merge. This, I repeat, is the metaphysical import Barthes wishes his essay to have; yet in fact, we have already seen that he not only makes these levels typographically distinctive, but concludes with tabulations and lists not very different from those of *Système de la Mode* and later expressed his satisfaction at seeing that his method did not obscure the larger structures of the work (*GV*,73). I think that not only are the two types of reading, linear and tabular, possible here, but that they must coexist, in order to provide the tension which produces meaning, and that the dual arrangement of the book proves this.

The fact remains, of course, that what is most striking in *S/Z* is the 'structuration' part, since literary studies had until then always stressed the structure. What Barthes objects to is the idea that the 'plan' of the work, the bare bones of the story, are deemed more important than all the 'flesh' which he now seeks to integrate; nothing in art is insignificant or meaningless. He therefore gives a reading 'in slow motion', where Balzac's text is divided empirically into 561 lexias, or units of reading. These are fragments of unequal length, whose sole purpose is to keep the number of overtones in each one manageable (four at the most). The choice of a piece of 'classical' prose makes this procedure legitimate; a modern text like Guyotat's *Eden, Eden, Eden* could not be subjected to such a treatment since the signifier has become to a great extent what it seeks to signify. Seymour Chatman's study of Joyce's *Eveline* (1969) may have provided a transition between the method advocated in Barthes's article on narrative and *S/Z*.

The analysis therefore bears on the signified, which is divided into five headings, or 'codes': 1. The code of actions, or *proairetic*, since we saw that Barthes sees actions as sequences which offer many possibilities for meaningful choice. 2. The *hermeneutic* code, made up of all the elements which serve to establish and solve riddles. 3. The quasi-quotations from the accepted knowledge or wisdom of the period, or *cultural* code(s) (Balzac is especially prone to such knowing asides, which are here effectively deflated by summaries such as: 'Ethnic psychology: the naive German/the mocking Parisian', or 'Passion and its abysses'. 4. The *semic* code, made up of qualities connoting characters or actions, often condensed by Barthes as neologisms (*sélénité, craintivité, pensivité*) as in *Mythologies*. These semes are shown to be unstable, migrating from one character to another; but where the concept of isotopy might find in this a factor of cohesion, Barthes wishes to demonstrate exactly the opposite. He stresses the fact that characters, places, actions and objects are thus dispersed and yield to the undifferentiated flicker of meaning; for the same reason they should not be regrouped thematically either. Finally there is 5, the *symbolic* code which it is even more imperative not to systematize, since the aim is to keep all the interpretations equal and thus cast doubt on there being any 'depth' or 'secret' in the text which could be revealed and named once and for all. The logic of symbol is multivalence and reversibility, the logic of dreams and fantasies.

The structuration is broken at crucial points by ninety-three very short chapters of commentary, which help to make the book lively and readable. The nature and status of the codes is further discussed there. Barthes makes use of several metaphors, as in *Critical Essays* when he tried to formulate his new doctrine of literature; the same ambiguity between the spontaneous order of nature and the arbitrary will of human beings is observed in both texts, as it is in the two types of fashion evolution. The text is said to pass through the network of these codes, which therefore must have existed before the text. Elsewhere, the codes are described as forces which seize hold of the text, or voices which are woven into it. These voices are given names: Voice of Empirics or experience, in the *proairetisms* (which we recognize from life because we have learnt them from art); Voice of the Person, in the semes (which shows that this notion is chiefly directed against the character); Voice of Science, in the cultural codes (which demotes not only commonsensical knowledge but science to hearsay); Voice of Truth, in the hermeneutisms (this truth is not that of symbol, but the mirage which makes us wish to learn the secret of origins in all matters, and which suspense manipulates); finally, Voice of the Symbol (*S/Z*, 17-21).

This last code is not the subject of commentary — the whole book is in fact its commentary; nonetheless this reticence has resulted in a good deal of mystification. The fact that for the first time Barthes referred globally to the intellectual 'intertext', instead of quoting chapter and verse when using one of the current *topoi*, also contributed to the uncertainty as to his purpose and achievement. As the commentary on the title tells us — it is placed at the heart of the book, as Chapter XLVII — the monogram 'S/Z', with its falsely symmetrical initials (those of the two protagonists, Sarrasine and Zambinella, and its reminder of Jakobsonian phonological oppositions, is itself a multi-faceted symbol. It refers to the production of meaning by binary oppositions, to the censorship Lacan sees in the stroke which separates the signifier from the signified, to the unbridgeable gap between nature and culture as epitomized in the contract (the incestuous overtone in the text was not exploited by Barthes as the theme of castration and death was, but it was noted by Lévi-Strauss (1979)). 'S/Z' symbolizes, at every level, the desire and the impossibility of going through the looking-glass: it is the rule which produces the structuration.

Can a structuration not produce a structure? Barthes advises against structuring the codes, each being 'a mirage of structures'; and against structuring the text by giving a hierarchy of the codes themselves. The order in which he deals with them, however (S/Z,17-21, and especially 261-3), shows a progression from the two codes in which the arrow of time cannot be stopped or reversed — the code of actions and that of riddles — towards those which deal with truth about the world and the person, leaving no question that the symbolic code is more equal than the others. The same bias recurs within the symbolic code itself. Centred on the body, which is the locus of the three equal 'entrances' to the symbolic, namely meaning, sex and creation, and finally money, it gives a privilege to the middle term, through which the other two are perceived. This is in a way built into the very use of Lacan's notion of castration as entrance into meaning and society, and epitomizes the transient power of psychoanalysis over Barthes at this period in his career. Thus all codes turn out to be cultural and are hence disparaged as stereotypes. Barthes does not distinguish a convention from a hypothesis: from his point of view, science is as bad as ideology. Yet the symbolic code, though contrasted with the other four, turns out to be simply the synthesis which has become the *vraisemblable* of our time.

In fact, Barthes often speaks about the symbolic not as a code, but as a *field*, though he does not hold to this distinction rigidly. The word 'code' has derogatory undertones in *S/Z*, referring to the schema of communication, whereas 'field' suggests the freedom to roam at will, which is the idea Barthes wants to foster. For what must be experienced is the polyphony of the voices, the possibilities they offer us to dream, digress and wander, by being perceived as 'an immense fading'. This term, which is used in telecommunications and was taken up by Lacan to denote the psychoanalytic concept of the vanishing of the subject, shows what is at stake in *S/Z*. Despite its source, it points to the transition between Barthes's allegiance to mainstream Lacanism and the more radical theses of *Tel Quel* writers, where (psycho)analysis is no longer seen as a psychology of the subject and the Other but as an access to the infinite permutations of a language without subject. The Oedipal crisis is then less important than the earlier 'mirror phase', the stage, described by Lacan, when the young child for the first time recognizes himself in a mirror and, comparing against his own lack of co-ordination, the ease with which this image copies his movements, conceives a permanent and alienating ideal self-image, albeit a flattering one. This, it will be remembered, was seen by Kristeva as similar to the imposition of a stable signifier onto the shifting pattern of experience. (See Kristeva 1980 for an even more drastic reorganization based on the notion of abjection.)

Strictly speaking, the *scriptible* text, when seen in terms of structuration, is not an object as such (although some texts contain more *scriptible* than others); it is *'ourselves writing'* (S/Z,5). Like the geno-text, it has to be created anew in each reader, the observer being part of the observed. Reading brings codes into being as needed, and cares little for completeness and exhaustiveness; indeed 'it is precisely because I forget [some codes, or some of the things which could also be said] that I read' (S/Z,11). We saw that Barthes contemplated a sixth code, called 'of schools and universities', which would list, in the traditional manner, the biographical elements deemed to be immediately relevant. He abandoned this polemical intention, but it would be interesting to compare the codes he used for *Mr Valdemar* with those used in *S/Z*. It cannot be done here because they do not seem to have the broad validity of the *S/Z* codes; for instance the *Valdemar* notes sometimes put on the same plane codes which seem to be sub-codes of those I have discussed. Of course, this seeming universality is difficult to interpret: it has deluded many people into thinking that Barthes was proposing new universal categories of literary experience; on the other hand, the codes used in connection with Poe do seem by and large to cover the aspects of life and the devices of art which we all fall back on eventually. Only concrete research — as Barthes suggests — would settle the matter. The question is: does he want it?

One part of him obviously does; quite apart from the necessity of earning one's living, the mark of pleasure is obvious in the study on Poe, for instance. It is absurd to reduce *S/Z* simply to an ingenious way of solving the problem of how to handle a lengthy stretch of prose, (as opposed to the fact that most close analyses are devoted to poems and have proportionately more space at their disposal), though it is of course also that. But Barthes's main purpose is not altruistic, for all the rousing appeals to the reader's freedom at the beginning. Whatever his enslavement by ideology, the reader is always free in a certain sense, and when an author announces that he is granting him freedom, he invariably means that he is going to browbeat him into putting in a lot of hard work. But what *S/Z* can do is show this reader how to rationalize a desire and an ability to deny his Oedipal self while affirming his pre-Oedipal one in extremely ingenious ways. Objectivity and subjectivity are dismissed at the outset (S/Z,10) as castrating forces which can take hold of the text but have no affinity with its plurality. They are defined as imaginary constructs, and no doubt there is such an image in all of us, made by ourselves and our time. But Barthes's reading is not meant to impose on the text his image of subjectivity: it *is* subjectivity. The subject is as ungraspable by himself as the reader is free: to announce that he is irrecoverable from the text (S/Z,10) invariably means that he is appearing at that very moment. And to offer as 'proof' of a reading its cohesion and durability, as was earlier the case in *Critical Essays*, surely makes an appeal to some kind of objectivity. It is impossible, as 'Myth Today' recognized long ago, to escape *both* objectivity and subjectivity *and* their signs. To try to do so is simply to aim the arrow of desire, which takes Subject towards Object, in an uncommon direction.

L'Empire des signes is one image of Barthes's utopian desire to solve the problem of signs and meaning. It is about an imaginary country, produced by 'selecting, somewhere in the world, a certain number of features . . . and, with them, deliberately forming a system'. The system functions on a single axis: centred/decentred, profound/superficial, spontaneous/ritualized, pairs of features that have long been recognized as equivalent. The first term applies to the West, with its oppressive 'semiocracy'; the second to an imaginary country which Barthes decides to call 'Japan'. In case this semiological opening seems too daunting, let it be stressed at once that this is one of the most readable of Barthes's books. It obviously belongs to the tradition represented by Voltaire's book on England and Madame de Staël's on Germany: it aims to castigate one's own country by means of a utopian portrait of another. But the utopia is also personal; it offers a haven of peace, not dissimilar to the vistas which classical society in *Degree Zero* — with the same feudal connotations — offers to the modernist exhausted by the responsibility of signs.

The Japanese meal, composed at random, and with no more centre to it than the Japanese capital; Japanese courtesy, as highly formalized as those elaborate packages containing mere trifles; the counterpoint of actions, voices and ancillary gestures in Bunraku puppetry; the haiku, intelligible but not amenable to Western classifications like concision, spontaneity, syllogism, metaphor; the 'calligraphy' of Japanese eyes, which is contrasted with the 'fire' and 'depth' valued in the West: all these are offered as pretexts for spiritual exercises.[2] But such utopian solutions cannot be practised at home; there, the only way is the laborious deconstruction of signs by means of the science of signs: the solution of pointing to the mask. Or is it? Perhaps the story does not finish there. The walnut, which in *Degree Zero* was meant to convey only itself, and the bean, which in *S/Z* is meant to convey all the stories of the world, may yet turn out to be aspects of the same elusive object of writing.

15

The body under the body

Ever sensitive to new theories, Barthes had constantly sought to integrate them into his doctrine of literature and his practice as a critic. And now, a few years after *S/Z*, these theories were marking time. Semanalysis had accomplished its critical task, and made many an unthinking semiologist aware of his own assumptions, and above all of the decision involved in adopting the scientific attitude. The naturalness of science, the supreme idol of the nineteenth century, had gone the way of all myths. The books written by the 'third generation' of structuralists began to appear in 1972 and 1973, indicating that a new paradigm had come into being; but the point on which everybody readily agreed was the lack of a proper theory of the subject and of history. A pervasive nihilism began to emerge, fostered by the desperate search for philosophical gadgets which marked the declining credibility of the philosophical enterprise, or at least of its old model — the hope for a discourse able to account for the totality of the truth, both intelligible and historical. The collapse of many political hopes was an obvious underlying factor. Unless, that is, one considers it evidence of progress to have the couturier Pierre Cardin go to present his new collection in China (which had twice offered misleading models to the West, first for the Enlightenment, then for 1968 Cultural Revolution) and enlighten the bemused Chinese in his turn by giving them this splendidly Barthesian definition: 'Fashion is what goes out of fashion.'

A first response to the state of intellectual play was what came to be known as 'the philosophy of desire', as embodied in Deleuze and Guattari's *Anti-Oedipus*.[1] Though it went out of its way not to criticize Lacan by name, it attacked his disciples on points of theory recognizably those of the master too. Soon the criticism became more explicit and gathered momentum from the general rebellion against all forms of power and 'mastery'. What F. Châtelet has called a 'bold renascence of scepticism' was combined with certain concrete forms appropriate to this new stress on freedom — chiefly stylistic experiment, a relaxation of sexual taboos and a rehabilitation of bodily pleasures — to provide a milieu which seemed custom-built for Barthes. *The Pleasure of the Text* is a typical product of this period, with its scepticism about the development of history, its sexual language, its questioning of all norms.

The opposition between pleasure and *jouissance*, on which *The Pleasure of the Text* is grounded, is both necessary and uncertain. For Lacan, pleasure is natural, gradual, extinguished both by deprivation and satiety; *jouissance* is the aim of desire, which comes from the discrepancy between an inarticulate need and the demand which articulates it in social language. Pleasure is organic, animal; *jouissance* is the fruit of the fundamental perversion which constitutes man. It is always new, disconcerting, unexpected; it can be satisfied only in transient and precarious fashion; its culmination, orgasm, is also a disappearance. But pleasure is also given cultural overtones, which complicates the picture. It then denotes an enjoyment fostered by a recognition of norms, an institutionalization of what was at first disorienting, while *jouissance* negates any kind of cultural maturation and cuts across social images of eroticism by ignoring the protocols surrounding nudity or 'erogenous zones' (a phrase which Barthes finds boring, probably because it amounts to a structural analysis of the body!). *Jouissance* is essentially individual and unpredictable. But what provides yet another source of tension between the two key terms is that in common parlance *jouissance* might very well be continuous with pleasure and not its converse. Moreover, as Barthes observes, desire, from which *jouissance* comes, appears to be a class-based idea; 'the people' (in his idea at least) only know pleasures, not the fashionable harping on a Desire which is essentially impossible to satisfy (*PT*,58).

The Pleasure of the Text was duly interpreted as theory by respectful disciples, and rightly so since it tries to unite the latest ideas about the generation of the text as seen in psycholinguistics and literary theory with Barthes's own life-long intuitions. But it was theory with a difference, and posed some problems to those who could not change registers as nimbly as Barthes himself and were not used to speaking of the strip-tease of the text, or of modernity as a body excitingly glimpsed where the classical garment leaves gaps. The sexual figures of the book would be weak if they were mere conceits; but they are meant to apply at all levels, social, sexual and literary, and to play their part in the deflation of values which were also those of *S/Z*. These values are all seen as part of a constellation which can be called Oedipal, or even phallic. Pleasure (or *jouissance*: at their most innovative, the two notions are synonymous in the text, *PT*,19, 30) is not impressed by violence, muscle, heroism; it resists even the subject's wish to dazzle and to please. Commonplace sadism, the rational sentences which are the staple of linguistics, conventional narrative where satisfaction is carefully erected, are all deflated in favour of the idiosyncratic cuts and foreshortenings which each individual practises in secret on the body of the world. Pleasure is fickle but stubborn, like reality itself; it is a veritable *epoche* which reveals the essence of the latter (*PT*,7, 18, 65).

If we follow this principle of pleasure, it supplies, like the *scriptible* in *S/Z*, the sharp knife of evaluation which alone allows us to think (*PT*,41). It strips reality from all possible *vraisemblables*; indeed we should use two words to denote the two objects of different types of realism: the first deciphers the 'real', which can only be demonstrated and not seen; the second sings of 'reality', which is not intelligible but 'just there' (*PT*,45-6). And in order to account for the unpredictability of *jouissance* in art, we need to distinguish the notion of *figuration*, (the object of our desire, which can be the author as guest in his own text, a character, a fetishized 'word' or any other 'figure') from that of *representation*, which is this same object but under the heavy disguise of various ideological alibis (*PT*,55-6). Barthes gives as an example a description of a Memling Virgin by an author who is obviously sexually attracted to the virgin but needs to believe that what draws him to her is her upright position, which he reads as a sign of purity. For a text to live, the circulation of desire must not be confined within the configuration of actants in the text; the reader needs to be an actant himself (*PT*,57). Shall we say that he needs to be a subject?

The theoretical bankruptcy of so many systems encouraged Barthes to rely on his own hunches instead of thinking, as he put it in *Barthes by Barthes*, 'under the guardianship of a great system', those of Marx, Sartre or Saussure (*RB*,102). Yet the critic Françoise Gaillard (1974) perceptively observed that Barthes's use of sexual imagery constituted a kind of 'subject of pleasure' which offered welcome compensations for all the deconstruction of subject and author which Barthes was preaching elsewhere. Yet this theoretical solitude sometimes took forms which verged on anomie; the perfect image of reality and of the incomprehensible pleasure it gives (not only obvious evocations of sex but also of food, of 'daily life' in various times and places, of the past as such, or of forms like the haiku which convey the quality of being 'there' and 'such') is after all stupidity (*PT*,19, *RB*,51), forever opaque to empathy. No wonder if this new position generated in Barthes a kind of fear, which he stated in *Barthes by Barthes* (*RB*,56, 144) and had already suggested in the epigraph of *The Pleasure of the Text*.[2]

Another cause for fear is the consequence of theoretical self-reliance, self-revelation, itself the theme of subsequent works. The need for 'self-expression' — this heretical phrase is used in *Barthes by Barthes*, one does not know how consciously (*RB*,22, 86) — and for 'lyricism' (*RB*,86) must have been there all along. But it had been prevented from reaching fruition by all the inhibiting factors listed in his autobiography: social (since his bourgeois status is compromised by the fact that his mother, for unexplained reasons, got no financial help from her family after being widowed and had to learn bookbinding); sexual (since right to the end Barthes alludes to his sexual tastes so obliquely that he forces the reader, like Henry James in *The Turn of the Screw*, to name what had remained unnamed and to adopt the role of voyeur); biological (he was left-handed); religious (since he was brought up as a Protestant in a Catholic country); educational (since his illness allowed him to take only a first degree, which does not guarantee employment); historical (since illness also prevented him from taking part in the war); and worst of all, linguistic (since the language of the intellectual exposes him to a quasi-racial kind of exclusion) (*RB*,85, 98, 131).

But why should 'subjectivity' be such a taboo word? Because, as we can see in texts such as the 1960 review of Velan, the subject to Barthes means not so much an imaginary and deceptive view of ourselves as a vision of the individual essentially cut off from the community, not so much alone as lonely. Anything is better than the sensation of being abandoned at the bottom of a hole (as his schoolmates once did to him, *RB*,121). One solution is the supposed disintegration of the subject brought about by *jouissance*, whether obtained by reading or writing, this blackness where the film-watcher can give free rein to his fantasies (*PT*,39). Another, of course, is to accept a self partly fashioned by society, and seek integration within the latter.

And this is where the 'subject of pleasure' helps. Acceptance can be obtained without undue betrayal of one's theories, since the equating of all 'substances' with a 'text', an interweaving of codes,[3] allows one to dwell on these substances, at a time when society tends to express its revulsion against all systematic thought by rediscovering pleasures such as the opera. Such a society can only have been gratified to read that Barthes now saw ideological commitment as a 'stupid blush' over the skin of the text, which may attract those who are that way inclined (*PT*,31). The blushing writer of *Degree Zero* was now, all passion spent, ready to savour the sight of this juvenile symptom in others and adopt the stance of the amateur. The fact that he had used the word *pleasure* (soon followed by words like *charm, wisdom, aesthetic*, etc.) made headlines in the literary sections of the liberal press. Suddenly, intelligence did not seem so threatening. The two former adversaries, who had frightened each other so much, now found each other quite likeable and Barthes was on the way to being fully integrated into the bourgeoisie. Reconciliation could be effected through the image of the mother, merging first with the bourgeoisie and then the provinces, a step nearer to nature than the intellectual capital. This still left the petite-bourgeoisie as convenient scapegoat for all sins. *Barthes by Barthes* shows the intellectual on the whole reconciled with his own language; the fact that the baker's wife neither speaks it nor understands it is of course regrettable, but her popular charm places her higher than her more educated petit-bourgeois daughter. *Barthes by Barthes* presents a euphoric and idyllic view of the family background, quite different from that of a few years before in the Thibaudeau interview. All we see now is the famous 'discreet charm', and Barthes even goes so far, when writing on Michelet, as to dream about the feudal romance of Blood and state a preference for personal allegiance over the notion of contract. And anyway, how could one speak against the bourgeoisie, since it is the language of the mother, the mother-tongue?

The bourgeoisie, not to be outdone, suddenly discovered that this admirable stylist, so consistently derided in its journals, was indeed a writer. This was of course made easier by the subjects Barthes now selected: the inner life, the sorrows of love, childhood, maternal devotion or scenes of provincial life are topics which invite pronouncements on the true nature of an author more than the most profound remarks on syntagms and functives. Barthes had already made dazzling analyses of substances; but these still had the anonymity of matter, whereas now his descriptions were applied to recognizable activities. He did not write about sound, he wrote about going to the opera, playing the piano or composing; he did not write about colour but was photographed at the easel and designed his own cover for *Barthes by Barthes*. Most symbolic of all, he wrote on food, giving an affectionate presentation of Brillat-Savarin; and though he had written before in the same vein on Sade, Fourier or Loyola, a gourmet is more congenial than an eccentric utopian, an ascetic, or a coprophagist.[4]

From this new integrated standpoint, Barthes now adopted, in intellectual and stylistic matters, an attitude which was a mixture of passivity and aggression, no longer sallying forth to seize hold of texts but sitting back and taunting those who failed to catch his elusive allegiance with being 'frigid'. The paradox contained in this inversion of roles was duly underlined by some feminists (Hermann, 1974) who moreover refused to find this kind of symbolic transgression without influence on how women are valued by society. They had even less sympathy with the claim that it was useless to try and conquer rights equal to men, since men had only made a mess of our society, which is fundamentally aggressive and 'homosexual', that is, male-centred. It is certainly true that the machismo now detectable even in supporters of feminism like Sartre may have contributed to fostering in Barthes the idea that social arts and graces like painting or playing the piano are fundamentally feminine — the recent revelation that Sartre had for a time earned some pocket-money by giving piano lessons came as quite a shock. But Barthes still saw hysteria as essentially feminine, even suggesting that the cunning Chinese, while affecting to raise woman's status by entrusting heroic parts to them in their operas and ballets, are subtly holding them up to ridicule. The ideal remained that of the strong silent man of the Western and gangster films described in *Mythologies*.

One had to be very careful therefore not to ruffle the calm surface of gracious living. This was made easier by the general loss of faith in ideologies. Barthes now derided those who used the neologisms for which he had done battle. He poked fun at his own former habit of suggesting new sciences all the time. He mocked Saussure for his belief in the gold standard. And finally, significantly, he mocked Brecht. Whereas before he had praised the Berliner Ensemble for using a blow-torch on theatre costumes, now, reading Brecht's instructions to an actress to carry a heavy linen-basket in order to suggest proletarian fatigue, Barthes sneered, isn't it naive to hope to represent the weight of history with a laundry-basket?[5]

But the autobiographical writing contains even more unflattering observations about Barthes himself, of a kind which, coming from anyone else, would amount to a ferocious slating. But this is precisely the point; it could not come from anyone else, at least not quite like that. And what does Barthes accuse himself of? This is where a little structuralism is useful; we shall then avoid the mistake of taking these damaging 'admissions' at face-value. The portrayal of Barthes by Barthes is not a casual one, although doubtless he had no understanding of its true meaning. It is a portrait of the writer as seen by bourgeois tradition; it is as 'imaginary' as the portrait of the scientist Barthes denounces in *S/Z*. In the folklore of literary history, the writer, as we all know, is a lovable rascal, with no intellectual integrity whatsoever, willing to sacrifice everything for the sake of a pleasant-sounding phrase; he is hopeless at maths, bored by his lonely work, and endowed with a phenomenal capacity for diversion in order to escape his routine. Nor is he content with signalling his identity in a way 'which can be seen from afar' (as he used to say about Naturalist writing); Barthes even adopts the governessy tone of the teacher's remarks on one of the schoolboy essays photographed in his autobiography, and like Proust, chides himself for a lack of will-power in wanting pleasure instantly. If he called his thematic study of Michelet a 'pre-criticism', it is only because he did not have the endurance or knowledge to write a real piece of criticism; if he writes in fragments, it is because he cannot stand boredom and is incapable of sustained work. Readers of *Système de la Mode* will need to pinch themselves at this point. And even more when they learn that the only reason for Barthes's interest in structuralism was that its binary principle made it possible to speak about everything without having anything to say. Barthes goes on to state that he has in fact read very little, and that he has read neither Blanchot or Hegel, whom he had elsewhere quoted abundantly.

To sum up, Barthes did not simply find room to integrate a new note of humanity into his writing. As in linguistics, introducing a new element led to a reorganization of the whole system; some things were gained, others lost. One critic (Catesson, 1977) has recently pointed out that in any autobiography one must constantly be aware of a four-term structure:

Intratextual	Extratextual
Narrator	Writer
Character	Model

What Barthes as narrator tells us about Barthes as character may not apply to Barthes as the model of this character, or even about Barthes the writer who lends his voice to the narrator. Barthes sacrificed his aggression in order to gain acceptance for all the aspects of himself which had for so long been repressed, and he constantly tested the limits of this acceptance. One way of doing this is to denigrate oneself first. Thus he now claimed the right to be 'silly', just as he dared to write on good food; the figure of the professor correspondingly appeared as lean and intelligent, a description now as derogatory in Barthes's mouth as it had been for those who used to characterize him as a Cassius. Writing on love, he claimed 'the right to be out of fashion'; not without the hope, however, of relaunching this old theme as a new fashion acceptable at least as kitsch.

The vocabulary of this latest period is psychoanalytical, and Barthes handles it with considerable sophistication, wondering for instance whether the excellent health he enjoys on holidays is not a kind of hysterical bodily manifestation. The problem of acceptance is complicated by what Barthes calls perversion, in order to claim this description in its psychoanalytical sense, namely, as the opposite of neurosis. It is a mode of adaptation which consists in imposing one's way of life on the world instead of being divided within oneself. This can only be done at the cost of ignoring certain aspects of oneself and projecting them outside, and we have just seen this mechanism at work. Everything Barthes wrote in the seventies showed a desire to defuse or deflect aggression from outside and to control his self-image, even if this finally required a general attack on mastery itself. The psychoanalytical interpretation of self-analysis is that of a narcissistic resistance; Barthes avoids this retort by deliberately grounding his autobiographical writing on Lacan's notion of the Imaginary; but the essence of the Imaginary is to pass itself off as truth. Barthes remarks that psychoanalysis, like all metalanguages, needs something to bite on, a more naive discourse. How can one produce it when one is conversant with psychoanalysis? The answer is by regressing. Meaning therefore results, in these late fragments, from the interplay between 'regressive' themes and 'progressive' interpretations. Both positions, that of perversion and that of psychoanalytic *bricolage*, imply a pleasurable self-sufficiency. Yet the psychoanalytical vocabulary is derogatory; it recognizes psychic aspects and processes such as sublimation or identification with ideals, but with a built-in reductionist tone. That Barthes chose such an approach is perhaps no accident.

Exemption from meaning was subsequently sought not in language but in the new magic notion, the body. Writing is desirable when it can aspire to the status of matter, and render the grain of a voice or the feel of an animal's muzzle. And most of all, 'write the body', and better, 'the body under my body', the clumsy and indeterminate something which the last illustration in *Barthes by Barthes*, an anatomical representation of all the blood vessels, tries to suggest. The same desire tempts him to present his childhood almost purely through photographs, chosen among those which fascinate him and put a stop to speculation. Or again, to write 'anamneses', short evocations of the unique flavour of a person or event which aim to be matte like a haiku, and are placed in the middle of the book as a rest from meaningful writing. Barthes tells us that he cannot take leave of his senses; his vision, like his view of writing, is 'fatally clear'. It is this madness that he values in love; he defines it, as Malraux did, as the possibility of revealing the insane part of ourselves to a privileged person, abolishing the barrier of individuation, and exposing the body under the body.

We have come a long way from the relaxed hedonist of the immediately preceding phase. He is doubtless still there, but he has not banished passion, guilt and masochistic self-mutilation. Yet among so many distractions, Barthes's autobiography offered for the third time a key which no critics had cared to use. It is a remark to the effect that 'destiny is an intelligent pattern' (*RB*,103). It is said to have inspired the whole of *On Racine*, and to be at the heart of *S/Z* as well (*S/Z*,175). What then does this passage in *S/Z* tell us? Something Mauron had already discovered in Racine, and which recalls the last episode in Cazotte's *Diable amoureux*, the image of someone who takes refuge in the arms of the very person who wants to murder him. Barthes, like Racine, had lost his father and sought substitutes to identify with. Sartre or Brecht obviously fulfilled that function, encouraging the aggression of theory against the bourgeoisie identified with the Mother — mother-nature and mother-tongue. How did they fail him? We do not know, but we find Barthes after *Mythologies* on the one hand taking refuge in the worship of language, to which he reduces everything while being very careful to stress that with this language he is in fact saying, that is doing, 'nothing'. On the other hand, he is giving his allegiance to structuralism, where he seeks another series of ideal fathers. He seems to have met a disappointing reception in admired thinkers like Lévi-Strauss and Lacan. Moreover, innovation always carries the risk of being superseded by the very intellectual movement it has helped to bring forth, and this happened to

Barthes too. In any case, the objects of this new identification found themselves contested in the end, just as Sartre had been by the wave of the New Novel. It is at this point that Barthes takes refuge in passivity and the pleasures identified with the mother. But still, they are in his mind impossible to reconcile with socialism, and therefore guilty; on the other hand, reaching at last the promised land of fiction does not compensate for the vacuum of theory and the loss of belief in science. Fiction is reached via the notion of the Imaginary, which is a renunciation of self-knowledge.

Besides, 'language (*langue*) is fascist', so that one should first concentrate on liberating it (*L*,14). This assertion has understandably struck some readers as a facile opting out of social and political commitment; but the examples Barthes gives show that it has a deeper meaning for him. His mother-tongue forces him to choose between masculine and feminine, between the intimacy of *tu* and the formality of *vous*, and to use a subject-predicate form, so that what he is defines him once and for all, and can never be altered by anything he does.

Just as Mauron's Racine, who, after a phallic bid for independence, falls back into the clutches of Port-Royal, the archaic mother figure, owing to the failure of his paternal identifications (an interpretation so heartily endorsed by Barthes that *On Racine* favours all the young male characters trying to achieve happiness in spite of possessive females); just as Sarrasine, who, fleeing from virile, castrating women into the arms of Zambinella, discovers too late that what awaits him there is an even more certain castration — so Barthes discovers that 'destiny is an intelligent pattern'. How strange that he should have stressed this (while not understanding it, since in his summary of Mauron's book he interprets Port-Royal as a substitute *father* — but see the French edition (p. 267) (since the sentence is omitted in *E*,270). This is something many readers must feel when confronting his latest works, whatever the renewal of inspiration and the stylistic distinction one finds in them. For in view of his insistence on this hermeneutic clue, the question must be asked: has Barthes, in becoming a 'personality' been truly recognized? In his autobiography, he sometimes wonders whether the type of writing he is trying to achieve *can* be understood, or whether it is locked in itself like the work of a madman (*RB*,114). *Barthes by Barthes* and *A Lover's Discourse* both start from an acknowledgement of that discursive and theoretical loneliness.

Yet in a text on Sollers which has obvious personal overtones Barthes makes this essential solitude definitive of the writer: 'We accept the particular, but not the singular; types, not individuals.' What of him who is 'absolutely isolated? Who is neither a Breton, nor a Corsican, nor a woman, nor a homosexual, nor a madman, nor an Arab; who *does not even* belong to a minority? Literature is his voice' (*SE*,8). The difficulty of his own texts is not only due to their elaborations on some very personal themes and code words, but, in the best cases, to the originality of his vision. As he says, quoting Proust's defence of his own work, 'You say these distinctions are subtle; these distinctions are real' (1978b). Barthes can say this with assurance since he is writing about an exhibition showing aspects of his beloved Japanese culture, which not only is aware of such subtleties but, like the Greeks, has a word for them (Barthes's review bears the strange and beautiful title 'Between love and anguish'). Are *The Pleasure of the Text, L'Empire des signes, A Lover's Discourse* really *read*, or are they immediately transcribed into a predictable orthodoxy? *Subtle* comes from *sub-tela*, a finely woven web far less easy to pontificate about than the much-vaunted 'Text', for it must be untangled each time with a fresh approach. One wonders if Barthes did not in part create this situation by not trusting enough in the individual reader's ability and desire to confront in silence the strangeness of his texts. But perhaps this was how he himself wanted it, since he was aware of his own insoluble contradictions (*RB*,137). Perhaps his insistence on being recognized as a writer could only result, in the present state of media-controlled culture, in his being recognized as a *traditional* writer, as opposed to what he seemed to want when he stressed the continuity of literary and critical discourses.[6]

For there is also an historical dimension to all this, which Barthes himself preferred to stress. His autobiography ends, with force, in a rejection of Totality as an imaginary closure of the gaps in desire and knowledge. Barthes gives several 'figures' which show foreclosure as an act of violence. The genre of the maxim, for instance, which names in order to hide uncertainty and chaos. Or, as he is finishing his book on a fine summer day, the image of nature: the sun, the heat, the flowers, the silence, the reassurance of work, all seem to repel the negative and uncertain — desire and aggression — and this foreclosure means violence, however seductively and mythically disguised. Totality is a grotesque yet frightening monster, which can only be held in check with an 'aesthetics of carnival' (*RB*,180).

Barthes convinced himself that only a revolutionary situation, by standing outside bourgeois language, could destroy it. The only thing which can be done meanwhile is to help it to disintegrate, as a lump of sugar dissolves in water. The example of Nietzsche shows that when it is impossible to conceptualize an alternative, one can at least try to suggest a field where new concepts could emerge. This is the nearest Barthes came to theorizing the originality of his own position: the failure of the theoretical father conferred on the son an adulthood of sorts. When theory falls silent, nothing but history can restore the flow of speech; it is therefore idle to speculate on what form the future will take. What this study has tried to provide is a reading of Barthes which records both desires and their contradictions. Both existed abundantly in him, providing a multitude of paths which all lead to different meanings. As the preface of *Mythologies* puts it, 'The reader will easily see where I stand.' But other paths are possible: after all, we are all part of Roland Barthes.

*   *   *

This study was finished when there came, almost simultaneously, the news of the publication of *La Chambre claire* and of Barthes's fatal accident. *La Chambre claire* proves the predictive value of a dual approach which seeks to account at one stroke for the intellectual and the existential in Barthes. It is his only novel, and a love story. It achieves at last the synthesis of theory and narrative, of language and life, of the mother and the father principles, of reality and reproduction, of past and present — indeed the whole book seems to tend towards what Breton called the supreme point where all antinomies disappear (compare to *MI*,160-1). Like *Nausea* and *Remembrance of Things Past*, it is the story of a quest, a hermeneutic thriller; but unlike Sartre's and Proust's masterpieces, it also shows the flight of the subject before the very advance of knowledge which it tries to promote. The book has a Beatrice, the mother, but its theoretical framework is provided by the first good father, Sartre: the book is written as a homage to *L'Imaginaire*, in which Sartre opposes the 'certainties' of phenomenology, which directly apprehends essences, to the mere 'probabilities' of science.

Yet the book exhibits a relaxed syncretism where the methods of phenomenology and structuralism are conjoined, with some Lacan thrown in as well. Trying to account for the fascination photographs have for him, Barthes thinks he will achieve his aim through an understanding of the essence of photography; but this 'eidetic science' is also conceived on structuralist lines: photography must be turned into a *langue* extracted from a corpus, itself obtained thanks to the application of a classifying principle which allows one to attribute a mark to some items. True, the first part of the book ends on Barthes's acknowledgement of failure: no classification has proved to be the real mediator, neither that produced by science nor that produced by pleasure as recommended by the early and the later Barthes. But this is simply because the principle of this exploration was wrongly chosen. The trust in the supremacy of the self, advised by Nietzsche and also Sartre (since only an intention, a personal interest makes the photography come alive) was sound in itself; but the hedonistic self cannot reach the universal: the true guides are the Romantic twins, love and death.

The strong narrative structure of the book underlines this. It is in two parts, and the second opens with a fragment entitled 'One evening ...' One evening he found the photograph of his recently deceased mother as a little girl, and this revealed to him the secret which he had until then sensed but obscurely. Only this photograph fulfilled his desire to find a true representation of the mother's essence; he had thus found her again. But in doing so, he was losing her a second time. For what photography tells above all else and in an ultimately material way (through optical and chemical processes) is that what it represents, its referent, was *once* there. And because the real is felt to have an absolute superiority, we interpret it as *alive*; even a corpse, in a photograph, is alive as corpse, so to speak. So that what characterizes photography is a conflation of past and present which is graphically illustrated by the image of a man waiting, in the condemned cell, for the execution which has long taken place.

Hence photography's kinship not only with death but with madness: the psychotic fears a catastrophe which has already happened. This madness is akin to what Barthes in his Inaugural Lecture called the essential delusion in the writer's calling, the desire to conjoin reality with truth, embodied in language. This turning of life into destiny is of course intolerable to him when he sees his freedom to interpret himself curtailed by a photographer who freezes his image. The humour of this passage does not conceal an anguish which overflows into revulsion against his own time, its illusions of progress and its feverish tempo (the plea for a slower tempo pervades this late period and provides an index of modernity for reading or writing; 1977b). The theme of the book, and perhaps a kind of post-partum depression as publication drew near, sometimes gives the impression that Barthes, from beyond the grave, is anathematizing 'the excitable world of the living' (an impression confirmed by the accidie revealed in his last interview, 1980c).

This even takes a polemical turn despite the flaunted irenic attitude of the later Barthes, when he chooses photography 'against' cinema and film studies. Not only is a photograph isolated, vertical, so to speak, lending itself to all our meanings instead of coercing us into accepting those of a narrative which sweeps us along, but it can also be produced by an amateur. Film, on the contrary, is produced by professionals, and 'read' by sciences, semiology, Marxism, psychoanalysis, which Barthes had come to view as so many policemen. Yes, as he had stated in his first semiological articles, photography is a message without a code, so that it is when Barthes turns himself into a savage and forgets all culture, standing on the only certainty he ever knew, 'the desperate resistance to any reductive system', that he holds the best clue to its essence, which is a realism more satisfying than the 'uncertain text'.

And indeed the forces of theory and fiction combine to produce a god-like, self-justifying discourse whose attendant risks of subjectivism are obvious. For although Barthes is correct when he says that it is easier to dream about photographs than about films, he is obviously wrong in seeing photography as unique in imposing the realization that 'this once was'. For this is the impression we get, especially after his death, when we see Barthes on film or hear his voice on tape. What he describes applies to all the products of mechanical reproduction of natural beings or phenomena. Yet the subjectivism which is, in *La Chambre claire*, enjoyed by the son under the benevolent gaze of both mother and father, is hardly an encumbrance; we are sufficiently protected against it by our own observations and biases. But as is shown by this theoretical work, which is also Barthes's most moving book, the insights of an individual subject are irreplaceable.

Appendix

This Appendix is not not an introduction to linguistics; many excellent introductions exist, by more competent authors. The following notes simply draw attention to a set of topics, problems and implications without which the actual discussion of Barthes's work, background and main project could not proceed. Accordingly, the four sections of the Appendix are arranged with regard more to ideological than to purely linguistic considerations. I beg the reader to accept some rather bald statements at this stage; most of the concepts defined here are also discussed in the main text where their strategic or symbolic use makes this relevant.

I: Structuralism

Structuralism is used here in its most general philosophical sense which earned the movement the label of myth even before it was contested. Since structuralism played a crucial part in Barthes's works both as myth and reality, such a broad interpretation is indispensable. That some vital contributors to the movement made a great show of dissociating themselves from structuralism is itself part of its mythical quality and had also been observed in connection with existentialism.

Structural linguistics is practically synonymous with modern linguistics; despite their wide divergences, the term covers most post-Saussurean schools. But the adjective *structural* should not be used in its linguistic sense just because a science uses some notion of structure — all sciences do. (In French, the adjectives *structural* and *structurel* respectively would be used in these two contexts.) Jean Piaget for instance cast his net too widely in his *Structuralism* and missed the specificity of recent developments. Thus it is advisable to read Piaget in conjunction with Pierre Guiraud's *Semiology*, despite its somewhat eclectic definitions of the sign.

'Structuralist' is sometimes also used in a more restricted sense, chiefly by followers of Noam Chomsky's transformational generative school, to characterize a particular branch of linguistics based chiefly in the United States in the 1940s and 1950s, inspired by the behaviorism of Leonard Bloomfield (1933), and best represented in the work of Zellig Harris. Its main assumption was that the task of linguistics is the formulation of discovery procedures for linguistic description, with minimal help from informants (even perhaps automatically), and starting from a corpus of attested utterances. It paid particular attention to the contextual distribution of the units (obtained by cutting up the utterances in order to classify them), hence the name *distributionalism* by which it is also known. While this sense of 'structuralist' is not found in French usage except among linguists and in this limited context, distributionalism is roughly contemporary with Barthes's linguistic studies, and the two operations of segmenting and classifying utterances are the basis of his semiological work, and that of his followers and colleagues. The difference is that Chomsky's efforts to make 'mentalism' respectable again were to a large extent unnecessary in the different tradition of Continental linguistics.

Hence the ease with which Chomsky's theory (I use the singular because translations of his work reached France together and more or less immediately after the publication of his second major work, *Aspects of the Theory of Syntax*, 1965) was integrated into what was there known as 'structural linguistics', whereas its impact has been described as traumatic in Anglo-American linguistics. It is therefore a mistake to attribute any failures in semiology to the fact that it harks back to a pre-Chomskyan era in France, since, as we shall see, the philosophical background was very different there and the advent of Chomsky did not really contradict the Saussurean heritage of European linguists. On the other hand, the Chomskyan theory has been called 'structuralist' even within the Anglo-Saxon context because, as the more recent stress on semantics has shown, its syntactic model does not fundamentally question the structuralist assumption, namely, the separation of form and content (see Howard Maclay in Steinberg and Jakobovits, 1971, 165 and especially 177). While this basic philosophical reason was not grasped by French linguists in the mid-1960s, they remembered very well that distributionalism was the foundation on which Chomsky's system had been built, and sometimes exaggerated this fact in order to minimize the gap between Harrisian and Chomskyan linguistics. Battle-scarred from their efforts to replace traditional grammar and historical linguistics by structural linguistics, they were not ready for yet another revolution. Today of course, Chomsky himself is being contested by his own disciples in the name of semantics and other recent developments in linguistics and the theory of literature.

II: Semiology, the sign, relations and functions

Sémiologie was the word independently chosen by Saussure around 1894, while the philosopher and logician Charles Sanders Peirce, the other founding father, had used the word *semiotic* around 1897, to designate the 'quasi-necessary, or formal, doctrine of signs' with which he had concerned himself since the 1860s. 'Semiotic' was traditional English usage, this Stoic term having been reintroduced in 1690 into English philosophical discourse by John Locke (see the 'Terminological Note' appended by Thomas A. Sebeok to his edition of Charles Morris's *Writings on the General Theory of Signs*). The use of a Greek word by Locke has particular piquancy; it shows that what passes for needless pedantry varies throughout the ages, and that a seventeenth-century empiricist could be more uninhibited than some twentieth-century critics. Semiotic for Morris was the study of *semiosis*, the 'process in which something is a sign to some organism' (1971, 366). The International Association for Semiotic Studies chose to adopt *semiotics* in 1969 while keeping to the prudent Latin compromise *Semiotica* as the name for its international journal. Barthes tends to keep to *semiology* for the general science postulated by Saussure, and this is the usage which will be followed here. Must one deduce that the *New Concise Oxford Dictionary* is converted to Barthes's view from the fact that its sixth edition (1976) defines semiology as a 'branch of linguistics'?

Words like *meaning* and *sign* are found in all the philosophical traditions of the world; hence the necessity of defining them clearly before beginning to discuss them. Barthes never defines the 'meaning of meaning', although the word *sens* (the French term for 'meaning') occurs extremely frequently in his writings, while the notion of meaning can be said to govern the whole of his thinking (*sens* is used in *Elements of Semiology* on pp. 35, 66, 71, 95 and especially p. 55, for instance) and even — from what he tells us — his behaviour. But he does define his notion of the sign in *Elements* (*S*,35ff), where such a step is indispensable, since once semiology is defined as the object of a projected science, its unit must also be defined.

Noting the occurrence of the word *sign* in many vocabularies from theology to medicine, and throughout history, from the Gospels to cybernetics, Barthes comes to the not unusual conclusion that a sign refers us to a relation between two *relata*. This however is not precise enough for most purposes, so that the word *sign* is commonly found as one of a series (which also includes *signal, index, icon, symbol, allegory,* etc.), leading to many terminological contradictions. Barthes proves this by a brief study of the uses of *sign* in four authors: Hegel, Peirce, Jung and Wallon. Though he discovers that the terminological contradictions obtain only between authors — within the individual's work, they are compensated by transfers of meaning — this merely underlines the imperative of ascertaining the code an author is using before trusting words like 'sign' and 'symbol'. It is these two words in particular which are the worst offenders, often having exactly opposite meaning in different authors (on this semantic field, see Todorov, 1977, drawing on Sperber, 1974).

It is a relief for Barthes, we feel, to move from such confusions to the well-ordered world of Saussure and linguistics — for, we notice in retrospect, the four authors above were philosophers and psychologists. Not only does the word 'sign' have no competitors in linguistics since Saussure, but the Saussurean definition itself would remove many of the problems tackled by philosophy and psychology. The sign is defined by Saussure as the union of a *signifier* and a *signified*, a sound image and a concept. This definition differs from what obtains in other codes (and indeed in common usage) where 'sign' is often used in the sense of Saussure's 'signifier', and even sometimes as the material stimulus. But for Saussure, both signifier and signified are mental and the sign is a two-sided Janus-like entity: signified and signifier are in one gesture cut out from 'the shapeless masses' of thought and sound. This removes problems of adequacy between the *relata*, and Saussure's work was for this reason dismissed at the outset by Ogden and Richards in *The Meaning of Meaning*, who themselves missed the point of such a strictly linguistic definition.

Many thinkers since Antiquity have maintained like Saussure that language cannot be reduced to extra-linguistic factors, whether in the nature of things or of thought, in other words, that it is *arbitrary*. Others have argued that it is partially or totally *motivated* by these same factors. Peirce's classification of signs is sometimes used by some authors to refer to these aspects: the *icon* is a sign determined by its object by virtue of its own internal nature; the *index* by virtue of the real relation it has with it; and the *symbol* by virtue of a law or convention (as in Saussure's *sign*, in fact). The description of a sign in Saussure therefore involves only the relation between its two components, signifier and signified, and not that between the unit resulting from their union and what it stands for or *refers* to in the extra-linguistic world. (On this most important point for an understanding of Barthes and his disciples, see Engler, 1973). For words not only *signify* but *refer*, they have a *referential function*, which at its simplest has traditionally been conceived as a naming relation with things. The being, thing, quality, event, etc., referred to by the sign is its *referent*, and can of course be abstract or imaginary despite the solid-looking illustrations one usually finds, such as trees or horses in Saussure's *Course*. The relationship of reference is sometimes called *denotation*; this term and its correlate *connotation*, as well as the terms *object-language* and *metalanguage* are discussed in the main text in Part III. The logician G. Frege opposed *reference (Bedeutung)* to *sense (Sinn)* in his discussion of the truth-value of propositions; in some contexts, the truth-value is affected when one word is replaced by another which might be considered a synonym. As a French logician jocularly put it, the truth-value of some propositions varies when the name 'General de Gaulle' is replaced by either 'the man of 18 June 1940' or 'the man of 13 May 1958'. The sense of a word is derived exclusively from its relationship with other words and does not predicate anything about the extra-linguistic world.

The relationship between signifier, signified (or their equivalents in other vocabularies) and referent is sometimes called the *semiotic triangle,* as in the well-known diagram in Ogden and Richards's *Meaning of Meaning* (1923, 11), which is probably the most complete.

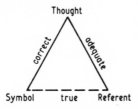

We find at the summits of the triangle the *thought,* whose relationship with the symbol is direct and can be *correct,* and whose relationship with the *referent* is direct and can be *adequate,* while the relationship of the referent with the *symbol* is only indirect (and thus represented by a dotted line) and can be *true.* Although Barthes stresses validity, not truth, and sense rather than reference, the notion of referent and the semiotic triangle are essential to his thinking, if only negatively; for instance, he denounces the 'referential illusion' in Realist and Naturalist writing, where author and reader alike labour under the illusion that the referent can be directly introduced into language without the mediation of a signified.

Some theorists argue that literary discourse can only have signifieds and not referents, despite occasional use of real locations or historical characters and events. The problem of the referent seems to have been swept under the carpet rather than really solved in much modern criticism. In order to avoid this evasion, Barthes resorts in *Elements* to the Stoics' triadic analysis, which distinguished 'the mental representation', 'the real thing' and 'the utterable' (S,43). The last closely resembles Saussure's *signified,* but (if this assimilation is made) it can then only have a functional definition, as one of the components of the sign, a definition Barthes himself calls 'quasi-tautological'. The only difference between signified and signifier is then that the latter is a mediator. And indeed, whoever accepts the idea of sign must accept, first and foremost, the idea of a difference between its two components, although it proves rather elusive to pin down, and has been radically challenged by some modern theorists, such as Derrida and Kristeva.

Inasmuch as Barthes gives a definition of meaning, it is on p. 55 of

Elements, as the sum of *signification* (by which he means the union of signifier and signified) and *value*. The notion of value characterizes the sign by its setting among other signs. In Saussure's famous formulation, 'in language (*langue*) there are only differences *without positive terms*' (*Course*, 120, quoted in *S*,72). This notion of value has been so exploited in structuralist ideology in order to characterize language as purely differential, devoid of all 'positive' or 'substantial' aspects, and existing independently of experience, that it is worth re-examining in its own setting in the *Course*. 'Value' is first used in order to introduce the notion of synchrony (see Section III), through a comparison of linguistics with economics (*Course*, 79). Both need to be tackled along two axes, for economics, the diachronic axis of economic history and the synchronic axis of political economy. Later in the *Course* (106), we come across value again in a comparison of linguistics with certain other sciences, which allegedly have an easier task because their units are found ready-made instead of having to be discovered. Several observations on Barthes's and Saussure's ideology can be made at this point:

1. Saussure confuses *units* with *objects* of science: to say that 'the animal' is the unit of zoology and 'stars "separated" in space' that of astronomy is begging the question: why not tissues common to many animals as Foucault asked in *The Birth of the Clinic*, or the whole formed by space and stars, as in Einstein's theory? We see here the same tendency to select solid units (in linguistics, signs rather than sentences), and also the synchronic bias which drives Saussure to ignore the long process of defining units in all sciences. While there certainly is a need for a working separation of synchrony and diachrony, it is easy to guess that not much useful reorganization of scientific fields could be based on such a rigid separation (against which Jakobson had already protested). Yet Saussure in the same passage asks questions concerning the size of units which anticipate those Barthes later asked about literary studies seen as semiology (*R*,165), but he comes out with a surprising answer: if concrete units are not immediately recognizable, it is because they are not necessary: 'We can study history without knowing the answer' (*Course*, 107). The paradox is that when Barthes cites this passage and alludes to the crucial part played by the *Annales* school of history in structuralism, because of its long-term outlook and the new objects it poses for history — economics, demography, techniques, climate, mentalities — he manages to turn this into a defence of synchrony! (*S*,101, note 55).

2. Economics (which because of its two axes is the model for linguistics and the crucial concept of value) has an immediate link both with nature and with human history. Yet Saussure immediately disavows this double link (linguistics is a system of pure values, where 'natural data have no place' — *Course*, 80) while Barthes praises the concept of value

because its economic origin allows one to 'depsychologize linguistics' (S,54). Interestingly for someone with such a Marxist past, he repeats Saussure's formulation of the example of political economy (the synchronic axis of economics) and sees money as being exchanged for labour, not labour-power. Those who think such considerations out of place should be reminded that Barthes himself was not above scoffing at Saussure's trust in the gold standard as symptomatic of his ideology.

3. Value involves the ideas of exchanging and comparing. One compares similar entities (words or banknotes), while one exchanges first labour and money, then money and goods, so that one might humorously see semiology, which trades social and natural objects for non-verbal signifieds, as a kind of barter, a situation whose difficulties will be discussed in Chapter 10. The effects of Saussure's privileging of synchrony and *langue* over diachrony and *parole* have been multiplied by similar choices on the part of all the structuralists including Barthes; I shall come back to this point in Section IV. This is important because of Barthes's denial that thought can exist without language, or at least his assertion that it is 'born encoded'. The stress on positive substances rather than negative forms generated many disputes among linguists and those who sought to extrapolate linguistics to other fields; they were eventually subsumed under the phenomenology/structuralism dispute (see Chapter 2).[1]

Let us now rapidly point out some similarities between all these linguistic concepts and those Barthes uses from other fields.

1. The opposition between signified and referent cannot but bring to mind Sartre's theory of imagination, which greatly impressed Barthes, perhaps via Maurice Blanchot's work which refers to their common model, Mallarmé. For Sartre, the work of art is 'un imaginaire' whose existence depends entirely on the reader/spectator's freely invested interest. What he sees or reads is only a material *analogon*. Sartre's attitude to imagination is extremely ambivalent. Imagination differs from perception in so far as it is a fundamentally different orientation towards the world, which it negates (as opposed to perception). This negation makes it like language, at the same time presence and absence (the sign is both a mark and a lack). Yet the products of imagination are somehow truer to reality than those of perception, since for phenomenologists man creates values as a free subject. Thus language is inherently action; hence the artist's responsibility and necessary commitment.

Consciousness, besides, has a built-in *pour autrui (for others)* dimension: communication is inescapable, although a Hegelian struggle among consciousnesses is also a given, and attempts can be made on the other hand to institute a kind of *folie à deux* — a kind of private language — based on bad faith: an attempt unavoidably foiled by the presence of a third person. Thus there is in Sartre's outlook something which one might call *performative* in the sense introduced by the philosopher J.L.

Austin (1962). 'Performative' utterances not only describe an event but in their very uttering perform an action (for instance 'I promise', or again 'I declare war' — Barthes's examples). The theory of speech acts, as developed by P.F. Strawson, J.R. Searle and H.P. Grice was introduced in France by the linguist E. Benveniste and found a ready audience in Barthes, since the ubiquitous social overdetermination is the core of his own experience; he had already tried to account for it by means of the notion of connotation and even before that the notion of *writing* in his first work *Writing Degree Zero*.

2. A ternary approach similar to the above (art, its objects, its public) is also found in Lacan. The three registers he distinguishes, namely the Real, the Imaginary and the Symbolic, would map neatly onto referent, signified and signifier; however, Lacan objects to the semiotic triangle in *Ecrits*, substituting for it two mobile chains where signifier and signified coincide only at certain anchor-points (see *S*,49). Lacan also stresses the primacy of the signifier and shows ambivalence towards the Imaginary and any attempt to stress positive elements in linguistics. The difference between this slant and Freud's teaching is pointed to by J. Laplanche and J.B. Pontalis in *The Language of Psychoanalysis*, for instance in the entries under *Imaginary* and *Symbolic*. Other instances of this bias are Lacan's heavy reliance on Freud's *Beyond the Pleasure Principle* (where the birth of meaning is linked with absence — that of the mother) to the exclusion of other Freudian texts which emphasize experience of plenitude or communication; or the tendency to epitomize Freud's discovery as that of the unconscious — a notion which was very popular at the end of the nineteenth century — rather than that of the structures through which we can relate to this unconscious. Finally, the psychoanalyst's 'symptomatic reading' of his patient's discourse is described as an ability to spot the gaps in the latter, as if the discourse of a paranoiac was not manifested by positive elements as well. This notion of reading was taken up by Althusser and literary theorists like Macherey and R. Balibar. One should note that *ideology* in Althusser is as indispensable as the *Imaginary* in Lacan (unlike what we find in Barthes); but it is treated with the same ambivalence.

3. Lastly, as pointed out by various linguists, the three philosophical positions which stress each summit of the semiotic triangle recall those taken in the famous medieval quarrel of the universals: realism, nominalism and conceptualism. Universals of course are in the news again, more than ever since the advent of Chomsky's theories.

I shall now say a few words about the various functions of language as proposed in modern linguistics and used by semiologists. I shall start with information theory which supplied the pattern for Jakobson's schema for these functions. This theory had a great influence on Barthes, since it seemed to give a scientific foundation to his oscillation between conceiving modernity as originality and seeing this infinite freedom as necessarily curtailed by the play of a finite number of elements.

In the philosophical essay which follows C. Shannon's theory of communication, W. Weaver defines communication in its broadest sense as 'all of the procedures by which one mind may affect another'; it includes language, the arts, the whole of human behaviour, and even the procedures by which a mechanism affects another mechanism. Weaver is well aware of the aesthetic and cultural aspects which such a definition of communication might seem too abstract to encompass. This definition can in fact easily be extended to a theory of reading or aesthetic perception even when the aim is to *fail* to achieve accuracy of transmission or correct interpretation, as in the Nouveau Roman, in Sartre's idea (in *A Plea for Intellectuals*) that the writer uses the possibilities for 'disinformation' in language, or of course in Barthes's *S/Z* or an unpublished course at the Collège de France on the notion of 'the neutral', where he showed how to contravene all the 'rules' for a successful 'normal communication' or conversation.

Here are the definitions given by Weaver and relevant for a reading of Barthes:

> The word *information*, in this theory, is used in a special sense but must not be confused with its ordinary usage, and in particular, with meaning. It relates not so much to what one *does* say as to what one *could* say; it is a measure of one's freedom of choice when one selects a message. It makes sense not really about one message but about the total situation. (1949, 99)

Thus this concept may seem at first 'disappointing and bizarre' (1949, 116). This caveat went unheeded by quite a few theorists of literature and culture until they were, indeed, disappointed in their hopes. The *quantity of information* (1949, 103) is related to the notion of *entropy*, which comes from thermodynamics: it is the function which expresses the degradation of energy and, in the kinetic theory of gases, results in an increase of disorder among molecules. The *relative entropy* of a system is the proportion of actual information transmitted, as opposed to the maximal value which could have been passed; its complement is called *redundancy* (1949, 104). Redundancy is the part of the structure of the message which is determined not by the free choice of the sender but by the accepted statistical rules governing the use of the symbols chosen. Redundancy has an important role in communication inasmuch as it gives more information than the strict transmission of the message needs, and thereby allows one to offset the effects of *noise*. This latter word denotes the parasitical elements which, being as unexpected as genuine information, at first look like the latter (Weaver for this reason calls it the 'joker'). But whereas information is defined only in relation to an intention, noise increases not information but uncertainty and acts as an obstacle (1949, 109). *Equivocation* is the name given to the uncertainty which remains, however clever the coding process (1949, 111).

Lévi-Strauss is probably responsible for the success of the concept of entropy in contemporary French thinking; in his *Tristes tropiques* he calls it 'inertia'. The second law of thermodynamics states that entropy always increases, and Eddington argued that it may be the supreme law of nature, that which gives time its arrow. The implications of this early model are important, not only for the static view of history in 'primitive' or 'cold' societies found in Lévi-Strauss (who for this reason spells his discipline 'entropology' because of the disruptive impact of Western culture on the societies it studies and the ensuing sameness between all cultures) but on the early models for the structural analysis of narrative. Besides, if one views literary excellence, like Barthes, as typically manifesting itself in totally new metaphors, which can never be integrated into a tradition, one can have a fairly despondent view of originality; for the difference with Lévi-Strauss's cultural pessimism is that in the field of culture and politics one could react by conservatism, whereas the modernist outlook in art makes originality a categorical imperative.

Many attempts have been made to classify and describe the functions of language, in some cases while speculating about its nature, origin, purpose and structure. If we take as a fundamental option the choice between the *representation of thought* and *communication* as the principal functions of language, we find that the former, found for instance in the theories of Port-Royal and in Humboldt, is less often mentioned recently (except by Chomsky) than the latter, found in Bühler and especially Jakobson. For Bühler, the communicative act always includes three dimensions: that of *representation*, or content which is communicated (the meaning of representation here is *reference*, not that meant by the Port-Royal linguists and used above), that of *appeal* to the receiver or interlocutor, and that of *expression* on the part of the speaker, who thus conveys his attitudes. Jakobson took up this schema but completed it by reinterpreting it within the framework of information theory.[2]

Jakobson lists the fundamental factors of all communication as follows: a sender sends a message to a receiver; in order to be operative, the message needs a context or referent, and a code which is at least partially common to encoder and decoder; finally, the message needs a contact, both a physical channel and a psychological connection between sender and receiver. Each of these six factors gives rise to a different function of language, although every message does not make use of all of them, and when several appear together, they form a hierarchy. The orientation towards the context is the *referential* (or denotative, or cognitive) function. The orientation towards the speaker is the *expressive* (or emotive) function, which typically appears in interjections but also in many factors, such as intonation, which were previously regarded as falling outside the study of *langue* proper, and belonging only to its execution. The *conative* function is centred on the receiver, on whom it aims to make an impression; the vocative and the imperative, including its modern guise of advertising, are typical examples.

Some messages seem to convey information but in fact are simply meant to keep the contact going, a typical example in certain cultures being a description of the weather! Jakobson calls this the *phatic* function (a term he took from 'The Problem of Meaning in Primitive Languages', a Supplement by the anthropologist B. Malinowski to Ogden and Richards's book). Any time two interlocutors wish to ascertain that they are using the same code, they make use of the *metalinguistic* function, which is therefore not confined to an esoteric occupation for logicians. Finally, when the stress is put on the message itself, we find the *poetic* function, which was the main subject of Jakobson's essay. Unlike some modern theorists who would reduce the whole of modern art, or even art itself, to this function, Jakobson stresses that it is only the dominant but not exhaustive function of 'poetry'; conversely any attempt to equate poetic function and poetry means that one will miss many fascinating phenomena observable in everyday language, as in the case of the metalinguistic function. In fact, all the poles of the schema can be merged or permutated, as is the case with the main roles based on syntax which are the elements in the schema for the structural analysis of narrative.[3]

Jakobson stresses the existence of a common code, whether it is found ready-made or whether it results from the efforts of both interlocutors to communicate. He maintains, against C.F. Hockett, that the notion of *idiolect*, the linguistic habits characterizing a given individual at a given moment, is a somewhat perverse fiction and that everything is socialized in language. Barthes however made use of this notion of idiolect, in the belief that the writer today no longer has a common code at his disposal, and that modern writing is essentially a scattering of idiolects.

Although Jakobson's diagram of communication (like that in Saussure's *Course*, 11, 12) shows only two interlocutors, communication is not to be conceived as an isolated act. Jakobson stressed the importance of Peirce's theories repeatedly, and in particular (1963, 27 and especially 40) the idea that a sign, in order to be understood, needs not only the two participants in the speech act, but also an *interpretant*, that is, another sign or group of signs which could be substituted for this first sign. This 'translation' into another sign can be interlingual as well (into another language) or even intersemiotic (into a pictorial sign system, for example); this is of obvious interest for semiology, whose necessity Jakobson stresses at the outset. He shows the inadequacy of ostensive definitions by the famous example of the monolingual Indian, to whom one shows a packet of Chesterfields, and who cannot know one's meaning for sure. There is, then, no direct relationship between word and thing. The need for interpretants in the understanding of signs has as its corollary, unfortunately, the circularity of semantics, but recent theorists such as Derrida do not see this as negative. Where there are still objections that Lacan and others do not explain how one breaks into the system, in most cases this is explained by the fact that sense and reference are learned together.[4]

The whole model of communication has been criticized by theorists like Kristeva because it makes use of the notion of sign and implies the idea of a 'full' subject who is expressed by his language instead of being partly or totally constituted by his language. This view of the productivity of language is easily connected with works like Proust's, where the writer is constituted at the end of his book — a model dear to Barthes for many reasons. The earlier model is however still valid for practical, transitive, conscious and voluntary communication, which is based on a logic of identity, unlike poetic or psychotic types of discourse which are based on another logic. The model of the sentence, which with Chomsky had seemed to supersede the sign as the cornerstone of linguistics, is being attacked in its turn, at least the Indo-European model, which is said by Kristeva (1975) to carry an unwanted ideology in its canonic form. Paul Ricoeur (1967) at the apogee of structuralism, had already argued that the notion of discourse might be the most fruitful starting-point, using the ideas of the linguist Paul Guillaume. Benveniste's work on discourse has been very influential, and his notion of *significance* is discussed in the main text.

III: Synchrony, diachrony, the subject and society

Saussure in his *Course* (79ff) distinguished two sciences of language, *static linguistics* which studies language-states, and *evolutionary linguistics*, an expression he preferred to *historical linguistics* (since the term *history* covers in fact two practices, description and narration — a point of interest to Barthes). However he soon preferred to speak of these as *synchronic* and *diachronic linguistics* (and hence of *synchrony* to denote a language-state and *diachrony* to denote an evolutionary phase) in order to stress 'the opposition and crossing of two orders of phenomena that relate to the same object' according to whether they are considered on 'the axis of simultaneities' or 'the axis of successions'.

However, what is stressed in the notion of synchrony is not so much simultaneity as the view that language forms a *system*, that it is cohesive. Thus this notion is inseparable from another of Saussure's momentous ideas, his distinction between *langue* and *parole*, and his taking the former as the object of linguistics. As Barthes explains at the beginning of *Elements of Semiology* (*S*,13), quoting Saussure (*Course*, 9ff), *langue* must not be confused with *langage* (language in general), a 'multiform and heterogeneous' reality partaking at the same time of the physical, the physiological, the mental, the individual and the social. Saussure's inspired reaction was to create order out of this chaos, and make it amenable to scientific enquiry by extracting 'a purely social object, the systematized set of conventions necessary to communication' at any given moment of history, 'indifferent to the *material* of the signals which compose it', and which he called *langue*; 'as opposed to which *parole* (*speech*) covers the purely individual part of language (phonation, application of the rules and contingent combination of signs)', in other words, language in use, manifested by actual speech acts, as so many messages made possible by a code.

The similarities between the *langue/parole* dichotomy and the Chomskyan dichotomy between *competence* and *performance* have been pointed out by Chomsky himself (1965, 4). *Competence* is a subject's 'knowledge' of the language (which may well be unconscious but allows him to decide whether a sentence is grammatical, or at least acceptable); *performance* is his actual use of this language in real-life situations. Chomsky's speaker/hearer is an ideal subject, a theoretical construct which was recently compared to Piaget's 'epistemic subject' (F. Bresson and G. Vignaux in B. Pottier, 1973, 413). But there are important differences between the Saussurean and the Chomskyan dichotomies.

Saussure defines *langue* as a set of necessary *conventions*, 'linguistic habits which allow an individual to understand and be understood' (*Course*, 9, 77), not as a set of *rules* (except in the traditional grammatical sense); in other words, it is the result of a somewhat mysterious social contract or of a purely passive process. Although the criterion of grammaticality shows that Chomsky accepted the view of *langue* as an institution, he started instead from the activity of the speaking subject (to the extent of suggesting it perhaps had a partly innate origin). Perhaps for this reason, he stressed a part of grammar, syntax, which Saussure had left practically untouched. Sentences were for Saussure a part of *parole*, which he might well have studied if he had had the time to engage in the constitution of the 'linguistics of speech' he announced. He was embarrassed meanwhile by the presence of set phrases and regular sentence patterns, an embarrassment which is reflected in Barthes's *Elements of Semiology* when he tries to assign the respective limits of institutions and individual creativity.

For Chomsky, on the contrary, both freedom and constraint can theoretically be integrated into the notion of a grammar as a system of formal rules, in finite number, which would generate (that is, describe or predict) al the possible correct sentences in a language (which are infinite in number), and only these. It is this capacity of the subject to pronounce and understand sentences he has never encountered before which becomes the object of linguistic study.

The stress on the infinite creativity of the subject involves the linguist in the necessity of dealing with *competence* in a logico-mathematical fashion and the success of Chomsky's theories came in part from the fact that he could thus prove the inadequacy of earlier types of grammar. The fact that Kristeva's theories of poetic language also rely on logico-mathematical models, seems to have caused in Barthes a sense of inadequacy which he stresses somewhat exaggeratedly in *Barthes by Barthes* as a total incompatibility with 'algorithms' (*RB*,99). An imagination more geometric than algebraic seems also to have characterized Saussure, judging by the numerous diagrams which appear in the *Course*. In particular, his fondness for distributing linguistic facts on two perpendicular axes, a predilection shared to some extent by Jakobson, seems to have struck echoes in Barthes, who constantly invests such a schema with theoretical or symbolic implications (see Section IV).

It is clear, in view of this ideological exploitation of linguistics, that the sociological sources of Saussure's thought cannot be overstressed in studying Barthes. The influence on Saussure of Durkheim's conception of *the social fact* as independent of its individual manifestations, which marked the scientific beginning of sociology, is one of the first topics discussed by Barthes in connection with semiology (*S*,23). In Saussure's *Course*, as for Durkheim, a language, like the social fact, is essentially coercive. Barthes mentions the view that Saussure had derived his model of *langue* from Durkheim and that of *parole* — a far less developed concept — from Durkheim's opponent Tarde, who argued that the individual is 'the alpha and the omega of the system'. Durkheim's acrimonious retort was that the dispute sprang 'above all from the fact that I believe in science and M. Tarde does not'. This encapsulates a great part of the controversies around *langue/parole* and *competence/performance*, since a number of theorists have felt recently that the distinction might be methodologically inevitable but was theoretically suspect. When extrapolated to define a literary competence, let alone a socio-political norm, the pitfalls become obvious. One of Durkheim's acknowledged sources was after all Auguste Comte, whose idea when he tried to establish a 'statics' and a 'dynamics' of society on synchronic and diachronic axes, was to provide a firm foundation for a science which would rule out revolutionary upheavals by identifying the permanent organs of the body politic.[5]

The risk of starting by assigning oneself a working object of knowledge and ending up by worshipping the status quo in literature or politics are increased if one adds the notion of an ideal informant — who often turns out to be the enquirer himself. This may well occur in spite of the scientist's personal beliefs and opinions, and Chomsky's inability to relate his liberal convictions to his linguistic theory which has the opposite ontological structure has been pointed out by Kristeva (1971, 24). It remains to be seen however, whether Chomsky's explicit appeal to the Cartesian and Sartrean theories is not an adequate answer.[6]

IV: The units of language and the organization of meaning

The initial impetus towards structuralism came from Lévi-Strauss when he conceived the idea of making sense of myths by assuming that they could be explored on lines derived from structural phonology, at that time the most advanced part of linguistics ('L'Analyse structurale en linguistique et en anthropologie', 1945 and 'La structure des mythes' 1955, now Chapters II and XI of *Structural Anthropology*). Making the hypothesis that myths, while apparently giving free rein to the imagination, were concrete realizations of an underlying system, the *paroles* of a *langue*, he set out to discover the units and rules of combination of this system, making the further hypothesis that these might be universals of the human mind. These units or 'mythemes' were conceived on the model of the *phoneme*, that is, as a bundle of *distinctive features*; the oppositions account for the role of the phoneme as the minimal unit of phonology. Not all the features of a phoneme play a part in its distinctive role; Lévi-Strauss in addition adopted Jakobson's theory of the binary classification of these distinctive features.

A language can be decomposed first into significant units, words (or more accurately, *morphemes*), which have a phonic shape and a meaning, both expression and content: this is the first articulation. Then these phonic shapes can be further decomposed into the sounds which are distinctive of the language in question; these are the *phonemes*, which have no meaning by themselves but serve to make up the expression side of the morphemes (which are the minimal grammatical units); this is the second articulation. But Jakobson proposes in addition (probably owing to the inspiration he derived from information theory, which functions in terms of binary choices) to reduce a general list of distinctive features to twelve binary oppositions. Barthes does not in fact make direct use of the notion of distinctive feature, which he calls 'sub-phoneme'.[7] This may seem surprising in view of the pioneering part played by Lévi-Strauss, but the reason is soon apparent. What Lévi-Strauss took from the concept of the phoneme as a bundle of distinctive features was the idea that mythical elements could first be selected because they were characterized by the presence or absence of a given quality, then grouped as bundles or mythemes. The part of this two-stage operation could equally well be played, in structuralist theory, by the double articulation between phonemes and morphemes.[8]

The phoneme, taken in its general sense as a minimal distinctive unit, has been an extremely productive concept, not only in linguistics (where even sober-minded theorists like Bloomfield introduced terms like *phememe, taxeme, tagmeme, glosseme, noeme, sememe* for units of various aspects of language) but in the approaches it inspired, both before and after Lévi-Strauss, and which can today be subsumed under the term semiology: it has spawned, for instance, *kineme* for body expression, *gusteme* in Lévi-Strauss and others for units of the food-system in various cultures, *vesteme* in Barthes and others, and more recently *logeme* (in Barthes) to denote a functional unit of discursive strategy. The opposition between the *etic* and the *emic* approaches (from the adjectives *phonetic*, applied to the description of sound in general, and *phonemic*, applied to the significant sounds of a language) was explicitly set out in the work of the American linguist K.L. Pike (1954-60) whose work is one of the sources of Barthes's *Elements*.

Distinctive features had already been the occasion for Jakobson to suggest a modification in another of Saussure's tenets, and to point out that the signifier was not always essentially linear in character, since distinctive features occur simultaneously; *concurrence* can be a type of combination as well as *concatenation*. This brings us to another essential aspect of Barthes's discussion of linguistics with a view to constituting a semiology. In his first structuralist article, 'The Imagination of the Sign', he defined the sign, after Saussure, by three types of relation, one internal, which unites the signifier and signified, and two external. Of the latter, the first is virtual and constitutes, for each sign, an organized reservoir or 'memory' of forms which are distinguished only by the smallest difference which is necessary and sufficient to alter the meaning within a particular system. Red, amber and green form such a system in the Highway Code. This relational plane is that of the *paradigm*, and this relation is therefore called *paradigmatic*. On the second relational plane, the sign is situated in relation to its 'neighbours' and no longer to its 'brothers'. These are the signs which precede and follow it in an actual utterance. In *Homo homini lupus*, 'Man is a wolf to man', *lupus* is related in certain ways to *homo* and *homini*. In the garment system, a sweater and a skirt can be associated, when worn together, in ways analogous to that which unites the words in a sentence. The plane where signs are actualized side by side is called by Saussure that of the *syntagm*, and this relation is therefore called *syntagmatic*.[9]

A prevalent model for the relationship between syntagm and paradigm when Barthes started writing was the Jakobsonian one, manifestly inspired by Saussure's idea of two types of mental activity in the use of signs but underpinned by the recent rise of information theory. Successive choices from paradigms constitute the syntagmatic axis; hence the tendency to conceive the latter as horizontal. Given the problematics of constraint and freedom which rule so much of Barthes's thinking, this conventional view of the syntagmatic axis as horizontal and the paradigmatic axis as vertical was very suitable, because of his Saussurean image of speech as totally free, hence sallying forth into the world, so to speak, and of *langue* as totally constricting, not only because of its social but also because of its systematic character, which weighs on the speaker and limits him in space.

The logical model of a syntagmatic axis constituted from successive paradigmatic choices (that of the so-called Markov chain) was proved to be too weak by Chomsky. This model is adequate as far as certain statistical aspects of language are concerned since they involve only left-hand constraints, but it neglects syntactic (and semantic) aspects for which one needs to take into account right-hand constraints and self-embedding possibilities as well as recursion (the recurrent application of some rules). The earlier model persisted in Barthes's thinking for a long time, however, because of his modernist stress on orginality. But in *S/Z* the model became much more complex, partly because of Chomsky's influence (his works are mentioned in Barthes's article on the 'Structural analysis of narratives') but also no doubt because Barthes had by then chosen to centre his analysis on the experience of reading, and thus had to take both surprise and anticipation into account.

The most important application of the perpendiculars of the syntagmatic/paradigmatic schema, as far as Barthes is concerned, was probably Jakobson's 1956 article on 'Two Aspects of Language and Two Types of Aphasic Disturbances' (now Chapter 2 in *Essais de linguistique générale*). Jakobson set out to discover, forty years after Saussure conceived the framework of two perpendicular axes of language, whether the latter could not supply a principle of classification whose implications were not even wider than appears at first. Applying a common heuristic procedure, he turned to the pathology of language in order to throw light on its normal use. Considering the manifestations of aphasia as described by neurologists, he thought there was evidence for pointing to the existence of two types of aphasia corresponding to the two axes of language.

These two basic types are distinguished according to whether the major deficiency lies in selection or combination. In the first, connecting links tend to survive, but not the substance of the discourse. The context is essential: patients do not initiate a conversation. They have difficulty with naming; words are replaced by their contextual description: a knife being called a 'pencil-sharpener' or 'apple-parer'. They cannot think of synonyms for words or equivalents in other languages. They lose the ability to classify or do it only metonymically or on a basis of contiguity, naming all the animals they saw in a zoo for instance. They can grasp literal meanings, but not metaphorical ones.

The other patients lack a major component of speech, that, precisely, which is not accounted for in Saussure's concept of syntagm: they cannot 'propositionize', although, as Jakobson observes, this loss can gradually affect entities simpler than the sentence. Here, despite the commonplace sense of aphasia, there is no 'wordlessness', since the only remaining entity in most cases is precisely the word. Syntactical rules are lost and the sentence is reduced first to telegraphic style, then to a mere 'word-heap'. The 'kernel subject word', which was the first to disappear in the first type of disturbance, is here the last. The 'residues of speech' before the final advent of *aphasia universalis*, the total loss of the power to use or to apprehend speech, are one-phoneme-one-word-one-sentence utterances, where the patient has regressed to the pre-linguistic stage of infants. These patients tend to use metaphors to refer to objects, saying 'spyglass' for microscope, and 'fire' for gaslight.

One of Saussure's examples of associative relations has perhaps proved even more useful for recent theories of the creativity of poetic language. Taking as an example the word *enseignement* he states, 'the mind creates as many associative series as there are diverse relations', the functional element belonging to either signifier or signified: the radical (*enseigner, enseignons,* etc.), the suffix (arme*ment*, change*ment*, etc.), the concept (*instruction, apprentissage, éducation,* etc.), so that the word is like the centre of a constellation (*Course,*125-6). Thus there is a constant interchange between sound and sense. It is ironic, in view of the stress Barthes, Lacan, Kristeva and many others will come to place on the primacy of the signifier, to find Saussure's editors pointing out firmly in a footnote that the last series mentioned by Saussure (*enseignement, justement, clément,* etc.) is 'rare and abnormal, for the mind naturally discards associations that becloud the intelligibility of discourse' (*Course,*126-7), an assertion which makes no bones about the inferior status of poetic discourse! At the same time the 'et ceteras' in each of the series themselves point to the difficulties of semantics, since it is difficult to structure a field which can be progressively covered by the associations of sound and meaning. The earlier Barthes deplored and the later Barthes welcomed this difficulty.

The real difference between syntagm and paradigm, since in a sense there are several paradigmatic axes, is what Saussure already called relations *in praesentia* and *in absentia* respectively: the real mystery is the actualization of meaning. This question of the combination *in praesentia* of elements available *in absentia* raises problems from at least two points of view: that of semantics, and that of its own application to semiology. In the image as object of semiological analysis, for instance, the syntagm is spatial, not temporal as in the 'spoken chain', Saussure's linear signifier.

Let us begin with the general question of semantics. We saw that when

Barthes began to write on semiology, the main model was Lévi-Strauss's analysis of myth, inspired from structural phonology. But there was another model, that of structural semantics, advocated by Hjelmslev and taken up in Greimas's attempt at a thoroughgoing semantic approach, the only one extending from the study of the structure of lexical items to that of texts, discourses and narratives. His stencilled 'Course' (which was to become his *Sémantique structurale*, 1966) is alluded to in Barthes's *Elements of Semiology* (1964).

Now semantics, when seriously tackled, immediately shows the limitations of the notion of sign as a starting-point. Signs undoubtedly exist as phenomena; words in particular (and especially nouns), as Saussure acknowledged, 'strike the mind' (*Course*, 111, 113-14). But Saussure's diagrams on pages 104 and 112, which show the 'coupling of thought with phonic substance' as a carving out of these two floating, labile, continuous and parallel substances, are too optimistic. However, it would be extremely unfair just to categorize Saussure thus and dismiss him. On the one hand, his *Course* showed that he was only too aware of the practical difficulties in finding the units of a language (*Course*, 104-5), since 'as a rule we do not communicate through isolated signs, but rather through groups of signs, through organized masses which are themselves signs' (*Course*, 123). On the other hand, the abundant series of unpublished studies on anagrams manifested the subtlety of his perception of semantic mechanisms at, so to speak, the atomic as well as the molecular level.

It is therefore more rewarding to take his suggestion seriously and start from the idea of language as bi-planar (*Course*, 104), the plane of signifiers constituting the plane of *expression*, and that of signifieds that of *content* (using the names Hjelmslev gave these planes). The difference is that the structure of these two planes is not necessarily the same; the planes are non-conformal, there is no one-to-one correspondence between them except perhaps at privileged moments, even though their forms might present some general structural similarities. Barthes in *Elements* (S,39) adopts Hjelmslev's version, as did Greimas, explaining that within each plane Hjelmslev distinguishes two further strata, that of *form* and that of *substance* making four strata in all.[10]

However, in *Elements*, Barthes makes no theoretical use of one of Hjelmslev's crucial notions, that of the minimal units of language, which Hjelmslev calls *figurae* (this has been seen above (p. 231) apropos of distinctive features). These are the elements, on the planes of both content and expression, through which new signs can be formed. A language is in terms of its purpose a sign system; but in terms of its structure — and here lies its essential peculiarity — it is a system of *figurae* which can be used to construct signs. Thus signs are relevant if we consider the 'external' functions of a language, its relation to non-linguistic factors, but not if we consider its 'proper internal functions' (Hjelmslev, 1961, 41-7). This choice of terms shows that Hjelmslev agreed with Saussure's hierarchy, where value is stressed more than signification, and signification more than reference. We saw that for Saussure, 'in language (*langue*) there are only differences *without positive terms*'; it is difficult in practice for semantics to get started on such principles, however, and this is why Greimas paid homage to Hjelmslev for recognizing nevertheless the importance of content.

Barthes in *Elements* mentions some attempts to explore the semantic substance through the method of 'fields' (*S*,44) and especially that of componential analysis, which stresses the 'form of content'. A morpheme like 'mare' can be decomposed into atoms of meaning called semantic components or *semes*, like 'horse' + 'female'. By commuting each one of these, one can obtain new morphemes: 'pig' + 'female' = 'sow'; 'horse' + 'male' = 'stallion'. Greimas has suggested the notions of a *semic kernel*, which together with *contextual semes* constitute *sememes*, a term reserved for meanings one finds in specific contexts or situations, as distinct from *lexemes* or lexical items. The sememe is the unit on which the sentence is built, hence the hopes of Greimas and others of linking the semantics of sentences with the more recent semantics of texts in the structural analysis of narrative. The text is then viewed as an expanded sememe, the sememe as a text in miniature.

Barthes was hampered by the fact that a general semantic theory was and is still missing; but his naming of connotations by means of neologisms like *craintivité* or *sélénité*, shows a first-rate perception of culturally or stylistically relevant semes. In each section of *Elements*, semantics is the missing link between the existing linguistics and the semiology which Barthes is trying to outline. In *Système de la Mode* he comes entirely on his own to the conclusion that the non-conformal character of the two planes of language means that they must be analysed separately. A difficulty of semantics is that the semes are by definition meaningful and not meaningless like the distinctive features, so that the idea of a double articulation is somewhat lame here. As F.P. Dinneen puts it: 'On the level of expression, the figurae are the nonsign constituents of signs, but on the level of content, they are the more generic sign-components of more specific signs' (1967, 413). Content figurae, however, do not exist in a free state but only in a bound state, even if they can sometimes be represented by a word. For instance *walk*, *ride*, *drive* and *fly* all contain the seme 'movement', but the latter cannot be considered a signified since there is no corresponding signifier even though the word between inverted commas can approximately be used to describe it.[11]

The question of the actualization of meaning, which would otherwise have remained implicit, through the play of relations *in praesentia* and *in absentia* arises explicitly when it is transposed from linguistics to semiology. How can the axes of syntagm and paradigm be transposed to spatial 'purports' or to multi-channelled media, like film? One suggestion Barthes, makes is the notion of 'typical sign' for each 'substance': the verbal sign, the graphic sign, the iconic sign, the gestural sign, are all 'typical signs' (S,47). Making use of it, however, sometimes turns out to be problematic.

Another problem for semiological studies concerns the fact that many seemingly analogical arrangements on syntagmatic and paradigmatic axes turn out to be simple tabulations lacking the main and most mysterious ingredients of language: the integration of syntax and semantics and the semantic synthesis itself. What still remains to be explained is why we find such tabulations illuminating despite their patently simplistic character. The idea was already implicit in psychoanalytic studies like Charles Mauron's on Racine which was an inspiration for Barthes's own 'Racinian Man' (R). Mauron's suggestion was to 'superimpose' literary works on one another (as used to be done with photographs in order to reveal generic features) and this also allowed one to grasp an evolution in Racine's inspiration. For despite Jakobson's objection — the fact that concurrence as well as concatenation could occur as a combinatorial mode — there might still be a basic sense in which the syntagm, although not one-dimensional, remains sequential, as G. Lepschy points out (1970, 49). How then can this apply to spatial syntagms? Perhaps one needs to decide whether one is going to adopt an *articulatory, acoustic* or *auditory* model of communication, one which puts the emphasis on the sender, the structure of the message or the reader. Barthes switched from the first to the third via the second in the course of his career.

Many would argue that the reader's point of view is the main one since as *Système de la Mode* suggests, it is perhaps the path between possible routes which constitutes the meaning, just as the path chosen among several possible routes constitutes the painting (or, as some radical theorists, praised by Barthes, have argued, the verbal rendering of such routes, so that a painting is ultimately nothing but the sum of its descriptions). L. Jenny (1978b) argues persuasively that the reading of texts may be illuminated by the study of the processes at work in reading an image. Perhaps what is missing is the proper logico-mathematical model; Piaget in his *Structuralism* (1968, 113) observed that, even in the seventeenth century, mathematical thought had gone beyond linear taxonomy and conceived infinitesimal calculus. Thus Leibniz's differential notion of *situs* has been contrasted with Descartes's substantialist outlook by J.L. Houdebine (1971), with an eye to recent debates in semiology.

The two axes lend themselves to various and sometimes contradictory ideological uses. The specific roles attributed by Martinet to syntagmatic and paradigmatic pressures in his theory of language change are used by Barthes in an early study, 'Rhetoric of the Image' (*IMT*) to bolster a dialectic of freedom and constraint. Two areas in which linguistic tenets are exploited ideologically are the claims that language is diacritical and that it is made of discrete units.

I have already stated that semantics makes it difficult to maintain the view that in languages there are only differences without positive terms. This is in fact a genuine area of indeterminacy in Saussure, which led to a split between the two main schools among his followers, the functionalists based in Prague and Paris and the glossematicians based in Copenhagen. The latter defined linguistic units only by their differential, diacritical, relational, 'negative' value; the former maintained that the unit is not *only* what the other units are not, but has in addition some positive reality. Barthes discusses this not only because of its intrinsic linguistic interest and the ideological investment he has made in both substance and form, but because he has to, in view of the essentially second-order character of the semiological sign, which as we shall see can be either renaturalized or refunctionalized, depending on whether the user wishes to disguise its semantic value or not.

The diacritical character of linguistic units finds favour with non-linguists, who associate it with a greatly exaggerated and idealized notion of the systematic character of *langue*. In fact, when one moves away from phonological units, where the oppositive and functional aspects perforce coincide, one finds the differential point of view impossible to apply strictly to grammar, let alone semantics. Even in phonology, phonetic considerations have to be introduced. Over-emphasis on the diacritical aspect also leads to neglect of other aspects of language which are crucial in the arts, such as redundancy and expressiveness. Finally, the field of linguistics may be radically extended if one chooses to include not only what language is taken to *be* but what one can besides *do* with it; this point is made with great force in Ducrot and Todorov (1972).

The assumption that linguistics deals only with discrete units can be traced to the same preoccupations with difference. Barthes's ambivalence on this question is greater than ever, but his reservations are perhaps more explicit. They chiefly concern Jakobson's binarism, which overdetermines Saussure's fondness for dichotomies (and its presumed Hegelian source), in spite of its having been wholeheartedly adopted by Lévi-Strauss and Greimas (see for instance *S*,12 and 99*n*3). Here again, the transposition of phonology to the other aspects of language, and especially to semantics, has not proved very successful. Meanwhile, the study and recognition, at long last, of elements like suprasegmentals or prosodic features (see p. 256) can only help to mitigate, as Barthes notes (*S*,20), the 'digitalism' he objects to. The ideology of the digital has even given rise to a counter-ideology of the analogical, for instance in P. Wollen's *Signs and Meaning in the Cinema* and A. Wilden's *System and Structure*. Barthes too had a definite tendency to think in dichotomies, but he often counterbalanced it by a stress on the *neutral* and *complex* poles where such oppositions are cancelled.

In the face of such complexities, one can readily understand Saussure's procrastination and Barthes's obsession with aphasia. One of the paradoxical consequences of the rise of the computer has been a healthy respect for the achievements of the human brain, when at first it looked as if it could easily be emulated by its mechanical progeny. As for the oversimplifications and ideological biases which can be detected in all thinkers, one can only be grateful for them, since they are an aspect of the drive which allowed not only linguistics but semiology to come about in the first place — what Barthes called 'the great adventure of desire'.

Notes

Chapter 1: Where to begin?

1. Barthes means that the 'object' is the deeper subject. For instance, in Brecht's *The Mother*, the object is Marxism but the subject, as the title indicates, is motherhood (*E*,139). A joint reprint of *Le Degré zéro de l'écriture* and *Eléments de sémiologie* states that the two books have very different subjects but the same object, namely the notion of connotation, which is the linch-pin of Barthes's thought (*G*,5). The subject/object distinction clearly corresponds to his awareness of the duality of the messages he sends, and is again used in the recent preface to the Catalogue of the Cy Twombly exhibition (1979b). In this study, it is used in the more usual sense, which goes back to scholasticism via Kant, and opposes man as subject of knowledge to all that is not the knowing self. This epistemological sense is the origin of the paradoxical denotation of the active and autonomous knowing agent as a 'subject', despite the etymology which defined man as 'subjected' to his passions. To the psychoanalyst Lacan, the word 'subject' means the 'speaking subject' of linguistics; the question of the active or passive status of this subject, however, is crucial to an understanding of contemporary thought and of Barthes in particular. Henceforth, the 'subject' will always mean here the human subject in that sense, except when the context makes it clear that the ordinary meaning of 'subject matter' is intended.

2. Barthes was still included in an *Anthologie des sociologues français contemporains* (by Jean Duvignaud) as recently as 1970, long after his evolution led him to deprecate scientific pursuits like sociology and *Mythologies* (an extract of which figures in this anthology) in particular.

3. The work of N. Ruwet (1972, 1975) illustrates this evolution particularly well. See also on the renewed interest in signifying practices in the Chinese, Indian, Islamic, Judaic and other traditions, Kristeva (1969b) and (1975).

4. On the way in which literary criticism was subjected to the imperatives of the Cold War, see for instance Ponge (1970), which preceded by nearly a decade the spate of autobiographies by French Communist intellectuals. Sartre's relations with Communists is well documented, for instance in Burnier (1966). Sartre's ambivalence towards science foreshadows recent trends, but see Houbart (1964, 26) George (1976, 13) and Poster (1975, 273). *Arguments* was published from 1957 to 1962; see the two recent volumes published by Gallimard (1977) as well as

Poster (1975) (which has appeared since this was written, and in which the whole period is excellently analysed) and *Le Magazine littéraire* (1976, 1977).

5. For instance in the 'Human Relations Area Files' and G.P. Murdock's 'World Ethnographic Sample', as well as models like L. Guttman's (see Cuisenier, 1967).

6. Moscovici (1976) gives a sociologist's view of French reactions to psychoanalysis by the early 1960s. I have described the more common arguments and devices used by French writers in their fight against the threat of psychoanalysis in my *L'usurpateur et le prétendant* (1964), an essay written before the mass-conversion of the French intelligentsia. The rise of the psychoanalyst in real life was offset in literature by confining him to three principal roles: the detractor of metaphysical or religious revelation, the accomplice of bad faith, and the instrument of totalitarianism. These roles were so strongly established until the publication of Lacan's *Écrits* (1966) that one must wonder how they ever came to be superseded. The answer is roughly as follows: the revelation now is that of the unconscious itself, while bad faith consists in denying its primacy. As for the totalitarian potentialities of psychoanalysis, the general response is more ambivalent. In its early days the only enthusiasts of psychoanalysis were the surrealists, and this should be remembered when reading the specific objections made to surrealism by the *Tel Quel* writers (1971). One should not forget the historical importance of a movement which provoked the enthusiasm of authors like Leiris and Michaux who prefigured so many aspects of modern writing. Indeed, Lacan's famous formulation, that the unconscious is structured like a language, may well have been suggested by the surrealists' attention to the linguistic expression of psychic phenomena (for instance, Breton and Eluard's suggestion, in *L'Immaculée conception* (1930), that the language patterns observed in the various psychoses could profitably replace the hackneyed genres of the time).

7. A striking feature of contemporary books is that whatever their actual subject they include a crash-course in epistemology as a means of stating the relationship of their concepts to a new intellectual paradigm. See especially many works by Chomsky, Šaumjan (1971), Costes (1973), or the tables of concepts appended to Lacan (1966), Sollers (1968a), Kristeva (1969a, 1977), and Barthes's *S/Z*. A glossary was also appended by B. Brewster to his translation (1969) of Althusser's *Pour Marx* (1966). Recent trans-translations into French of Popper, Kuhn and Feyerabend confirm this epistemological revival. The conjunction of Althusser's *Pour Marx* (1966). Recent translations into French of Popper, Kuhn and Feyerabend confirm this epistemological revival. The conjunction of Supérieure, whose periodical, *Cahiers pour l'analyse* published several crucial articles, one of which was the basis of *S/Z* (see Reboul, 1967).

8. The existence of an Asiatic mode of production seemed to interfere with the official Marxist version of the development of history as a linear succession of types of society determined by the same causes. See on this Godelier (1975), and for a semiotic overview, Kristeva (1975). The tenets of the *Annales* school, founded in 1929, made it a precursor of structuralism. Its rejection of what it called *histoire événementielle* (chiefly political and diplomatic history) in favour of the study of slow processes and the basic elements of social life (see Appendix, p. 222) can lead, as it did in Barthes, to a critique of narrative exposition and a plea for an analytic method and presentation. The whole approach is now

paradoxically under fire because of its positivism, on the grounds that the discourse of history (on which Barthes was writing when this reassessment was under way) is itself part of history. As historians agree, a major part in this reassessment was played by Foucault, despite his acknowledged debt to contemporary historical practice. The historian must therefore psychoanalyse his own discourse; see on this Nora's discussion with Pontalis (Nora, 1977) in an issue of the *Nouvelle Revue de Psychanalyse* significantly entitled 'Mémoires' and also *Faire de l'histoire* (1974) edited by J. Le Goff and P. Nora). Historians are familiar with what psychoanalysts call *effets d'après-coup*, the deferred action of past events (*nachträglichkeit*) which are reinterpreted in the light of present experiences and desires; this explains the plurality of interpretations, since any kind of memory is a search for origins and legitimation on the part of a group or an individual. The notion of verisimilitude is therefore as important in history as it is in literary studies (as we shall see in relation to the role of memorization in the constitution of meaning), although reactions to the relativization of historical reality can vary: history may seem to be little different from fiction, or narrative may be presented, as it is by J.-P. Faye (1972a and b) as an ideal instrument to understand political ideologies, which have an undoubted reality and productivity.

9. See Monod (1968), and Lacan (1968) for Lacan(?)'s correctives whenever Monod seems to stray from the path of ideology into positive science, as he does elsewhere on the question of language (Monod, 1970, 144).

10. Notable examples of philosophers dissatisfied with their activity or its institutionalized form are Politzer (1973), Nizan (1960), Revel (1954), Piaget (1968b) and Châtelet (1970). The contestation of philosophy seen as the crown of humanist studies, a pursuit for adolescents 'mature' enough to withstand its critical effects, has however been toned down since the government's intention to phase out the teaching of philosophy in secondary schools (a uniquely French institution) has become obvious. Hence the recently constituted Groupe de Recherches sur l'Enseignement Philosophique (see GREPH, 1977).

11. See Lévy-Leblond and Jaubert (1975), the periodicals *La Recherche* (for instance Jurdant, 1975) and *Impa Science*, or *Discours biologique et ordre social*, a collective work in the interesting 'Science ouverte' series published by Le Seuil (Achard *et al.*, 1977).

12. Poulet (1967) gives an interesting survey of the contending schools. Other collections, which reflect a slightly later state of play, are Doubrovsky and Todorov (1971) and two special issues of the Communist periodical *La Nouvelle Critique* (1968, 1970) containing papers given at two conferences organized in conjunction with the *Tel Quel* group.

Chapter 2: The structuralist debate

1. Contributions to or assessments of this debate can be found in Sebag (1964), *Les Temps modernes* (1966), *L'Arc* (1966), *Yale French Studies* (1966), *Esprit* (1967), Wahl (1968), Piaget (1968), Leduc (1970), *Psychanalyse et marxisme* (1970), Lane (1970), Macksey and Donato (1970), *Twentieth Century Studies* (1970), Guiraud (1971), Ducrot and Todorov (1972), Jameson (1972), Hollier (1973), Robey (1973), *The Human Context* (1973), Scholes (1974), Culler (1975),

Benoist (1975), Pettit (1975), Hawkes (1977), Sturrock (1979), etc., in addition, of course, to all the books and articles by the protagonists themselves.

2. The status of language is obviously crucial in this debate. It had already been discussed in Marxist and psychoanalytical terms. Barthes was happy in *Mythologies* to be able, for once, to agree with Stalinist orthodoxy on the matter of the 'reticence ... of language according to Stalin' (*M*,158). Stalin, when he had become more and more remote from public life, suddenly manifested his presence in print once more on the unlikely subject (for him) of linguistics. He asserted that language is not part of superstructure, as had been stated by N.Y. Marr, whose disciples formed the main school of Soviet linguistics. This unexpected support for the idea of language as beyond the reach of conscious control was welcomed by Barthes, Lacan and others. It has become obvious today, with the reaction against the structuralist wave, that the *fact* of Stalin's intervention underlined at any rate the political nature of language, and that its *content* was evidently geared to the internal policy of the USSR, since it had a direct bearing on the question of official languages in the various Soviet republics (see on this Lepschy (1967), Calvet (1975), Houdebine (1977b).

Yet although linguistics lent its prestige to Lacan's theory, in another sense psychoanalysis functions as the foundation of linguistics. It is only because of phenomena like slips of the tongue or dreams that we can accept tenets which have a great importance in Barthes's later theories, like that of the primacy of the signifier. The question of the scientific status of psychoanalysis is therefore crucial. In recent French texts, it is often simply asserted, but efforts have been made to ground psychoanalysis in various conceptions of science (see for instance Bouveresse (1976), Kermode (1976) or Soper (1978).

Science is defined by A. Badiou (1969b) as the 'subject' of philosophy, precisely because there is no 'subject' of science; this is why science is experienced by philosophy as a torture chamber.

3. 1966 proved to be a vintage year, a veritable watershed, with the publication of major structuralist works like Foucault's *Les mots et les choses* and Lacan's *Écrits* (Laplanche and Pontalis's *Vocabulaire de la psychanalyse* (1967) also contributed to the dissemination of Lacan's work) which followed hard on the heels of the work of Althusser and his disciples. The same year saw the appearance of *Critique et vérité* and Doubrovsky's book on the Quarrel (Todorov's anthology of texts by Russian formalists had come out the year before), Greimas's *Sémantique structurale*, Benveniste's *Problèmes de linguistique générale* and the first translations of Chomsky (following his *Aspects of the Theory of Syntax*, 1965). The periodicals *Cahiers pour l'analyse* and *Langages* were founded (on the linguistic plane, Jakobson's *Essais de linguistique générale* (1963) and the first publication of Saussure's *Anagrams* (1964) were just beginning to make an impact as well). Last but not least, a special number of the periodical *L'Arc* devoted to Sartre, and containing his attack on structuralism, appeared in the same year (see Note 1). Finally, on another but no less important plane, 1966 was also the year of the Cultural Revolution in China, and of the appearance of a pamphlet by the Situationist International which denounced Western society, in terms reminiscent of *Mythologies*, as a 'Society of the Spectacle'.

4. Piaget's outstanding polymathy is offset by blind spots which unfortunately

concern vital aspects of the subject. He stresses cognitive psychology at the expense of any study of affective life. He omits all mention of the manifestations of imaginative and linguistic creativity, namely literature, art and ideology. Finally, his indifference to historicity (the sense of the irreversibility of time and its effects) in socio-political life, as against his vivid awareness of it in the biological, cognitive, and perhaps ontological fields, results in a totally negative assessment of Foucault's work (as against his interesting though quirky treatment of Althusser's). (See also Appendix, p. 217.)

5. Making allowance for an unconscious has led to a characteristic use of the word *effect*, which before structuralism was found mostly in scientific discourse (unless it was, prophetically, in Brecht's alienation-effect). Lacan speaks of *truth-effects*, Althusser of *society-effects*, Barthes of *reality-effects*, Greimas of *meaning-effects* and other critics of *beauty-effects* (the latter will probably irritate traditional critics most of all, although the formalists used the word *effect* in similar fashion). A question of major relevance in this connection is obviously that of the relations between language and thought. Barthes right from the start, and whatever ambiguities he evinces on related subjects, was adamant about the impossibility of there being thought without language (Z,89), thus 'solving' this thorny problem (as against this, see for instance Gardner (1972) on Lévi-Strauss and Piaget). In this sense, structuralism could be said to have substituted a new dualism founded on Lacanian psychoanalysis for the old existentialist one founded on ontology; a continuum between man and nature is, on the contrary, the premise of the 'nouvelle anthropologie naturaliste' of thinkers like S. Moscovici and E. Morin.

6. Gaston Bachelard is one of the most remarkable thinkers of the twentieth century. He enjoyed two successive careers, as a psychoanalyst of science and as one of the founding fathers of the *nouvelle critique* (see Lecourt, 1975).

7. The 'patient silence of structuralism in the face of History' finally exorcised history as superego, according to Barthes (GV,51). Spatialization now seemed liberating, as opposed to its previous association with alienation by philosophies which equated temporality and authenticity (as in J. Gabel (1962), whose work was advertised in *Arguments* in the very issue containing one of Barthes's first structuralist articles).

8. See also on this debate Ricoeur's *De l'Interprétation* (1965), a work of lucidity and integrity, containing some definitive passages on the compatibility and incompatibility of structuralist and phenomenologist perspectives. M. Tort's critique (1966), although cogent and in parts devastating, ignores the fact that the long examination Ricoeur devotes to the criticisms behaviourists and empiricists level at psychoanalysis will seem redundant only to people who, like Tort, have been relatively insulated from them — by phenomenology, in fact.

9. A *doublet* is one of two words which have the same etymology but different meanings; *hôtel* and *hôpital* are relevant examples in view of Foucault's *Histoire de la folie*. Foucault, in *Les mots et les choses* (*The Order of Things*) inverts the definition, tracing the heterogeneous genealogy of a supposedly single notion rather than stressing the common origin of two different ones. Foucault's definition comes as the conclusion of the 'archaeology' carried out in *Les mots et les choses* which uncovers a succession of intellectual configurations he calls *epistemes*. The *episteme* is defined as the tacit experience of order which stands

between the fundamental codes of a culture (which govern its language, perceptions, modes of exchange, techniques, values and practices) and the scientific and philosophical interpretations it produces. This experience always appears in a definite mode at a given moment in history, and constitutes a *sol positif*. Positivity is the manifest or latent relation to the current mode of order which is necessary for the various forms assumed by empirical knowledge throughout the ages to be recognized as such. These forms are complex and relatively stable conglomerates of concepts, traditions, practices, institutions and uses of language. Such were, for instance, in the classical age, general grammar, the analysis of wealth, natural history, and in the nineteenth century, philology, political economy, biology. Can it be said that the latter replaced the former? Up to a point only, since each element in both triads can be shown to have more to do with the other two than that which later stood in the same structural position as itself.

The change from one *episteme* to the next is characterized as 'enigmatic' — surely the understatement of the year, but one which effectively holds ready-made explanations at bay. Foucault's archaeological enquiry reveals two great discontinuities in Western culture: that which marks the beginning of the classical age towards the middle of the seventeenth century, and that which, at the start of the nineteenth, marks the beginning of our modernity. Intimations of a fourth episteme can be felt in the recent 'death' of man.

By a skilful structural equation, he shows the arrival of man in the locus formerly occupied by classical discourse, as well as the entrance of man's correlate, the unconscious, which is not a separate entity, empirically discovered, but simply the Other of this new scientific object. The 'human sciences' are not and never will be 'sciences'; they are forms of knowledge which will last as long as 'man' does. They are constantly threatened by the proximity of the other two components of the modern *episteme*: the exact sciences, wistfully held up as an ideal, and a type of philosophical reflection which conceives history as the 'harmonious science of totality'. Conversely, the human sciences represent a danger for the other sciences, which must forever guard against 'psychologism', 'sociologism' or 'historicism'. The only challenge to an uncritical acceptance of this situation consists therefore in wondering whether 'man' really exists; the removal of this 'crease' in knowledge would open the way to a new sort of thinking.

10. It is interesting to find that Laplanche and Pontalis show in *Vocabulaire de la psychanalyse* (*The Language of Psychoanalysis*) that Freud, for all his seemingly absolute determinism, still needed notions like 'object choice' or 'choice of neurosis' in order to explain how constitutional and historical factors acquire a meaning and a motivational value.

11. Although he published a text on Fourier (*Sade, Fourier, Loyola*, 1971) Barthes was too distrustful of spontaneity and concerned with the proper place of ritual to be a libertarian. Recent interpretations have argued that Fourier was not as permissive as was generally thought, and this agrees with the current realization that all utopian thought perforce has a dogmatic streak. The dedication of *S/Z* to the members of Barthes's seminar who had caused the flow of speech through their attentive *écoute*, might have been interpreted in a rather revolutionary way in the post-1968 years, but Barthes set the record straight unambiguously (*T*,100).

12. Comte is at present a favourite target for among other things, the highly systematic character of his thought, which is now interpreted as a paranoid denial of femininity, both in himself and as one of the poles of all thought. See the latest edition of his *Cours de philosophie positive* (1975) and Kofman (1978).

13. After years of fruitful dialogue between Sartre and Lévi-Strauss (the traces of which can be found in *Critique de la raison dialectique* and *La pensée sauvage*), Sartre bluntly and perhaps thoughtlessly but, as hindsight shows, not without a certain perception, suddenly lashed out in an interview published in *L'Arc* (1966) which finalized the rearrangement of the battle-lines. But as D. Grisoni (1975) pointed out the immediate and radical transcending of the structuralist position is to be found in the under-read *Critique* rather than in such polemical pronouncements, which do not do justice, for instance, to the profundity of Foucault's analyses. Foucault lightheartedly retorted that he was not trying to explain events by means of the 'pratico-inert' — a key notion in *Critique*, the dead weight of what was once a living praxis — but by the 'theoretico-active'. After 1968, Sartre and Foucault were united by their common activism and *gauchisme*. Sartre is the only model who survives a tidal wave of iconoclasm in the later Barthes (see Chapter 15). A very balanced assessment of the respective merits and roles of phenomenology and structuralism can be found in Metz (1979, especially 163). One year after 1968, the fascinating episode of the 'Man with the Tape Recorder' allowed Sartre to re-state his position in relation to psychoanalysis and the subject as agent in *Les Temps modernes* (1969).

Chapter 3: A narrative with a hero

1. This is almost inevitable in any case since Barthes at various times published works after he had moved on to a different theoretical position, so that their prefaces and blurbs are at variance with the contents. Notable examples are *On Racine*, *Critical Essays*, *Système de la Mode* and the essay on ancient rhetoric in *Communications 16*.

2. Poetics (this ancient word had already been chosen by Valéry as the title of his course at the Collège de France) could then be defined as the science of what the Russian formalists called 'literariness' (*literaturnost*), what makes a text specifically literary. The positivist assumptions in such a notion are obvious, which does not mean that it has no immediate usefulness. As Barthes pointed out, it is up to historians to prove whether what we call 'literature' has a transhistorical existence; the word, as he stressed in *Writing Degree Zero*, is of recent origin (late eighteenth century in both English and French).

An anamorphosis is a distorted projection of an object, which can be seen in its correct proportions only when it is looked at from a certain point of view, or reflected in a suitable mirror. An exhibition of such anamorphoses at the Musée des arts décoratifs in Paris in 1976 allowed the critics to take up many themes of current theory of literature, some of which had already been launched at the time of the *nouvelle critique* after the rediscovery of the baroque outlook (see Rousset, 1947, and more recently a writer praised by Barthes, Sarduy, 1975). Anamorphoses imply that there is an *orthodox*, a right opinion, or way of looking at things; yet it is well known that they have often been used in order to question all norms by the introduction of transgressive contents: sex, scatology or death.

Their role is thus comparable to the type of cultural practices highlighted by Bakhtin in his study of carnival (1970a).

The Chomskyan concept of competence, which takes up the old rhetorical idea of norm and deviation descriptively, not normatively, has been extended as, for instance, Dell Hymes's 'communicative competence' (see Giglioli 1972). The notion of a literary competence is therefore an object of study suggested by a triple background. It is probably explored most systematically in J. Culler's *Structuralist Poetics*, which transcends literary study and leads towards an examination of cultural competence (compare with Greimas's work on the 'semiotics of the natural world' (1970a) or to Perelman and Olbrechts-Tyteca, 1958).

3. The prototype of the teleological version of Barthes's career was transmitted in Marc Buffat's article 'Le simulacre', in the *Tel Quel* special issue which marked a turning-point in Barthes's attitude. One of the most striking aspects of this change is the presence of a type of discourse which Bakhtin calls 'hidden polemics' (1970a). The reader senses that Barthes is carrying on an acrimonious argument with adversaries who are not clearly identified; this contrasts with the single-mindedness and vulnerability so evident in, say, *Critique et vérité*, even in the face of bitter attacks. On Gide's 'disappointing' attitude, see P. Herbart's non-theoretical but acute study (1952).

Chapter 4: He is a writer, who wants to be one

1. On modernism, see Bradbury and McFarlane (1976) who give the dates 1890-1930 and, characterizing this period by a tradition of introversion and experiment, are thus able to account for the chiliastic effect of the idea of *fin-de-siècle*. Yet the authors acknowledge that this antagonism to the referential bias of both the preceding and succeeding periods does not prevent continuities with committed art. See also on this Josipovici in Cruikshank (1970), as well as Kermode (1971) on paleo- and neo-modernism. The mimetic or experimental character of modern(ist) fiction is perhaps ultimately less important than a belief in a cataclysmic rupture. Thus Walter Benjamin (1973, 152) sees Brecht's non-Aristotelian drama as a progress comparable to Riemann's non-Euclidean geometry while Barthes needs to believe in an absolute opposition between new theories and those they supersede. Another criterion is an ontological preference for either the promotion of the mighty *modernist* creator and his subtle characters or the demotion of author and character as subjects in *modernity*.

2. The periodical *Tel Quel*, founded in 1960, and the group of the same name, assumed an ever greater importance in Barthes's thought, despite the changing allegiances of both parties. Its best-known members are Philippe Sollers, Julia Kristeva and Marcelin Pleynet. The collection of articles *Théorie d'ensemble* (1968) gives a representative overview of its positions at the time when its influence was at its peak.

3. This trend has been powerfully reinforced by Lacan's work, all the more so since his doctrine is supported by a very distinctive exploitation of style. Although this style has obvious psychological roots, Lacan claims that its main features (chiefly based on etymological and phonetic punning — see Lavers, 1971b) demonstrate the materiality of the signifier and the mechanisms of the

unconscious. Reading him thus constitutes a major aspect of analytical training. In his classification of discourses and the attitudes they reveal, Lacan, like the surrealists, makes use of a typology based on psychotic uses of language (see also Irigaray, 1967 and Green, 1973) combined with another typology inspired by Hegel's dialectic of Master and Slave (see for instance its applications in Nemo, 1974).

Although a typology of discursive strategies is at the heart of Barthes's early inspiration and thus can hardly be devoid of psychoanalytical roots, he was at first more outwardly concerned with social determinants, like Queneau (1965), or recently Duneton (1978). As for textual practice, which in writers like Philippe Sollers, Hélène Cixous or Lucette Finas is fused with their acute theoretical awareness, Barthes's depends on a representational element which his extremism alone would consider less advanced. It foreshadowed various deconstructive strategies in Derrida; see Part IV.

Chapter 5: The network (synchrony)

1. And an outstanding example of *après-coup*! See J. Godechot (1974) which covers four generations of historians. The reviews of F. Furet (1978) all bore titles like 'Is the Revolution over?', 'It's over!', etc. What gave point to the matter was the current effort to establish a causal connection between nineteenth-century progressivism, the Enlightenment, even rationality, and totalitarianism.

2. One sometimes wonders whether Saussure's name has not become a kind of shorthand favoured over more immediately relevant names (although this does not apply to Barthes, whose *Elements of Semiology* and *Système de la Mode* show he was familiar with the full array of sources available when he began to write). It certainly would not be possible to understand the parts of linguistics which Barthes found most useful by reading Saussure's *Course* alone. Greimas, whom Barthes had met in 1950 at Alexandria where they were both teaching, had introduced him to the work of Jakobson, Lévi-Strauss's major linguistic source. Merleau-Ponty, in his discussion of language (1945, 1960), makes use of concepts put forward by the proponents of Gestalt theory, by Cassirer, by the French and German phenomenologists, by Bühler, whose theory of linguistic functions was extended by Jakobson, by Piaget, and even by Proust, which shows that, in his refreshingly catholic outlook, literature could make a contribution as valid as philosophy and experimental psychology. This must have greatly encouraged Barthes, in whose pantheon Proust figures prominently.

3. Barthes's texts could easily today fit into a volume of essays like Giglioli (1972) or Turner (1974), and were forerunners of recent studies on the role of language in colonial, sexual or social oppression. See for instance Gobard (1976) which analyses linguistic imperialism in its four dimensions: *vernaculaire* (the language of a territorial unit), *véhiculaire* (that of trade), *référentiaire* (that of a national culture) and *mythique* (that of a spiritual country).

4. Here is therefore another source of Barthes's central insight, together with the nausea which he said bourgeois myth caused in him. In both cases, however, language means action; the privileged locus of his insights is therefore perhaps not so much sociolinguistics as pragmatics. See his preface to Flahault (1978) for a recent recognition of this. In his critique of the Stalinist 'terror before all

problematics' Barthes is a clear precursor of the present mood. He has given excellent analyses of both Marxist and bourgeois writing, showing amazing sensitivity to the stratifications and sects within Marxism (as Sartre was doing at the same moment in *Nekrassov*, with the same effects of high comedy) as well as to the corrupting effects of a fundamentally fraudulent project in the bourgeois discourse on colonialism.

Chapter 6: The voyage (diachrony)

1. On Sartre's comments on Barthes's version of his distinction between poetry and prose as the activity of, respectively, the *écrivain* and the *écrivant*, see *A Plea for Intellectuals*, which also shows Sartre's reinterpretation in terms of information theory. (When I refer to *What is Literature?* I include the other articles on the same subject published in *Situations II*.)

2. In *Critique et vérité* Barthes opposes to positivist ideas on creation and criticism the medieval 'management of the text' split into four roles: the *scriptor*, the *compilator*, the *commentator* and the *auctor*. Yet this arrangement ended up in yielding interpretations which would look today no less 'delirious' than those of the *nouvelle critique*. This is because the critical vision begins with the *compilator* (*CV*,76-7). Barthes also points out that multiple interpretation was so well understood that it was institutionalized in the medieval theory of the four meanings (literal, moral, allegorical and anagogical) (*CV*,51). His paradigmatic opposition between classical and modern therefore requires some adjustments. A more serious objection is that the plural model contradicts the picture of classicism as straightforward choice with all hesitancy repressed — a proof that Barthes views both values with ambivalence.

3. The somewhat problematic concept of petite-bourgeoisie and the evolution of the political climate and of Barthes's attitudes give an extra dimension to this hesitancy (see on this Rancière 1974, 274n). Barthes in *Mythologies* defines the bourgeoisie in psychological/ontological terms (as the class which cannot recognize the Other but seeks to reduce everything to the Same) and never by means of its place in the process of production. His analyses contain however a structural aspect inasmuch as he sees society, like art, as ineluctably divided into trend-setters and epigones, and this is backed by an obvious economic element: the bourgeoisie can afford to buy the partridge which the petite-bourgeoisie must be content to contemplate in the glamorous photos of *Elle*.

In the Thibaudeau interview (1971) Barthes indicated a wish to undertake a serious sociological study of this subject. Various studies since then have attempted this task, for instance Poulantzas (1974) and Baudelot, Establet and Malemort (1974) who start from the same Marxist basis but see as central those sections of the population which neither sell their labour-power, like the proletariat, nor directly extract surplus-value, like the owners of means of production, but benefit from a retrocession of this surplus-value. As a number of critics pointed out, this economic account must nevertheless be supplemented with an analysis of the ideology of these classes (a belief in meritocracy, in the neutrality of the state, etc.).

4. The ground had been prepared by Bourdieu and Passeron (1964 and 1970); see also Baudelot and Establet (1971). The major contribution to Barthes's

privileged field is Renée Balibar (1974), a study of the process of acquisition of the national language and its accepted uses. The common language as *national* language is the result of a specific historical conflict. Like bourgeois law, its chief function was to give a unified, universalist, and thereby (in the interpretation of the post-Revolutionary period) progressive form to a content, which was in fact the domination of the bourgeoisie. The social contradiction in the two networks studied by Baudelot and Establet, *primaire-professionnel* and *secondaire-supérieur*, is reflected in opposite uses of this common language, 'style' being the preserve of the upper network (*secondaire-supérieur*). The famous division between preterite and present perfect, which Sartre, then Barthes, for all their acumen, took as a starting point, a 'Nature', here reveals its strategic function. A reality-effect is automatically obtained when the supposedly simpler, present perfect, form is used by a character or about him. Since literary effects are due to a built-in contradiction (between two modes of language use which the reader has been conditioned to interpret as norm and exception), they can be described in psychoanalytical terms as compromise formations, where the real state of affairs is repressed and disavowed by means of all the Freudian mechanisms: condensation, displacement, reversal, punning or the hallucinatory conjuring-up of the real. These analyses by Balibar (whose debt to Barthes is obvious and acknowledged) can also be compared, in a wider perspective, to Lévi-Strauss's account of myth as the imaginary solution to contradictory accounts of reality, the analysis of the cultural components of perception in Panofsky (1967) or Auerbach (1974) or Mary Douglas's (1970) use of Basil Bernstein's notion of elaborated and restricted codes in her theory of natural symbols in society.

5. See *SFL*, 34-7 for the elements and rules of the combinatorial game in Sade. This is not a simple metaphor since 'syntactic' rules such as reversibility (which states that anybody can be agent and object in turn) correspond to Barthes's notion of a plural text which is held up as an ideal. Yet, as Barthes agrees, the libertines who decided on those rules are the only ones who can speak and murder the others without retaliation — a crucial reservation considering that he cites the management of pleasure in Sade as a wise sharing out of roles in 'Writers, intellectuals, teachers' (*IMT*).

Chapter 7: The responsibility of forms

1. *Déçu* in French means 'disappointed', but Barthes's spelling *dé-ception* (in the French text) shows that he meant it as a multiple pun based on the etymological source *decipio*. It then means also 'deceived' and 'made to let go of' (*E*,259). *Décevoir* is also taken as the opposite of *concevoir*. Barthes also uses another semantic cluster around the words *défait* (undone, both deconstructed and vanquished) and *défection* (with its overtones of defaulting, being defective, or deserting).

Ashby's homeostat is a cybernetic model illustrating an 'ultrastable' system, that is, one which is homeostatically controlled, but which is in addition capable of taking circumstances into account (Ashby, 1960, 58 and 100; see also Wilden (1972).

2. Yet in *Mythologies* Barthes had already stressed that in Adamov's play *Ping-Pong* objects are not symbols, that is, clichés which serve to obliterate the

strangeness of their support. Objects for Adamov start a semantic drift which the later Barthes praised as a 'third meaning' (*IMT*). The substratum of this constant theme in his work is the ontology of existentialism with its Marxist and Oedipal connotations, but also his view of matter and language, as we shall see in Parts III and IV. The poetic Word is pregnant with unheard-of possibilities, so much that it merges with the 'silence' by which Barthes characterizes matter. Objects are then suitable symbols of modern alienation and 'desacralization' (as in essays in *Mythologies* on the Citroen DS-19, plastic, the Jet-Man or Jules Verne's *Nautilus*) because they are limited by individuation.

3. Various problems immediately arise (some of which are discussed in Parts III and IV), for instance the relative 'volumes' of signifier and signified — a problem already mentioned by Benveniste in the first number of *La Psychanalyse* (see *S*,166), and mainly, what is to be taken as a unit for both planes. Take the signifier: 'Precisely, what is it that signifies? A word? A line? A character? A situation? A tragedy? An entire body of work?' (*R*,164). Since literature is a code for which we have no Rosetta stone, we have to posit the signified before the signifier. More difficulties:

> If the work signifies the world ... [what level must we choose:] contemporary events (the English Restoration for *Athalie*)? The political situation (the Turkish crisis of 1671 for *Mithridate*)? The current of opinion? The 'vision of the world' (Goldmann)? And if the work signifies the author, the same uncertainty begins all over again; at what level of the person are we to establish the signified? The biographical circumstances? The emotional level? A psychology of age? An archaic psyche (Mauron)? (*R*,165)

Chapter 8: Everything, then, can be a myth?

1. This is also one aspect of the surrealist image, although Barthes prefers to draw comparable lessons from the haiku. When Breton said that 'the cat-headed dew was swaying', he meant, as Genette (1966a, 206) pointed out, that the cat-headed dew was swaying.

2. Later Barthes was to state that it is difference alone which produces meaning (*SM*,21). The more balanced precept is found in texts written at the beginning of his structuralist period: meaning comes from the interplay between difference and similarity.

3. Even without the explicit reference to 'structuralism' in 'Myth Today' (*M*,111), the association of myth with de-historicization and de-politicization would point to Lévi-Strauss as a source of inspiration; this interpretation pervaded *Tristes tropiques*, which appeared while Barthes in 1955 was writing *Mythologies*.

4. Barthes later often quoted this phrase, but the model he proposes for the structure of myth shows that he had rediscovered the idea of compromise formations and their relevance in the study of fiction. Mannoni's *Fictions freudiennes* put his theoretical insights to work in a particularly intelligent and entertaining way.

5. In order to distinguish between the first and the second system, Barthes suggests a terminology (*M*,116-17) which is added here to the diagram (*M*,115). The spatial representation is of course a simple metaphor for Barthes's original

intuition of a second-order language, first conceptualized as *writing* in *Degree Zero*.

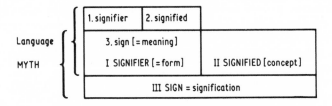

In *Mythologies* Barthes calls the two systems *object-language* and *metalanguage*. Yet the diagram rather corresponds to the later notion of *connotation*, since in metalanguage the sign of the first system is taken as *signified*, not signifier. This opposition is clear in Hjelmslev (*S*,89); here in *Elements* we find a representation (*S*,90) which I reproduce upside down in order to show the similarity with the earlier one above.

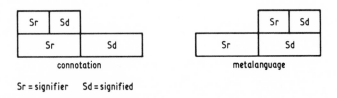

In the case of connotation, the first system is called *denotation*. The striking difference between the earlier and the later formulations is that Barthes at first stressed the unit formed by signifier and signified, and later the indefinite superimposition of such 'staggered system'. Traces of both conceptions are found in *Système de la Mode*, showing Barthes's evolution.

6. This even applies to 'natural' objects. In a famous passage (*M*,112n) Barthes shows that the natural activity of sea-bathing takes place in an atmosphere saturated with social signs, but he excepts the sea itself. Yet to receive, in rainy London, a Christmas card from a tropical country representing a landscape lashed by monsoon rains makes one realize that cultural expectations of what constitutes a pleasant experience shape our perceptions themselves.

7. *Mythologies* is full of tragi-comic examples of society turning well-meant actions into mere gestures (*gesture* and *spectacle* often express this alienating mechanism). The charitable Abbé Pierre who tries to achieve a 'zero degree of haircut' and a nondescript appearance because 'the idea of fashion is antipathetic to the idea of saintliness' (*M*,47) ends up covered with a veritable forest of signs. Barthes here has renovated a major poetic theme, the lament on our worldly condition; but in this case man is seen as subject not so much to change and decay as to the innumerable signs which reify him.

8. This is borne out by the fact that the concepts of denotation and object-language, supposedly logically prior to connotation and metalanguage, are in fact invariably introduced in treatises of linguistics as an afterthought and only when they are needed. Yet still the myth persists of a prior knowledge of a language directly geared to things as they are, and this can only be encouraged by training the spotlight on connotation.

9. It is evidence of Barthes's dual inspiration that he uses *motivation* both in its psychological sense (*M*,118) and in its linguistic sense (*M*,126, where the oppostion between bourgeois false nature and artistic anti-physis makes use of this ambiguity).

10. This could be represented as follows, adding a layer to Barthes's diagram to represent his own language, in accordance with his indication (*S*,93-4; see also *SM*,292, where he uses Hjelmslev's more convenient terms, *content* and *expression* — see Appendix, p. 235). NB: the number of layers is not fixed, other arrangements can exist and layer 2 can itself be called *denotation* (or *terminological system*) if layer 1 is not already constituted by language.

4. metalanguage	Sr			Sd		
3. connotation			Sr		Sd	
2. metalanguage		Sr	Sd			
1. denotation or object-language		Sr	Sd			

11. Interestingly, the famous *Verfremdungseffekt*, the estrangement or alienation-effect, had been partly suggested to Brecht by the way the Chinese actor Mei Lan-fang, whom he saw perform in Moscow in 1935, 'seemed to stand aside from his part and 'make it quite clear that he knows he is being observed' (quoted in Willett, 1959, 208-9). Here is a way to cope with the dual messages constantly sent by society: make it possible for the spectator to practice a dual reception of such messages. Barthes's analyses of Japanese Bunraku and Kabuki are written with the same re-training in mind. He had already argued in *Mythologies* that a Charlie Chaplin offset his woolly humanism by spontaneously adopting techniques akin to Brecht's: he demonstrated blindness by presenting at the same time a man who is blind and what he does not see (*M*,40). In Brecht, this dissociation was entrusted to the actor's technique as well as to the presentation of the content, and this has been identified with the 'device of making strange' (*Priem ostrannenija*) of the Russian formalists. It is intriguing, however, in view of Bruce Morrissette's Oedipal reinterpretation (1963) of the 'fable' in Robbe-Grillet, and of Barthes's later definition of the effect of the modern text as 'showing its behind to the Father', the law or authority, to find that the two examples of alienation-effect Brecht gives after explaining the notion are: seeing one's mother becoming another man's wife when one acquires a step-father, and seeing one's superior in the hierarchy being bullied in his turn.

As for Barthes's ambivalence on the subject of mediations and immediacy (holding meaning at bay by mediating devices, while dreaming of doing without ideology), it perhaps reflects the tension inherent in the revolutionary attitude when applied to art. It says both that its version of reality is true to life and that its own duty is to make this version come true. Barthes praised Brecht's 'efficiently ambiguous word: *Einverstandnis'* which seeks to render this (*M*,156). Despite their long involvement with Barthes's theories, Greimas and Robbe-Grillet have professed themselves unconvinced by a genealogy of myth which attributes it solely to man's alienation in a capitalist regime, and we saw that Barthes himself does not always rule out a beneficial effect of myth. Greimas sees myth as an inevitable aspect of the *vécu*, and Robbe-Grillet chooses 'freely' to 'speak' the fantasies of the modern world instead of submitting to them. But this is all in the mind; the spectator of Robbe-Grillet's films does not have the impression of any heroic assertion of freedom.

Chapter 9: Homo significans

1. See Goldmann (1971, 62 and 66). For a chronology of Goldmann's work which ofters a very perceptive comment on the changing intellectual scene, see Leenhardt (1979). Barthes had already written against a 'psychological' interpretation of Racine. In order to play Thésée, it is enough to speak as if one had seen the gods.

Chapter 10: Both diffident and rash

1. These two layers are called the *pictorial* and the *iconic* by the Groupe μ in their study of the image (1978b, 16). Another distinction which is of great importance is that between what the Russian formalists called the *fable* and the *subject*. The number of these ideal 'layers' and the way in which the planes of content and expression can be structured are discussed in this chapter and the next, as well as in Part IV.

The question of whether Barthes ever was a structuralist in literature depends on the meaning one gives to 'structuralist'. In some recent theoretical works as well as in Barthes's last phase, the word has come to denote the ambition of writing a grammar on the Chomskyan model: by means of rules generating a deep structure which is then transformed into the various narratives we observe, we could then account for all possible narratives. It is a pity that the scope of 'structuralism' has thus been limited by its association with one particular theory. Even in the narrow sense, Barthes has brought to the structuralist study of literature a good epistemological grounding, a practical list of transposable concepts, an effort to show these in use in 'Racinian Man' and *Système de la Mode*, as well as his studies on Sade, Loyola (*SFL*) and Verne (*NEC*).

2. These terms are particularly confusing since signification automatically exists in any use of signs (the question is whether these signs are explicitly accepted by both interlocutors, and the message intentional) and communication is not necessarily explicit. Some latter-day 'semiologists of communication' showed no interest in the subject before it became fashionable; others have made use of the problematic elaborated in *Elements of Semiology* without even

including if in their bibliographies. More interesting than these polemics is the observation that the semiological idea was already in the air, contained in suggestions of the founding fathers of linguistics, but also in studies like Hall (1959) and Birdwhistell (1971). The description of the various branches of semiotics can be found in Eco (1972), and representative articles in Kristeva, Rey-Debove and Umiker (1971). Other relevant articles can be found in Benthall and Polhemus (1975) and Polhemus (1978).

3. Such passages show that despite the gradual recentring of every problem on language, Barthes still viewed it with considerable ambivalence. This is obvious if we compare him to Lacan, who stresses that psychoanalysis is a 'talking cure' and does not accept non-verbal communication as currency.

4. The interest of many poets in synaesthesias is based on an intuitive understanding of such semiological facts. Many cartoonists can sum up a situation without speech better than a whole sociological study. In Saul Steinberg's illustrations of words, the essence of 'Swindle' is conveyed by a magnificent capital S followed by less and less impressive graphics until the end sells you short by its illegibility. Jean Anouilh indicates at the end of some scenes in his plays that an ironical tune (one which our cultural habits, and perhaps some universal sound symbolism, have taught us to interpret as funny) could be used to provide a 'disbelieving' connotation.

5. All this shows that Barthes is well aware that looking ridiculous is the occupational disease of the semiologist. Butor has interpreted most of Barthes's activity as a strategy to conquer the right to use the three vocabularies which are taboo to the young boy in our society: sexual language, learned language, and the language of women (Butor, 1968, 33, 43). There are external taboos as well, for instance those which prescribe that certain subjects belong only in certain publishers' series (what Barthes calls the 'protocols of reception'). *Elements of Semiology* was first published in a learned periodical, *Communications*, and hardly caused a ripple outside research circles, where it began a steady underground career. But its English version appeared in a series meant for the educated layman who, judging by the reviews, was considerably baffled by it. A comparable situation arose in France when *Système de la Mode* came out, this time in a popular series; but whether because of a different cultural picture or because they were determined to rise to the challenge, fashion writers betrayed no sign of dismay and made knowing references to the book, having, one imagines, quietly dropped the linguistic apparatus and concentrated on its thematic interpretation.

6. An article on food published by Barthes in *Les Annales* (1961) contains other amusing examples. Barthes classifies the main themes of the rhetorical messages of the advertisements studied into three groups: the national past (French cooking never innovates), anthropological data (as in Lévi-Strauss's studies, some foodstuffs are not considered suitable for men) and health values. The latter, however, are beginning to be altered by the development of dietetics, while the development of the post-industrial society interferes with the first group, since it is geared to adaptation to the modern world. The polysemy of food is then specified by culture (as shaped by advertising) to produce 'two situations of perfect readability': the business lunch and the snack — a word which, like many Anglicisms in French, connotes smartness and effciency: 'Il y a

un certain napoléonisme du snack'! It is by now a common joke to note that coarse bread, pottery plates and unvarnished pine are 'read' as middle class, while white bread, china plates and French polish (former signs of social distinction) perforce mean working class (see also *SM*,135). The same applies to the wearing of sloppy clothes at week-ends instead of one's Sunday best (*SM*,254). The middle-class kitchen is in keeping with the new ecological mood, but the latter in turn is explained by Jean Baudrillard (1968, 1972 — books which elaborate on the problematics of Barthes's semiological studies) as part of a syndrome of the artificial preservation of nature, which can only be kept in token form, 'in quotation marks', in an overpopulated world dominated by social signs.

7. For instance he will ask some subjects what meaning they attribute to a piece of music by submitting to them a list of verbalized signifieds such as *anguished, stormy, sombre, tormented*, etc. But in fact all these denote a single musical signified which ought to be designated by a single cipher. The latter would still be a metalanguage, but this is probably inevitable and makes the analysis of signifieds problematic, Barthes says (*S*,46). This is in keeping with his interpretations of social signs as inherently connoted, just as psychoanalysts see the whole of psychic life as inherently overdetermined (see the notion of *étayage* or anaclisis, the relation of sexual drives and vital functions). On the semiological analysis of music, see Ruwet (1972), the work of the Groupe de Recherche in Montreal e.g. Lidov (1975), and Nattiez (1975 — an interesting book marred by anti-Barthesian polemics more approporiate to the excesses of some latter-day disciples), L. Bernstein (1976), and F. Lerdahl and R. Jackendoff (1977). I thank Natasha Spender for drawing my attention to the latter.

8. On the correspondence between the signified of a visual sign and different linguistic signifiers, see Engler (1973) where many remarks bear out Eco (1970); see also Lindekens (1976) on visual semiotics. It would be interesting to try and apply the ten codes listed by Eco (1970) to literature, in view of the latter's representational element, even though Eco's aim was to free visual semiotics from an overdependence on verbal categories. Eco's ten codes are: 1. perceptual codes; 2. codes of recognition, which allow us to recognize the object represented; 3. codes of transmission, which study for instance the lines in televised images; 4. tonal or suprasegmental codes, which extend over the whole of the message and transmit conventional intonations such as 'strength', 'graceful' or 'expressionistic'; 5. the iconic codes, articulated as *figurae*, signs and utterance-signs; 6. iconographic codes, which choose the signifieds of the iconic codes to connote more complex cultural objects (what is identified as a half-naked woman carrying a human head on a salver connotes Salome, whereas a woman wearing more clothes, holding a head in her left hand and a sword in her right hand connotes Judith); 7. codes of taste and sensibility, which specify the connotations of iconographic codes (a flag can connote 'patriotism' or 'war' depending on the situation); 8. rhetorical codes, which result from the institutionalization of originally iconic solutions and have now become norms of communication; 9. stylistic codes, which connote their original author (some types of filmic sequence could connote 'Chaplin' or '1900s eroticism'); 10. the codes of the unconscious, which structure the other codes in a way that favours certain identifications or projections.

9. The study of the reading process and of semantics depends to some extent on a better understanding of memory. See Lenneberg (1967), Le Ny (1979) and

Johnson-Laird (1974). I thank Peter Wason for drawing my attention to the last article as well as to the work of Eleanor Rosch. On the hologram as analogon of memory see Piattelli-Palmarini (1977), drawing on the work of Karl Pribram. A hologram is the photographic record which allows one to reproduce a three-dimensional image when illuminated by light of the same wavelength as the original laser beam — as the reader re-generates a text.

Chapter 11: It is the path that makes the work, or, Between things and words

1. When did fashion start? It all depends on how one defines the phenomenon, and we saw that Barthes had at least two models in mind. The question itself exemplifies the modern tendency to explain all facts by the material and social infrastructure rather than by inherent traits of human nature, for instance a desire for change. There certainly are many examples of sumptuary laws meant to codify social stratification, encourage specific sectors of trade or enslave aristocrats by giving them an absorbing pastime. To take a single recent theory, Yvonne Deslandres (1976, 86 and 107) sees fashion as a purely Western phenomenon starting at the end of the fourteenth century.

Chapter 12: In those days, intellectual history was going very fast

1.

The signifier (S) is global, made up of a multilevelled chain (metaphorical chain): signifier and signified have only a floating relationship and coincide only at certain anchor points. The line between the signifier (S) and the signified (s) has its own value (which of course it did not have in Saussure): it represents the repression of the signified. (*S*,49)

2. On this synthesis, which has already been outlined here (see p. 19) in connection with Foucault's work and Hollier's *Panorama* (1973), see also Baudry (1968) and Goux (1973). Its outstanding creative offshoots are probably Sollers's *Lois, H* and *Paradis*, as well as Barthes's *S/Z* in view of its unique position between conceptual discourse and literature. This synthesis has perhaps in recent years characterized the English more than the French scene, and a different ideological picture perforce gives it a new meaning: more tactical and less anarchistic. See for instance Coward and Ellis (1977), Burniston and Weedon (1978), Belsey (1980) and above all the work done in film studies by the contributors to the periodical *Screen*.

3. Let us note in this connection that the new Derridean concepts ended up in a contestation of some Lacanian tenets (Derrida 1972b and 1975) as epitomized by Derrida's amusing conflation of two major Lacanian attitudes in his neologism *phallogocentrism*. Some critics have argued that Lacan has no real theory of language, but this objection ignores the fact that many professional linguists have been inspired by him and have constantly updated his doctrines (see for instance Milner, 1978a, and Flahault, 1978). But one may legitimately wonder whether the cardinal principle of the primacy of the signifier might not quite simply come

from the fact that Lacan's 'The Insistence of the Letter' was written as early as 1957, under the influence of Lévi-Strauss, at a time when the main model was phonological, not semantic. Kristeva, who initially cited this article (1972) soon meant something quite different by the term 'signifier'. For other criticisms of Lacan, see Deleuze and Guattari (1972), Wilden (1972) and Irigaray (1977). These often take up feminist critiques of Freud himself; see Kofman (1980).

4. This is all the more remarkable since it is the negation of Saussure's theory of the sign. He may thus have twice fathered modern semantics, once with the *Course* he left in note form, and again with the Anagrams on which he lavished his care but which still seem to be the object of social censorship. Saussure thought he could discover the name of a chief or god disseminated throughout Latin poems, calling this hidden message *paragram*, *hypogram* or *anagram*. Yet Kristeva (1971) draws attention to a diagram published in Godel (1957) which seems to show that, for Saussure, the production of meaning started with the signifier, which presses on it constantly like the unconscious 'primary process'. Meaning is then maintained only by a forcible compromise.

Chapter 13: A whole landscape in a bean

1. Constant reference is made in this chapter to the following works: Propp (1970), Souriau (1950), Tesnière (1959), Lévi-Strauss (1960), *Communications* (especially Nos 4, 8, 11), Bremond (1973), Chabrol (1973), Hamon (1977), Kermode (1974), Scholes (1974), Culler (1975), Fowler (1977), Hawkes (1977). See note 2 for specific developments in Greimas's theory.

2. This sketch of Greimas's theories is limited to the state it had reached when Barthes was writing his article on the structural analysis of narratives (*IMT*). For its subsequent development, which casts light in retrospect on the problems addressed by Barthes, see Bibliography under Greimas, as well as Greimas and Courtès (1979), the Documents and Bulletins du Groupe de Recherches Sémio-Linguistiques de l'Ecole des Hautes Etudes en Sciences Sociales, Courtès (1976), Hénault (1979), Nef (1976), Rastier (1974), Ricoeur (1980). Ricoeur's is a sympathetic but searching critique of Greimas's effort to generate narrative from a semiotic and logical model which is fundamentally a static taxonomy, that is, a model where relations are not oriented. Although this model often has great heuristic value, its application sometimes relies on an unacknowledged semantics of action (of the kind which analytic philosophy is now elaborating) and on the 'praxic' and 'pathic' categories of polemics and exchange. He argues that meaning and narrativity are grasped directly through an intuition whose support, in reader and characters, is necessarily a subject, as taught by phenomenology.

3. Despite the importance of the semantic data obtained from a study of memorization, no one to my knowledge has used the hologram (see above Chapter 10, *n* 9) as a model for the character, which is a memory construct. Hamon (1977) examines its constitution by the reader from discontinuous signifiers and signifieds, a process which Barthes had described earlier about the total meaning of a work (see above Chapter 7, *n* 3) and examined closely in *Système de la Mode*. Let us note that the anti-humanist streak in the structural analysis of narrative is essentially different from that found in the New Novel, as

is proved by Barthes's different reactions to them: where the latter tried to destroy the very idea of character, the former tries to identify roles and basic plots which sound very constrictive to someone who had come to view the psychoanalytic archetypal story as very near the bone.

4. A banal love-story without impediments has two characters who each represent two actants:

He	Subject + Sender
She	Object + Receiver

and presumably vice versa! But the disjunction of the Object and the Sender produces a well-known story with three actants:

A man, a woman,
An apple, a drama.

as *Les Parapluies de Cherbourg* puts it (Greimas, 1966, 177). The disjunction of the four main actants produces many well-known plots which can be subsumed under the general description of the story of a quest. 'Produces' is to be understood in the metalanguage of the analyst, although many a writer must have consciously or unconsciously constituted something like Greimas's table of actants. Souriau (1950) shows how incredibly overworked his scheme of six roles had been in nineteenth-century drama, and this goes a long way towards explaining the recent revulsion against psychological literature. Souriau could however still suggest a few permutations by working methodically through the table of possibilities, like Lévi-Strauss working on myth, or Kroeber on costume.

5. Similarly Goldmann (1964) charted in Malraux's work an evolution from an abstract to a figurative (and realist) treatment of some themes (and a change from individual to collective hero), followed by an involutionary reversal to abstraction, which he connects with the author's belief and loss of belief in certain values. This analysis was grounded in Lukács's proto-structuralist interpretation of forms, and the novel in particular.

6. 'Death' produces a re-evaluation of all the preceding words, actualizing their funereal potential 'rhetorically', that is, by means of connotations: *stranger* = who is still alive; *smell* = putrefaction; *to pick* = kill; *remorse* = after killing; *violet* = funereal colour; *smile* = of a death's head. The third isotopy 'Love' poses a methodological problem; the erotic overtones of the poem are felt by practically everybody but hardly figure on the plane of denotation. *Smile* is the exception; *pick me* is already metaphorical. This isotopy results from a wealth of projective analogies generated by factors like the different gender (in French) of *stranger* and *violet*, the given name *Violet*, the feminine gender of *death* in French (which sounds exactly like *dead* in either singular or plural), the seductive behaviour, the traditional metaphor of orgasm as *la petite mort*, the 'paragrammatic' reading — of the kind recommended by Kristeva — of *violate*, where the dominant isotopy pre-selects the sounds, etc. Disambiguation — the process of choosing between several readings — is only necessary for certain types of communication (see Kristeva, 1974a, on an opposite strategy in Mallarmé and Lautréamont). The virtues of 'undecidable' cases (a term which comes from the vocabulary of mathematics, and which since Chomsky has become part of that of linguistics) have been exploited particularly by Derrida.

7. This distinction between story and discourse corresponds to slightly different projects in contemporary theorists (see above, Chapter 10, *n* 1). It rests on various criteria, the most important of which are the presence or absence of the marks the speaker leaves in his discourse and the differences in the distorting potential of different media. Both have existential as well as theoretical importance for Barthes, as is shown by the strange ending of his article. He notes that the structural analysis of discourse and narrative has put another restriction on combinative freedom, so that the latter increases when one rises in the hierarchy of units from phoneme to morpheme to sentence, only to decrease when sentences are organized into a text.

Chapter 14: The starred text

1. Let us note that in Cazotte the devil appears asking: 'Che vuoi?' and that Lacan takes up this sentence to symbolize the voice of the subject's desire, unrecognizable at first to himself. Cazotte seems to have been, up to a point, aware of the significance of this episode which has also inspired Baudelaire.

2. Although Barthes openly admits that he offers an anamorphosis, some passages of his book are unquestionably referential (and far less Europeocentric than Michaux's, 1967) if only when he deplores the fact that modern Japan is 'losing its signs just as one loses one's hair or one's teeth'. But the book has another axis, whose full relevance will appear only in the next chapter and which could be characterized as father-aggressive/mother-supportive. This opposition is the basis of the contrast between, for instance, Western food and cutlery and Eastern meals and chopsticks. This is a common theme in travel books; but it is more unusual to interpret the experience of Japanese civilization as motherly, one aspect of this being the non-directive structure of its language, as opposed to the coercion of what Barthes calls, neologistically and significantly, his 'father-tongue' (*ES*,28). In this connection, he does not seem to be aware of the concept of *amae*, the overreliance on someone's unconditional love and support, which the Japanese apparently need in order to feel at ease and which has been invoked by some authors in order to explain cases of breakdowns in communication between foreign businessmen and their Japanese counterparts (I thank Hidé Ishiguro for helping to define this notion). See also Barthes's last article on Stendhal (1980e), his French *patrie* and his Italian *matrie*.

Chapter 15: The body under the body

1. See also by the same 'schizo-analysts', the second volume of *Capitalisme et schizophrénie*, called *Mille plateaux* (1980) and *Rhizome* (1976), a short and aphoristic book which both acknowledges and promotes the replacement of monism by pluralism thanks to a tongue-in-cheek classification of books modelled on that of root-types: classical (tap-root), modernist (rootlets), and the truly modern, which should be based on the rhizome, a subterranean stalk with aerial roots, where every point can be connected with any other.

2. 'The sole passion of my life has been fear'. It is by Hobbes, but may well have been taken from the erotic best-seller *Emmanuelle*, which gives it in this unusual form (Emmanuelle Arsan, *Emmanuelle*, Eric Losfeld, *Le Terrain Vague*,

1967, 148); the passage which refers to the epigraph, in Barthes's book, is worded ambiguously (*PT*,48). If this is correct, how one imagines Barthes chuckling over this transgressive intrusion!

3. So that just as these new signifying practices will superannuate 'literature' and 'painting', their metalinguistic correlates, criticism and aesthetics, will be replaced by a general *ergography*: 'the text as work, work as text' (1969a, a review of J.-L. Schefer's *Scénographie d'un tableau* (1968); see also 'Musica Practica' (*IMT*) on Beethoven). The 'text' can of course, as we saw in *S/Z*, be the depersonalized subject himself, who is the stereography of significant processes: see the descriptions Barthes gives of himself in a café or coming out of the cinema (*PT*,49; 1975b) or his affirmation: 'There are writers who don't write books' (1974d; *SE*,78). Such passages show that pleasure can be obtained from what was originally a defensive reaction; but this pleasure depends on a refusal of the historicity of the subject, of the recognition and interpretation of any pattern in the choice of object and the occurrence of *jouissance* (as against its simple and instantaneous acknowledgement). This quintessential repetitiveness of pure encounters with the world overdetermines, in Barthes's later works, his original conception of poetry as rhythm and discontinuous insights (see for instance 'Rasch' (1975e) or the ending of *The Pleasure of the Text*). This also explains the increasingly frequent reference to the *satori* of Zen, even if sometimes Barthes interprets as synonymous aspects of Japanese culture which are in fact antithetical (as shown by Ruth Benedict's classic analyses, 1977, 173-4, on the release from the 'observer-self' necessary in order to taste life fully — a release sought by Barthes in what he calls 'this writing aloud, which is not speech', *PT*,66).

Barthes's self-imposed fight against discursive *consistance* (consistency being punningly seen as a thickening glue) does not always, however, result in a dispersal of the subject. A growing trust in the same process when it leads to the re-generation of a subject through fiction can be charted throughout this late period, from the debunking observer in *S/Z* and *The Pleasure of the Text* (*PT*,27), through *Barthes by Barthes* (*RB*,95, 162) and 'Ça prend' (1978c) to 'Délibération' (1979e) on the project of keeping a diary, and finally to *La Chambre claire*. This change in attitude could be described in Smith and Apter's terms (1975) as a change from the *telic* (concerned with achieving goals) to the *paratelic* (concerned with expressive behaviour — compare the epithet *autotelic* to describe the narcissism inherent in the poetic function). From the self-doubts which Barthes expressed at the end of his first period (see a crucial passage in *E*,154), he managed to make himself a writer of fiction, of 'the novelistic without the novel' through the immense detour of his theoretical work. Would this, however, have occurred without the self-assurance generated by his theories (whose intrinsic worth is unaffected by their genesis)? To invert one of his pronouncements (1974d), 'It is because he had spoken [didactically] that he wrote'. And yet his constant talk, in recent years, about writing a novel, and critics' regrets at his not having had the time to do this, show that his regression from a view of all writing as poetry — a term which since surrealism could cover an immense spectrum stretching from concept to image — had undone all the results of his former efforts to confer on the critic the status of writer and re-established the old pecking order.

4. The performance on stage by Pierre Leenhardt of fragments from *A Lover's*

Discourse, Barthes's playing the part of Thackeray in André Téchiné's film on the Brontë family (and one might add, a posthumous exhibition of his drawings and paintings) partake of the same movement towards the world. The eroticization of food is a common feature in authors like André Pieyre de Mandiargues, Georges Bataille, Emmanuel Péreire, and films like W. Borowczyk's or *La grande bouffe*. As for the conflict latent in these opposite responses, and epitomized in the dual characterization of *langue* as 'mother-' and 'father-tongue', it corresponds to Barthes's life-long 'splitting of the object', which results in his alternately trusting a good mother and trying to propitiate a phallic mother while dreaming about what an idyllic relationship with his father might have been (see also his review of Gérard Blain's film *Le pélican* (1974a) in which he sees an 'inverted Oedipus complex', with the father in love with the son). Derrida's comments on Mallarmé (1972c, 300-1) could serve here; he quotes Freud on the fantasy of being born to the father alone, and of giving him a child even at the cost of one's virility. Compare with Barthes's treatment of Michelet, who is punished for having, in quasi-Poujadist fashion, accused intellectuals of lacking virility (*RB*,103) and castrated by seeing his ideology dismissed with a stroke of the pen and being feminized in Barthes's book.

5. Sartre alone survives this hecatomb. This may be due to his reconsideration of Marxism, to his having blazed an autobiographical trail placed under the sign of 'Words' and the mother, or to the plans he had for a while, according to some commentators, to write a love story. Sartre's masochistic declarations on his late commitment (and now his last interview in *Le Nouvel Observateur*, 1980) were taken at face value just like Barthes's. (On the ambiguity of the confessional discourse which perhaps caused this, see C.C. O'Brien, 1965, 96 and 108). On the question of the gold standard, let us point out that this euphoric praise of the floating of currencies, held up by various philosophers as a model for that of all values, ignored the fact that the 'demonetarization' of gold was engineered to turn the dollar into the new standard.

6. His late texts abound in weird notations, which release their full meaning not so much when we connect them with his usual themes as when we let their weight of reality slowly sink in. One single example, which has to be in French: it is taken from a letter about Derrida sent to *Les Lettres francaises* (1972a):

> Nous lui devons des mots nouveaux, des mots actifs (ce en quoi son écriture est violente, poétique) et une sorte de détérioration incessante de notre confort intellectuel. . . . Il y a enfin dans son travail quelque chose de *tu*, qui est fascinant: sa solitude vient de ce qu'il va dire.

This could not be better put about Barthes himself.

Appendix

1. This emphasis on the negative and differential aspect of language can be illustrated by means of one of Saussure's famous examples, that of the 8.25 p.m. Geneva-to-Paris trains which leave at twenty-four-hour intervals. 'We feel that it is the same train each day, yet everything — the locomotive, coaches, personnel — is probably different' (*Course*, 108). We feel it to be the same because it is defined in relation to other trains. It is true that we would still feel the same if it

left or arrived late and altered its route (as Saussure also notes); yet there is *one* condition for an identity to be felt, even though its material realization changes, and it is that the train should at some.time leave Geneva and at some time arrive in Paris.

2. *Essais de linguistique générale* (1963), 28ff (written in 1952) and especially 213ff written in 1960. I refer to the French collection of Jakobson's essays since it is chiefly in that form that they achieved their influence in France; the 1960 essay was originally published as 'Linguistics and Poetics', in T.A. Sebeok (ed.) *Style in Language* (1960).

3. Jakobson suggested a universal criterion for recognizing the poetic function, which applies at all levels, from that of sound and rhythm to that of syntax and meaning (1963, 220). He postulated that what is normally found on the axis of selection was in this particular case put side by side on the axis of combination (see Section IV). Thus similar sounds, which usually form a mental reserve, here appear in sequence as rhymes, and similar meanings, of which only one is normally chosen, here are found together, for instance in metaphors. What is more, parallelism in expression tends to suggest parallelism in content.

4. See on this Lyons (1968, 458). Pending the constitution or a satisfactory theory of culture, he prefers to use 'application' rather than reference in the case of certain words and expressions (1968, 434). See also Quine on 'The Inscrutability of reference', which is fundamentally indeterminate, in Steinberg and Jakobovits (1971, 142). See also D. Steinberg's 'Overview' (1971, 489-91), about the three main theories on the origin of 'ideas', and about the relationship between language and cognition: the neo-behaviorist, the Chomskyan and the empiricist-generative, which is associated with Piaget (see also Part IV on recent semantic theories).

5. See Lukes (1973, especially 302-12) and, for Comte's influence on Durkheim (1973, 67ff, especially 68n11). See also Lévy-Bruhl (1903, especially Book III, Chapters III and IV on social statics and social dynamics).

6. See Kristeva (1971) and Chapter 12 in the present study. Among French sources on Chomsky, see an interview with J.-M. Benoist in *La Quinzaine littéraire* (1969); *Hypothèses* (1972), where discussions with Jakobson, Halle and Chomsky are presented by J.-P. Faye, J. Paris, J. Roubaud and M. Ronat; and *Dialogues* between Chomsky and M. Ronat (1977).

7. The example he gives in *Elements* (*S*,20) is in fact due to H. Frei, one of Saussure's successors in Geneva and, Barthes claims, is a face-saving subterfuge to gloss over an area of indeterminacy in Saussure, which concerns the possibility of positive elements in language.

8. The example given by Lévi-Strauss in his 1955 article was the Theban version of the Oedipus myth, where the successive events in the story, which are, so to speak, the distinctive features, are arranged in vertical columns (the mythemes) under descriptions like: overestimation or underestimation of kinship relations, etc., a model which Todorov took up later (1966b). On the question of the double articulation in semiology, see Chapter 10; Lévi-Strauss has condemned most forms of modern music and painting as victims of the 'utopia of the century', i.e. trying to do away with one of the levels of articulation (1964, 28-32).

9. In 'The Imagination of the Sign' (*E*) Barthes discusses paradigmatic relations

before syntagmatic ones because this order has symbolic connotations for him; but in Saussure's *Course*, the order is the opposite because Saussure wished to stress the linear nature of language. Furthermore, he spoke of 'associative' relations; the term 'paradigmatic' was suggested by Hjelmslev. Barthes used the latter term in *Elements*, yet abandoned it later in the same book, in the section 'Syntagm and System' where he extended the notion, using 'systematic' instead; this is particularly confusing in the diagram on p. 63, where the word 'system' is used in two different senses, to denote on the one hand an area of experience (the food, garment, car systems, etc.) and on the other the paradigmatic axis. The term 'paradigm' is not without drawbacks either. As defined in *Elements* (*S*,102*n*59) it comes from '*paradeigma*: a model, table of the flexions of a word given as model', and this traditional sense could interfere with the more recent usage. Moreover, this original meaning has been extended by Thomas Kuhn in a way which is highly relevant to Barthes's problematic and to recent intellectual history; see Kuhn (1970, viii) where a paradigm is defined as constituted by the 'universally recognized scientific achievements that for a time provide model problems and solutions to a community of practitioners' and further definitions in the 1969 Postscript to his book, as well as Kuhn in Lakatos and Musgrave (1970) and Suppe (1971).

10. These notions are defined by Barthes (*S*,40) in terms of language but can apply to other areas. They are: 1. The *substance of expression* (the phonic substance studied by phonetics). 2. The *form of expression* (made of the paradigmatic and syntactic rules), which is the same in one language whether it is spoken or written, that is, realized in different substances. 3. The *substance of content* (the emotional, ideological or simply notional aspects of the signified, which can be considered as a positive element in language). 4. The *form of content*, which distributes the same semantic substance differently in different languages (for instance, distinguishing a different number of colours in a continuous reality). Barthes suggests that this last category is easier to grasp in semiology, where a meaning is invested in an object used for some other purpose; but this is because he does not take up the full scale of Hjelmslev's distinctions, and omits the notion of *matter*. This, which is expressed in Danish as *substans* or *mening*, is usually translated into English as *purport*, and in French as *matière*; none of these terms is satisfactory and unambiguous. The consequence of Barthes's difficulties with that notion is that the idea of *substance*, that is, the purport once divided by the form, like a net (Hjemslev, 1961, 52ff) is robbed of its main value for semiology: that of allowing one to consider the autonomous structuration of a given field, which would not depend on either the divisions of language or those of the areas selected for semanticization (food, garments, etc.)

11. Semanticists and semioticians used to ransack chemistry for metaphors (e.g. the notion of valency); they have now had to switch to sub-atomic physics and pin their hopes on elementary particles and even quarks. This probably points to a need for a rapprochement between linguistics and psychology, since the latter can often give 'deeper' definitions of linguistic concepts which are relevant when considering the existential investments in linguistic theory or literary practice, by Barthes and others (see for instance Milner (1978) whose object is 'linguistics inasmuch as it is affected by psychoanalysis', on the Lacanian notion of *lalangue*, of which *langue* is only a facet. Pottier (1980) resorts to the

notion of *noeme*, or meaning particle at the conceptual level, as opposed to the three other levels of content features: on the one hand, referential features, and on the other, semantic units of existence belonging to *langue* ('glottic' as Barthes would have said), the semes and sememes. Literary semiotics works at the noemic level, dealing with the content by means of metalinguistic labels like 'war' and 'peace'. Le Ny (1979) in his excellent overview of recent semantic research, gives definitions of signifier and signified (showing that the latter is not a concept) and introduces the notion of *meme*, or mnemic entity which is a component of an individual's lexemic signifieds (the semes are those memes which are common to all the speakers). Semantic structures are for him a subset of mnemic, and generally cognitive, structures; understanding a continuous discourse is a finalized activity which includes reaching a terminal aim. But although he deals with metaphor, he does not specify what psychological support a reading practice based on a deconstructing intention and the use of undecidable elements instead of contextualization and disambiguation could be.

Biography

As explained in Chapter 1, the sources of Barthes's biography at present all originate with him and were released in his late period. He had by then come to consider autobiographical discourse as 'imaginary' and concerning 'a character in a novel'. But this imaginary quality varies: the biographical summary in *Barthes by Barthes* represents 'a life' by a social skeleton consisting of academic appointments and the illnesses which delay them, a 'work' which leaves out the 'text' of 'encounters, friendships, loves, travels, readings, pleasures, fears, beliefs, satisfactions, indignations, distresses: in a word: repercussions?' Whereas an earlier summary (Mallac and Eberbach, 1971) included intellectual models, these figures were demoted in the later Barthes to transient crazes, a change epitomized by the metaphorical switch from the 'growth' image of humanism to the Lacanian image of the 'revolutions of desire' (*T*,99-100).

1915 12 November: born in Cherbourg, son of Louis Barthes, a naval officer, and Henriette Binger. Father killed in a naval battle in 1916. Childhood in Bayonne.

1924 Move to Paris, but school holidays in Bayonne with the Barthes grandparents. Mother, partly because of an impoverished family and partly for unexplained reasons, has to learn a manual skill, bookbinding, despite her middle-class origins. Barthes obtains his baccalauréat in 1933 and 1934.

1934-5 First attack of tuberculosis; lesion in the left lung and treatment in the Pyrénées.

1935-9 Studies at the Sorbonne for a degree in French and Classics. Helps to found the Groupe de Théâtre Antique, and travels with them to Greece. Exempted from military service. Lecteur in Hungary in the summer of 1937.

1939-41 Teaches literature in lycées at Biarritz then in Paris. Diplôme d'études supérieures (M.A.) on Greek tragedy.

Oct. 1941: Relapse of tuberculosis. Has to give up the preparation of the agrégation, the competitive qualifying examination for teaching in state schools.

1942 First stay in the Sanatorium des étudiants de France, at Saint-Hilaire-du-Touvet, in the Isère.

1943 Convalesces in Paris and finishes his licence (B.A.).

July 1943: Relapse in the right lung.

1943-5 Second stay in the Sanatorium des étudiants, then at Leysin. Several months of pre-medical study with the intention of becoming a psychiatrist.

During treatment, relapse. Right extra-pleural pneumothorax.

1946-7 Convalescence in Paris.

1947 Publishes in *Combat*, formerly Camus's newspaper, a series of literary chronicles which will become *Writing Degree Zero*.

1948-9 Assistant in the library, then teacher, at the French Institute in Bucharest, and lecteur at Bucharest University.

1949-50 Lecteur in Egypt at the University of Alexandria. Meets A.J. Greimas. Writes for *Combat, Esprit, Lettres Nouvelles, France Observateur*, all left-wing papers and periodicals.

1950-2 At the *Direction générale des Relations culturelles* (Ministry of Foreign Affairs) in the Education Department.

1952-4 Attached to the C.N.R.S. (Centre National de la Recherche Scientifique) (lexicology). Takes part in the foundation of the magazine *Théâtre populaire* where he defends the plays and theories of Brecht after the first visit to Paris of the Berliner Ensemble in 1954.

1954-5 Literary adviser to the Editions de L'Arche.

1955-9 Attached to the C.N.R.S. (sociology). Sub-editor and contributor to *Arguments* (1956-63).

1960-80 Chef de travaux in the VIth and most famous section (Sciences économiques et sociales) of the Ecole Pratique des Hautes Etudes (E.P.H.E.), a somewhat marginal establishment in the state system of higher education, where he gets tenure as a Directeur d'Etudes in 1962, offering a seminar on the 'sociology of signs, symbols and representations'. In 1974, the VIth section became a separate establishment, the Ecole des Hautes Etudes en Sciences Sociales (E.H.E.S.S.) with the right to award its own diplomas, thus modifying slightly its marginal status.

1966 Visiting Professor at Johns Hopkins University.

1967 Lectures in Japan.

1969-70 In Morocco. Lectures at the University of Rabat.

1976 Professor at the Collège de France, chair of 'Sémiologie littéraire'.

1978 Death of Henriette Barthes.

1980 26 March: Dies in Paris after a road accident which occurred on 25 February.

Bibliography

This is a select bibliography. Only translations of books written by Barthes have been included (in the text the wording is sometimes slightly altered). In the secondary sources, I try to suggest the backcloth against which his thought has evolved; an effort has been made both to document the intellectual picture when he started writing and to emphasize the most recent state of various controversies. Original publication dates are given only when of interest, and French sources are stressed since, as Barthes acknowledged, they often are the most relevant.

Unless otherwise indicated, all books are published in Paris.

Works by Barthes

Books

Le Degré zéro de l'écriture, 1953, Seuil.
—reprinted 1965 together with *Eléments de sémiologie* and a new foreword, Gonthier.
—reprinted 1972 together with *Nouveaux essais critiques*, Seuil, Collection 'Points'.
—translated 1972 by Annette Lavers and Colin Smith as *Writing Degree Zero*, London, Cape; New York, Hill & Wang, preface by Susan Sontag.
Michelet par lui-même, 1954, Seuil.
Mythologies, 1957, Seuil.
—reprinted 1970 with a new preface, Seuil, Collection 'Points'.
—selection, with the theoretical essay 'Myth Today', translated 1972 by Annette Lavers as *Mythologies*, London, Cape; 1973, New York, Hill & Wang.
—reprinted 1973, Paladin paperback.
—balance of original essays (except 'Astrologie' and together with five other essays) translated 1979 by Richard Howard as *The Eiffel Tower and Other Mythologies*, New York, Hill & Wang.
Sur Racine, 1963, Seuil.
—translated 1964 by Richard Howard as *On Racine*, New York, Hill & Wang.
Elements de sémiologie, 1964, *Communications*, 4
—reprinted 1965 with *Le Degré zéro de l'écriture* and a new foreword, Gonthier.
—translated 1967 by Annette Lavers and Colin Smith as *Elements of Semiology*, London, Cape; New York, Hill & Wang.
Essais critiques, 1964, Seuil.
—translated with new introduction 1972 by Richard Howard as *Critical Essays*, Evanston, Northwestern University Press.

Critique et vérité, 1966, Seuil.

Système de la Mode, 1967, Seuil.

—translation forthcoming, London, Cape; New York, Hill & Wang.

L'Empire des signes, 1970, Geneva, Skira ('Les Sentiers de la création').

—reprinted 1980, Flammarion, Collection 'Champs'.

S/Z, 1970, Seuil.

—translated 1974 by Richard Miller, New York, Hill & Wang; 1975, London, Cape.

Sade, Fourier, Loyola, 1971, Seuil.

—translated 1976, New York, Hill & Wang; 1977 by Richard Miller, London, Cape.

—reprinted 1980, Seuil, Collection 'Points'.

Nouveaux essais critiques

—collected in 1972 and published in paperback together with *Le Degré zéro de l'écriture*, Seuil, Collection 'Points'.

—translated 1980 by Richard Howard as *New Critical Essays*, New York, Hill & Wang; London, Cape, forthcoming.

—translated 1975 by Richard Miller as *The Pleasure of the Text*, New York, Hill & Wang; 1976, London, Cape.

Alors la Chine?, 1974, Bourgois.

Roland Barthes par Roland Barthes, 1975, Seuil.

—translated 1977 by Richard Howard as *Roland Barthes by Roland Barthes*, London, Macmillan; New York, Hill & Wang.

Fragments d'un discours amoureux, 1977, Seuil.

—translated 1978 by Richard Howard as *A Lover's Discourse: Fragments*, New York, Hill & Wang; 1979, London, Cape; forthcoming, Penguin.

Image-Music-Text, 1977, London, Fontana/Collins; New York, Hill & Wang (essays selected and translated by Stephen Heath).

Leçon: Leçon inaugurale de la chaire de sémiologie littéraire du Collège de France, prononcée le 7 janvier 1977, 1978, Seuil.

—translated 1979 by Richard Howard, *Oxford Literary Review*, Autumn; *October* (USA), October.

Sollers écrivain, 1979, Seuil (a collection of essays written 1965-79).

La Chambre claire. Note sur la photographie, 1980, *Cahiers du cinéma*, (Editions de l'Etoile)/Gallimard/Seuil.

—translated 1981 by Richard Howard as *Camera Lucida*, New York, Hill & Wang; 1982, London, Cape.

Sur la littérature (with Maurice Nadeau), 1980, Presses de l'université de Grenoble (the text of a dialogue broadcast on the French radio).

Le Grain de la voix. Entretiens 1962-1980, 1981, Seuil.

Carte e segni, 1981, Milan, Electa (a catalogue of Barthes's drawings and paintings).

Barthes Reader, 1982, New York, Hill & Wang; London, Cape (selections by Susan Sontag).

In preparation

1. A new volume of critical essays on photography, painting and music, edited by François Wahl, called *L'obvie et l'obtus*.

2. One or perhaps two volumes of literary texts, and perhaps eventually complete works, edited by François Wahl.

Selected articles*

1933

'En marge du *Criton*', *L'Arc*, 56, Special issue on Barthes.

1942

'Notes sur André Gide et son Journal', *Existences*, reprinted in *Le Magazine littéraire*, 97, Special issue on Barthes.

1954

'*L'Etranger*, roman solaire', *Bulletin du club français du livre*, 12 April.

1955

a 'La Peste: annales d'une épidémie ou roman de la solitude?', *Club* (Bulletin du Club du Meilleur Livre), January.
b 'Réponse à Albert Camus' (about the above), *Club*, April.
c '*Nekrassov* juge de sa critique', *Théâtre populaire*, 14, July-August.

1961

'Pour une psycho-sociologie de l'alimentation contemporaine', *Annales*, 5, September-October.

1962

'A propos de deux ouvrages de Cl. Lévi-Strauss: sociologie et socio-logique', *Information sur les sciences sociales*, 1, 4 December, reprinted in Bellour and Clément (1979).

1963

'Les deux sociologies du roman' (on Lucien Goldmann), *France-Observateur*, 5 December.

1966

a 'Les vies parallèles' (review of *Proust* by G. Painter), *La Quinzaine littéraire*, 15 March.
b 'La mode, stratégie du désir' (a debate between Barthes, Jean Duvignaud and Henri Lefebvre — 'three sociologists'), *Le Nouvel Observateur*, 23 March.

1967

a 'Le discours de l'histoire', *Information sur les sciences sociales*, VI, 4 August.
b 'Science versus literature', *Times Literary Supplement*, 28 September.
c 'Le match Chanel-Courrèges arbitré par un philosophe', *Marie-Claire*, September.

1968

'L'effet de réel', *Communications*, 11.

---

* A complete bibliography up to 31 December 1973 can be found in Stephen Heath, *Vertige du déplacement*. I omit the articles included in *IMT*, *NEC* and *GV* which are designated by their titles in the text.

1969

a 'La peinture est-elle un langage?' (on J.-L. Schefer), *La Quinzaine littéraire*, 1-15 March.

b 'Un cas de critique culturelle' (on hippies), *Communications*, 14.

1970

a 'La linguistique du discours', in A.J. Greimas (1970c).

b 'Masculin, féminin, neutre', *Echanges et communications, mélanges offerts à Cl. Lévi-Strauss*', The Hague, Mouton.

c 'Ce qu'il advient au significant' (preface to Pierre Guyotat, *Eden, Eden, Eden*, Gallimard).

d 'Preface', *Erté*, Parme, Franco-Maria Ricci.

e 'L'Etrangère' (on J. Kristeva), *La Quinzaine littéraire*, 1 May.

f 'L'ancienne rhétorique (aide-mémoire)', *Communications*, 16.

1971

a 'Réflexions sur un manuel', in S. Doubrovsky and T. Todorov (1971).

b 'Style and its Image', in Chatman (1971).

c 'Conversation with Roland Barthes', in Heath, McCabe and Prendergast (1971).

d 'Réponses' (to a questionnaire prepared by Jean Thibaudeau), *Tel Quel*, 47, Autumn, Special issue on Barthes.

1972

a 'Lettre à Jean Ristat', *Les Lettres françaises*, 29 March, Special issue on Derrida.

b 'Jeunes chercheurs', *Communications*, 19.

c 'Sociologie des signes, symboles et représentations', *Programme d'enseignement 1972-73*, Ecole Pratique des Hautes Etudes, VIth Section. See also the (anonymous) *Généralités* on the School.

1973

a 'Aujourd'hui, Michelet', *L'Arc*, 52.

b 'Saussure, le signe, la démocratie', *Le Discours social*, 3-4 April.

c 'Réquichot et son corps', in *L'Oeuvre de Bernard Réquichot*, Bruxelles, Editions de la Connaissance.

d 'Les sorties du texte' (on Bataille), in Sollers (1973).

e 'Comment travaillent les écrivains' (interview), *Le Monde*, 27 September.

f 'Analyse textuelle d'un conte d'Edgar Poe', in Chabrol (1973).

1974

a 'Un père amoureux' (review of Gérard Blain's film *Le Pélican*), *Le Nouvel Observateur*, 4 February.

b 'Pourquoi j'aime Benveniste', *La Quinzaine littéraire*, 16-30 April.

c 'Premier texte' (introducing Barthes's 'En marge du *Criton*' [1933]), *L'Arc*, 56. Special issue on Barthes.

d 'Au séminaire', *L'Arc*, 56.

1975

a 'Barthes critique le "Barthes" de Barthes' (review by Barthes of his own autobiography, also entitled elsewhere in the same issue 'Barthes puissance trois',
'Barthes to the third power', and introduced by the editor Maurice Nadeau's
own review), *La Quinzaine littéraire*, 1-15 March.
b 'En sortant du cinéma', *Communications*, 23.
c Preface to Gérard Miller, *Les Pousse-au-jouir du Maréchal Pétain*, Seuil.
d 'Lecture de Brillat-Savarin' in Brillat-Savarin, *Physiologie du goût*, Hermann.
e 'Rasch' in Kristeva, Milner, Ruwet (1975).
f 'Roland Barthes met le langage en question' (an interview with Laurent Kissel,
preceded by a spiteful but perceptive note by Robert Kanters, tracing a change
in Barthes and presenting him as the prospective author of a love story — and
with a photograph of Barthes playing the piano), *Le Figaro littéraire*, 5 July.
g 'Que liront-ils en vacances?' (Barthes's answer to this question put to several
writers), *Le Nouvel Observateur*, 12 July.

1976

'Accordons la liberté de tracer', *Le Monde de l'éducation*, 13 January.

1977

a 'Le grain d'une enfance' (on J. Daniel's *Le refuge et la source*), *Le Nouvel
Observateur*, 9 May.
b 'Question de tempo', *Gramma*, 7, Special issue on Lucette Finas.
c 'La lumière du Sud-Ouest', *L'Humanité*, 10 September.

1978

a Preface to F. Flahault, *La Parole intermédiaire*, Seuil.
b 'Entre l'amour et l'angoisse' (review of the exhibition at the Festival d'automne of
the Musée des Arts décoratifs, Paris, called *Ma — Espace/Temps au Japon*), *Le
Nouvel Observateur*, 23 October.
c 'Ça prend' (on Proust), *Le Magazine littéraire*, 144, December.
d 'Chroniques' (on topical events, on his work, etc.), *Le Nouvel Observateur*, 18
December 1978-26 March 1979.

1979

a Preface to R. Camus, *Tricks*, Mazarine.
b 'Sagesse de l'art' in *Cy Twombly, paintings and drawings, 1954-1977*, Catalogue
of the Whitney Museum of American Art, New York, for the 1979 exhibition.
c 'Le sexe passe' (on André Téchiné's film *Les soeurs Brontë*), *Le Nouvel Observateur*, 14 May.
d 'Les rendez-vous du *Nouvel Observateur*: avec Roland Barthes', (interview by
N. Boulanger), 8 October.
e 'Délibération' (on keeping and publishing a diary), *Tel Quel*, 82, Winter.

1980

a 'Note sur un album de Lucien Clergue' (from Barthes's reflections as examiner
when Clergue obtained his Doctorate), *Sud*, 31.
b Interview with Laurent Dispot on food, health and 'maigritude', *Playboy* (French
edition), March.
c 'La crise du désir' (interview by Philip Brooks who, with Patrick Sarfati, spoke
with Barthes four days before his accident), *Le Nouvel Observateur*, 14 April.

The substance of this interview had already appeared, with comments, as:

d 'Barthes signs off', *Time Out*, 11-17 April. (The differences between these two pieces are of great interest to all text-watchers.)

e 'On échoue toujours à parler de ce qu'on aime' (on Stendhal), *Tel Quel*, 85, Autumn. (Barthes's last text, published posthumously.)

f 'Cher Antonioni', *Les cahiers du cinéma*, 311, May.

1981

'Italo Calvino vu par Roland Barthes', *Le Monde*, 20 February. (An extract from an interview by the radio station France-Culture, 20 October 1978.)

'Une leçon de sincérité', *Poétique*, 47, September.

Books and special issues on Barthes

Tel Quel, 47 (Autumn 1971) articles by P. Sollers, J. Kristeva, M. Pleynet, F. Wahl, S. Sarduy, M. Buffat, A. Lavers. Bibliography. Contains 'Réponses', interview by J. Thibaudeau.

Mallac, Guy de and Margaret Eberbach (1971) *Barthes*, Editions Universitaires.

Critique, 302, (July 1972) articles by R. Laporte, P. Duvernois, B. Vannier.

Calvet, Louis-Jean (1973) *Roland Barthes, un regard politique sur le signe*, Payot.

L'Arc, 56 (1974) C. Clément and B. Pingaud (eds).

Heath, Stephen (1974) *Vertige du déplacement. Lecture de Barthes*. Fayard.

Le Magazine littéraire, 97 (February 1975).

Thody, Philip (1977) *Roland Barthes: A Conservative Estimate*, London, Macmillan.

Compagnon, Antoine (ed.) (1978) *Prétexte: Roland Barthes*, Acts of a colloquium at Cérisy-la-Salle, Union générale d'editions, 10/18.

Fages, J.-B. (Jules Gritti) (1979) *Comprendre Roland Barthes*, Toulouse, Privat.

Lund, Steffen Nordahl (1981) *L'aventure du signifiant. Une lecture de Barthes*, Presses Universitaires de France.

Poétique, 47 (September 1981). Contains articles by J. Derrida, J.-P. Richard, F. Flahault, G. Genette, T. Todorov, S. Doubrovsky, R. Bensmaïa, M. Charles.

Culler, Jonathan (1982) *Barthes*. Fontana Modern Masters series, London, Collins.

Communications, special issue on Barthes, forthcoming, 1982.

Critique, special issue on Barthes, forthcoming, 1982.

Mention should also be made of:

Reichler, Claude. *La diabolie. La séduction, la renardie, l'écriture*, Minuit, 1979, one whole section of which is devoted to Barthes, and, as a sign of mythical recognition:

Burnier, Michel-Antoine and Patrick Rambaud (1978) *Le 'Roland-Barthes' sans peine*, Balland. Alas, it falls rather flat: both Burnier in this book and François George in his *Effet 'Yau de poêle* against Lacan are more interesting when they write on Sartre and his side than when they attack the opposition — see the next section of this bibliography on both.

Other works consulted*

Achard, P., A. Chauvenet, E. Lage, P. Nève, G. Vignaux (1977) *Discours biologique et ordre social*, Seuil.

* Articles on Barthes, books discussing his work or containing texts by him indicated by *.

Action poétique, 53 (1973) 'L'idéologie dans la critique littéraire', Le Pavillon, Roger Maria.

Adorno, Theodor W. (1974) *Théorie esthétique*, Klincksieck.

—— (1979) *Dialectique négative*, Payot.

Afterimage, 5 (1974) Special issue on 'Aesthetics, Ideology, Cinema', Noel Burch (ed.), London.

Althusser, Louis (1966) *Pour Marx*, Maspero.

—— (1966) with Etienne Balibar, Roger Establet, Pierre Macherey, Jacques Rancière, *Lire le Capital*, Maspero.

—— (1976) 'Idéologie et Appareils Idéologiques d'Etat' [1970], in *Positions*, Editions Sociales.

Les Annales: Economies, Sociétés, Civilisations (1971) Special issue on 'Structure et histoire', May-August, A. Colin.

* Antonioni, Michelangelo (1980) 'Lettre à Roland Barthes', *Cahiers du cinéma*, 311, May.

Apollinaire, Guillaume (1947) 'L'ami Méritarte', in *Le Poète assassiné*, Gallimard.

L'Arc, 30 (1966) Special issue on 'Sartre aujourd'hui', B. Pingaud (ed.), Aix-en-Provence (contains the interview 'J.-P. Sartre répond').

—— 58 (1974) Special issue on Jacques Lacan, C. Clément (ed.), with only women contributors.

Arguments (1977), Minuit [1957-62], reprint of main issues, Gallimard, 10/18, 2 vols.

Aron, Jean-Paul (1973) *Le mangeur du dix-neuvième siècle*, Laffont.

Ashby, Ross W. (1960) *Design for a Brain* [1952] 2nd edition, London, Chapman and Hall.

Aubral, François and Xavier Delcourt (1977) *Contre la nouvelle philosophie*, Gallimard, Idées.

Auerbach, Erich (1974) *Mimesis* [1946], Princeton, Princeton University Press.

Austin, J.L. (1962) *How to Do Things with Words* [1955], London, Oxford University Press.

Bachelard, Gaston (1938) *La psychanalyse du feu*, Gallimard.

—— (1940) *La philosophie du non*, Presses Universitaires de France.

Badiou, Alain (1969a) *Le concept de modèle*, Maspero.

—— (1969b) 'Marque et manque: à propos du zéro', *Cahiers pour l'Analyse*, 10, Special issue on 'La Formalisation', Seuil.

Bakhtin, Mikhail (1970a) *La poétique de Dostoïevski* [1928], Seuil. Trans. of 2nd edition, Moscow, 1963 (Introduction by J. Kristeva).

—— (1970b) *L'Oeuvre de François Rabelais et la culture populaire au Moyen-Age et sous la Renaissance*, Gallimard.

—— (pseudonym V.N. Vološinov) (1977) *Le Marxisme et la philosophie du langage* [1929], Minuit (Introduction by Roman Jakobson).

* Balibar, Renée (1974) with Geneviève Merlin and Giles Tret, *Les français fictifs. Le rapport des styles littéraires au français national*, Hachette.

—— (1974) and Dominique Laporte, *Le français national. Constitution de la langue nationale commune à l'époque de la révolution démocratique bourgeoise*, Hachette.

Bann, Stephen, (1970) 'A Cycle in historical discourse: Barante, Thierry, Michelet', *Twentieth Century Studies*, 3, Special issue on 'Structuralism',

Canterbury, University of Kent.

* —— (1977) 'Barthes Britannicus', *PN Review*, 5 (2).

—— and S. Bowlt (eds) (1973) *Russian Formalism*, Edinburgh, Scottish Academy Press.

Bataille, Georges (1967a) *Histoire de l'oeil* [1928], Pauvert.

—— (1967b) *La part maudite* [1949], Minuit.

—— (1970) Preface to *Le bleu du ciel* [1936], Union générale d'éditions, 10/18.

Bateson, Gregory (1973) *Steps to an Ecology of Mind*, St Albans, Paladin.

Baudelot, Christian and Roger Establet (1971) *L'école capitaliste en France*, Maspero.

—— and Jacques Malemort (1974) *La petite bourgeoisie en France*, Maspero.

Baudrillard, Jean (1968) *Système des objets*, Gallimard.

—— (1972) *Pour une critique de l'économie politique du signe*, Gallimard.

—— (1976) *L'échange symbolique et la mort*, Gallimard.

Baudry, Jean-Louis (1968) 'Ecriture, fiction, idéologie', in *Tel Quel, Théorie d'ensemble*, Seuil.

* Beaujour, Michel (1980) *Miroirs d'encre*, Seuil.

* Bellour, Raymond (1971) *Le livre des autres*, L'Herne.

* —— and Catherine Clément (eds) (1979) *Claude Lévi-Strauss, Textes de et sur Cl. Lévi-Strauss*, Gallimard.

* Belsey, Catherine (1980) *Critical Practice*, London, Methuen.

Benedict, Ruth (1977) *The Chrysanthemum and the Sword: Patterns of Japanese Culture* [1946] London, Routledge & Kegan Paul.

Bénichou, Paul (1948) *Morales du Grand Siècle*, Gallimard.

Benjamin, Walter (1973) *Illuminations*, London, Collins/Fontana.

Bennett, Tony (1979) *Formalism and Marxism*, London, Methuen.

Benoist, Jean-Marie (1975a) *La révolution structurale*, Grasset.

—— (1975b) *Tyrannie du logos*, Minuit.

—— (1969) Interview with Chomsky in *La Quinzaine littéraire*, 1-15 June.

Benthall, Jonathan and Ted Polhemus (eds) (1975) *The Body as a Medium of Expression*, London, Allen Lane.

Benveniste, Emile (1966 and 1974) *Problèmes de linguistique générale*, Gallimard, 2 vols.

Bernstein, Basil (1971) *Class, Codes and Control*, London, Routledge & Kegan Paul.

Bernstein, Leonard (1976) *The Unanswered Question*, Cambridge, Mass., Harvard University Press.

Birdwhistell, Ray L. (1971) *Kinesics and Context: Essays on Body-Motion Communication*, London, Allen Lane.

Blanché, Robert (1966) *Les structures intellectuelles*, Vrin.

Blanchot, Maurice (1949) *La part du feu*, Gallimard.

—— (1955) *L'espace littéraire*, Gallimard.

* —— (1959) *Le livre à venir*, Gallimard.

Bloch, Ernst, *et al.* (1977) *Aesthetics and Politics*, London, New Left Books.

Bloch, Marc (1949) *Apologie pour l'histoire, ou Métier d'historien*, A. Colin.

Bloom, Harold, Paul de Man, Jacques Derrida, Geoffrey Hartman and J. Hillis Miller (1980) *Deconstruction and Criticism*, London, Routledge & Kegan

Paul.

Bloomfield, Leonard (1933) *Language*, New York, Holt, Rinehart & Winston.

* Bonitzer, Pascal (1980) 'Le hors-champ subtil', *Cahiers du cinéma*, 311, May.

Boons, Marie-Claire (1968) 'La fuite du "vrai" dans la cure psychanalytique', *Communications*, 11.

Bouazis, Charles (ed.) (1973) *Essais de la théorie du texte*, Galilée.

Bourdieu, Pierre and Jean-Claude Passeron (1964) *Les héritiers*, Minuit.

———— (1970) *La reproduction*, Minuit.

Bouveresse, Jacques (1976) 'Une illusion de grand avenir: la psychanalyse selon Popper', *Critique*, 346.

Bradbury, Malcolm and James McFarlane (1976) *Modernism*, Harmondsworth, Penguin.

Brecht, Bertolt (1970) *Ecrits sur la politique et la société*, L'Arche (often cited by Barthes).

Bremond, Claude (1973) *Logique du récit*, Seuil.

Bresson, François and Georges Vignaux (1973) 'La Psycholinguistique', in B. Pottier, *Le langage*, Denoël.

Breton, André (1961) *Ode à Charles Fourier* [1947], edition by Jean Gaulmier, Klincksieck.

———— and Paul Eluard (1930) *L'Immaculée conception*, Editions surréalistes.

Brewster, Ben (1969) Glossary appended to *For Marx* (translation of Althusser's *Pour Marx*), Harmondsworth, Penguin.

Brøndal, Viggo (1943) *Essais de linguistigue générale*, Copenhagen, Munskgaard.

Brooke-Rose, Christine (1958) *A Grammar of Metaphor*, London, Secker & Warburg.

* Buffat, Marc (1971) 'Le simulacre', *Tel Quel*, 47.

Burnier, Michel-Antoine (1966) *Les existentialistes et la politique*, Gallimard.

Burniston, Steve and Chris Weedon (1978) 'Ideology, subjectivity and the artistic text', in *On Ideology*, Birmingham, Centre for Contemporary Cultural Studies.

* Butor, Michel (1968) 'La Fascinatrice', *Les cahiers du chemin*, October, Gallimard.

———— (1970) *La Rose des vents. 32 Rhumbs pour Charles Fourier*, Gallimard.

Buyssens, Eric (1943) *Les langages et le discours. Essai de linguistique fonctionnelle dans le cadre de la sémiologie*, Bruxelles, Office de publicité.

Calvet, Louis-Jean (1975) *Pour et contre Saussure. Vers une linguistique sociale*, Payot.

Canguilhem, Georges (1967) 'Mort de l'homme ou épuisement du Cogito?', *Critique*, 242.

———— (1970) *Etudes d'histoire et de philosophie des sciences*, Vrin.

Carloni, Jean-Claude et Jean-Claude Filloux (1969) *La critique littéraire* [1955], Presses Universitaires de France (point of view very similar to the early Barthes's).

Cassirer, Ernst (1944) *An Essay on Man*, New Haven, Yale University Press.

———— (1953-7) *The Philosophy of Symbolic Forms* [1923-9], New Haven, Yale University Press.

Castel, Robert (1973) *Le Psychanalysme. L'ordre psychanalytique et le pouvoir*, Maspero.

Catesson, Jean (1977) 'Auto, Bio et Graphie', *Critique*, 357.

Caws, Peter (1968) 'What is Structuralism?', *Partisan Review*, 35.

—— (1979) *Sartre*, London, Routledge & Kegan Paul.

Cazotte, Jacques (1950) *Le Diable amoureux* [1772], Athena.

Centre for Contemporary Cultural Studies (University of Birmingham) (1978) *On Ideology*, London, Hutchinson.

Certeau, Michel de, Dominique Julia and Jacques Revel (1975) *Une politique de la langue. La Révolution française et les patois*, Gallimard.

* Chabrol, Claude (1973) *Sémiotique narrative et textuelle*, Larousse.

Charlton, Donald (1959) *Positivist Thought in France during the Second Empire*, Oxford, Clarendon Press.

Châtelet, François (1970) *La philosophie des professeurs*, Grasset.

Chatman, Seymour (1969) 'New Ways of Analysing Narrative Structure, with an example from Joyce's *Dubliners*' [on 'Eveline'], *Language and Style*, 2.

* —— (ed.) (1971) *Literary Style: A Symposium*, London, Oxford University Press.

—— and Samuel B. Levin (1967) *Essays on the Language of Literature*, Boston, Houghton Mifflin.

Cherry, Colin (1978) *On Human Communication: A Review, a Survey and a Criticism*, 3rd edition, Cambridge, Mass., MIT Press.

Chiodi, Pietro (1976) *Sartre and Marxism* [1965], Brighton, Sussex, Harvester. Tr. by Kate Soper.

Chomsky, Noam (1964) Review of B.F. Skinner, *Verbal Behavior* [1959], in J. Fodor and J. Katz (eds) *The Structure of Language*, Englewood Cliffs, N.J., Prentice-Hall.

—— (1965) *Aspects of the Theory of Syntax*, Cambridge, Mass., MIT Press.

—— (1969) Interview with J.-M. Benoist, *La Quinzaine littéraire*, 1-15 June.

—— (1970) 'Some Observations on the Problems of Semantic Analysis in Natural Languages', in A.J. Greimas (ed.) *Sign, Language, Culture*, The Hague, Mouton.

—— (1972) 'Entretien avec Jean Paris' and 'Réponses au questionnaire de la RTB' in Jean-Pierre Faye, Jean Paris, Jacques Roubaud and Mitsou Ronat, *Hypothèses*, Seghers/Laffont.

—— (1977) *Dialogues* between Chomsky and Mitsou Ronat, Flammarion.

Cixous, Hélène (1976) *La*, Gallimard.

Clément, Catherine (1978) *Les fils de Freud sont fatigués*, Grasset.

—— and R. Bellour (eds) (1979) *Claude Lévi-Strauss, Textes de et sur Cl. Lévi-Strauss*, Gallimard.

Cohen, Jean (1966) *Structure du langage poétique*, Flammarion.

—— (1979) *Le haut langage. Théorie de la poéticité*, Flammarion.

Cohen, Ralph (ed.) (1974) *New Directions in Literary History*, London, Routledge & Kegan Paul.

Cohn, Robert Greer (1977) 'Mallarmé contre Genette', *Tel Quel*, 69.

* *Communications* (Review of the C.E.C.MAS (Centre d'Etudes des Communications de Masse), now C.E.T.S.A.S. (Centre d'Etudes Transdisciplinaires: Sociologie, Anthropologie, Sémiologie), VIth Section of the Ecole Pratique des Hautes Etudes (now the Ecole Pratique des Hautes Etudes en Sciences Sociales)).

See especially the following issues:
4 (1964) 'Recherches sémiologiques'
8 (1966) 'L'analyse structurale du récit'
11 (1968) 'Le vraisemblable'
15 (1970) 'L'analyse des images'
16 (1970) 'Recherches rhétoriques'
19 (1972) 'Le texte. De la théorie à la recherche'
20 (1973) 'Le sociologique et le linguistique'
22 (1975) 'La nature de la société'
23 (1975) 'Psychanalyse et cinéma'
30 (1979) 'La conversation'.

Compagnon, Antoine (1979) *La seconde main ou le travail de la citation*, Seuil.
* —— (1981) 'Roland Barthes', *Universalia 1980, Encyclopaedia Universalis*.
Comte, Auguste (1975) *Cours de philosophie positive, 1829-*, ed. M. Serres, F. Dagognet, A. Sinaceur, J.-P. Enthoven, 2 vols., Hermann.
Coquet, Jean-Claude (1973) *Sémiotique littéraire. Contribution à l'analyse sémantique du discours*, Tours, Mame.
Costes, Alain (1973) *Albert Camus ou la parole manquante*, Payot.
Courtès, Joseph (1976) *Introduction à la sémiotique narrative et discursive*, Hachette.
* Coward, Rosalind and John Ellis (1977) *Language and Materialism: Developments in semiology and the theory of the subject*, London, Routledge & Kegan Paul.
Craig, David (1975) 'Towards Laws of Literary Development', in D. Craig (ed.) *Marxists on Literature, An Anthology*, Harmondsworth, Penguin.
Cruikshank, John (1970) *French Literature and its Background [6] The Twentieth Century*, London, Oxford University Press.
Cuisenier, Jean (1967) 'Le structuralisme du mot, de l'idée et des outils', *Esprit*, 35.
* Culler, Jonathan (1975) *Structuralist Poetics: Structuralism, Linguistics and the Study of Literature*, London, Routledge & Kegan Paul.
—— (1976) *Saussure*, Fontana Modern Masters series, London, Collins.
Curran, J., M. Gurevitch and J. Wollacott (eds) (1977) *Mass Communication and Society*, London, Edward Arnold.
Daix, Pierre (1968) *Nouvelle critique et art moderne*, Seuil.
Damisch, Hubert (1972) *Théorie du nuage*, Seuil.
Debord, Guy (1967) *La Société du Spectacle*, Buchet-Chastel.
* De George, Richard T. and M. Fernande (eds) (1972) *The Structuralists: From Marx to Lévi-Strauss*, New York, Doubleday.
Delas, Daniel and Jacques Filliolet (1973) *Linguistique et poétique*, Larousse.
Deleuze, Gilles and Félix Guattari (1972, 1980) *Capitalisme et schizophrénie* [I] *L'Anti-Oedipe*. [II] *Mille plateaux*, 2 vols, Minuit.
—— (1976) *Rhizome*, Minuit.
Derrida, Jacques (1967a) *De la grammatologie*, Minuit.
—— (1967b) *L'écriture et la différence*, Seuil.
—— (1972a) *Marges de la philosophie*, Minuit.
—— (1972b) *Positions*, Minuit.
—— (1972c) *La dissémination*, Seuil.

———— (1975) 'Le facteur de la vérité', *Poétique*, 21.

———— (1977) 'Ja, ou le faux-bond', *Digraphe*, 11, April.

Descombes, Vincent (1977) 'Pour elle un Français doit mourir', *Critique*, 366, November.

———— (1979) *Le même et l'autre. Quarante-cinq ans de philosophie française (1933-78)*, Minuit.

Deslandres, Yvonne (1976) *Le costume, image de l'homme*, A. Michel.

* Dijk, Teun van (1972) *Some Aspects of Text-Grammars*, The Hague, Mouton.

Dinneen, Francis P. (1967) *An Introduction to Linguistics*, New York, Holt, Rinehart & Winston.

Domenach, Jean-Marie (1967) 'Le système et la personne', *Esprit*, 35.

* Doubrovsky, Serge (1966) *Pourquoi la nouvelle critique. Critique et objectivité*, Mercure.

* ———— and Tzvetan Todorov (eds) (1971) *L'Enseignement de la littérature*, Plon.

Douglas, Mary (1970) *Natural Symbols: Explorations in Cosmology*, London, Barrie & Jenkins.

———— (ed.) (1973) *Rules and Meanings: The Anthropology of Everyday Knowledge*, Harmondsworth, Penguin.

———— (1974) with Michael Nicod, 'Taking the Biscuit: The structure of British meals', *New Society*, 19 December.

———— and Baron Isherwood (1979) *The World of Goods*, London, Allen Lane.

Ducrot, Oswald and Tzvetan Todorov (1972) *Dictionnaire encyclopédique des sciences du langage*, Seuil.

Du Marsais (1967) *Traité des tropes* [1818 edition], Geneva, Slatkine Reprints, 2 vols (of which the 2nd is Fontanier's *Commentaire raisonné sur les tropes de Du Marsais*).

Dumézil, Georges (1977) *Les dieux souverains des Indo-Européens*, Gallimard.

Duneton, Claude (1978) *Parler croquant*, Stock.

* Duvignaud, Jean (1970) *Anthologie des sociologues français contemporains*, Presses Universitaires de France.

Eagleton, Terry (1976) *Criticism and Ideology*, London, New Left Books.

Eco, Umberto (1965) *L'œuvre ouverte*, Seuil.

———— (1970) 'Sémiologie des messages visuels', *Communications*, 15.

———— (1972) *La structure absente*, Mercure.

———— (1976) *A Theory of Semiotics*, Bloomington, Ind., Indiana University Press.

Empson, William (1961) *Seven Types of Ambiguity* [1930], Harmondsworth Penguin.

Engler, R. (1973) 'Rôle et place d'une sémantique linguistique saussurienne', *Cahiers Ferdinand de Saussure*, 28, Geneva.

Epstein, E.L. (1978) *Language and Style*, London, Methuen.

Erlich, Victor (1955) *Russian Formalism: History-Doctrine*, The Hague, Mouton.

Esprit, 3 (1963) Special issue on Lévi-Strauss: 'La pensée sauvage et le structuralisme'.

———— 35 (1967) Special issue on 'Structuralismes. Idéologie et méthode'.

Fages, J.-B. = Jules Gritti.

Faye, Jean-Pierre (1972a) *Théorie du récit*, Hermann.

―――― (1972b) *Langages totalitaires. Critique de la raison/l'économie narrative*, Hermann.

Feyerabend, Paul (1975) *Against Method*, London, New Left Books.

Finas, Lucette (1979) *Le bruit d'Iris*, Flammarion.

* Flahault, François (1978) *La parole intermédiaire*, Seuil.

Fónagy, Ivan (1970-1) 'Les bases pulsionnelles de la phonation', *Revue française de psychanalyse*, 34-35.

Fontanier, Pierre (1968) *Les figures du discours* [1821-30], G. Genette (ed.), Flammarion.

Forster, E.M. (1923) *Pharos and Pharillon*, London, Hogarth.

Foucault, Michel (1961) *Folie et déraison. Histoire de la folie à l'âge classique*, Plon.

―――― (1963) *Naissance de la clinique*, Presses Universitaires de France.

―――― (1966) *Les mots et les choses*, Gallimard.

―――― (1969) *L'archéologie du savoir*, Gallimard.

―――― (1971) *L'ordre du discours*, Gallimard.

Fowler, Roger (1977) *Linguistics and the Novel*, London, Methuen.

Francastel, Pierre (1967) *La figure et le lieu*, Gallimard.

France, Peter (1972) *Rhetoric and Truth in France: Descartes to Diderot*, Oxford, Clarendon.

Frye, Northrop (1965) *Anatomy of Criticism* [1957], New York, Atheneum.

Fumaroli, Marc (1980) *L'âge de l'éloquence. Rhétorique et 'res literaria' de la Renaissance au seuil de l'époque classique*, Geneva, Droz; Paris, Champion.

Furet, François (1978) *Penser la Révolution française*, Gallimard.

Gabel, Joseph (1962) *La fausse conscience. Essai sur la réification*, Minuit.

* Gaillard, Françoise (1974) 'Roland Barthes "sémioclaste"?', *L'Arc*, 56.

Gardner, Howard (1972) *The Quest for Mind*, London, Coventure.

Genette, Gérard (1966a) 'Vertige fixé', *Figures*, Seuil.

―――― (1966b) 'Bonheur de Mallarmé?', *Figures*.

* ―――― (1966c) 'L'envers des signes', *Figures*.

―――― (1966d) 'Figures', *Figures*.

―――― (1969a) 'Rhétorique et enseignement', *Figures II*, Seuil.

―――― (1969b) 'Frontières du récit', *Figures II*.

―――― (1972) *Figures III*, Seuil.

―――― (1976) *Mimologiques*, Seuil.

―――― (1979) *Introduction à l'architexte*, Seuil.

George, François (1976) *Deux essais sur Sartre*, Bourgois.

―――― (1979) *L'effet 'Yau de poêle*, Hachette.

Giglioli, Pier Paolo (ed.) (1972) *Language and Social Context*, Harmondsworth, Penguin.

Girard, René (1961) *Mensonge romantique et vérité romanesque*, Grasset.

―――― (1972) *La violence et le sacré*, Grasset.

Gobard, Henri (1976) *L'aliénation linguistique, analyse tétraglossique*, Flammarion.

Godechot, Jacques (1974) *Un jury pour la Révolution*, Laffont.

Godel, Robert (1957) *Les sources manuscrites du Cours de linguistique générale de F. de Saussure*, Geneva, Droz & Minard.

Godelier, Maurice (1975) Preface to C.E.R.M. (Centre d'Etudes et de Recherches

Marxistes), *Sur les sociétés précapitalistes*, Editions Sociales.

—— (1977) *Horizon, trajets marxistes en anthropologie*, new edition, Maspero.

Goldmann, Lucien (1955) *Le dieu caché*, Gallimard.

—— (1964) *Pour une sociologie du roman*, Gallimard.

—— (1971) *La création culturelle dans la société moderne. Pour une sociologie de la totalité*, Denoël/Gonthier.

Gombrich, E.H. (1960) *Art and Illusion*, London, Phaidon.

Gorz, André (1980) *Adieu au prolétariat*, Galilée.

Goux, Jean-Joseph (1973) *Freud, Marx — Economie et Symbolique*, Seuil.

—— (1978) *Les Iconoclastes*, Seuil.

Gramsci, Antonio (1971) *Prison Notebooks*, London, Lawrence & Wishart.

Green, André (1973) *Le discours vivant*, Presses Universitaires de France.

Greimas, A.J. (1966) *Sémantique structurale*, Larousse.

—— (1970a) *Du sens*, Seuil.

—— (1970b) 'L'écriture cruciverbiste', *Du Sens*.

—— (ed.) (1970c) *Sign, Language, Culture*, The Hague, Mouton.

—— (ed.) (1972) *Essais de sémiotique poétique*, Larousse.

—— (1973) 'Les Actants, les acteurs et les figures', in C. Chabrol, *Sémiotique narrative et textuelle*, Larousse.

—— (1976a) *Maupassant. La sémiotique du texte: exercices pratiques*, Seuil.

—— (1976b) *Sémiotique et sciences sociales*, Seuil.

—— (1976c) Interview with F. Nef in F. Nef (ed.), *Structures élémentaires de la signification*, Bruxelles, Complexe.

—— (1976d) Preface to J. Courtès, *Introduction à la sémiotique narrative et discursive*, Hachette.

—— with J. Courtès (1979) *Sémiotique. Dictionnaire raisonné de la théorie du langage*, Hachette.

* —— (1980) 'Roland Barthes: une biographie à construire', *Bulletin du Groupe de recherches sémio-linguistiques*, 13, March.

GREPH (Groupe de recherche sur l'enseignement philosophique) (1977) *Qui a peur de la philosophie?*, Flammarion.

Grisoni (1975) 'Sartre, de la structure à l'histoire', *Le Magazine littéraire*, 103-4.

Gritti, Jules (pseudonym J.-B. Fages) (1968) *Le Structuralisme en procès*, Toulouse, Privat.

—— (1966) 'Un récit de presse: les derniers jours d'un "grand homme"', *Communications*, 8.

—— 'Deux arts du vraisemblable: la casuistique, le courrier du coeur', *Communications*, 11.

Groupe de recherches sémio-linguistiques de l'Ecole des Hautes Etudes en Sciences Sociales (EHESS-CNRS, U.R.L.7 de l'Institut de la Langue Française). The Group, whose Director is A.J. Greimas, publishes *Bulletins* and *Documents*.

Groupe μ (sometimes called 'Groupe de Liège', including, at different times: Jacques Dubois, Philippe Dubois, Francis Edeline, Jean-Marie Klinkenberg, Philippe Minguet, François Pire, Hadelin Trinon, Arpad Vigh).

—— (1970) *Rhétorique générale*, Larousse.

—— (1976) 'La chafetière est sur la table. Eléments pour une rhétorique de l'image', in *Communications et langages*, 29.

———— (1978a) *Rhétorique de la poésie. Lecture linéaire, lecture tabulaire,* Bruxelles, Complexe.

———— (eds) (1978b) *Collages,* an issue of the *Revue d'esthétique,* 3-4, 10/18.

———— (eds) (1979) *Rhétoriques, sémiotiques,* an issue of the *Revue d'esthétique,* 1-2, 10/18.

Guillaume, Gustave (1964) *Langage et science du langage,* Montreal, Presses de l'Université du Québec.

Guiraud, Pierre (1971) *La sémiologie,* Presses Universitaires de France.

Habermas, Jürgen (1970) 'Towards a Theory of Communicative Competence', *Inquiry,* 13.

Hall, Edward T. (1959) *The Silent Language,* New York, Doubleday.

Hall, Stuart, *et al.* (1973) 'Mapping the Field', *Working Papers in Cultural Studies,* Birmingham, Centre for Contemporary Cultural Studies, 4.

Halliday, M.A.K. (1969) 'Language in a Social Perspective', *Educational Review,* 23(3).

———— (1970) 'Language Structure and Language Function', in J. Lyons (ed.) *New Horizons in Linguistics,* Harmondsworth, Penguin.

———— (1975) *Explorations in the Functions of Language,* London, Edward Arnold.

———— (1978) *Language as Social Semiotic,* London, Arnold.

Halperin, John (ed.) (1974) *The Theory of the Novel,* New York, Oxford University Press.

* Hamon, Philippe (1977) 'Pour un statut sémiologique du personnage', in *Poétique du récit* (also contains articles by Barthes — 'Introduction to the Structural Analysis of Narratives' — C. Wayne Booth and W. Kayser).

* Harari, Josué V. (ed.) (1980) *Textual Strategies: Perspectives in Post-Structuralist Criticism,* London, Methuen.

Haroche, Claude, P. Henry and M. Pêcheux (1971) 'La sémantique et la coupure saussurienne. Langue, Langage, Discours', *Langages,* 24.

Harris, Zellig S. (1963) *Discourse Analysis,* The Hague, Mouton, Reprints: Papers on Formal Linguistics, 2.

Hartman, Geoffrey (1970) *Beyond Formalism,* New Haven, Yale University Press.

* Hawkes, Terence (1977) *Structuralism and Semiotics,* London, Methuen, (in the New Accents series of which T. Hawkes is editor; each book has a full bibliography).

Heath, Stephen (1972) 'Ambiviolences', *Tel Quel,* 50 and 51.

* ———— Colin McCabe and Christopher Prendergast (eds) (1971) *Signs of the Times. Introductory Readings in Textual Semiotics,* Cambridge, Granta.

Hegel, G.W.F. (1939-41) *La phénoménologie de l'esprit* [1807]. Trans. and notes by Jean Hyppolite, Aubier-Montaigne.

———— (1878) *Lectures on the Philosophy of History,* London, Bell.

Hénault, Anne (1979) *Les enjeux de la sémiotique. Introduction à la sémiotique générale,* Presses Universitaires de France.

Herbart, Pierre (1952) *A la recherche d'André Gide,* Gallimard.

* Hermann, Claudine (1974) 'Le sexe du langage', *La Quinzaine littéraire,* 1-31 August.

Hindess, Barry and Paul Hirst (1977) *Mode of Production and Social Formation,*

London, Macmillan.

Hjelmslev, Louis (1959) *Essais linguistiques. Travaux du Cercle linguistique de Copenhague*, 12.

—— (1961) *Prolegomena to a Theory of Language*, revised edition, Madison, University of Wisconsin Press.

* Hollier, Denis (ed.) (1973) *Panorama des sciences humaines*, Gallimard.

L'Homme et la société, (1966) 1 and 2, July-December.

Houbart, Jacques (1964) *Un père dénaturé*, Julliard.

Houdebine, Anne-Marie (1976) 'Langue nationale et politique', *Tel Quel*, 68.

Houdebine, Jean-Louis (1971) 'Lecture(s) d'une refonte', *Critique*, 287.

—— (1977a) 'Jdanov ou Joyce?', *Tel Quel*, 69.

—— (1977b) *Langage et marxisme*, Klincksieck.

Howells, Christina (1979) *Sartre's Theory of Literature* (MHRA Texts and Dissertations, 14), London, MHRA.

Human Context (The) (1973) Special issue on 'The Impact of Structuralism', 5(1).

* IASS-AIS (International Association for Semiotic Studies — Association Internationale de Sémiotique) (1979) *Actes du premier Congrès* [1974], S. Chatman, U. Eco and J.-M. Klinkenberg (eds), The Hague, Mouton.

—— (forthcoming) *Proceedings of the Second Congress* [1979], T. Borbé (ed.), The Hague, Mouton.

Ingleby, David (1972) 'Ideology and the human sciences. Some comments on the role of reification in psychology and psychiatry', in T. Pateman, *Countercourse*, Harmondsworth, Penguin.

Irigaray, Luce (1967) 'Approche d'une grammaire d'énonciation de l'hystérique et de l'obsessionnel', *Langages*, 5.

—— (1977a) 'Misère de la psychanalyse', *Critique*, 365.

—— 'Women's Exile' (1977b) Interview in *Ideology and Consciousness*, 1, May.

Jakobson, Roman (1963) *Essais de linguistique générale*, Minuit.

—— (1973) *Questions de poétique*, Seuil.

—— with Claude Lévi-Strauss (1962) '*Les Chats* de Charles Baudelaire', *L'Homme*, 2.

Jameson, Fredric (1971) *Marxism and Form*, Princeton, Princeton University Press.

—— (1972) *The Prison-House of Language: A Critical Account of Structuralism and Russian Formalism*, Princeton, Princeton University Press.

—— (1981) *The Political Unconscious*, London, Methuen.

Jefferson, Ann (1980) *The Nouveau Roman and the Poetics of Fiction*, Cambridge, Cambridge University Press.

Jenny, Laurent (1978) 'Sémiotique du collage intertextuel, ou la littérature à coups de ciseaux', in Groupe μ, *Collages*.

Johnson-Laird, P.N. (1974) 'Experimental Psycholinguistics', *Annual Review of Psychology*, 25.

Josipovici, Gabriel (1970) 'The Birth of the Modern: 1885-1914', in Cruikshank, *French Literature and its Background*.

* —— (1971) *The World and the Book*, London, Macmillan.

—— (ed.) (1977) *Literature, Society and the Sociology of Literature*, Proceedings of the Conference held at the University of Essex.

Joyaux, Julia = Julia Kristeva

Jurdant, Baudouin (1975) 'La vulgarisation scientifique', *La Recherche*, 53.

Kermode, Frank (1971) *Modern Essays*, London, Fontana.

* —— (1974) 'Novel and Narrative', in J. Halperin (ed.) *The Theory of the Novel*, New York, Oxford University Press.

—— (1976) 'Fighting Freud', *New York Review of Books*, April 29.

* —— (1979) *The Genesis of Secrecy. On the Interpretation of Narrative.* Cambridge, Mass., Harvard University Press.

Klinkenberg, Jean-Marie (1973) 'Vers un modèle théorique du langage poétique', *Degrés* I.

—— (1979) 'Communication et signification: l'unité de la sémiologie', in IASS, *Actes du premier Congrès* [1974].

Kofman, Sarah (1978) *Aberrations. Le devenir-femme d'Auguste Comte*, Aubier/Flammarion.

—— (1980) *L'énigme de la femme*, Galilée.

Kojève, Alexandre (1969) *Introduction to the Reading of Hegel. Lectures on the Phenomenology of Spirit (assembled by R. Queneau)* Allan Bloom (ed.) [Gallimard, 1947], New York, Basic Books.

* Kristeva, Julia (1969a) *Sémeiotiké. Recherches pour une sémanalyse.* Seuil.

—— (pseudonym J. Joyaux) (1969b) *Le langage, cet inconnu*, SGPP and Planète.

—— (ed.) (1971) *Langages*, 24, (contains the article 'Du sujet en linguistique', now also in *Polylogue*).

—— (1972) 'Sémanalyse et production de sens', in Greimas.

—— (1974a) *La révolution du langage poétique*, Seuil.

—— (1974b) *Des Chinoises*, des Femmes.

—— (ed.) (1975) *La traversée des signes*, Seuil (contains the articles 'Pratique signifiante et mode de production', and 'Remarques sur le "mode de production asiatique"').

—— (1977) *Polylogue*, Seuil.

—— (1979) 'Il n'y a pas de maître à langage', *Nouvelle Revue de Psychanalyse*, 20, Special issue on 'Regards sur la psychanalyse en France'.

—— (1980) *Pouvoirs de l'horreur. Essai sur l'abjection*, Seuil.

—— J. Rey-Debove and D.J. Umiker (eds) (1971) *Essays in Semiotics/Essais de sémiotique* (reprints from *Social Science Information/Information sur les sciences sociales*), The Hague, Mouton.

—— J. Milner and N. Ruwet (eds) (1975) *Langue, discours, société. Pour Emile Benveniste*, Seuil.

Kuhn, Thomas (1970) *The Structure of Scientific Revolutions*, 2nd revised edition, Chicago, University of Chicago Press.

Lacan, Jacques (1966) *Ecrits*, Seuil.

—— (1968) 'La leçon inaugurale du professeur Jacques Monod au Collège de France', *Scilicet* 1 [the journal of Lacan's Ecole freudienne] (most articles in *Scilicet* are anonymous and it is not clear whether this one is or is not part of a note signed by Lacan).

—— (1973) *Télévision*, Seuil.

—— (1975a) *Le Séminaire, XX, Encore*, Seuil.

—— (1975b) *De la psychose paranoïaque dans ses rapports avec la personnalité* [1932], Seuil, (Lacan's doctoral thesis).

La Capra, Dominick (1978) *A Preface to Sartre*, Ithaca, N.Y., Cornell University Press.

Lacoue-Labarthe, Philippe (ed.) (1975) *Poétique*, 21, Special issue on 'Littérature et philosophie mêlées'.

Ladrière, Jean (1967) 'Sens et système', *Esprit*, 35.

Laing, Ronald and David Cooper (1964) *Reason and Violence: A Decade of Sartre's Philosophy 1950-1960*, London, Tavistock.

Lakatos, Imre and Alan Musgrave (1970) *Criticism and the Growth of Knowledge*, Cambridge, Cambridge University Press.

Landowski, Eric (ed.) (1981) *Le Carré Sémiotique* (Special issue), *Bulletin du Groupe de recherches sémio-linguistiques*, 17, March.

* Lane, Michael (1970) *Structuralism, A Reader*, London, Cape.

Langages, 13 (1969) Special issue on 'L'analyse du discours' Jean Dubois and Joseph Sumpf (ed.).

―――― 24 (1971) Special issue on 'L'épistémologie de la linguistique', J. Kristeva (ed.).

―――― 31 (1973) Special issue on 'Sémiotiques textuelles', Michel Arrivé and Jean-Claude Coquet (ed.).

―――― 33 (1974) Special issue on 'S.K. Šaumjan et la grammaire générative applicative', René L'Hermitte and Hélène Wlodarczyk (eds).

―――― 35 (1974) Special issue on 'Problèmes et méthodes de le sémiologie', Jean-Jacques Nattiez (ed.).

Lanson, Gustave (1912) *Histoire de la littérature française*, 12th revised edition, Hachette.

Laplanche, Jean and Serge Leclaire (1963) 'L'inconscient', *Les Temps Modernes*, 183.

―――― Jean-Bertrand Pontalis (1965) *Vocabulaire de la psychanalyse*, Presses Universitaires de France.

Lavers, Annette (1964) *L'usurpateur et le prétendant. Essai sur le psychologue dans la littérature contemporaine*, Minard, Lettres Modernes.

* ―――― (1970) 'France: The End of the Terreur? The Evolution of Contemporary Critical Attitudes', *The Human Context* II(1) (on Barthes in relation to Paulhan and Blanchot).

* ―――― (1971a) 'En traduisant Barthes', *Tel Quel*, 47.

―――― (1971b) 'Some Aspects of Language in the Work of Jacques Lacan', *Semiotica*, 3 (a partial rewriting of 'Freud in his own Write, or Language in Lacan', in *Cambridge Opinion/Circuit*, Summer 1969).

Leach, Edmund (1969) *Genesis as Myth*, London, Cape.

Lecourt, Dominique (1975) *Marxism and Epistemology: Bachelard, Canguilhem, Foucault*, London, New Left Books.

Leduc, Victor (ed.) (1970) *Structuralisme et marxisme*, Union générale d'éditions, 10/18.

* Leenhardt, Jacques (1973a) *Lecture politique du roman. 'La Jalousie' d'A. Robbe-Grillet*, Minuit.

―――― and Brigitte Navelet (eds) (1973b) *Psychanalyse et sociologie*, Bruxelles, Editions de l'université de Bruxelles.

―――― (1979) 'Lecture critique de la théorie goldmanienne du roman', in C. Duchet (ed.), *Rencontres sur la socio-critique et l'analyse idéologique des textes littéraires*, Nathan.

* —— (1981) Preface to R. Heyndels, *Littérature, idéologie et signification*, L'Age d'Homme.

Lefebvre, Henri (1947) *Descartes*, Editeurs français réunis.

—— (1949-54) *Pascal*, Nagel.

—— (1958-61) *Critique de la vie quotidienne, Introduction*, L'Arche.

—— (1966) 'Claude Lévi-Strauss et le nouvel éléatisme', *L'Homme et la Société*, 2.

Le Goff, Jacques and Pierre Nora (eds) (1974) *Faire de l'histoire*, Gallimard.

Leiris, Michel (1956) *Bagatelles végétales*, Jean Aubier.

Lejeune, Philippe (1975) *Le pacte autobiographique*, Seuil.

* —— (1980) *Je est un autre*, Seuil.

Lenneberg, Eric H. (1967) *Biological Foundations of Language*, New York, Wiley.

Le Ny, Jean-Francois (1979) *La linguistique psychologique*, Presses Universitaires de France.

Lepschy, Giulio (1967) 'Nota sullo strutturalismo e sulla linguistica sovietica recente', *Studi e Sagge Linguistici*, 7.

—— (1970) *A Survey of Structural Linguistics*, London, Faber & Faber.

—— (1979) 'Saussure e gli spiriti', in Lepschy, *Intorno Saussure*, Turin, Stampatore.

Lerdahl, F. and R. Jackendoff (1977), 'Towards a formal theory of tonal music', *Journal of Music Theory*, Spring.

Leroi-Gourhan, André (1965) *Le geste et la parole*, A. Michel.

Lévi-Strauss, Claude (1955) *Tristes tropiques*, Plon.

—— (1958, 1973) *Anthropologie structurale*, 2 vols, Plon.

—— (1960) 'La structure et la forme. Réflexions sur un ouvrage de V. Propp', in *Anthropologie structurale*, Vol. II.

—— (1962) *La pensée sauvage*, Plon.

—— (1964) *Le cru et le cuit*, Plon.

—— (1971) *L'homme nu*, Plon.

* —— (1979) 'Sur *S/Z*' [1970], in R. Bellour and C. Clément (eds) *Claude Lévi-Strauss, textes de et sur Lévi-Strauss*, Gallimard.

—— with G. Charbonnier (1961) *Entretiens avec Lévi-Strauss*, Plon/Julliard.

—— with R. Jakobson (1962) 'Le Chats de Baudelaire', *L'Homme*, 2.

Lévy-Bruhl, Lucien (1903) *The Philosophy of Auguste Comte* [1900], London, Swan Sonnenschein.

Lévy-Leblond, Jean-Marc and Alain Jaubert (1975) *(Auto)critique de la science*, Seuil.

Lidov, David (1975) *On Musical Phrase*, Monograhies de sémiologie et d'analyse musicales, I, Université de Montréal.

Lindekens, René (1976) *Essai de sémiotique visuelle*, Klincksieck.

Lodge, David (1970) *The Language of Fiction: Essays in Criticism and Verbal Analysis of the English Novel*, London, Routledge & Kegan Paul.

* —— (1979) *The Modes of Modern Writing*, 2nd edition, London, Edward Arnold.

Lukács, Georg (1966) *Histoire et conscience de classe* [1923], Minuit.

—— (1971) *Realism in our Time: Literature and the Class Struggle*, with a Preface by George Steiner, New York, Harper & Row.

Lukes, Steven (1973) *Emile Durkheim, His Life and Work, A Historical and Critical Study*, London, Allen Lane.

Lyons, John (1968) *Introduction to Theoretical Linguistics*, Cambridge, Cambridge University Press.

—— (ed.) (1970) *New Horizons in Linguistics*, Harmondsworth, Penguin.

Lyotard, François (1968) *Discours, figure*, Klincksieck.

—— (1974) *Dérive à partir de Marx et de Freud*, 10/18.

—— (1975) 'De l'apathie théorique', *Critique*, 333.

Macciocchi, Maria-Antonietta (ed.) (1976) *Eléments pour une analyse du fascisme*, 10/18.

Macherey, Pierre (1966) *Pour une théorie de la production littéraire*, Maspero.

* Macksey, Richard and Eugenio Donato (ed.) (1970) *The Language of Criticism and the Sciences of Man: The Structuralist Controversy*, Baltimore, Johns Hopkins Press.

McLeod, Ian (1978) 'Writing Biography: Sartre's Method', *Oxford Literary Review*, 3(1), Special issue on 'Theoretical Criticism'.

Magazine littéraire, 103-4 (1975) Special issue on 'Sartre dans son histoire', J.-J. Brochier (ed.).

—— 112-13 (1976) Special issue on 'Le mouvement des idées, Mai 1968-Mai 1976'.

—— 127-8 (1977) Special issue on 'Vingt ans de philosophie en France' (published separately (1979) as *Les dieux dans la cuisine*, Aubier, 10/18).

Mallarmé, Stéphane (1945) *Oeuvres complètes*, Gallimard, Pléiade.

*Man, Paul de (1971) *Blindness and Insight, Essays in the Rhetoric of Contemporary Criticism*, London, Oxford University Press.

Mannoni, Maud (1979) *La théorie comme fiction*, Seuil.

Mannoni, Octave (1969) *Clefs pour l'imaginaire*, Seuil.

—— (1978) *Fictions freudiennes*, Seuil.

Marcellesi, J.B. and B. Gardin (1974) *Introduction à la sociolinguistique*, Larousse.

Marin, Louis (1970) 'La description de l'image', *Communications*, 15.

—— (1979) *Le récit est un piège*, Minuit.

Martinet, André (1961) *Eléments de linguistique générale*, 2nd edition, A. Colin.

Mauron, Charles (1969) *L'inconscient dans l'oeuvre et la vie de Racine* [1954], Corti.

—— (1962) *Des métaphores obsédantes au mythe personnel. Introduction à la psychocritique*, Corti.

Mehlman, Jeffrey (1974) *A Structural Study of Autobiography: Proust, Leiris, Sartre, Lévi-Strauss*, Ithaca, Cornell University Press.

Meletinski, E. (1970) 'L'etude structurale et typologique du conte', in V. Propp *Morphologie du conte*, Seuil.

Merleau-Ponty, Maurice (1945) *Phénoménologie de la perception*, Gallimard.

—— (1960) *Signes*, Gallimard.

Meschonnic, Henri (1979) 'Situation de Sartre dans le langage', in M. Sicard (ed.) *Obliques*.

Mészáros, István (1979) *The Work of Sartre*, Vol. 1, Brighton, Sussex, Harvester.

Metz, Christian (1970) 'Au-delà de l'analogie, l'image', *Communications*, 15, Minuit.

────── (1979a) *Essais sémiotiques*, Klincksieck.

────── (1979b) *Le signifiant imaginaire (Psychanalyse et cinéma)*, Union générale d'éditions, 10/18.

Michaux, Henri (1967) *Un barbare en Asie* [1933], Gallimard.

Miller, Jacques-Alain (1966) 'Index raisonné des concepts majeurs', in J. Lacan, *Ecrits*, Seuil.

────── (1968) 'Action de la structure', *Cahiers pour l'analyse*, 9.

Milner, Jean-Claude (1978a) *L'amour de la langue*, Seuil.

────── (1978b) *De la syntaxe à l'interprétation*, Seuil.

Moles, Abraham (1956) *Théorie de l'information et perception esthétique*, Flammarion.

────── (1971) *Art et ordinateur*, Casterman.

Monod, Jacques (1968) 'De la biologie moléculaire à l'éthique de la connaissance', Leçon inaugurale au Collège de France, in *L'Age de la Science*, 1.

────── (1970) *Le Hasard et la nécessité*, Seuil.

Mordier, Jean-Pierre (1981) *Les débuts de la psychoanalyse en France, 1895-1926*, Maspero.

Morin, Edgar (1973) *Le paradigme perdu: la nature humaine*, Seuil.

Morris, Charles (1971) *Writings on the General Theory of Signs*, The Hague, Mouton.

Morrissette, Bruce (1963) *Les romans de Robbe-Grillet*, Minuit.

Moscovici, Serge (1976) *La psychanalyse, son image et son public*, new revised edition, Presses Universitaires de France.

────── (1972) *La société contre nature*, Union générale d'editions, 10/18.

Nattiez, Jean-Jacques (ed.) (1971) 'Sémiologie de la musique', *Musique en jeu*, 5.

────── (ed.) (1974) 'Problèmes et méthodes de la sémiologie' *Langages*, 35, September.

* ────── (1975) *Fondements d'une sémiologie de la musique*, Union générale d'editions, 10/18.

Nef, Frédéric (ed.) (1976) *Structures élémentaires de la signification*, Bruxelles, Complexe, (contains his important 'Presentation').

Nemo, Philippe (1974) *L'homme structural*, Grasset.

Nizan, Paul (1960) *Les chiens de garde* [1932], Maspero.

Nora, Pierre (1977) 'Entretien avec J.-B. Pontalis: mémoire de l'historien, mémoire de l'histoire', *Nouvelle Revue de Psychanalyse*, 15.

Norris, Christopher (1978a) *William Empson and the Philosophy of Literary Criticism*, London, Athlone.

* ────── (1978b) 'Roland Barthes: the view from here', *Critical Quarterly*, 20(1), Spring.

* *La Nouvelle Critique*, Two special issues, jointly with *Tel Quel*:

────── (1968) 'Linguistique et littérature', April.

────── (1970) 'Littérature et idéologies', April.

O'Brien, C.C. (1965), *Writers and Politics*, Harmondsworth, Penguin.

Ogden, C.K. and I.A. Richards (1923) *The Meaning of Meaning*, London, Routledge & Kegan Paul.

Osgood, Charles E. (1971) 'Where do sentences come from?', in D. Steinberg and L. Jakobovits, *Semantics*, Cambridge, Cambridge University Press.

Ossola, Carlo (1979) 'Les "ossements fossiles" de la lettre chez Mallarmé and chez Saussure', *Critique*, 391.

Oxford Literary Review

────── (1978) Theoretical criticism issue, 3(1).

———— (1978) Derrida issue, 3(2).

OULIPO (1973) *La littérature potentielle*, Gallimard.

Painter, George (1959) *Proust: The Early Years*, London, Chatto & Windus.

Panofsky, Erwin (1967) *Essais d'iconologie*, Gallimard.

Parkin, Frank (1971) *Class, Inequality and Political Order*, London, MacGibbon & Kee.

* Pateman, Trevor (1973) Review of *Mythologies*, *The Human Context*, 5 (reprinted in 1980a).

———— (1980a) *Language, Truth and Politics*, Lewes, Jean Stroud, 2nd edition.

———— (1980b) 'How to Do Things with Images, an essay on the pragmatics of advertising', *Theory and Society*, 10 (reprinted in 1980a).

Patte, Daniel (1981) 'Carré sémiotique et syntaxe narrative', in Documents du Groupe de recherches sémio-linguistiques, III, 23.

Paulhan, Jean (n.d.) *Clef de la poésie* [1924], Gallimard.

———— (1973) *Les fleurs de Tarbes, ou la Terreur dans les lettres* [1941], (suivi d'un dossier réuni par Claude Zilberberg), Gallimard.

———— (1977) *Traité des figures*, in Du Marsais, *Traité des tropes, avec une postface de Claude Mouchard*, Le Nouveau Commerce.

Pêcheux, Michel (1969) *Analyse automatique du discours*, Dunod.

———— (1975) *Les vérités de La Palice*, Maspero.

Peirce, Charles Sanders (1931-58) *Collected Papers*, Cambridge, Mass., Harvard University Press.

La Pensée, 135 (1967) Special issue on 'Structuralisme et marxisme', October.

Perelman, Chaim and Lucie Olbrechts-Tyteca (1958) *Traité de l'argumentation*, Presses Universitaires de France.

Perelman, Chaim (1979) *The New Rhetoric and the Humanities: Essays on Rhetoric and Its Applications*, Dordrecht and London, Reidel.

Pettit, Philip (1975) *The Concept of Structuralism: A Critical Analysis*, Dublin, Gill & Macmillan.

Piaget, Jean (1968a) *Le Structuralisme*, Presses Universitaires de France.

———— (1968b) *Sagesse et illusions de la philosophie* [1965], 2nd edition with a preface, Presses Universitaires de France.

Piattelli-Palmarini, Massimo (1977) 'L'entrepôt biologique et le démon comparateur', *Nouvelle Revue de Psychanalyse*, 15.

Picard, Raymond (1965) *Nouvelle critique ou nouvelle imposture*, Pauvert.

Picon, Gaëtan (ed.) (1957) *Panorama des idées contemporaines*, Gallimard.

Pierssens, Michel (1977) 'L'interstice et la dissidence' (review of L.-J. Calvet (1975) *Pour et contre Saussure. Vers une linguistique sociale*, Payot), *Critique*, 361-2, June-July.

Pike, Kenneth (1967) *Language in Relation to a Unified Theory of Human Behavior*, The Hague, Mouton.

Pingaud, Bernard (1979) 'Les contrebandiers de l'écriture', *Nouvelle Revue de Psychanalyse*, 20.

Pleynet, Marcelin (1977) *Art et littérature*, Seuil.

* ———— (1980) *Le voyage en Chine*, Hachette.

Polhemus, Ted (ed.) (1978) *Social Aspects of the Human Body: A Reader of Key Texts*, Harmondsworth, Penguin.

Politzer, Georges (1973) *Ecrits I. La philosophie et ses mythes*. Editions Sociales.

Ponge, Francis (1970) *Entretiens avec Philippe Sollers*, Gallimard/Seuil.

Pontalis, Jean-Bertrand (1978) *Entre le rêve et la douleur*, Gallimard.

Poole, Roger (1966) 'Introduction' to Cl. Lévi-Strauss, *Totemism*, Harmondsworth, Penguin.

——— (1970) 'Structuralism and Phenomenology: a literary approach', *Journal of the British Society for Phenomenology*.

Popper, Karl (1966) *The Open Society and its Enemies* [1945], London, Routledge & Kegan Paul.

Posner, Roland 'Poetic communication versus literary language, or the linguistic fallacy in poetics', in IASS-AIS, *Actes du premier Congrès*.

Poster, Mark (1975) *Existential Marxism in Post-War France: From Sartre to Althusser*, Princeton, Princeton University Press.

Pottier, Bernard (ed.) (1973) *Le langage*, Denoël.

——— (1980a) 'Comment dénommer les sèmes', *Bulletin du Groupe de recherches sémio-linguistiques* (13), March.

——— (ed.) (1980b, 1981) 'Les universaux du langage', Special issues of *Bulletin du Groupe de recherches sémio-linguistiques* (14), June, (19), September.

Poulantzas, Nicos (1974) *Les classes sociales dans le capitalisme aujourd'hui*, Seuil.

* Poulet, Georges (ed.) (1967) *Les chemins actuels de la critique*, Plon.

Pribram, Karl H. (1980a) 'The Place of Pragmatics in the Syntactic and Semantic Organization of Language', in *Temporal Variables in Speech: Studies in Honour of Frieda Goldman-Eisler*, Janua Linguarum, The Hague, Mouton.

——— (1980b) 'The Role of Analogy in Transcending Limits in the Brain Sciences', *Daedalus*, Spring.

Prieto, Luis (1964) *Principes de noologie*, The Hague, Mouton.

——— (1966) *Messages et signaux*, Presses Universitaires de France.

——— (1975) *Etudes de linguistique et de sémiologie générales*, Droz.

Propp, Vladimir (1970) *Morphologie du conte* [1928], Seuil, from the 2nd edition, Leningrad, 1969.

Proust, Marcel (1954) *Contre Sainte-Beuve*, Gallimard.

Psychanalyse et Marxisme I and II (1970) *Cahiers du Centre d'Etude et de Recherche Marxistes*, 81, 82.

Queneau, Raymond (1965) *Bâtons, chiffres et lettres* [1947], 2nd enlarged edition, Gallimard.

——— (1947) *Exercices de style*, Gallimard.

Quine, Willard Van Orman (1953) *From a Logical Point of View*, Cambridge, Mass., Harvard University Press.

——— (1971) 'The Inscrutability of reference', in D. Steinberg and L. Jakobovits, *Semantics*, Cambridge, Cambridge University Press.

* Ragon, Michel (1973) *Histoire de la littérature prolétarienne en France*, A. Michel.

Rancière, Jacques (1974) *La leçon d'Althusser*, Gallimard.

Rastier, François (1974) *Essais de sémiotique discursive*, Tours, Mame.

Reboul, Jacques (1967) 'Sarrasine ou la castration personnifiée', *Cahiers pour l'Analyse*, 7, Special issue on 'Du mythe au roman'.

Rée, Jonathan (1976a) 'Half a critique', *Radical Philosophy*, 15, (review of Sartre's *Critique de la raison dialectique*).

——— (1976b) Sub-titles and Glossary appended to the translation of *Critique de la raison dialectique* by A. Sheridan-Smith, London, New Left Books.

Reich, Wilhelm (1972) *The Mass Psychology of Fascism* [1942] London, Souvenir Press.

Revel, Jean-Francois (1954) *Pourquoi des philosophes?*, Pauvert.

Ricardou, Jean (1971) *Pour une théorie du nouveau roman*, Seuil.

Ricoeur, Paul (1965) *De l'interprétation. Essai sur Freud*, Seuil.

—— (1967) 'La structure, le mot, l'événement', *Esprit*, 35.

—— (1980) 'La grammaire narrative de Greimas', *Documents du Groupe de recherches sémio-linguistiques* (15).

Riffaterre, Michael (1971) *Essais de stylistique structurale* (with a Presentation by Daniel Delas), Flammarion.

* Robbe-Grillet, Alain (1981) 'Le parti de Roland Barthes', *Le Nouvel Observateur*, 30 March.

Robert, Marthe (1972) *Roman des origines et origines du roman*, Grasset.

* Robey, David (ed.) (1973) *Structuralism: An Introduction*, London, Oxford University Press. (Contains essays by J. Culler, U. Eco, R. Gandy, E. Leach, J. Lyons, J. Mepham, T. Todorov and the editor.)

Roudinesco, Elisabeth (1979) *Pour une politique de la psychanalyse*, Maspero.

Rousset, Jean (1947) *La littérature de l'âge baroque en France*, Corti.

—— (1978) 'Au coeur de l'aventure française du baroque', *Critique*, 373-4.

Ruprecht, Hans-George (1981) 'Du formant intertextuel. Remarques sur un objet ethnosémiotique', *Documents du Groupe de recherches sémio-linguistiques*, (3)21.

Ruwet, Nicolas (1972) *Langage, musique, poésie*, Seuil.

—— (1975) 'Parallélismes et déviations en poésie', in J. Kristeva, J. Milner and N. Ruwet (eds) *Langue, discours, société*, Seuil.

Sarduy, Severo (1975) *Barroco*, Seuil.

Sartre, Jean-Paul (1938) *La nausée*, Gallimard.

—— (1939) *Esquisse d'une théorie des émotions*, Hermann.

—— (1940) *L'imaginaire*, Gallimard.

—— (1943) *L'être et le néant*, Gallimard.

—— (1946a) *Baudelaire*, Editions du Point du Jour.

—— (1946b) *L'existentialisme est un humanisme*, Nagel.

—— (1946c) 'Matérialisme et révolution, reprinted in *Situations III*, Gallimard.

—— (1947a) *Situations I* (contains the review of M. Blanchot's novel *Aminadab*).

—— (1947b) *Qu'est-ce que la littérature?*, reprinted in *Situations II*, Gallimard.

—— (1952) *Saint Genet, comédien et martyr*, Gallimard.

—— (1955) *Nekrassov*, Gallimard.

—— (1960) *Critique de la raison dialectique, précédé de Questions de méthode*, Gallimard.

—— (1963) *Les mots*, Gallimard.

—— (1966) 'Jean-Paul Sartre répond', *L'Arc*, 30.

—— (1969) 'L'homme au magnétophone', *Les Temps modernes*, 274.

—— (1972a) 'Sartre 1972', texts published in *L'Idiot International* and *Der Spiegel* edited and translated by George Gross, *The Human Context*, 4(3).

—— (1972b) *Plaidoyer pour les intellectuels*, Gallimard.

—— (1980) 'L'espoir, maintenant . . .', interview by Benny Lévy, *Le Nouvel Observateur*, 10, 17, 24 March.

Owing to the importance of Sartre's work in Barthes's elaboration of the semiological idea and in the structuralist debate, the reader is referred to Michel Contat and Michel Rybalka's *Les écrits de Sartre* (1970) (a conscious parallel with Lacan's *summa*?), Gallimard.

Šaumjan, Sebastian K. (1971) *Principles of Structural Linguistics*, The Hague, Mouton.

Saussure, Ferdinand de (1973) *Course in General Linguistics* [1915, ed. Charles Bally, Albert Séchehaye with Albert Riedlinger] with notes by Tullio de Mauro, trans. Louis-Jean Calvet, Payot. *Course in General Linguistics* (1960). London, Peter Owen, (1974) Fontana (with an Introduction by J. Culler). (The edition referred to in this study is this translation; the pagination is identical in hardback and paperback.)

———— *Anagrams* Jean Starobinski (ed.) (1971) *Les Mots sous les mots: Les anagrammes de Ferdinand de Saussure*, Gallimard (the first partial publication was in 1964; much of the manuscript remains unpublished).

Schefer, Jean-Louis (1968) *Scénographie d'un tableau*, Seuil.

* ———— (1980) 'Barthes', *Cahiers du cinéma*, 311, May.

* Scholes, Robert (1974) *Structuralism in Literature: An Introduction*, New Haven, Yale University Press.

* *Screen* (1973) Double issue on Cinema Semiotics, Spring/Summer.

Searle, John (1969) *Speech Acts*, Cambridge, Cambridge University Press.

———— (1980) *Expression and Meaning: Studies in the Theory of Speech Acts*, Cambridge, Cambridge University Press.

Sebag, Lucien (1964) *Structuralisme et marxisme*, Payot.

Sebeok, Thomas (ed.) (1960) *Style in Language*, Cambridge, Mass., MIT Press.

———— (1972) *Perspectives in Zoosemiotics*, The Hague, Mouton.

Serres, Michel (1968) *Hermès ou la communication*, Minuit.

Shannon, Claude and Warren Weaver (1949) *The Mathematical Theory of Communication*, Urbana, University of Illinois Press.

Sicard, Michel (ed.) (1979) *Obliques*, 18-19, Double issue on Sartre, vol. 2 (1981).

Simonis, Yvan (1968) *Lévi-Strauss ou la 'passion de l'inceste'*, Aubier/Montaigne.

Smith, K.C.P. and Michael Apter (1975) *A Theory of Psychological Reversals*, Chippenham, Wilts, Picton Press.

Sollers, Philippe (1968) *Logiques*, Seuil.

———— (1972) *Nombres*, Seuil.

* ———— (ed.) (1973) *Bataille*, Union générale d'editions, 10/18.

———— (1979) 'Sur la notion de paradis', *Tel Quel*, 68.

Sontag, Susan (1967) *Against Interpretation and Other Essays*, London, Eyre & Spottiswoode.

Soper, Kate (1978) 'Note on the scientificity of Freud's *Interpretation of Dreams*', *Radical Philosophy*, 20, Summer.

Soriano, Marc (1972) *Le dossier Perrault*, Hachette.

Souriau, Etienne (1950) *Les deux cent mille situations dramatiques*, Flammarion.

Sperber, Dan (1974) *Le symbolisme en général*, Hermann.

———— and Deirdre Wilson (forthcoming) *The Interpretation of Utterances: Semantics, Pragmatics and Rhetoric*.

Spitzer, Leo (1962) *Linguistics and Literary History. Essays in Stylistics* [1948], New York, Russell & Russell.

———— (1970) *Etudes de style*, Gallimard.

Stalin, Joseph V. (1974) *Le marxisme et les problèmes de linguistique*, Peking, Editions en langues étrangères.

Steinberg, Danny D. and Leon A. Jakobovits (1971) *Semantics*, Cambridge,

Cambridge University Press.

* Stern, J.P. (1973) *On Realism*, London, Routledge & Kegan Paul.

* Sturrock, John (1977) *Paper Tigers: The Ideal Fictions of Jorge Luis Borges*, Oxford, Clarendon Press.

* ——— (1979) *Structuralism and Since: from Lévi-Strauss to Derrida, five studies in French Thought*, London, Oxford University Press (contains essays by the editor (on Barthes), D. Sperber, H. White, M. Bowie, J. Culler).

Suppe, Frederick (ed.) (1971) *The Structure of Scientific Theories*, Urbana, Ill., University of Illinois Press.

* 'Tante Ursule' (1979) 'Lettre ouverte à Roland Barthes', *La Quinzaine littéraire*, March.

* *Tel Quel* (1968) *Théorie d'ensemble*, Seuil.

——— 46, (1971) Special issue on surrealism.

Les Temps modernes, 246 (1966), issue on 'Problèmes du structuralisme' (contains articles by M. Barbut, P. Bourdieu, J. Ehrmann, M. Godelier, A.J. Greimas, P. Macherey, J. Pouillon).

Tesnière, Lucien (1959) *Eléments de syntaxe structurale*, Klincksieck.

Todorov, Tzvetan (1965) *Théorie de la littérature* (texts by the Russian formalists, edited by Todorov), Seuil.

——— (1966a) 'Les anomalies sémantiques', *Langages*, 1.

——— (1966b) 'Les catégories du récit littéraire', *Communications*, 8.

——— (1968) Introduction to *Communications*, 11, on 'Le vraisemblable'.

——— (1969) *Grammaire du Décaméron*, The Hague, Mouton.

——— (1971) 'Les formalistes en occident', *Poetics*, 1 (a description of the main collections of texts by Russian formalists).

——— (1975) 'La notion de littérature', in J. Kristeva, J. Milner and N. Ruwet (eds) *Langue, discours, société*.

——— (1977) *Théories du symbole*, Seuil (especially Chapter 9, 'Le symbolique chez Saussure').

——— (1978a) *Symbolisme et interprétation*, Seuil.

——— (1978b) *Les genres du discours*, Seuil.

* ——— (1979) 'La réflexion sur la littérature dans la France contemporaine', *Poétique*, 38, April, Special issue on 'Théories du Texte'.

Tort, Michel (1966) 'De l'interprétation ou la machine herméneutique', *Temps modernes*, 21.

——— (1970) 'La psychanalyse dans le matérialisme historique', *Nouvelle Revue de Psychanalyse*, 1.

Tortel, Jean (ed.) (1952) *Le Préclassicisme français*, Les Cahiers du Sud.

Tristani, Jean-Louis (1977) 'La théologie comme science au vingtième siècle', *Critique*, 367.

Turner, Roy (ed.) (1974) *Ethnomethodology: Selected Readings*, Harmondsworth, Penguin.

Turkle, Sherry (1978) *Psychoanalytic Politics: Freud's French Revolution*, London, A. Deutsch (partly published in *The Human Context*, 7, 1975).

Twentieth Century Studies, 3 (1970) Special issue on 'Structuralism'.

——— 7/8 (1972) Special issue on 'Russian Formalism'.

* Updike, John (1975) 'Roland Barthes', *The New Yorker*, 24 November.

Valéry, Paul (1957-60) *Oeuvres*, Gallimard, Pléiade.

Vaneigem, Raoul (1967) *Traité de savoir-vivre à l'usage des jeunes générations*,

Gallimard.

Vološinov, V.N. = Bakhtin.

Veron, Eliseo (1973) 'Vers une logique naturelle des mondes sociaux', *Communications*, 20.

Vincent, J.M. (ed.) (1974) *Contre Althusser*, Union générale d'editions, 10/18.

Wahl, François (ed.) (1968) *Qu'est-ce que le structuralisme?*, Seuil (contains essays by O. Ducrot, M. Safouan, D. Sperber, T. Todorov, as well as his own 'La philosophie entre l'avant et l'après du structuralisme').

—— (1972) 'Appendice. Autour d'une critique du signe', in Ducrot and Todorov.

Walton, Paul and Stuart Hall (eds) (1972) *Situating Marx*, London, Human Context Editions.

Watzlawick, Paul, Janet Beavin and Don D. Jackson (1967) *The Pragmatics of Human Communication*, New York, W.W. Norton.

—— (1976) *How Real is Real? Communication, Disinformation, Confusion*, New York, Random House.

Wellek, René (1963) *Concepts of Criticism*, New Haven, Yale University Press.

—— and Austin Warren (1949) *Theory of Literature*, New York, Harcourt Brace Jovanovich.

White, Hayden (1973) 'Foucault decoded: notes from underground', *History and Theory*, 12 (1).

* White, Kenneth (1979) 'Le cortège de Roland Barthes', *La Quinzaine littéraire*, 295, 1-15 February.

Wiener, Norbert (1948) *Cybernetics, or Control and Communication in the Animal and the Machine*, Cambridge, Mass., MIT Press.

Wilden, Anthony (1968) *The Language of the Self*, Baltimore, Johns Hopkins Press.

—— (1972) *System and Structure: Essays on Communication and Exchange*, London, Tavistock.

Willett, John (1959) *The Theatre of Bertolt Brecht: A Study from Eight Aspects*, London, Methuen.

Williams, Raymond (1977) *Marxism and Literature*, London, Oxford University Press.

Wollen, Peter (1972) *Signs and Meaning in the Cinema*, London, 3rd edition, Secker & Warburg.

Wollheim, Richard (1971) *Freud*, London, Fontana Modern Masters series, Collins.

—— (1979) 'The Cabinet of Dr. Lacan', *New York Review of Books*, 25 January.

* *Working Papers in Cultural Studies* (*WPCS*) (Journal of the Centre for Contemporary Cultural Studies, Birmingham), 4 (1973) Special issue on 'Literature and Society' (especially S. Hall, *et al.* 'Mapping the Field').

* —— 6 (1974) 'Cultural Studies and Theory' (especially Iain Chambers, 'Roland Barthes: Structuralism/Semiotics').

Yale French Studies, 36-7 (1966) Special issue on 'Structuralism'.

Zéraffa, Michel (1971) *Personne et personnage*, Klincksieck.

Zhdanov (Jdanov), Andrei (1972) *Sur la littérature, la philosophie et la musique* [1947], Editions Norman Béthune (contains the text against Alexandrov's book, 'Sur la philosophie', cited by Barthes in 'Myth Today').

Index

This index includes adjectives and substantives derived from proper names, e.g. Freud, Freudian, Freudianism, etc.

Achard, P., 242
Adamov, Arthur, 50, 250, 251
Aesop, 109, 115
Alexandrov, G.F., 117
Althusser, Louis, 9, 14, 15, 18, 19, 20, 22, 68, 77, 78, 98, 124, 178, 183, 224, 241, 243, 244
Annales school of history, 10, 95, 97, 182, 222, 241, 255
Anouilh, Jean, 255
Apollinaire, Guillaume, 67, 140
Apter, Michael, 261
Aristophanes, 81
Aristotle, 11, 42, 75, 189, 191, 198, 247
Arsan, Emmanuelle, 260
Ashby, W. Ross, 93, 95, 97, 250
Auerbach, Erich, 250
Austin, J.L., 11, 224

Bachelard, Gaston, 17, 19, 37, 62, 108, 116, 244
Badiou, Alain, 18, 243
Bakhtin, Mikhail, 247
Balibar, Renée, 224, 250
Bally, Charles, 53
Balzac, Honoré de, 148, 149, 154, 180, 190, 196–203
Bataille, Georges, 30, 163, 168, 197, 262
Bateson, Gregory, 8
Baudelaire, Charles, 109, 129, 260
Baudelot, Christian, 78, 249, 250
Baudrillard, Jean, 33, 163, 164, 256
Baudry, Jean-Louis, 257
Beauvoir, Simone de, 48
Beckett, Samuel, 14
Bédier, Joseph, 181
Beethoven, Ludwig van, 261
Bellour, Raymond, 194

Belsey, Catherine, 257
Benedict, Ruth, 261
Bénichou, Paul, 71
Benjamin, Walter, 247
Benoist, Jean-Marie, 20, 34, 243, 263
Benthall, Jonathan, 255
Benveniste, Emile, 37, 158, 172, 174, 189, 193, 194, 224, 243, 251
Bergson, Henri, 140
Bernstein, Basil, 250
Bernstein, Leonard, 256
Birdwhistell, Ray, 255
Blain, Gérard, 262
Blanché, R., 182
Blanchot, Maurice, 32, 51, 61, 62, 63, 64, 66, 70, 92, 209, 223
Bloch, Marc, 10, 96
Bloomfield, Leonard, 218, 232
Boccaccio, Giovanni, 179
Boileau, Nicolas, 34, 71
Boons, Marie-Claire, 184
Borges, Jorge Luis, 32
Borowczyk, Walerian, 262
Bourdieu, Pierre, 148, 249
Bouveresse, Jacques, 243
Bradbury, Malcolm, 247
Braudel, Fernand, 10
Bréal, Michel, 182
Brecht, Bertolt, 48, 50, 66, 67, 91, 122, 123, 164, 209, 211, 240, 244, 247, 253, 254
Bremond, Claude, 133, 186, 191, 258
Bresson, François, 229
Breton, André, 214, 241, 251
Brewster, Ben, 98, 241
Brillat-Savarin, Anthelme, 208
Brøndal, Viggo, 51, 182
Brontë family, 262

Brooke-Rose, Christine, 134
Buffat, Marc, 247
Bühler, Karl, 226, 248
Burnier, Michel-Antoine, 240
Burniston, Steve, 257
Butor, Michel, 34, 74, 255
Buyssens, Eric, 136

Calvet, Louis-Jean, 137, 243
Camus, Albert, 22, 40
Canguilhem, Georges, 19
Cardin, Pierre, 204
Cassirer, Ernst, 10, 248
Castries, Général de, 82
Catesson, Jean, 210
Cavafy, C.P., 36
Cazotte, Jacques, 198, 199, 211, 260
Céline, Louis-Ferdinand, 85
Chabrol, Claude, 177, 258
Chaplin, Charlie, 79, 253, 256
Char, René, 59, 66, 121
Chateaubriand, François-René, 61, 74,
    168, 174
Châtelet, François, 204, 242
Chatman, Seymour, 199
Chomsky, Noam, 16, 37, 58, 110, 111,
    143, 149, 150, 152, 173, 185, 190, 191,
    192, 194, 218, 224, 226, 228, 229, 230,
    231, 233, 241, 243, 247, 259, 263
Christie, Agatha, 194
Cixous, Hélène, 248
Cocteau, Jean, 61
Comte, Auguste, 15, 17, 230, 246, 263
Cooper, David, 10
Costes, Alain, 241
Coty, René, 140
Courtès, Joseph, 258
Coward, Rosalind, 257
Cruikshank, John, 247
Cuisenier, Jean, 8, 241
Culler, Jonathan, 242, 247, 258

Dadoun, Roger, 23
Deleuze, Gilles, 204, 258
Derrida, Jacques, 10, 14, 19, 27, 31, 50,
    99, 130, 138, 162, 169–72, 221, 228,
    248, 257, 259, 262
Descartes, René, 17, 71, 197, 231, 237
Descombes, Vincent, 78
Deslandres, Yvonne, 257
Destutt de Tracy, Antoine, 184
Dijk, Teun van, 41
Dinneen, Francis P., 236
Donato, Eugenio, 242
Donne, John, 29
Dos Passos, John, 50
Doubrovsky, Serge, 12, 133, 242, 243
Douglas, Mary, 141, 143, 250
Dreyfus, Alfred, 88

Duchamp, Marcel, 32
Ducrot, Oswald, 145, 238, 242
Du Marsais, César C., 74
Dumas fils, Alexandre, 34
Dumézil, Georges, 178, 181
Duneton, Claude, 248
Durkheim, Emile, 14, 230, 263
Duvignaud, Jean, 240

Eberbach, Margaret, 4
Eco, Umberto, 146, 148, 255, 256
Eddington, Arthur S., 226
Einstein, Albert, 85, 91, 222
Eleatism, 20, 21
Ellis, John, 257
Eluard, Paul, 241
Engler, R., 220, 256
Erlich, Victor, 77
Establet, Roger, 78, 249, 250
Euclid, 247

Faye, Jean-Pierre, 242, 263
Febvre, Lucien, 10
Fénelon, François de Salignac, 75
Feyerabend, Paul, 241
Finas, Lucette, 248
Fini, Léonor, 48
Flahault, François, 248, 257
Flaubert, Gustave, 24, 50, 61, 86, 89, 92,
    134, 192, 193, 197
Fónagy, Ivan, 174
Forster, E.M., 36
Foucault, Michel, 10, 14, 15, 19, 20, 23,
    24, 27, 31, 35, 67, 170, 194, 222, 241,
    243, 244, 245, 257
Fourier, Charles, 31, 74, 172, 208, 245
Fowler, Roger, 258, 263
Francastel, Pierre, 148
Frankfurt school, 164
Frazer, Sir James, 129
Frederika, Queen of Greece, 82
Frege, Gottlob, 220
Frei, Henri, 263
Freud, Sigmund, 9, 16, 22, 23, 29, 60, 73,
    82, 109, 116, 129, 162, 170, 172, 174,
    180, 191, 198, 224, 245, 250, 258, 262
Furet, François, 248

Gabel, Joseph, 244
Gaillard, Françoise, 206
Galois, Evariste, 18
Garbo, Greta, 105
Gardner, Howard, 244
Gaulle, Général de, 21, 221
Genet, Jean, 109
Genette, Gérard, 65, 72, 73, 99, 133, 251
George, François, 23, 240
Gestalt theory, 15, 16, 248
Gide, André, 22, 28, 29, 60, 79, 95, 247

Giglioli, Pier Paolo, 247, 248
Gobard, Henri, 248
Godard, Jean-Luc, 132
Godechot, Jacques, 248
Godel, R., 258
Godelier, Maurice, 241
Goethe, Johann Wolfgang von, 76
Goldmann, Lucien, 11, 96, 99, 130, 132,
  180, 251, 254, 259
Gorz, André, 92
Goux, Jean-Joseph, 257
Graham, Billy, 82, 90
Gramsci, Antonio, 78, 79
Green, André, 248
Greimas, Algirdas Julien, 42, 133, 149,
  150, 169, 171, 178, 181–4, 185, 186,
  187, 198, 235, 236, 238, 243, 244, 247,
  248, 254, 258, 259
GREPH, 242
Grice, H.P., 11, 224
Grisoni, Dominique, 246
Gritti, Jules, 73, 133
Groupe μ, 73, 134, 188, 254
Guattari, Félix, 204, 258
Guillaume, Paul, 228
Guiraud, Pierre, 217, 242
Guttman, L., 241
Guyotat, Pierre, 194, 199

Hall, Edward T., 255
Halle, Morris, 263
Hamon, Philippe, 258
Harris, Zellig, 149, 218
Hawkes, Terence, 243, 258
Hébert, Jacques-René, 48, 49, 52, 109
Hegel, Georg F.W., 8, 22, 50, 68, 69, 93,
  108, 116, 123, 180, 209, 219, 223, 238,
  248
Heidegger, Martin, 10
Hénault, Anne, 258
Hepburn, Audrey, 105
Herbart, Pierre, 247
Hermann, Claudine, 208
Hjelmslev, Louis, 5, 52, 57, 136, 147, 152,
  155, 156, 158, 159, 168, 169, 190, 235,
  236, 252, 253, 264
Hobbes, Thomas, 260
Hockett, C.F., 227
Hofmannsthal, Hugo von, 32
Hollier, Denis, 19, 242, 257
Houbart, Jacques, 240
Houdebine, Jean-Louis, 172, 237, 243
Humboldt, Wilhelm von, 52, 167, 226
Husserl, Edmund, 10, 169
Hymes, Dell, 247

Ionesco, Eugene, 14
Irigaray, Luce, 182, 248, 258

Jackendoff, R., 256
Jackson, Hughlings, 58
Jacob, François, 10
Jakobovits, Leon A., 218, 263
Jakobson, Roman, 9, 42, 58, 61, 73, 108,
  118, 126, 128, 129, 168, 173, 182, 185,
  195, 200, 222, 224, 226–8, 231, 232,
  233, 234, 238, 243, 248, 263
James, Henry, 207
Jameson, Fredric, 242
Jansenists, 181
Jaspers, Karl, 170
Jaubert, Alain, 242
Jenny, Laurent, 237
Johnson-Laird, P.N., 257
Josipovici, Gabriel, 247
Joyaux, Julia = Kristeva
Joyce, James, 23
Jung, Carl G., 108, 219
Jurdant, Baudouin, 242

Kafka, Franz, 91, 92, 93
Kant, Immanuel, 37, 240
Karčevski, S., 135
Kermode, Frank, 243, 247, 258
Khomeini, Ayatollah, 23
Klinkenberg, Jean-Marie, 137, 174
Kofman, Sarah, 246, 258
Kojève, Alexandre, 8
Koyré, Alexandre, 19
Kristeva, Julia, 14, 26, 27, 31, 35, 125,
  138, 150, 160, 172–5, 176, 193, 196,
  201, 221, 228, 230, 231, 234, 240, 241,
  247, 255, 258, 259, 263
Kroeber, A.L., 97, 153, 259
Krushchev, Nikita, 77
Kuentz, Pierre, 73
Kuhn, Thomas, 20, 241, 264

Lacan, Jacques, 9, 10, 14, 17, 18, 20, 21,
  23, 24, 29, 38, 43, 68, 73, 79, 116, 123,
  125, 129, 168, 173, 176, 191, 194, 195,
  196, 197, 198, 200, 201, 205, 210, 211,
  214, 224, 228, 234, 240, 241, 242, 243,
  244, 247, 248, 255, 257, 258, 260, 264
Lacoue-Labarthe, Philippe, 25
Ladrière, Jean, 18
Laing, Ronald D., 10
Lakatos, Imre, 264
Lane, Michael, 242
Lanson, Gustave, 71
Laplanche, Jean, 168, 224, 243, 245
La Rochefoucauld, François de, 174
Lautréamont (Isidore Ducasse), 172, 259
Laver, James, 162
Lavers, Annette, 62, 241, 247
Leclaire, Serge, 168
Leduc, Victor, 242
Leenhardt, Jacques, 92, 254

Leenhardt, Pierre, 261
Lefebvre, Henri, 21, 71
Le Goff, Jacques, 242
Leibniz, Gottfried W., 169, 237
Leiris, Michel, 43, 68, 241
Lenin, Vladimir I., 22, 96
Lenneberg, Eric H., 256
Le Ny, Jean-François, 171, 256, 265
Lepschy, Giulio, 237, 243
Lerdahl, F., 256
Leroi-Gourhan, André, 169
Lévi-Strauss, Claude, 6, 8, 9, 16, 17, 24,
    34, 36, 67, 94, 97, 108, 114, 125, 126,
    129, 130, 131, 132, 142, 151, 152, 156,
    180, 181, 186, 201, 211, 226, 231, 232,
    235, 238, 244, 246, 248, 250, 251, 255,
    258, 259, 263
Lévy-Bruhl, Lucien, 263
Lévy-Leblond, Jean-Marc, 242
Lidov, David, 256
Lindekens, René, 256
Locke, John, 219
Loyola, St Ignatius, 74, 208, 254
Lukács, Georg, 50, 60, 90, 259
Lukes, Steven, 263
Lyons, John, 263
Lyotard, François, 31

McFarlane, James, 247
Maclay, Howard, 218
Macherey, Pierre, 224
Macksey, Richard, 242
Malemort, Jacques, 249
Malinowski, Bronislaw, 227
Mallac, Guy de, 4
Mallarmé, Stéphane, 33, 61, 62, 64, 65,
    66, 84, 87, 94, 161, 172, 188, 191, 192,
    193, 195, 223, 259, 262
Malraux, André, 62, 65, 86, 132, 179,
    211, 259
Manet, Edouard, 161
Mankiewicz, Joseph L., 76
Mannheim, Karl, 96
Mannoni, Octave, 107, 251
Mao-Tse-tung, 22, 23
Marcus, Solomon, 174
Marin, Louis, 147
Markov, A.A., 191, 233
Marr, N.Y., 243
Martinet, André, 126, 146, 149, 192, 237
Marx, Karl, 6, 7, 8, 9, 14, 16, 17, 20, 21,
    22, 23, 24, 27, 30, 56, 60, 66, 67, 68,
    69, 71, 76, 78, 79, 80, 82, 90, 92, 94,
    96, 98, 115, 116, 117, 118, 123, 129,
    130, 164, 172, 183, 198, 206, 214, 223,
    240, 241, 243, 249, 251, 262
Maupassant, Guy de, 198
Mauron, Charles, 96, 99, 180, 181, 211,
    212, 237, 251

Medvedev, P.N., 172
Mei Lan-fang, 253
Memling, Hans, 207
Mendeleev, Dimitri I., 18
Mendès-France, Pierre, 104, 140
Mérimée, Prosper, 75
Merleau-Ponty, Maurice, 18, 51, 52, 53,
    108, 248
Metz, Christian, 133, 146, 147, 246
Michaux, Henri, 43, 241, 260
Michelet, Jules, 34, 35, 37, 48, 49, 67, 79,
    88, 91, 94, 123, 193, 208, 209, 262
Milner, Jean-Claude, 257, 264
Moebius, A.F., 195
Monod, Jacques, 10, 242
Morin, Edgar, 244
Morin, Violette, 133
Morris, Charles, 219
Morrissette, Bruce, 94, 253
Moscovici, Serge, 241, 244
Murdock, G.P., 241
Musgrave, Alan, 264

Nattiez, Jean-Jacques, 256
Nef, Frédéric, 258
Nemo, Philippe, 248
Nietzsche, Friedrich, 10, 35, 163, 172,
    195, 213, 214
Nizan, Paul, 116, 242
Nora, Pierre, 242

O'Brien, Conor Cruise, 262
Ogden, C.K., 220, 221, 227
Olbrechts-Tyteca, Lucie, 247

Painter, George, 3, 4
Panofsky, Erwin, 148, 250
Paris, Comte de, 82
Paris, Jean, 263
Parkin, Frank, 82
Pascal, Blaise, 56, 71, 111, 191
Passeron, Jean-Claude, 249
Pateman, Trevor, 115
Paulhan, Jean, 62, 63, 73
Peirce, Charles Sanders, 108, 139, 147,
    152, 169, 219, 220, 227
Péreire, Emmanuel, 262
Perelman, Chaim, 247
Pettit, Philip, 243
Phaedrus, 109
Piaget, Jean, 15, 16, 17, 18, 19, 217, 229,
    237, 242, 243, 244, 248, 263
Piattelli-Palmarini, Massimo, 257
Picard, Raymond, 11, 12, 133, 180, 187
Pierre, Abbé, 252
Pierssens, Michel, 135
Pieyre de Mandiargues, André, 262
Pike, Kenneth, 232
Plato, 11, 22, 29, 31, 42, 170, 189

Pleynet, Marcelin, 247
Poe, Edgar Allan, 148, 191, 197, 202
Polhemus, Ted, 255
Politzer, Georges, 242
Ponge, Francis, 240
Pontalis, Jean-Bertrand, 224, 242, 243, 245
Popper, Karl, 11, 22, 241
Port-Royal, 181, 212, 226
Poster, Mark, 240, 241
Pottier, Bernard, 229, 264
Poujade, Pierre, 71, 81, 82, 120, 262
Poulantzas, Nicos, 249
Poulet, Georges, 99, 242
Prévert, Jacques, 58
Pribram, Karl H., 257
Prieto, Luis, 136
Propp, Vladimir, 181, 182, 184, 186, 258
Proust, Marcel, 3, 4, 94, 186, 192, 209, 213, 214, 228, 248

Queneau, Raymond, 39, 41, 43, 62, 86, 91, 92, 99, 134, 248
Quine, W. Van Orman, 35, 263

Racine, Jean, 11, 80, 94, 124, 179, 180, 181, 211, 212, 237, 254
Rancière, Jacques, 249
Rastier, François, 178, 179, 184, 258
Reboul, Jacques, 198, 241
Rée, Jonathan, 164
Reich, Wilhelm, 82
Reichler, Claude, 34
Revel, Jean-François, 242
Rey-Debove, Josette, 255
Richard, Jean-Pierre, 99
Richards, I.A., 220, 221, 227
Ricoeur, Paul, 181, 228, 244, 258
Riemann, Georg, 247
Riffaterre, Michael, 38
Rimbaud, Arthur, 131
Robbe-Grillet, Alain, 14, 65, 94, 95, 131, 253, 254
Robey, David, 242
Ronat, Mitsou, 263
Rosch, Eleanor, 257
Roubaud, Jacques, 263
Roudaut, Jean, 32
Rousseau, Jean-Jacques, 36, 180, 192
Rousset, Jean, 71, 246
Russian Formalists, 12, 79, 117, 130, 172, 189, 243, 246, 253, 254
Ruwet, Nicolas, 240

Sade, D.A.F., Marquis de, 74, 208, 250, 254
Safouan, Moustapha, 182
Sarduy, Severo, 246

Sarraute, Nathalie, 50
Sartre, Jean-Paul, 6, 7, 8, 10, 12, 15, 17, 18, 20, 22, 24, 31, 38, 50, 51, 57, 60, 61, 62, 64, 65, 66, 67–70, 72, 73, 76, 77, 78, 79, 80, 82, 85, 86, 87, 89, 92, 99, 105, 108, 109, 115, 116, 121, 122, 123, 130, 132, 164, 206, 208, 211, 212, 214, 223, 225, 231, 240, 243, 246, 249, 250, 262
Šaumjan, Sebastian K., 241
Saussure, Ferdinand de, 5, 9, 15, 37, 39, 42, 51, 52, 53, 54, 57, 58, 59, 73, 75, 95, 107, 108, 109, 110, 126, 128, 129, 135, 136, 138, 139, 141, 142, 143, 144, 146, 147, 150, 152, 167, 169, 172, 173, 181, 189, 192, 193, 206, 209, 217, 218, 219, 220, 221, 222, 223, 227, 228, 229, 230, 232, 233, 234, 235, 236, 238, 239, 243, 248, 258, 262, 263, 264
Schefer, Jean-Louis, 147, 261
Scholes, Robert, 242, 258
Schumann, Robert, 193
Searle, John, 11, 92, 224
Sebag, Lucien, 242
Sebeok, Thomas, 263
Shannon, Claude, 225
Situationists, 138, 243
Smith, K.C.P., 261
Socrates, 28
Sollers, Philippe, 59, 163, 171, 175, 176, 194, 212, 241, 247, 248, 257
Solzhenitsyn, Alexander, 22, 23
Soper, Kate, 243
Soraya, ex-Queen of Iran, 82
Souriau, Etienne, 181, 182, 183, 189, 258, 259
Sperber, Dan, 220
Spitzer, Leo, 53
Staël, Germaine de, 203
Stalin, Joseph V., 22, 68, 77, 82, 243, 248
Starobinski, Jean, 99, 193
Steinberg, Danny D., 218, 263
Steinberg, Saul, 255
Stendhal (Henri Beyle), 192, 260
Stoics, 108, 219, 221
Strawson, P.F., 11, 224
Sturrock, John, 243
Suppe, Frederick, 264
Surrealists, 21, 62, 68, 79, 172, 241, 251

Tarde, Gabriel, 230
Téchiné, André, 262
Tel Quel, 4, 37, 88, 92, 117, 177, 201, 241, 242, 247
Tesnière, Lucien, 182, 258
Thackeray, William M., 262
Thibaudeau, Jean, 4, 51, 88, 125, 180, 208, 249
Todorov, Tzvetan, 42, 132, 145, 189, 220,

238, 242, 243, 263
Tomashevsky, B., 189
Tort, Michel, 244
Tortel, Jean, 71
Toulet, Paul-Jean, 188
Turner, Roy, 248
Twombly, Cy, 240

Umiker, Donna J., 255

Valéry, Paul, 12, 73, 188, 194, 195, 246
Valle Inclan, Ramon del, 167
Velan, Yves, 91, 207
Verne, Jules, 131, 251, 254
Veselovsky, A.N., 181
Vignaux, Georges, 229

Voltaire (François-Marie Arouet), 71, 203

Wahl, François, 19, 20, 242
Wallon, Henri, 108, 219
Weaver, Warren, 225
Weedon, Chris, 257
Wellek, René, 12
Whorf, Benjamin L., 141
Wiener, Norbert, 11
Wilden, Anthony, 239, 250, 258
Willett, John, 253
Wittgenstein, Ludwig, 10
Wollen, Peter, 239

Zhdanov (Jdanov), Andrei, 77, 117, 118